Teaching Marketing

ELGAR GUIDES TO TEACHING

The Elgar Guides to Teaching series provides a variety of resources for instructors looking for new ways to engage students. Each volume provides a unique set of materials and insights that will help both new and seasoned teachers expand their toolbox in order to teach more effectively. Titles include selections of methods, exercises, games and teaching philosophies suitable for the particular subject featured. Each volume is authored or edited by a seasoned professor. Edited volumes comprise contributions from both established instructors and newer faculty who offer fresh takes on their fields of study.

Titles in the series include:

Teaching Cultural Economics
Edited by Trine Bille, Anna Mignosa and Ruth Towse

Teaching Nonprofit Management
Edited by Karabi C. Bezboruah and Heather Carpenter

Teaching the Essentials of Law and Economics
Antony W. Dnes

Teaching Strategic Management
A Hands-on Guide to Teaching Success
Sabine Baumann

Teaching Urban and Regional Planning
Innovative Pedagogies in Practice
Edited by Andrea I. Frank and Artur da Rosa Pires

Teaching Entrepreneurship, Volume Two
A Practice-Based Approach
Edited by Heidi M. Neck, Candida G. Brush and Patricia G. Greene

Teaching Environmental Impact Assessment
Angus Morrison-Saunders and Jenny Pope

Teaching Research Methods in Political Science
Edited by Jeffrey L. Bernstein

Teaching International Relations
Edited by James M. Scott, Ralph G. Carter, Brandy Jolliff Scott and Jeffrey S. Lantis

Teaching Marketing
Edited by Ross Brennan and Lynn Vos

Teaching Marketing

Edited by

Ross Brennan

Professor of Industrial Marketing, Hertfordshire Business School, University of Hertfordshire, UK

Lynn Vos

Associate Professor of Marketing, Southern Alberta Institute of Technology, Canada

Edward Elgar
PUBLISHING

Cheltenham, UK • Northampton, MA, USA

Cover image: Joshua Coleman on Unsplash

Published by
Edward Elgar Publishing Limited
The Lypiatts
15 Lansdown Road
Cheltenham
Glos GL50 2JA
UK

Edward Elgar Publishing, Inc.
William Pratt House
9 Dewey Court
Northampton
Massachusetts 01060
USA

Paperback edition 2022

A catalogue record for this book
is available from the British Library

Library of Congress Control Number: 2021946151

This book is available electronically in the **Elgar**online
Business subject collection
http://dx.doi.org/10.4337/9781789907896

MIX
Paper from
responsible sources
FSC   FSC® C013604

ISBN 978 1 78990 788 9 (cased)
ISBN 978 1 78990 789 6 (eBook)
ISBN 978 1 0353 0813 2 (paperback)
Printed and bound by CPI Group (UK) Ltd, Croydon, CR0 4YY

In honor of Professor David Ross Brennan, my dear friend, most esteemed colleague, man of profound integrity and humility, and loving husband and father to Jacqueline, Sarah and Emily. Ross was a rare example of the gentleman academic who demonstrated continuously that the best academic departments are built on goodwill – the extra contributions that go above and beyond the job description and include a genuine and profound commitment to the success of others. Ross believed that rigorous thinking, including the deep exploration of theory, ideas and perspectives in marketing are the foundations to better teaching. This work reflects his beliefs and values.

Contents

Figures

Tables

Boxes

Contributors

Dag Bennett is Associate Professor of Marketing at London South Bank University, UK. His research interests include buying behaviour, emerging markets, industrial buying behaviour, and marketing education. Dag's published work includes chapters in several textbooks, notably *Marketing: Theory, Evidence, Practice* (with Byron Sharp, John Scriven and others), *Sustainable Smart Cities* (with Marta Peris-Ortiz and Diana Perez-Bustamante Yabar) and research articles in such journals as *International Marketing Review*, *International Research in Marketing*, and *Business Horizons*.

Ross Brennan was the former Professor of Industrial Marketing at the University of Hertfordshire, UK. His research interests included business-to-business marketing, industrial networks, social marketing, and marketing education. Ross's published work includes several textbooks, notably *Marketing: An Introduction* (with Gary Armstrong, Philip Kotler and Michael Harker) and *Business to Business Marketing* (with Louise Canning and Ray McDowell), and research articles in such journals as *Industrial Marketing Management*, the *European Journal of Marketing*, *Marketing Theory*, *Business Ethics: A European Review*, and the *Journal of Marketing Education.*

Barbara Czarnecka is Associate Professor of Marketing at the London South Bank University, UK. Her teaching interests are eclectic and include improving research methods teaching to students who think they do not like research. You can read more about her research and teaching interests on www.barbaraczarnecka.com.

Andrew Corcoran holds an MBA and an MA in Education, is a Fellow of the Chartered Institute of Marketing, and a Senior Fellow of the Higher Education Academy. He has worked in the Construction (1986–1989), Manufacturing (1989–2001) and Higher Education (since 2001) sectors. He held Business Development roles at Birmingham City University and the University of Worcester. He began his teaching career with Aston University in 2010 and is Assistant Professor in Marketing and Departmental Teaching Director at Nottingham University Business School, UK. He teaches Marketing Management, Consumer Behaviour, International Marketing, Environment of Business, Strategic Management, Innovation Management, and Marketing Consultancy.

Michael Harker is a lecturer in the Department of Marketing in the Strathclyde Business School, UK. His research interests lie in networks and relationships, and improving business education. To this end he has conducted several investigations funded by the Academy of Marketing into current practice, work appearing in *Academy of Management Learning & Education* and *Marketing Intelligence and Planning*, of which he is a former editor. Michael's published work also includes *Marketing: An Introduction* (with Gary Armstrong, Philip Kotler and Ross Brennan) and papers in the *International Small Business Journal* and the *Journal of Strategic Marketing*. He has taught the introductory class in marketing for the last 15 years at Strathclyde.

Teresa Heath is an Associate Professor in Marketing at the University of Minho, Portugal. She was previously Assistant Professor at the Nottingham University Business School. Her research focuses on critical marketing and its intersection with sustainability, consumption, and responsible management education. Her work has been published widely, including in the *Journal of Business Ethics*, *Journal of Business Research*, *European Journal of Marketing* and *Management Learning*. Teresa has extensive, international experience of teaching modules on Marketing Theory and Critical Marketing. She is a member of the Education Committee of the Academy of Marketing, Visiting Fellow at the University of Nottingham, and Fellow of the Higher Education Academy.

Ariadne Beatrice Kapetanaki is Lecturer in Marketing at the University of York Management School, UK. She has experience teaching social marketing and behaviour change to public health, marketing and nutrition/dietetics students at both undergraduate and postgraduate levels. Her research is interdisciplinary and focuses on social marketing, consumer culture, vulnerable consumers, food consumption, food practices and policies. Her projects have received funding from the ESRC, the British Academy and the British Academy of Management. She has published in journals such as *The Lancet*, *Journal of Cleaner Production*, *Cambridge Journal of Education* and *Journal of Consumer Affairs*.

Maria Rita Massaro is Lecturer in Marketing at the University of Westminster Business School, UK. She has taught Marketing, Branding, and Research Methods across different institutions in Italy and the UK. Currently, she is exploring the application of social media listening tools to the teaching of marketing research.

Andrew Paddison is a Teaching Fellow in the Department of Marketing in the Strathclyde Business School (University of Strathclyde, UK). His research interests focus upon marketing pedagogy, in particular signature pedagogies, and place marketing. His teaching interests focus upon consumer behaviour/consumption and small business marketing. Within SBS, Andrew is the Academic Director of the GA (Graduate Apprenticeship) in Business Management. Prior to SBS, Andrew worked at the University of Paisley, Middlesex University, University of Stirling and SRUC.

Anita Peleg is a National Teaching Fellow with more than 25 years' experience in university education. Her specialist teaching areas focus on business and marketing ethics, marketing and marketing research. Her research interests include ethics and moral education in marketing, and education for employability. She has presented and published papers and contributed to academic books on graduate employability, marketing ethics and moral education at seminars and conferences throughout the UK.

Fiona Spotswood is Senior Lecturer in Marketing at the University of Bristol, UK. She teaches social marketing to postgraduates. Her research seeks to advance critical understandings of social marketing. She focuses on physical activity and inactivity research, and is particularly interested in the configuration of everyday social practices that frame the possibility of physically active leisure. Her research has been published in the *European Journal of Marketing*, *Journal of Social Marketing*, *Critical Public Health* and *Sociology of Health and Illness*, amongst others. She edited a volume exploring interdisciplinary approaches to behaviour change entitled *Beyond Behaviour Change* (2016), based on her ESRC funded seminar series of the same name.

Caroline Tynan is Emeritus Professor of Marketing at the University of Nottingham, UK, President and a Fellow of the Academy of Marketing and a Fellow of the Chartered Institute of Marketing. She has represented the discipline of marketing on the UK's research assessment exercises RAE2008 and REF2014. Over the last 15 years she has taught various postgraduate modules on Marketing Theory. Her research interests focus on consumer identity, consumption meanings, value creation, experience marketing and luxury consumption. She has published in a wide range of journals including the *Journal of Business Research*, *European Journal of Marketing*, *Journal of Marketing Management* and *Journal of Travel Research*.

Lynn Vos is Associate Professor of Marketing at SAIT (Southern Alberta Institute of Technology) in Calgary, Canada. She researches marketing and higher education and has contributed works on simulation games, improving postgraduate dissertations, integrating learning, cross-disciplinary curriculum, assessment, and the marketisation of higher education, among others. Lynn worked at four universities in the UK prior to returning to her native Canada in 2020. She also held a national role as Discipline Lead for Marketing and Accounting/Finance at the Higher Education Academy (2011–2014) where she visited over 60 UK universities, discussing and promoting improvements in teaching and learning.

Jonathan Wilson is Associate Professor in Marketing and Business Research at the University of East Anglia (UEA), UK. He is a recipient of the UEA 2018 Sir Geoffrey and Lady Allen prize in teaching and a University Teaching Fellow. Jonathan is author of the best-selling book *Essentials of Business Research: A Guide to Doing Your Research Project* and has been a Fellow of the Chartered Institute of Marketing (CIM) since 2004. He has taught on marketing and business programmes to employees from leading multinational companies, such as: Barclays, British Airways, Sinopec and Deutsche Bank.

Ben Wooliscroft is Professor of Macromarketing at Auckland University of Technology, Auckland, New Zealand. He is also President of the Macromarketing Society, Inc. and Associate Editor of the *Journal of Macromarketing*. He has taught the history of marketing to students at various levels (undergraduate through doctoral) for two decades. His research focuses on the interactions between marketing, markets and society, with Quality of life as the dependent variable. Ben has published in a variety of journals including the *Journal of Macromarketing, Marketing Theory, Journal of Business Research, Journal of Sustainable Tourism*, the *Journal of Happiness Studies* and *Applied Research in Quality of Life*.

1. Introduction to *Teaching Marketing*

Ross Brennan and Lynn Vos

Marketing involves a vast range of participants, processes and perspectives. Linguistically it is used interchangeably as a verb – "to market" ideas, people, places, products or services, and a noun – "marketing" – all of the activities involved in transferring goods and services from producer to buyer or user such that mutually beneficial, voluntary exchange takes place. With the publication of Wroe Alderson's (1957) work *Marketing Behavior and Executive Action*, marketing as a discipline moved from a focus on distribution and the classification of relevant institutions to that of the marketing manager or seller's perspective (see Wooliscroft in Chapter 7 of this volume). The breadth of topics and processes considered as part of the discipline grew as Alderson's work began an expansion of the field from mainly theoretical perspectives drawn from economics to include insights from many social and behavioural science disciplines (Shaw and Lazer, 2007). By the 1960s, this influx of ideas led to increased and more disciplinary diverse research into the mind and actions of the consumer, thus establishing the second most prominent school of thought after marketing management, that of consumer behaviour. In the 1970s the societal view of marketing and wider, more reflective and critical schools of thought, including macromarketing were growing sub-fields, including research into what Wilkie and Moore (1999) refer to as the broader, complex and evolving effects of the aggregate marketing system within and across societies that bring up questions of ethics, sustainability, moral responsibility, inequalities and failures in development (Hill and Martin, 2014).

Thus, marketing can be viewed as an integrating discipline (Bedeian, 2005) whose practical and research outputs have a large footprint. It edges into other fields of thought and inquiry and other fields edge into marketing, the outcome of which is to broaden both theory and practice. For deep knowledge and understanding of consumers, marketing scholars draw upon research in sociology, the neurosciences and clinical, cognitive and social psychology; for understanding of markets and exchange, macro, micro and now behavioural economics; for perspectives on evolving trends, not to mention the discipline itself, history. This is to name only a few and leaves out theoretical perspectives native to the discipline developed in marketing science, industrial marketing and marketing theory, among others; areas of interest explored further in chapters within this work (see the chapters by Bennett, by Brennan, and by Tynan and Heath). As a field, marketing is rich in ideas that are complex and contradictory and as a discipline these characteristics make it rich in the potential for both disciplinary and cross-disciplinary research, theory formulation and testing. Thus, Wilkie and Moore (1999: 198) remind us why researchers and educators are drawn to marketing: it is "among the most stimulating, complex and intellectually challenging of academic areas in a university setting" (as quoted in Chapter 3 by Tynan and Heath).

The complexity of marketing is also demonstrated in how it is practised across industries, organisations, societies, groups and/or by individuals. A vast and diverse array of functions, roles, processes and perspectives make up the marketing space. In one scenario a customised solution is being offered as "a team of professionals from an IT vendor work ... alongside a complementary team from a manufacturing organisation ... to deliver an enhanced logistics and inventory control system" (Brennan in Chapter 7). In another, a well-known producer of breakfast cereals is grappling with modifying its product line to address governmental and consumer concerns about sugar intake while reconsidering how it promotes its highly profitable range of high sugar cereals to its core customer groups. In yet another, a government body has invested millions first to understand the reasons behind COVID-19 vaccine hesitancy, then to develop online and offline messaging to encourage all citizens to get vaccinated.

As a function, the boundaries of marketing are fluid and thus within any organisation its constituent parts may fall to or be claimed by other functional areas, often so much so that the value contributed by marketing is questioned – someone else is doing sales, products are developed within the operations department, marketing research is commissioned out, logistics is managed within the supply chain, technologists and data analysts are deciding on the software and systems to best track and identify patterns in consumer data, and public relations is managing the bulk of external communications. The fact that marketing functions are often distributed across multiple departments rather than conducted exclusively in a marketing department is one of many issues that create challenges for marketing educators. The question arises – how can we tackle this breadth and complexity in the undergraduate marketing curriculum without under-representing the key ideas, perspectives, theories and processes that make up the field? Too often, unfortunately, the curriculum is modularised into narrow functional areas such as market research, marketing communications, and digital marketing; this approach may provide students with an overview of these areas and some technical skills but risks leaving them with a narrow and impoverished perspective on marketing.

Boundary issues are also present regarding who claims to speak authoritatively on the subject. Far more than other professional subjects – finance, architecture, biology, for instance – those who write and speak about marketing appear to come from all walks of life. A quick internet search brings up not millions, but billions of documents related to marketing, many of which greatly oversimplify complex ideas in terms of both understanding and application. The ease with which such works can be found creates additional challenges for marketing educators whose students generally have great facility searching for ideas and concepts through the main internet providers, but less with library databases or with discriminating between a credible, well researched source and a derivative, monetised source whose ideas are greatly simplified, misleading and often wrong. How often, for example, is social marketing confused with social media marketing, the opportunities in a SWOT analysis viewed as strategic alternatives, and/or the product-market development vectors of Igor Ansoff (1957) misunderstood, to name only a few of the more basic marketing ideas found in a quick internet search?

That the discipline is subject to such profound simplification, where core ideas and concepts are made into simple formulae for success and then repurposed and repeated in hundreds of internet blogs and videos is an issue that marketing educators must explore and allow students to reflect on. As Brennan points out, however, marketing "scholars [appear] less inclined to defend their conceptual domains against the abuses of journalistic commentators than scholars in most other fields" (Brennan, 2012: 5). Perhaps the problem stems from how marketing ideas are typically introduced to students – we remind them that they too are customers, and thus already familiar with many aspects of the discipline. While helpful in engaging students early on, this approach can quickly narrow the scope of examples and ideas presented, thus contributing to the abridged and often less complicated view of marketing that they encounter in other fora. In seeking to build student interest, the rich theoretical perspectives inherent in areas such as macromarketing, networked business relationships, critical consumption and other areas where the final customer is not the central focus become less prominent in the curriculum and in so doing, give students less knowledge and value than they deserve from this rich and composite discipline.

The challenge of how to structure and what to include in the marketing curriculum is complicated by different perspectives within the discipline over the purpose of a marketing education, including how it should be taught and who the priority stakeholder or stakeholders should be – questions that come up time and time again in the marketing education literature, reaching back to the commentaries of the earliest educators. In Chapter 7 on teaching marketing history, Wooliscroft reminds us that almost 120 years has passed since university scholars began to organise, research and teach concepts in marketing. Although marketing ideas have been written about and debated "back to the ancient Greek Socratic philosophers, Plato and Aristotle [who] discussed …

issues, such as how marketing was integrated into society" (Shaw and Jones, 2005: 241), when Hagerty (1936) taught one of the first classes in marketing, a three-hour course at Ohio State University in 1905, there was almost no available literature upon which to base his teaching. It took some years before the discipline developed scholarly perspectives and academic literature for the development of theory and for use in the classroom. Thus, Hagerty would spend any free time he had conducting interviews with "prominent men in different lines of mercantile trade in Philadelphia and in New York City" (Hagerty, 1936: 23) at department stores, in intermediary institutions including "manufacturer's agents, brokers, jobbers and travelling salesmen" (p. 22) to find examples and ideas to build the new curriculum.

The fact that marketing academics turn to industrial practice and prac-titioners as sources of classroom as well as research ideas, and that much scholarly research in the field seeks to grapple with business problems is to be expected given the professional nature of the discipline. However, as with other disciplines with a substantial practitioner community, there is a need to strike a balance in academic research and curriculum design between serving the interests of practitioners (by, for example, delivering skilled graduates and useful research) and serving the wider interests of both students and other stakeholders.

Indeed, the question of *what* to teach in marketing, or what counts as mar-keting knowledge, is an epistemological debate of long standing, reflected even in the Hagerty (1936) article. At the broadest level, marketing educators (and researchers) deliberate over whether to focus on teaching students *how* to do marketing (practical/applied) (e.g. Walle, 1991; Hulbert and Harrigan, 2011; Koch, 2013) or whether to focus on teaching *about* marketing (market-ing as theory, as social function, and from a critical perspective) (Catterall et al., 2002; Hill and McGinnis, 2007). Certainly, a review of the top marketing education journals bears this out.

In terms of the "how to" end of the spectrum, the literature in marketing education over the past four decades (the main period for which marketing education has had dedicated journals), produces a steady stream of calls for change because, the authors claim, the marketing curriculum, current at their time of writing, is failing to meet the needs of industry or to develop the knowledge and skills required by employers. This pressure for change is more often than not presented as an imperative; the language in article titles or abstracts implying that failure to consider the proposed innovations could have significant, negative consequences for both students and the discipline. Examples include Stanton's (1988) call for serious "restructuring", Koch's (1997) "designing a new logic and structure", Pharr and Morris's (1997) "time to rethink marketing education", Smart et al.'s (1999) call to "increase its relevancy", Hulbert and Harrigan (2011) proposing "a new marketing DNA" and more recently, the "need for radical innovations" (Schlegelmilch, 2020). The urgency and frequency of these calls implies that the relevance of what we teach our students and the relevance of research to solve current business problems is constantly under question and scrutiny. Is this simply the nature of a professional discipline or is there something more to it? It could be argued that all professional disciplines taught in research institutions are by nature, both ahead of and behind the sectors they serve. Ahead of, given that research into innovative practices are not restricted by the immediacy of earnings requirements, and researchers have the luxury of testing new theories and ideas over time; and behind what industry professionals see as their imperatives, particularly as technology develops at the pace of Moore's law while curriculum innovations in academic institutions follow other conventions and patterns that take time, involve so many stakeholders and have different aims and objectives. The former issue that argues for academic research as a real benefit to industry is held back by the opaque nature of most research output and its non-industry-friendly structure and language. It's not so much that things are lost in translation, but that they are simply never translated into useful or implementable ideas for business.

Clearly, however, there are those marketing scholars who believe that relevance to industry is a *sine qua non* of academic marketing research. And relevance to industry is often interpreted simplistically as providing guidance on effective marketing strategies for marketing practitioners. However, academic research need not serve a narrow interest group, and marketing practitioners are by no means the only people with an interest in marketing research anyway. As in other disciplines, there is no reason why academic marketing research cannot pursue the goal of understanding marketing better for purely scientific reasons, with scientific knowledge as the ultimate goal. Furthermore, a wide range of stakeholders besides marketing practitioners have interests in understanding marketing, since the marketing system interacts extensively with other important social systems, as summarised by Wilkie and Moore (1999) and considered within the sub-field of macromarketing. Clearly, policy-makers, regulators and consumer groups have considerable interest in marketing research. Indeed, other stakeholders whose interests may not be directly aligned with the capitalist paradigm also have an interest in serious research into marketing principles and practice. Likely examples are groups such as Extinction Rebellion, in connection with such issues as the contribution of marketing activity to climate change, and Black Lives Matter, in connection with issues like the representation of people of colour in advertising and marketing campaigns.

In the context of marketing education, this "relevance debate" is rather different since marketing students must be considered the primary stakeholder group. The question is not *if* the interests of marketing students should be given priority, but what those interests are and how they should be prioritised. Just as there are those who argue that academic marketing research should primarily serve the interests of marketing practitioners, so there are those who argue that marketing education should serve the interests of marketing students by endowing them with skills and knowledge that marketing practitioners claim to find useful. The common feature becomes the positioning of the marketing academy as a service industry to marketing practice: to deliver research and graduates that practitioners perceive to be useful. Just as this argument can be contested for research, so it can be contested for education. It is students' interests that are the priority, not practitioners' interests. First, there are those students who study marketing without the desire to become marketing professionals, for whom a narrowly defined industry-designed curriculum is pointless and unnecessarily restrictive. Secondly, there are the many students who will pursue a career that is broadly in marketing, but not narrowly within the confines of a conventional consumer-marketing context. Thirdly, it is important to remember that marketing educators are the responsible education professionals, and while it is important to listen to marketing practitioners, it is also important to remember that they are not education professionals. One can ask the practitioner what skills and knowledge they consider useful in the workplace today and what they expect to be useful tomorrow. However, one cannot ask the practitioner what the curriculum should look like to prepare students for the marketing workplace of today, and to endow them with the lifelong learning skills and growth mindset required to thrive in future years. The former is a question on which marketing practitioners can provide an informed opinion. The latter is a matter of expert educational design.

Thus, the objectives of education, be it in marketing or other disciplines, are not the same as the objectives of those managing organisations and unless that education is called training and is situated within and created by or in collaboration with an organisation or industry association, the objectives will never be the same. Education in the formal sense serves society, not a particular industry or individual target audiences, although professional disciplines add the latter groups as important stakeholders. Whatever the discipline, education is about developing citizens who have the capacity to think more broadly about issues within and beyond a discipline, and the broad subject matter and theoretical perspectives that come under the subject area of marketing attest to this.

Even as four decades of scholarship has many claims that the marketing curriculum does not meet the needs of industry stakeholders and that academic marketing research, as narrowly defined, is not useful to practitioners, marketing degrees nevertheless continue to draw students in large numbers, suggesting that students find the subject compelling and of sufficient interest to invest their resources. It is also one that may offer an interesting and rewarding career for many students. Of course, in terms of educational design, teachers of marketing must remain open to improving and upgrading the curriculum to reflect new research and to address broad and changing trends in the marketing system. As Wilkie and Moore (1999: 198) remind us, "marketing's contributions (1) accumulate over time, (2) diffuse through a society, and (3) occur within the context of everyday life [all of which] can make them hard to discern at any given time". They caution that as commentators and presumably as educators, we bring four perceptual barriers to understanding how these contributions can affect the discipline: "time, system limits, culture and personal experience" (p. 199). Time can make it difficult to discern the emergence and ultimate effects of these shifts and contributions. They may arise suddenly and have long effects, such as COVID, or emerge slowly over time but with increasing urgency for action, such as climate change and the need for diversity. System limits make it challenging to understand whether important trends emerge exclusively from actions within the marketing system, from the effects of other aggregate systems such as finance or technology or from systems interacting with each other – the interaction of marketing and technology systems today being an example. Cultural barriers remind us that marketing is a "social institution that is highly adaptive to its cultural and political context" and thus varies greatly in the world in terms of its stage of development and how it is applied, thus "we must take care to distinguish which lessons are generalisable and which are not (Wilkie and Moore, 1999: 199) but also to broaden the geographical scope of cases and examples we use in the classroom (Wilson, Chapter 11). Finally, our own personal experiences, preferences and scholarly interests can keep us so focused that we are imperceptive of or less interested in change, developments and effects, small or large that could be considered, not only so our students are better prepared for marketing careers, but so they are better prepared as thinkers, problem solvers and citizens.

Thus, educators need to consider where we can enrich our students' understanding in a changing world where marketing actions or inactions, both at the individual and systemic levels have a role to play. Sometimes this means focusing on particular skills, such as numeracy, given that solving both company and society level issues requires more and more sophisticated quantitative and research skills; at other times building in more opportunities for students to consider ethics, development, social and sustainability issues; and at still others to examine the growing role of technology in marketing decision making, customer responsiveness and innovation. In addition to theory and content we should also reflect continuously on how we teach and make use of the vast and growing evidence-base about ways to improve our pedagogy. Most importantly, however, we must continue to develop our students' breadth of knowledge across the broad and complex field of marketing and to use our teaching opportunities to challenge them and to develop their critical and higher-level thinking skills. These are among the main objectives of this edited work.

The work presented here should be of interest to both those new to teaching in marketing as well as more experienced educators who wish to enhance their teaching with new perspectives, teach new courses or assist in curriculum development. Many chapters provide examples and exercises that can be used in the classroom, suggest pedagogical approaches upon which to structure the teaching and learning, and all contain rich reference lists to allow educators to build their current courses or develop new ones. Given how diverse the field of marketing is, this work is not exhaustive in terms of subjects that are currently taught or could be taught. However, the chapters that make up the book provide many insights into subjects that make up the curriculum of most marketing programmes and also ones that, while not ubiquitous, could enrich the students' learning, understanding and critical thinking skills if added to a programme.

In Chapter 2 Anita Peleg advocates "ethics and responsibility from the outset". A wealth of research-informed advice and teaching resources on the subject of teaching ethics and related topics (such as CSR and sustainability) can be found in the marketing education literature (Allan and Wood, 2009; Nicholson and DeMoss, 2009; Beggs, 2011; Donoho and Heinze, 2011; Donoho et al., 2012). Prominent voices have called for the comprehensive integration of ethics, CSR and sustainability into the marketing curriculum (Beggs, 2011; Rundle-Thiele and Wymer, 2010). Despite the following rather pessimistic finding: "Studies of ethics education have shown that ethics training does not result in improved moral reasoning (ethical judgment) by students" Beggs (2011: 49), Beggs (2011) also cites evidence that ethics education can make a difference to students' ethical reasoning. However, he argues that the teaching of marketing ethics should not be explicitly flagged as such; ethical dilemmas are context-specific, and in the real world they do not come fully marked up as requiring ethical consideration. Hence, Beggs' advocacy of *seamless* integration of ethics into the curriculum: embedding ethical discussions into the discussion of traditional marketing topics as a natural part of the curriculum. In her chapter, "Ethics and responsibility from the outset", Peleg follows the same line of argument but takes it a great deal further and provides a detailed template for the implementation of such ideas. Influential organisations support this approach (for example, the UN Global Compact Principles for Responsible Management Education and the Association to Advance Collegiate Schools of Business (AACSB International)), major employers consider ethics and social responsibility to be a key component of the business school curriculum, and business students expect opportunities to study these topics (Crane, 2004; Reynolds and Dang, 2017). Consequently, Peleg proposes that in *every* taught marketing module responsible principles and practice should be considered alongside profitable economic outcomes; ethics and social responsibility should become central and not be considered as an option or a bolt-on extra in the curriculum. Specific examples and case studies are used to illustrate how this can be achieved in the practice of marketing education.

Caroline Tynan and Teresa Heath discuss how to teach marketing theory and critical thinking in Chapter 3. Building on a theme prominent in other chapters in this work, Tynan and Heath advocate developing students' critical thinking skills, in this case through grappling with the origins, development and diversity of marketing theory. The authors explore how teaching marketing theory allows students to develop not only higher-level thinking skills but also the confidence and facility to critique the discipline so they can both apply marketing concepts and processes under expected, typical conditions and, when these ideas fall short or do not work, adapt them or try something else. This facility comes from having had opportunities to question the received wisdom. They note, quite rightly, that many marketing programmes unfortunately take a "theory-light" approach to the discipline because educators assume that students find theory and theory formulation challenging and thus err on the side of teaching techniques and skills that when separated from the originating theories appear to students as immutable and determinate. Tynan and Heath argue that it is all a matter of how educators introduce theory, its purposes, uses and value. The authors provide recommendations on how to introduce the value of theory in marketing, first by having students consider the purpose of theory and theory formation, second by considering widely known theories and the significant contributions these theories have made to our lives, and third to consider how even well-known fictional detectives such as Sherlock Holmes use theories to solve their cases. Marketing has a rich theoretical heritage, with research grounded in diverse epistemological positions using a wide range of methodologies. Students are able to consider the main theoreticians whose work has made the field of marketing so rich and diverse and the course can also give them a solid grounding in philosophical perspectives that shape researchers' methods, thus going much further than most marketing research modules in providing insights and understanding relevant to their major project and/or dissertation work. In demonstrating that theories are all around us and a part of most solutions and innovations, Tynan and Heath also remind educators that theories and how they are tested should not be presented in unnecessarily complex ways that may appear obscurantist and intimidating to students.

In Chapter 4 Michael Harker and Andrew Paddison explore the marketing curriculum. They begin their investigation of the marketing curriculum with some fundamental questions: what is a curriculum, is there an established curriculum in marketing, what does it look like, and how is it changing? A review of 29 published studies of the marketing curriculum reveals that there is a core to the marketing curriculum, comprising the topics of marketing principles, marketing communications, marketing research and strategic marketing. Beyond this there are established topics (the standard curriculum) including well-established subject matter such as consumer behaviour, international marketing, e-marketing and retail marketing. Harker and Paddison express surprise (which may be shared by many readers) that consumer behaviour seems to fall outside the core although inside the standard curriculum. Harker and Paddison then turn to current developments in the UK marketing curriculum based on a survey of departments carried out on behalf of the Academy of Marketing. Consumer behaviour seems now to be establishing itself in the core marketing curriculum. Of increasing popularity in the curriculum are e-marketing (now usually referred to as digital), client-based projects, critical marketing, and issues around marketing and society, including marketing ethics. Declining in popularity are subjects that require numeracy skills (which many will regard as unfortunate since marketing decisions often require quantitative reasoning), and that take a broader organisational perspective on marketing (such as business-to-business marketing). However, there is evidence that certain marketing subjects, notably digital and international marketing, are increasingly being distributed across the curriculum and, therefore, subsumed into other topics. The supposition here is that curriculum designers increasingly see marketing as an inherently international and digital discipline so that these components must be ubiquitous in the curriculum. On the other hand, and perhaps surprisingly, there is no evidence of the same effect in the case of marketing ethics and sustainability despite prominent calls for this to happen (Peleg makes a persuasive case in Chapter 2).

Lynn Vos examines the educational value of marketing simulation games in Chapter 5. Along with other authors in this collection, Vos grounds her teaching recommendations within an explicit pedagogical approach. Authentic learning recommends applied tasks that can lead to deeper learning when students are given sufficient practice, challenge, formative feedback and time for reflection (Newmann et al., 1996; Gulikers et al., 2006; Herrington and Herrington, 2006; Ashford-Rowe et al., 2014; Lincoln and Cassidy, 2018; Villarroel et al., 2018). Marketing simulation games are by nature active learning tools that mirror elements of real-world business decisions while removing the main risks associated with decision making in practice, and thus simulations fulfil a core requirement of authentic learning – a simulated experience from the work environment that can develop students' higher-level thinking skills. Vos argues that simulation games offer other elements of effective pedagogy that are much discussed in the literature but not often practised simultaneously within a single module. She demonstrates how games allow students to practise their understanding of core concepts over a number of game iterations – something that our time-strapped curriculum does not always permit (Ericsson et al., 1993). Simulations also provide for a mediated learning environment where the game or the tutor can add graduated levels of complexity such that the students are regularly challenged to learn more and in greater depth while being given regular feedback on their progress with both game-generated reports (financial, sales, distribution effectiveness, customer satisfaction, among others) and tutor debriefing (Fanning and Gaba, 2007; Dieckmann et al., 2009). Moreover, given the number of rounds or iterations of the game, simulations provide ongoing opportunities for students to reflect on their approaches to decision making and to consider what they need to improve upon. In addition to demonstrating the inherent pedagogic values of simulations, Vos also argues strongly for a key learning benefit of simulations that is often assumed to occur over the course of a student's degree but is not always achieved – that of integration of learning (Kuh, 2008; Barber, 2014). Ideally, as students pass through their learning experience, they are deemed to be integrating the knowledge gained in one subject with that of another, such that when they graduate, they are able to skilfully deploy and weave together knowledge and learning from across modules to effectively and efficiently solve the kinds of cross-functional, multidisciplinary problems they will encounter in practice. Vos demonstrates that simulation games are one of the few learning tools that allow students to integrate their learning from across a range of marketing modules and other courses to actively develop cross-functional and critical thinking skills.

In Chapter 6 Andrew Corcoran offers those new to teaching consumer behaviour a guide to getting started. He begins by reminding us that of all the schools of thought within marketing, consumer behaviour is probably the most cross-disciplinary, with educators and researchers either coming from or grounding their research in different discipline areas. As Shaw and Jones (2005: 261) remind us, "[b]ecause it deals with human behavior, consumer behavior is one of marketing's most eclectic schools of thought" and as the field developed, many well-known theorists in psychology, sociology and economics, among other disciplines, have contributed ideas to our understanding of buyer behaviour. The main journals in the field, the *Journal of Consumer Psychology* and the *Journal of Consumer Research*, are highly esteemed by scholars and "recognised world-wide as exemplars of excellence" by the Chartered Association of Business Schools (charteredabs.org); both publish articles by researchers from across the social sciences. Certainly the field is rich in theory and models of decision making and buyer behaviour and Corcoran provides an overview of some of the best known and widely used, including Lavidge and Steiner's (1961) Hierarchy of Effects Model, Dewey's (1910) five stage consumer decision-making process, Maslow's (1943) Hierarchy of Needs, and McGuire's (1974) drives and motives. The author provides many helpful exercises and activities to use in the classroom, in addition to providing a structure for how the module could be taught, including learning outcomes, topics and core readings.

The topic of Chapter 7, by Ben Wooliscroft, is teaching marketing history. Few programmes in marketing include a dedicated course in marketing history, although elements may be discussed in contemporary issues or theory modules. Wooliscroft, who has been teaching the history of marketing thought for the past two decades, argues that students benefit from having a better understanding of how their discipline evolved because, after all, one of the key objectives of dedicated study in a particular field is to develop both the capacity and confidence to critique its theoretical foundations while also moving the field forward over time (Shaw and Jones, 2005; Hunt, 2011; Wooliscroft, 2011). For example, understanding how we came to teach marketing from a predominantly management perspective in contrast to looking at marketing from a broader societal perspective provides opportunities for students to understand how particular ideas become dominant in a discipline, thus allowing them to question not only why such ideas come to the forefront but also that other schools of thought might offer important insights and approaches to marketing problems from both theoretical and applied perspectives (Tadajewski, 2006). Wooliscroft suggests that students read from seminal works such as Sheth et al. (1998) *Marketing Theory: Evolution and Evaluation*, Alderson's (1957) *Marketing Behaviour and Executive Action* in addition to works by Bagozzi (1975) on value creation, Hunt and Morgan (1996) on the resource advantage of the firm, Ehrenberg (1995) on marketing science, and Vargo and Lusch (2004) on value-in-use, to name just a few. His course begins with key organising questions such as "what is marketing?", "what is theory?" and the five main questions that structure the core text used in the course (Sheth et al., 1998), including identifying the proper domain(s) of marketing, what is or should be the dominant perspective in marketing (if any), and whether marketing is an art or a science. These are questions that students are unlikely to have considered as they move from one subject area to the next, semester after semester. He then suggests a structure for the course that follows the "School's" approach, so well laid out in Shaw and Jones (2005). As the students move through an understanding of foundational ideas by reading works by key scholars in earlier schools, including the commodities, institutional, functional schools through later schools including the dominant managerial school, the large consumer behaviour school and macromarketing, they consider the origins of concepts still predominant as organising principles in today's marketing textbooks while allowing them to think critically about how marketing scholars have grappled with key ontological and epistemological perspectives and theory, most of which have never fully achieved their original grand objectives. Thus, they are able to contemplate the kinds of struggles for knowledge and knowing that confront thinkers in disciplines such as marketing, but more generally in all knowledge creation.

In Chapter 8, Ross Brennan considers the topic of teaching business-to-business marketing. Business-to-business marketing has never been the most popular course in the marketing curriculum, and indeed seems to be of diminishing importance in the curriculum, at least in the United Kingdom (according to Harker and Paddison in Chapter 4). One obvious reason for this relative unpopularity is that much business-to-business marketing fails to conform to the naive perception that many undergraduate students have of what marketing is. If you believe that marketing is something done to consumers by the providers of consumer goods and services in order to persuade them to buy, and therefore associate marketing with the characteristic embellishments of such practice (for example, an over-emphasis on the communications dimension of marketing, delivered through consumer media and emphasising affective rather than rational appeals), then this all makes sense. As Brennan points out, however, the characteristics of business markets and marketing are often very different from consumer marketing, both in practical and theoretical terms. One way to determine the most suitable approach to marketing starts with a contingency framework that identifies the key characteristics of markets, customers and customer relationships, and then suggests appropriate marketing strategies. Business-to-business markets are often characterised by enduring customer relationships involving multiple high-value transactions, within which trust and mutual dependence develop, leading to relationship-specific investments and mutual adaptations. Consequently, different theoretical frameworks, such as those of the IMP Group that focus on business-to-business relationships and the industrial networks of which they are a part (Håkansson, 1982; Håkansson and Snehota, 1995; Håkansson and Ford, 2002; Brennan et al., 2020), offer a sounder basis for both theorising and practical marketing strategy. From a pedagogic perspective, Brennan (Chapter 8) advocates a "deep end" rather than a "shallow end" approach to teaching business-to-business marketing. The deep end approach starts by focusing on business-to-business marketing situations that contingency frameworks show to be distinctly different from typical consumer marketing situations, so that students need to learn a distinctly different perspective on marketing and a new vocabulary suitable for the business-to-business context. This will better prepare the student to enter the professional world of business-to-business marketing than the simplistic notion that consumer marketing ideas can be easily transferred to the business marketing context.

Barbara Czarnecka and Maria Rita Massaro examine research methods teaching in Chapter 9. The subject of research methods is one that presents the marketing curriculum planner with particular dilemmas. Czarnecka and Massaro address these dilemmas, observing that on the one hand many marketing students are poorly prepared to undertake a rigorous course in research methods, while on the other hand employers consistently demand that marketing graduates should be competent in analysing and interpreting data and turning the analysis into actionable plans. It is easy to see how this dilemma, if poorly handled, could be reduced to a competition between the desire to avoid upsetting the student-customer (who might want to avoid too much maths) and the desire to demonstrate key employability outcomes in the course design. However, as Czarnecka and Massaro argue, there really can be no doubt that research evidence in its many forms is playing an ever-increasing role in professional marketing practice, and so whatever the background or preferences of marketing students may be, the learning outcomes from a marketing course simply must include competence in the handling of marketing data. The only serious question is how to achieve this. From a pedagogic point of view Czarnecka and Massaro strongly advocate an active-learning approach to research methods, with the learning process centred on finding solutions to practical marketing problems. At all points in teaching research methods for marketing, students should be exposed to practical as well as theoretical material. Many students, in subsequent employment, will be expected to use big data, and so the inclusion of data analytics in the research methods course is imperative. However, despite the ever-increasing focus on big data and analytics, Czarnecka and Massaro are equally insistent that qualitative methods remain an important part of the marketer's armoury and must be included in the research methods curriculum. This includes both traditional qualitative methods (such as focus groups and semi-structured interviews) and the relatively new field of netnography, the adaptation of ethnographic techniques for use in the online world (Kozinets, 2002, 2019).

In Chapter 10 Ariadne Kapetanaki and Fiona Spotswood consider how to teach social marketing. Kapetanaki and Spotswood are strong advocates for the inclusion of social marketing in the marketing curriculum. First, they address some of the more widespread confusions about social marketing. Social marketing may well use social media as a component of the communications mix but be sure not to confuse social marketing with social media, or social media marketing. Rather, social marketing is the use of marketing tools and techniques alongside other mechanisms (such as health communication and health education) to bring about social and behavioural changes that benefit individuals and wider society. This correctly implies that there is an ethical dimension at the core of social marketing, and Kapetanaki and Spotswood explicitly link social marketing to issues of marketing ethics, environmental sustainability and macromarketing. It is easy to see how the marketing student, used to the idea that the purpose of marketing activity is to increase sales, profitability and shareholder value by delivering value to customers (Doyle, 2000), may initially find the idea of social marketing difficult. However, as

Kapetanaki and Spotswood argue, this is a rapidly growing area of marketing practice, the worth of which has been recognised by prominent scholars and marketing professionals for several decades (Kotler and Levy, 1969; Kotler and Zaltman, 1971; Andreasen, 1994). Certainly, a social marketing course within the marketing curriculum provides the opportunity to expose students to both fascinating theoretical ideas (for example, social cognitive theory and the health belief model) and important practical problems (for example, reducing alcohol abuse and risky sexual behaviours) that they might not otherwise encounter during their studies. Kapetanaki and Spotswood present a convincing argument that the inclusion of social marketing can provide a valuable broadening of the curriculum, an exciting intellectual challenge for students, and contribute to the university's employability agenda.

The subject matter turns to teaching international marketing in Chapter 11 by Jonathan Wilson. International marketing is a core subject within most undergraduate and postgraduate marketing programmes. Wilson argues for two major approaches when teaching the subject: first, that educators must broaden their repertoire of resources and examples to include a range of international conditions, brands and companies (Crittenden and Wilson, 2006; Leonidou et al., 2007; Malhotra et al., 2013; Vos, 2013) and second, that the educator use an explicit pedagogic approach to teaching and assessment – authentic learning – an approach also discussed in Chapter 5 on marketing simulation games. In developing his argument for the former, Wilson provides a historical overview of the discipline to demonstrate that while the learning resources and materials used in teaching have developed along with the shifts in global trade and the rise of global brands, they have not done so as comprehensively and thus do not always reflect the realities of today's global marketplace. Most textbooks and cases continue to come from either the US or a handful of Western European countries, yet in 2021, 53 of the world's top global brands have their origins in countries other than the US, with 11 of the top 20 brands by value from China (https://brandirectory.com/rankings/global/table 2021). This reality, Wilson argues, requires educators to move beyond the available textbooks to include academic journals and to develop activities that draw from a breadth of country examples, not only other country brands but also different approaches to international marketing that are shaped by unique cultural, economic and political factors. He adds two further arguments for broadening the range of cases and examples. First, he discusses the current student reality: most students today use or are familiar with brands from around the world – TikTok (China), Spotify (Sweden), Zara (Spain), Samsung (South Korea) and L'Oreal (France), to name just a few. Secondly, he reminds us that globalisation has also profoundly affected higher education. Before COVID restricted international travel, 80 per cent of students in most UK postgraduate marketing programmes were from Asian countries (HESA, 2019/20).

The majority of undergraduate marketing courses also include students from around the world. Thus, Wilson argues, not only do we have an obligation to broaden the perspectives taught, but we also have a wealth of diverse experiences to draw upon. Wilson's second discussion point is that of using an explicit pedagogy to enhance the teaching and learning in international marketing. Authentic assessment is a whole course pedagogy that begins with using examples from professional practice, or scenarios that students will encounter in the field in order to increase student interest and enhance employability (Lombardi, 2007; Fook and Sidhu, 2010; Herrington et al., 2010). He provides five useful learning exercises that educators can employ in the classroom and provides student outputs from the exercises, including details on how to deploy them for greatest learning effectiveness while also demonstrating the authentic learning principles that are enhanced through each exercise.

In Chapter 12, "Teaching marketing science", Dag Bennett argues passionately for the scientific method as a fundamental guiding force within marketing. While his principal audience is marketing educators, there can be no doubt that his message is relevant to the entire marketing community. Bennett's plea is for marketers to renounce and refrain from magical thinking, faddish ideas and thoughtlessly following the latest marketing fashion, and to replace this with rigorous, disciplined thinking grounded in evidence-based practice and logical analysis. So, for the purposes of this book, Bennett trenchantly represents and defends the marketing-as-science school of thought (Converse, 1945; Hunt, 1976). Indeed, it is plausible to argue that the third decade of the twenty-first century is as good a time as any to revisit the science/art debate in marketing (Brown, 1996). The dust has settled on the fad for postmodern marketing and, ironically, postmodern ideas have arguably been woven seamlessly into modern marketing practice. Bennett, coming at this issue from the perspective championed by the late Andrew Ehrenberg (Keng and Ehrenberg, 1984; Ehrenberg et al., 1990; Ehrenberg, 1995), presents scientific marketing concepts that can be taught in the classroom (such as double jeopardy and the duplication of purchase law), advocates pedagogic methods suitable for making these concepts accessible to marketing students, and more generally defends the idea that there are important, replicable, empirical generalisations in marketing. These generalisations, although not carrying the same weight as the fundamental laws of physics, nevertheless represent useful, basic building blocks of marketing knowledge that can help protect marketing students (and practitioners) against falsehoods and unsubstantiated claims to knowledge.

REFERENCES

Allan, D. and Wood, N.T. (2009). Incorporating ethics into the marketing communications class: The case of Old Joe and New Jo Camel. *Marketing Education Review*, *19*(2), 63–71.

Alderson, W. (1957). *Marketing Behaviour and Executive Action: A Functionalist Approach to Marketing Theory*. Homewood, IL: Richard D. Irwin.

Andreasen, A.R. (1994). Social marketing: Its definition and domain. *Journal of Public Policy & Marketing*, *13*(1), 108–114.

Ansoff, I.H. (1957). Strategies for diversification. *Harvard Business Review*, *35*(5), 113–20.

Ashford-Rowe, K., Herrington, J. and Brown, C. (2014). Establishing the critical elements that determine authentic assessment. *Assessment and Evaluation in Higher Education*, *39*(2), 205–222.

Bagozzi, R.P. (1975). Marketing as exchange. *Journal of Marketing*, *39*(4), 32–9.

Barber, J.P. (2014). Integration of learning model: How college students integrate learning. *New Directions for Higher Education*, *2014*(165), 7–17.

Bedeian, A.G. (2005). Crossing disciplinary boundaries: A epilegomenon for Lockett and McWilliams. *Journal of Management Inquiry*, *14*(2), 151–5.

Beggs, J.M. (2011). Seamless integration of ethics. *Marketing Education Review*, *21*(1), 49–56.

Brennan, R. (2012). Educating professional marketers? *Marketing Education Digest*, *1*(1), York, Higher Education Agency. Accessed 30 March 2020 at: https://www.lynnvos.com/marketing-education-digests.

Brennan, R., Canning, L.E. and McDowell, R. (2020). *Business to Business Marketing* (5th edn). London: Sage.

Brown, S. (1996). Art or science?: Fifty years of marketing debate. *Journal of Marketing Management*, *12*(4), 243–67.

Catterall, M., Maclaran, P. and Stevens, L. (2002). Critical reflection in the marketing curriculum. *Journal of Marketing Education*, *24*(3), 184–92.

Converse, P.D. (1945). The development of the science of marketing – an exploratory survey. *Journal of Marketing*, *10*(1), 14–23.

Crane, F.G. (2004). The teaching of business ethics: An imperative at business schools. *Journal of Education for Business*, *79*(3), 149–51.

Crittenden, V. and Wilson, E.J. (2006). Content, pedagogy, and learning outcomes in the International Marketing course. *Journal of Teaching in International Business*, *17*(1–2), 81–101.

Dewey, J. (1910). *How We Think*. Boston, MA: Heath.

Dieckmann, P., Molin Friss, S., Lippert, A. and Ostergaard, D. (2009). The art and science of debriefing in simulation: Ideal and practice. *Medical Teacher*, *31*(7), 287–94.

Donoho, C. and Heinze, T. (2011). The personal selling ethics scale: Revisions and expansions for teaching sales ethics. *Journal of Marketing Education*, *33*(1), 107–122.

Donoho, C., Heinze, T. and Kondo, C. (2012). Gender differences in personal selling ethics evaluations. *Journal of Marketing Education*, *34*(1), 55–66.

Doyle, P. (2000). *Value-Based Marketing*. Chichester: Wiley.

Ehrenberg, A.S. (1995). Empirical generalisations, theory, and method. *Marketing Science*, *14*(3_supplement), G20–G28.

Ehrenberg, A.S., Goodhardt, G.J. and Barwise, T.P. (1990). Double jeopardy revisited. *Journal of Marketing*, *54*(3), 82–91.

Ericsson, K.A., Krampe, R.T. and Tesch-Romer, C. (1993). The role of deliberate practice in the acquisition of expert performance. *Psychological Review*, *100*(3), 363–406.

Fanning, R.M. and Gaba, D.M. (2007). The role of debriefing in simulation-based learning. *Simulation in Healthcare*, *2*(2), 115–25.

Fook, C.Y. and Sidhu, G.K. (2010). Authentic assessment and pedagogical strategies in higher education. *Journal of Social Sciences*, *6*(2), 153–61.

Gulikers, J.T.M., Bastiaens, T.J. and Kirschner, P.A. (2006). Student perceptions of assessment authenticity: Study approaches and learning outcome. *Studies in Educational Evaluation*, *32*(4), 381–400.

Hagerty, J.E. (1936). Experiences of an early marketing teacher. *Journal of Marketing*, *1*(1), 20–27.

Håkansson, H. (ed.) (1982). *International Marketing and Purchasing of Industrial Goods*. Chichester: John Wiley and Sons.

Håkansson, H. and Ford, D. (2002). How should companies interact in business networks? *Journal of Business Research*, *55*(7), 133–9.

Håkansson, H. and Snehota, I. (eds) (1995). *Developing Relationships in Business Markets*. London: Routledge.

Herrington, J. and Herrington, A. (2006). Authentic conditions for authentic assessment: Aligning task and assessment. In A. Bunker and I. Vardi (eds), *Research and Development in Higher Education* (Vol. 29, pp. 146–51). Milperra: HERDSA.

Herrington, J., Reeves, T.C. and Oliver, R. (2010). *A Guide to Authentic E-learning*. London: Routledge.

HESA (2019/20). Where do HE students come from? Accessed 3 March 2021 at https://www.hesa.ac.uk/data-and-analysis/students/where-from.

Hill, M.E. and McGinnis, J. (2007). Curiosity in marketing thinking. *Journal of Marketing Education*, *29*(1), 52–62.

Hill, R.P. and Martin, K.D. (2014). Broadening the paradigm of marketing as exchange: A public policy and marketing perspective. *Journal of Public Policy and Marketing*, *33*(1), 17–33.

Hulbert, B. and Harrigan, P. (2011). How can marketing academics serve marketing practice? The new marketing DNA as a model for marketing education. *Journal of Marketing Education*, *33*(3), 253–72.

Hunt, S.D. (1976). The nature and scope of marketing. *Journal of Marketing*, *40*(3), 17–28.

Hunt, S.D. (2011). On the intersection of marketing history and marketing theory. *Marketing Theory*, *11*(4), 483–9.

Hunt, S.D. and Morgan, R.M. (1996). The resource-advantage theory of competition: Dynamics, path dependencies, and evolutionary dimensions. *Journal of Marketing*, *60*(3), 107–114.

Keng, K.A. and Ehrenberg, A.S. (1984). Patterns of store choice. *Journal of Marketing Research*, *21*(4), 399–409.

Koch, A.J. (1997). Marketing curriculum: Designing its new logic and structure. *Journal of Marketing Education*, *19*(3), 2–11.

Koch, A.J. (2013). The future of marketing education: A practitioner's perspective. *Journal of Marketing Education*, *34*(1), 54–67.

Kotler, P. and Levy, S.J. (1969). Broadening the concept of marketing. *Journal of Marketing*, *33*(1), 10–15.

Kotler, P. and Zaltman, G. (1971). Social marketing: An approach to planned social change. *Journal of Marketing, 35*(3), 3–12.

Kozinets, R.V. (2002). The field behind the screen: Using netnography for marketing research in online communities. *Journal of Marketing Research, 39*(1), 61–72.

Kozinets, R.V. (2019). *Netnography: The Essential Guide to Qualitative Social Media Research* (3rd edn). London: SAGE Publications.

Kuh, G.D. (2008). Why integration and engagement are essential to effective educational practice in the twenty-first century. *Peer Review, 10*(4), 27–8.

Lavidge, R.J. and Steiner, G.A. (1961). A model for predictive measurements of advertising effectiveness. *Journal of Marketing, 25*(6), 59–62.

Leonidou, L.C., Kaminarides, J.S. and Panayides, P. (2007). The international marketing environment: Textbook content vs educators' views. *Journal of Teaching in International Business, 18*(2/3), 101–131.

Lincoln T.J. and Cassidy, R. (2018). Authentic assessment in business education: Its effects on student satisfaction and promoting behaviour. *Studies in Higher Education, 43*(3), 401–415.

Lombardi, M.M. (2007). Authentic learning for the 21st century: An overview (ELI Paper 1). Educause Learning Initiative.

Malhotra, N.K., Wu, L. and Whitelock, J. (2013). An updated overview of research published in the *International Marketing Review*: 1983 to 2011. *International Marketing Review, 31*(1), 7–20.

Maslow, A.H. (1943). A theory of human motivation. *Psychological Review, 50*(4), 370–96.

McGuire, W. (1974). Psychological motives and communication gratification. In J.F. Blumer and E. Katz (eds), *The Uses of Mass Communications: Current Perspectives on Gratifications Research* (pp. 106–167). Beverly Hills, CA: Sage.

Newmann, F.M., Marks, H.M. and Gamoran, A. (1996). Authentic pedagogy and student performance. *American Journal of Education, 104*(4), 280–312.

Nicholson, C.Y. and DeMoss, M. (2009). Teaching ethics and social responsibility: An evaluation of undergraduate business education at the discipline level. *Journal of Education for Business, 84*(4), 213–18.

Pharr, S. and Morris, L.J. (1997). The fourth-generation marketing curriculum: Meeting AACSB's guidelines. *Journal of Marketing Education, 19*(3), 31–43.

Reynolds, S.J. and Dang, C.T. (2017). Are the "customers" of business ethics courses satisfied? An examination of one source of business ethics education legitimacy. *Business & Society, 56*(7), 947–74.

Rundle-Thiele, S.R. and Wymer, W. (2010). Stand-alone ethics, social responsibility, and sustainability course requirements: A snapshot from Australia and New Zealand. *Journal of Marketing Education, 32*(1), 5–12.

Schlegelmilch, B.B. (2020). Why business schools need radical innovations: Drivers and development trajectories. *Journal of Marketing Education, 42*(2), 93–107.

Shaw, E.H. and Jones, D.G.B (2005). A history of the schools of marketing thought. *Marketing Theory, 5*(3), 239–81.

Shaw, E.H. and Lazer, W. (2007). Wroe Alderson: Father of modern marketing. *European Business Review, 19*(6), 440–51.

Sheth, J.N., Gardner, D.M. and Garrett, D.E. (1988). *Marketing Theory: Evolution and Evaluation*. New York: John Wiley and Sons.

Smart, D.T., Kelley, C.A. and Conant, J. (1999). Marketing education in the year 2000: Changes observed and challenges anticipated. *Journal of Marketing Education, 21*(3), 206–216.

Stanton, W.J. (1988). It's time to restructure marketing in academia. *Journal of Marketing Education*, *6*(1), 2–9.

Tadajewski, M. (2006). The ordering of marketing theory: The influence of McCarthyism and the Cold War, *Marketing Theory*, *6*(2), 163–200.

Vargo, S.L. and Lusch, R.F. (2004). Evolving to a new dominant logic for marketing. *Journal of Marketing*, *68*(January), 1–17.

Villarroel, V., Bloxham, D.B., Bruna, C. and Herrera-Seda, C. (2018). Authentic assessment: creating a blueprint for course design. *Assessment & Evaluation in Higher Education*, *43*(5), 840–54.

Vos, L. (2013). Improving international marketing programs to reflect global complexity and risk: Curriculum drivers and constraints. *Journal of Teaching in International Business*, *24*(2), 81–106.

Walle, A.H. (1991). Modern marketing: The shift from academic respectability to practitioner significance. *Management Decisions*, *29*(4), 39–40.

Wilkie, W.L. and Moore, E.S. (1999). Marketing's contribution to society. *Journal of Marketing*, *63* (Special millennium edn), 198–218.

Wooliscroft, B. (2011). Marketing theory as history. *Marketing Theory*, *11*(4), 499–501.

2. Ethics and responsibility from the outset

Anita Peleg

INTRODUCTION

In this chapter, I suggest a new approach to teaching ethics, where the business and marketing curricula develop a moral mindset that considers balancing the needs of social, environmental and economic concerns. To achieve this, I propose a curriculum that no longer treats ethics and responsibility as an add-on but integrates consideration of these issues across the whole curriculum. The aim of this approach is to achieve a more positive, proactive approach to the partnership between responsibility and business success driven by an approach that considers not only shareholders but all stakeholders.

The curriculum embeds the consideration of responsible marketing from the outset, with a dedicated module in the first year. Moreover, every subject module will introduce principles and values that become part of decision-making criteria to enable the alignment of social and environmental responsibility with business success.

To enable engagement with this approach, I discuss and demonstrate a variety of approaches and teaching initiatives that combine the cognitive, affective and conative approaches to learning, where students learn to think, feel and do. These teaching activities can be applied to a range of subject areas and drive the development of competencies in critical and moral reasoning, character and values, professionalism, emotional intelligence and personal reflection.

This approach can be delivered from the bottom up by individual champions that adapt their modules, share their practice with others and then lead the course team to consider necessary changes in structure. The course can then be promoted as an example of innovation and of good practice to be disseminated internally and externally.

For business schools, the marketing discipline and universities, the outcome can be an amendment of purpose, from a purely knowledge-driven agenda to an agenda where knowledge drives a social purpose, where universities can lead the education agenda to drive social and economic progress.

A NEW PURPOSE

On 19 August 2019, CEOs of 181 top US corporations officially changed the definition of the purpose of a corporation (Business Round Table 2019). They committed to lead their companies for the benefit of all stakeholders and not principally to serve shareholders. Alongside this declaration, the corporate world is embracing the term 'Woke Capitalism' (Merriam Webster 2020) and devoting much attention to social, environmental and economic factors, the triple bottom line (Elkington 1998), to demonstrate a positive contribution of business in society. For many this is a long-overdue response to public demand for business to behave responsibly and integrate economic, social and environmental goals. For others this is a trend already underway, with many companies promoting ethical values and responsibility to society as part of their mission and values statements, with sizeable investments in CSR programmes. For yet more, this may just be window dressing with little substance, or greenwashing, a way to manipulate public opinion in order to improve reputation.

Indeed, many of the largest and most well-known companies proudly state and demonstrate their commitment to social and environmental responsibility in value statements on their web pages. Often these statements are the first words that you see and are further emphasized on every page and in all major initiatives. They have become a fundamental part of the marketing communications and brand positioning of the organization.

Consumer expectations also demonstrate the importance of this trend. In a study by FleishmanHillard Fishburn (2019), 59 per cent of consumers said they expect companies to make a stand on climate and environmental issues. Furthermore, research on millennials identifies favourable attitudes towards CSR, personal involvement in social projects (McGlone et al. 2011) and support for companies integrating social, environmental and economic principles (Deloitte 2016). Equally, the Cone Communications (2015) study demonstrates that 61 per cent of millennials believe they have a responsibility to make a difference and 69 per cent say they would reject employment with a company that is not socially responsible.

So how is this change in purpose reflected in the Business and Marketing curricula of our universities that consistently claim to reflect emerging trends and priorities in business? Key organizations, such as the UN Global Compact Principles of Responsible Management, the US Association to Advance Collegiate Schools of Business (AACSB) and the UK Academy of Management and the UK Institute of Business Ethics, amongst many others, are attempting to drive the business school agenda, pressing for the integration of social and environmental responsibility across the curriculum. Indeed, the first business schools in the late nineteenth and early twentieth century claimed the need for social and moral education in business as the key to the justification and legitimization of business education (Abend 2013).

However, there has been consistent criticism of the very foundations of business education (Ghoshal 2005; Rasche et al. 2013), which emphasizes profit at any cost, absolving business students from moral responsibility, and of university rankings which only applaud analysis and scientific research. Ghoshal (2005) and Nelson et al. (2014) highlight erosion of trust in business and suggest a link to the business school education received by those involved in numerous business scandals. In response there is renewed talk of the importance of integrating ethics across the curriculum and commitment from universities, particularly business schools, to reflect this in their teaching (Matchett 2008; Kenny and Lincoln 2015).

In a recent review of 30 business schools in the UK (Peleg 2019), course descriptions and module descriptions identify strategies, concepts, skills and competencies to be learned with no mention of the complexity of considering economic, social and environmental principles in decision making and activities. Where ethics, responsibility or CSR feature, they are often an optional module in the final year, or a topic covered at the end of a module. These findings are supported by Weber (2013), who reports that there has been an increase globally in the number of courses with ethics content but not in the breadth or depth of coverage. Similarly, other surveys (Austin and Toth 2011) claim there are few stand-alone compulsory ethics modules and those in existence are often offered as electives with little effort to integrate ethics across the curriculum (Rasche et al. 2013). Moreover, the call for universities to prioritize ethics education and create an atmosphere conducive to ethical sensitivity and understanding remains wanting (Nelson et al. 2014).

The marketing discipline is no different. For an area constantly criticized for unethical behaviour, the majority of marketing education programmes do little to mirror consumer expectations or to consider social responsibility and the charge of window dressing as consistent themes. Where various marketing roles put social responsibility at the forefront of their messages, should marketing students not consider and scrutinize this activity across the curriculum? Should universities and, in particular, business and marketing education, not take a more proactive approach and lead this agenda?

Amongst academics and some business leaders, there are calls for universities to lead as moral institutions and for their staff to lead as moral exemplars (Sternberg et al. 2007). Maxwell (2007) emphasizes the need for academic education to move away from a focus on 'knowledge enquiry' towards developing responsible leadership and wise decision-making skills, or 'wisdom enquiry', so that universities become initiators and leaders of social change and social progress. These studies tend to echo the words of Barnett (1990) and Bok (1982), suggesting that university education must work harder to engage students to become socially responsible leaders.

In this chapter I propose an approach that recognizes the newly announced purpose of business and integrates ethics and responsibility for all stakeholders across the marketing curriculum. I suggest that for every module taught, responsible principles and practice are considered alongside profitable economic outcomes, and not as an afterthought. No longer will ethics and social responsibility be considered an option, or bolted on to the curriculum. Instead, students will be encouraged to prioritize responsibility to all stakeholders as part of their decision-making criteria across all marketing functions.

To present this approach, first I set out how this might be put into practice; I then discuss the challenges and suggest some practical initiatives for achieving integration of ethics and responsibility across the marketing curriculum. I review the current discourse on ethics education and identify suggestions for content, delivery approaches and techniques with examples of different teaching interventions. Finally, I highlight as an example, how the alignment of ethics, responsibility and business success can be applied throughout a Public Relations (PR) module.

A NEW APPROACH

If our aim is to produce marketing managers capable of making informed and responsible decisions, then the synergies between marketing, ethics and social responsibility must be identified and supported from the outset. To achieve this, I suggest a dedicated ethics and responsibility module in year one, complemented by the alignment of the goals of marketing with a responsible stakeholder approach throughout the curriculum.

Start as you Mean to Continue

In the first year of undergraduate studies, there will be a core module in business ethics and social responsibility delivered across all business courses. Whereas in most business and marketing curricula this module is an option in the final year, there is little reason for this. It is never too early to discuss ethics and social responsibility, and embedding these issues across the curriculum is required from the outset. The module would set the tone for all the first year modules and for the whole programme, focusing on the newly defined purpose of business which focuses on all stakeholders, the resulting need to balance social, environmental and economic goals and the importance and complexity of ethics and responsibility in business. All subsequent modules at every level will devote the first lecture to establishing the principles and values that guide success in that subject area. Those principles and values follow a stakeholder-based approach which aims to achieve social, environmental and economic goals that consider the impact on all stakeholders.

This module should normally be taught by a specialist in business ethics and social responsibility who can develop a greater consciousness and sensitivity of ethical issues and encourage application of ethical theory across a variety of issues and business functions. This specialist can then share ideas and advise academics trying to integrate responsibility into their subject module.

Students at every level find questions of responsibility engaging on both academic and personal levels (Peleg 2019), enabling every student to contribute their views. As issues of ethics and responsibility are not merely about knowledge or academic ability, there is a more level playing field. Students can be taught to develop their views through different lenses and be encouraged to analyse and reflect on their thinking, their feelings and their past and present behaviour. This introduces them to the importance of reflective practice and the complexities of achieving marketing and business goals responsibly and serving the needs of all stakeholders.

The other first year modules will focus on a particular subject area in marketing or business management integrating principles of economic, social and environmental responsibility and stakeholder analysis into the subject. As with the core module, each subject module is introduced by its key principles, goals and outcomes from the outset.

This structure will be repeated on a yearly basis with each subject-specific module integrating ethical issues and consideration and one core subject-specific module that develops the stakeholder approach more deeply.

Example of core modules at each level

- Level Four: Ethics, Responsibility and Business: A stakeholder approach (Core, introducing ethics, stakeholder approach, triple bottom line).
- Level Five: Product and Service Management: Core module with focus on micro and macro issues of safety, materials, sustainability, quality.
- Level Six: Brand Management: Core: Aligning brand reputation, values, trust and responsible business approaches.

Aligning the Goals of Marketing with a Responsible Stakeholder Approach

This proposal is based on the principle that a responsible stakeholder approach can be aligned with economic success (Freeman 1984; Godfrey et al. 2009; Henisz et al. 2014; Sundheim and Starr 2020). This principle will therefore be integrated across the curriculum and each subject module will ensure continuous consideration of multiple stakeholders, social and environmental outcomes when planning and executing marketing initiatives.

The above-mentioned structure and approach suggest a radical change in the way business and marketing curricula are planned and taught by the course team and individual module leaders. It requires buy-in from the organization and, most importantly, from individual academic staff over time.

EMPOWERING CHANGE

Change inevitably creates challenges. Here I identify challenges to this proposal and in response suggest a bottom-up approach to empower teachers and students.

Challenge: Changing Mindset and Resistance

For many, this new approach requires a change in mindset and culture. It starts from the top and is deliberately filtered down through the organization to create a new vision for higher education with widespread buy-in. For others, business education, and specifically business schools, are part of the problem, instructing in values of materialism and short-term profit to an amoral agenda. Thus, business education prepares students for the job market where knowledge and practical skills are seen as more marketable than an ethically responsible mindset. The result is a passive approach by business academics and teachers waiting for change from the top, teaching for current skills in the marketplace and demonstrating an amoral approach to business.

Where change is initiated from the top, however, as academics we can be resistant where there appears to be little consultation, little thought to the new workload it poses, or to the previous work that has gone into a currently successful design. We are all reticent to redesign modules that have been previously applauded by students and staff alike and as a result we tend to tweak our modules, adding in the current thinking as an additional topic. Moreover, the struggle for space and time in the curriculum is a constant challenge. Furthermore, module redesign is time-consuming, and where colleagues express a lack of confidence and a need for training in business ethics and social responsibility, the time constraints become an even greater obstacle.

Response: Leadership from the Bottom Up

My most positive experiences in university education have been built on the ability to be creative with the content and delivery of the modules I was responsible for. I have seen many examples where new approaches were adopted by others and became a feature of the course. Therefore, while an organizational approach and culture would certainly enhance the responsible mindset, developing or redeveloping a subject module that embeds issues of responsibility throughout can serve as an example to empower others and to create course change. As academics and teachers, we have the power to create change from the bottom up.

Response: Sharing Ideas and Teaching Approaches

Sharing and understanding the competencies that can be developed through ethics education can motivate greater participation in such an initiative. While not everyone is an expert in ethics, our own moral compass and understanding of our subject areas will act as a guide to which issues of responsibility deserve consideration. Module leaders can then benefit from learning, sharing ideas and teaching approaches from discussion with colleagues. In the curriculum design suggested in the previous section there would be a specialist ethics module in year one, taught by a specialist in business ethics and social responsibility. That specialist would be a particularly valuable resource for teaching ideas and would ensure that members of the academic team know what key concepts have been taught and discussed, so that they can apply them to their subject areas.

Challenge: The Purpose of Education

There has been continuous debate amongst academics as to whether a university education is a training of the mind, and therefore aimed at developing knowledge and cognitive ability, a training for the workplace aimed at developing employability skills, or a training in character, values and reflective self-development. Currently there is increasing consciousness of the demands of the workplace for key skills, for universities to be agents of social progress and to develop social and environmental responsibility amongst their students. For some, the focus on so-called soft skills – employability skills and moral development – is driven by societal needs but comes at the expense of deeper subject knowledge and theoretical inquiry (Vos and Page, 2020). In particular, the focus on employability skills is seen as bowing to a government and business agenda of productivity and performance as opposed to the goal of learning for its own sake. In former times the development of personal character and values was a focus of academic education. However, today many would argue that it is not the responsibility of university activity but something that is developed in one's early years.

This debate creates an ambivalence towards the role of the university educating towards moral and societal good and cynicism towards its potential success.

Response: Consider the Benefits of Ethics Education

Developing different types of learning

Issues of moral responsibility require learning that facilitates thinking (cognitive learning), feeling (affective learning) and behaviour (conative learning). Whilst much of the emphasis in our teaching is about knowledge and skills, we all agree that we want to challenge our students and we want to encourage them to challenge some of the existing knowledge. Issues of ethics and responsibility are particularly suitable for challenging the status quo and studying issues from different viewpoints. Here marketing students can think deeply and imaginatively, identify issues of concern, reflect on past and present behaviour, criticize, question and debate current practice with the purpose of identifying alternative solutions. Furthermore, affective learning emphasizes the importance of developing emotional intelligence, personal values and relationships, which facilitate understanding of difference and reflective practice. Finally, reflecting on past and present behaviour is considered an important element of educational development at all levels and facilitates learning to create change. These three approaches to learning and development are central to developing proactive, thoughtful and analytical learners as well as a responsible mindset.

Preparing students for the marketplace

Furthermore, recent surveys suggest that employability criteria are changing, and employers now look beyond just knowledge and skills, to candidates with competencies demonstrating leadership and responsibility (Breaugh and Starke 2000). In particular, values-based recruitment is increasingly common, where hiring is based on employees whose personal values, behaviour and beliefs align with the values of the company (Davis 2016; Kirman 2016).

Thus, empowering students to be reflective, sensitive to difference, responsible for their actions and aware of the consequences of business decisions will provide a maturity sought by businesses today (FleishmanHillard Fishburn 2019).

Challenge: A Sense of Powerlessness and Cynicism

In my 20 years of teaching Business Studies and Marketing students, I often found my students were aware of ethical issues and were keen to discuss the responsibility of business freely and passionately. At the same time, they were also very dismissive of organizations' attempts to demonstrate responsible behaviour and cynical of the idea that companies can embrace social, environmental and economic responsibility. These students would criticize business for its unethical nature but when challenged as to why they wanted to work in these so-called 'unethical environments' they appeared powerless and viewed the status quo as a necessary reality.

Conversely, the previously mentioned studies (Deloitte 2016) demonstrate a passion from millennials to work for socially responsible companies, which according to the cynical view of my students, do not exist. Similarly, studies (Herrington and Weaven 2007; Paul 2019) show that marketing academics state strong concern about poor marketing ethics and support for marketing education that takes ethics and responsibility seriously, but an equal level of cynicism as to its potential impact (Gentile 2017).

How do these opposing views co-exist? On the one hand a stated preference to work for an organization that demonstrates social responsibility alongside a deep scepticism about companies that do demonstrate responsibility and about the idea that profit and responsibility can coexist? This ingrained ambivalence and cynicism towards the coexistence of ethics and responsibility in business and marketing from both marketing colleagues and students is perhaps the greatest challenge.

Response: Alignment of Responsible Business Goals with Economic Success

Definitions of marketing emphasize the significance of stakeholders where 'organizations are now under pressure to demonstrate initiatives that take a balanced perspective on stakeholder interests' to include 'customers, clients, partners, and society at large' (Maignan et al. 2005: 957). More recently, Murphy et al. (2016: 5) identify the importance of 'practices that emphasize transparent, trustworthy, and responsible personal and/or organizational marketing policies and actions that exhibit integrity as well as fairness to consumers and other stakeholders'. These definitions, therefore, support the important role of marketing, ethics and responsibility in the development of strategy and planning (Greenley et al. 2004) and support course and module learning outcomes that emphasize the achievement of principles of social responsibility and stakeholder value alongside principles of effectiveness and profitability.

What does this concept of alignment mean in practice?

- Identifying the synergies between ethics, responsibility and business success, where ethical values, principles and practice are part of the success criteria of every company and not merely 'a limiting factor or constraint on strategy' (Macfarlane and Perkins 1999: 24).
- Understanding the influencing factors that help achieve ethics, responsibility and business success.
- Identifying areas of ethical concern and how to overcome them.

- Identifying examples of positive alignment, where responsibility to stakeholders contributes to long-term business outcomes.

Examples of this alignment are identified in the sample teaching activities
shown in this chapter and in the outline PR module presented in Appendix
A. The outline module suggests how alignment of ethics, responsibility and
success in communications can be integrated through synergies achieved
through building trust and thus enhancing brand reputation. Through the development of a live case study, students develop and execute a PR campaign by
considering these synergies, identifying areas of ethical concern and balancing
responsible communications with PR success.

DELIVERING ETHICS EDUCATION

Literature and views on the content and delivery of ethics education are often
hotly debated, with particular methods advocated to achieve a particular
educational purpose. In this section, I demonstrate how integrating ethics
and responsibility across the curriculum can enable a variety of teaching
approaches and content to be delivered using a variety of techniques.

Stand-alone vs. Integration

'Until a balancing ethical dimension is included within all subject study
rather than as a final year option, it is likely that discrete courses in business
ethics will fail to disturb the market orthodoxy of business studies students.'
(Macfarlane 1995: 35)
   There has been much academic debate over the question of the place of
ethics in the curriculum. Marketing and business programmes predominantly
offer stand-alone modules as electives, delivered in the final year of undergraduate studies or at postgraduate level (Peleg 2019). This gives the student little
time to consider, debate and develop their own understanding of the ethical
challenges in business and to transform their engagement with ethical issues
into intention and action. The proponents of stand-alone modules suggest that,
'in practice a separate module gives the subject the recognition it deserves and
allows the sustained attention needed to treat it formally, systematically and in
sufficient depth' (Warren 1995: 21). However, an integrated approach across
the curriculum (Matchett 2008) suggests attention to ethical issues throughout
the student's time at university and the provision of both stand-alone modules
dealing with the development of ethical thinking plus the embedding of moral
questioning and development of diverse competencies across a wide range
of business subjects to make it relevant and practical. Thus, 'business ethics

should be the conceptual glue holding together the curriculum' (Owens 1998, cited in Peppas and Diskin 2001: 349).

While the debate has focused on stand-alone vs. integration, I suggest that these two delivery modes are not exclusive. A stand-alone core ethics module should sit alongside integration of ethics and responsibility across the whole curriculum. The stand-alone module provides in-depth understanding of the ethics and social responsibility and integration applies those concepts to different marketing functions.

Suggested Content

Content areas can be identified in several ways: by micro and macro issues, by organizational and personal factors impacting decision making, by key themes across the subject area and by marketing roles within the organization.

Macro vs. micro issues

Macro issues are concerned with strategy and the firm's wider impact, including sustainability, CSR and globalization issues (see example of macro issue in Teaching Case 1). Much of the current content of ethics courses focuses on these philosophical and practical questions debating the role of the organization and its responsibility to wider society. In particular, the stakeholder approach to the organization, stakeholder mapping and analysis can be applied to ethical dilemmas and conflicts. Principles, values and their application to the strategic mission of the organization can also drive ethics content. Furthermore, reputation is often lauded as the key strategic outcome and driver of successful and responsible marketing. Finally, Elkington's (1998) principles of the Triple Bottom Line (economic, social and environmental) are often used to scrutinize and assess current organizational behaviour and to understand the complexities of business responsibility. These key themes are identified in Figure 2.1 as key themes and explained in more detail in the next section.

In contrast, micro issues focus on ethical behaviour and management within organizations and integration of ethics into specific business and marketing activity, for example, issues such as data usage, information misrepresentation, bribery and gift giving, and conflicting stakeholder responsibilities (see Teaching Case 2). Studying micro issues of ethics and responsibility focuses on decision making and behaviour within each of the marketing roles, such as market research, advertising, and product management. Figure 2.1 identifies these micro issues according to subject area within the curriculum and marketing role and they are further explained with examples.

While many business and marketing ethics modules focus on macro issues, this is often criticized as being less relevant to situations that students face or are likely to face in the early stages of their careers. Therefore, integrating ethics across a range of marketing subject areas and functions allows the curriculum to address both the broader ethical issues affecting society and the micro ethical concerns that employees will face early in their marketing careers and within their different marketing roles.

Organizational context

Research into the factors influencing ethical decision-making and experience of ethics in the workplace reveals a range of contextual and personal factors (Trevino et al. 2008). Understanding the influence of factors such as organizational context and culture, different roles and levels of seniority, enables students to consider different perspectives and understand the complexity of responsible decision making. Trevino et al. (2008) find that senior managers' perceptions of ethics in their organizations are more positive than those of lower-level employees, whereas there is greater cynicism, less trust and greater distance from employers amongst junior employees. Studying these varying perceptions through role play, case studies or film can sensitize students to these differences (see Teaching Case 2). Unsurprisingly, those in more senior roles identify broader management and strategic issues as part of their ethical decision making while practitioners in the early stages of their careers were challenged by micro issues that affected them, their performance and their relationships directly. Furthermore, evidence of the impact of organizational culture, leadership and national culture on decision making and behaviour provides areas of study. Understanding the impact of these factors on workplace behaviour and the resulting micro ethical issues can be studied through internal relationships with issues such as internal relations, people management, speaking up, diversity and discrimination; external relationships with diverse stakeholders and conflicting value systems.

Key Themes

Values, trust and reputation

Different perceptions of ethics in terms of its meaning and association can also influence content and approach to teaching. For many, ethics is about values developed through family and experience, identifying workplace values such as honesty, integrity, trust and professionalism. This suggests content that is focused on identifying how those values can be applied in professional situations and identifying situations and solutions in which values conflict across multiple stakeholders, as demonstrated in Teaching Case 2.

In particular, the concept of trust is often referred to as a key factor in building both personal reputation and organizational reputation and successful marketing and branding (Peleg 2019). Indeed, the Edelman Trust Barometer (2020) reveals consensus that a brand's impact on society promotes brand trust and identifies trust as the second most important factor in brand choice after price. From the outset, a dedicated ethics module in year one and marketing subject areas such as consumer behaviour, brand management, marketing communications and PR can focus on the links between brand reputation, trust and the ethical behaviour of the brand (Jost 2014; Syed Alwi et al. 2017) as key goals and criteria for success (Appendix A).

Differentiating ethics and law

Understanding where the law ends and ethics begins is fundamental to the study of both and helps differentiate the terms. Ethics, law and compliance are often referred to synonymously (Peleg 2019), with overlap identified between the study of ethics and the study of law. Habert and Ingulli (2012: 1) suggest that 'Law concerns what we *must* do and ethics concerns what we *should* do.' The role of compliance and regulation as a positive influence on ethical behaviour is often described by junior practitioners while those in senior positions often see law as more restrictive and complex to apply (Peleg 2019). The challenge of interpreting regulation into practice, differentiating between the letter and the spirit of the law and navigating the grey areas between ethics and law, principles and values are discussed at all levels of seniority and in all environments (Jensen et al. 2009; Levine 2015). These grey areas require critical thinking, discussion, sensitivity and application of values and can therefore offer particularly useful topics for discussion and analysis across the curriculum.

Stakeholder orientation

'Marketing is the activity, set of institutions, and processes for creating, communicating, delivering, and exchanging offerings that have value for customers, clients, partners, and society at large' (American Marketing Association 2013).

According to some definitions of marketing, the close interaction with consumers, suppliers and other parties drives a stakeholder orientation. This managerial approach prioritizes stakeholder analysis as key to responsible decision-making, which considers the effect of decisions and actions on all stakeholders. Stakeholder analysis is often undertaken as part of strategy and supply chain management and social responsibility modules. However, where the key purpose of business and marketing is to benefit all stakeholders, stakeholder analysis becomes a key theme across the curriculum.

The triple bottom line

The triple bottom line first expounded by Elkington (1998) goes beyond stakeholder analysis to consider a framework to evaluate performance of the organization in three areas. The traditional bottom line, monetary profit and the need to consider social responsibility to all stakeholders, sits alongside the environmental impacts of the company. For some, responsible business activity requires a delicate balancing of people, planet and profit, while others suggest that it is impossible to measure these three outcomes in a comparable way, and yet others hold the view that these three goals are incompatible. Despite the difficulty of using this model as a form of measurement, many companies declare their commitment to these three principles, and current ethics modules often use the triple bottom line as a framework to consider the impact of actions on shareholder, stakeholder and environmental concerns. Teaching Case 1 shows how Marshall's PLC considers the triple bottom line in how it sources its materials. Using a case study that poses the challenges Marshall's has faced in dealing with child labour and sustainable sourcing, students are tasked to propose solutions that balance people, planet and profit. They compare their responses with Marshall's activity and impact, as demonstrated in Figure 2.1. These key themes are not specific to one subject area and can therefore feature as topics in a dedicated ethics module or applied across the curriculum.

Marketing Function and Role

The various functions and topic areas in marketing demonstrate quite specific macro and micro issues in need of consideration. Figure 2.1 shows how each subject area has a unique set of ethical issues alongside some key themes that can be applied to all. It demonstrates the range of different ethical issues that can be considered alongside the theory and practice within that role. For a topic such as product management, micro issues such as health and safety, inclusive design, sustainable design and new product development, misleading labelling and packaging can be explored, with particular reference to the mediating role of law.

BOX 2.1   SUBJECT EXAMPLE 1

A debate over current health issues such as obesity can ask the question 'Do food manufacturers have a responsibility to produce products with lower fat, salt and sugar content?' or 'Is government intervention through law necessary?' This debate would consider the differing views of a variety of stakeholders, the underlying question of individual freedom vs. responsibility for society and the relationship between ethics and law.

When studying marketing research, micro issues of privacy, confidentiality, honesty and transparency are significant and can be studied with reference to the different research methods, such as ethnography and netnography and to the potential use and misuse of data.

BOX 2.2 SUBJECT EXAMPLE 2

A focus on netnography, which uses digital forums and platforms to collect information, raises questions of consent and anonymity. While most of the information posted on social media is public, it is not always anonymous, so how should it be used? Furthermore, should information about the private lives of celebrities and politicians be protected and research consent sought? Some would argue that privacy is a fundamental human right, so informed consent should be obtained even if it is not a legal requirement.

Within a supply-chain management module, macro issues of material sourcing, location of manufacturing, employee management and child labour can be included as part of strategic principles, values and decisions.

BOX 2.3 SUBJECT EXAMPLE 3

Stakeholder analysis can be a useful exercise when considering the location of a manufacturing plant or transportation hub. Students will consider the balancing effects of land usage, transport networks, pollution and waste on the local population and the local and national economy of this type of strategic decision. See also Teaching Case 1 for another detailed example.

In marketing communications modules, such as advertising, digital media and public relations, many key issues of honesty, misleading claims and transparency can be raised, amongst others.

BOX 2.4 SUBJECT EXAMPLE 4

Students can evaluate examples of existing advertising, social media and PR campaigns for their honesty and transparency. They can also discuss questions of privacy, online harms and fake news that are of particular relevance to digital media. These values can be considered for their importance in building trust and brand reputation.

The above examples also identify four key strategic considerations and themes that influence how all these issues may be tackled to align responsible marketing and business success across all subject areas: the stakeholder orientation; adhering to regulation, responsible principles and values; building trust, relationships and reputation; and, balancing economic, social and environmental concerns. These overarching themes are also identified in Figure 2.1.

Figure 2.1   *Principles, themes and topics for integrating ethics and responsibility across the curriculum*

APPROACHES TO DELIVERY

When considering how to deliver ethics education within the curriculum, the purpose of that teaching intervention must first be considered. Differing views concerning the purpose of ethics education are vigorously debated by both academics and teachers. The debate centres on different philosophies, frameworks and approaches that are either cognitive (Kohlberg and Turiel 1971), affective (Gilligan 1982) or conative (Prentice 2014; Gentile 2017). Cognitive approaches see the purpose of moral education to develop capacities for moral reasoning. Students learn how to make ethical decisions through reasoning to develop universal principles. Affective approaches suggest the importance of developing character through personal values, emotional intelligence and relationships to facilitate ethical behaviour. Finally, conative approaches focus on understanding individual behaviour in order to learn how to develop responsible behaviour.

Methods of delivery and teaching techniques are linked to the overall approach and purpose of the course and the competencies to be developed. Cognitive approaches often focus on the use of case studies and debates, affective approaches practise creative narratives, simulations and role play, while conative approaches devote much time to experiential learning and reflective practice.

In this section these different approaches to the purpose, content and delivery of ethics education are identified and delivery techniques are demonstrated through detailed examples of educational activities (teaching cases).

Developing Cognitive Reasoning

For many, moral and educational development is best achieved through the development of cognitive abilities to research, manage and evaluate information and use reason to take responsible decisions. This approach is based on the philosophers of reason, such as Immanuel Kant (1785) and the work of psychologist Lawrence Kohlberg (1971) who saw moral development as based on different stages of cognitive development over time. To enable cognitive development, reasoned discussion and debate are encouraged, often using ethical theory to make decisions and suggest behaviour. Thus, the power of critical reasoning is emphasized to develop the student's ability to reflect, analyse and deliberate meaningfully for the purpose of responsible decision making and supports the idea of public reason which welcomes questioning, dissent and difference for their educational benefits (Rawls 1972[2008]; Tveit and Sunde 2016).

Techniques and materials often utilized with this approach are case studies and news items, which are often used in equal frequency to academic textbooks (Murphy et al. 2016). These include live cases and cases developed by the students themselves. These techniques highlight the complexity of real-world situations, current ethical issues and moral conflicts and enable cognitive problem solving with guidance from decision-making frameworks.

BOX 2.5   TEACHING CASE 1

Approach: Cognitive

Technique: Case Study Applied to Ethical Theory

Competencies Developed: Developing Awareness, Reasoning and Decision Making

Approach
This approach aims to develop ethical awareness and critical thinking to enable responsible decision making. This activity is relevant to all educators in any discipline who want to experience the application of ethical theory to the development of critical reasoning skills. A case study focuses on ethical issues and performance in the supply chain and can be applied to a Supply Chain or International Marketing module or to a dedicated ethics module. It is an example of macro focused content that enables strategic decisions.

Ethical Theory to Enable Reasoning
Students are encouraged to look at problems through the different lenses of different ethical theories. Based on Emmet's (1979) metaphor of the prism, students can learn how a spectrum of different theories illuminate different aspects of morality, consider multiple ways of seeing the world and therefore reach different decisions.

Description of Activity
Students are presented with a short business dilemma that focuses on issues of child labour, and environmental concerns in an international context. Participants are allocated a work group and a particular moral theory. Each group uses their theory to suggest how to generate solutions to the business problem. This enables participants to understand and apply ethical theory to a specific moral issue in business and then debate their solution with others.
   The theories:

- Deontology – Duty Ethics (Kant): Students are tasked to identify universal principles and duties that can guide their actions and decisions irrespective of the outcome.
- Teleology – Utilitarianism: Students are tasked to understand the outcomes of various solutions for different stakeholders to achieve the greatest good for the greatest number of people.
- Shareholder Theory: Managerial Egoism. Students put shareholders first, where moral decision is what is best for the shareholder and the good of the company.

- Social Contract Theory: Students debate how to ensure that the least advantaged group benefits the most and how to minimize the difference between the least and most advantaged people.
- Virtue Ethics: Students identify specific values and discuss how these values might be applied to the way the company behaves.

Groups devise solutions by answering three guidance questions posed. The teacher proactively facilitates each group discussion to ensure they understand how to use the theory, explain misconceptions, challenge ideas and keep the students focused on developing a strategy that adheres to their allocated ethical philosophy. The teacher also encourages the students not to look at this problem through their own moral lens and merely suggest their personal favoured solution.

Each student group then presents their solutions to the class for discussion moderated by the teacher/seminar leader.

Finally, the path that the company chose in reality is presented, their philosophy considered and the extent of alignment between economic, social and environmental values evaluated.

Participants Take Away:

- an understanding of ethical theory and its application to practical problems;
- how consideration of different ethical approaches can sometimes produce different outcomes, or sometimes produce the same outcomes for different reasons;
- an understanding of the complexity of balancing the economic, social and environmental needs of the organization and considering all stakeholders;
- the early stages of development of critical reasoning skills.

Evaluation
Feedback demonstrates that students enjoy the challenge of understanding ethical theory and are impressed that each theory can achieve very different solutions. They find it a positive challenge to look at a problem through a lens that is not their own and require careful guidance not to revert to their personal biases. Some students adopt the use of ethical theory as an analysis tool in subsequent modules, to demonstrate consideration of diverse alternatives.

Developing Values, Relationships and Sensitivity to Others

This approach is based on two ethical philosophies, one that promotes character based on values that are developed through practice, virtue ethics (Aristotle c.325 BC), and the other that particularly focuses on affective values, care ethics (Gilligan 1982), such as a caring approach, that includes emotion and sensitivity towards others and rejects the significance of rational thinking. Here we will focus on the affective, care-based approach which can be developed in several ways using role play, games, film or literature that allow the reader or viewer or participant to consider the emotion, experience and views of the other. Role play for example is learner-centred activity that involves live decision making and action together with reflection on experiences to understand their implications (Jagger et al. 2016). Film, literature and graphic novels are also considered useful to understand customers through written, verbal and non-verbal communication (Fischbach and Conner 2016) and can nurture empathy for others (Michaelson 2016).

BOX 2.6   TEACHING CASE 2

Approach: Affective

Technique: Role Play

Competencies: Sensitivity, Developing Relationships, Cross-cultural Understanding

Approach
This approach aims to develop sensitivity of the other. Through role play students can develop imagination, sensitivity and cross-cultural understanding. This technique can be used within any module where decisions need to consider views of different stakeholders with different cultural orientations. The scenario for the role play is set either by a mini case, narrative or film excerpt which describes a scenario that may be interpreted differently by different stakeholders.

Developing Cross-cultural Understanding
In this case the subject is gift giving within the sales and marketing role. It can be delivered as part of a dedicated ethics module which focuses on gift giving, bribery and cross-cultural understanding, or in a dedicated sales, marketing communications, consumer behaviour or international marketing module.

Description of Activity

Students receive a short lecture on cultural orientation, using Hofstede and other models of importance. The case, scenario or film is presented and then students are divided into pairs. Each pair is allocated a character, culture and viewpoint. Each pair is invited to create a backstory to their character and culture that directs their view and actions with regard to gift giving.

Examples of the various stakeholders represented:

- The Company: Head office;
- The Sales Rep;
- The Manager;
- Local Community Leader;
- Potential Buyer;
- National Government Representative.

A representative from each pair is then invited to present their view and personal story to the class. The class will therefore hear several views, each from a different stakeholder as each speaker tries to explain their position. A discussion can then take place as to the merits of each viewpoint. Students from different cultures are also asked to contribute alternative views from those presented.

Finally, students are asked to reflect on what they have learned about each stakeholder, the influences shaping a personal outlook and what new insights they have developed. They will also be asked to compare the difference between the character that they presented and their own personal disposition and experience.

Participants Take Away:

- an understanding of how culture, family background, experience and other factors influence personal views and disposition;
- an appreciation of the lived experience of individuals in other cultures;
- a sensitivity towards views different from their own;
- an understanding of how different stakeholders are affected by and may affect personal and organizational decision making.

Evaluation

Role play requires students to shed inhibitions and be willing to take on a different persona from their own. Therefore, it is particularly effective in a small group who have been working together for some time. Students report learning about cultural orientation as very interesting and particularly like the opportunity to study a culture and background different from their own. They find writing the backstory to their persona challenging and often need tutor guidance. The ensuing role play is often presented tentatively at first but with interaction often develops into a lively debate. Finally, students often find it difficult to engage in open reflective activity but are happier to participate if it is part of regular classroom activity where they individually record their thoughts in writing at the end of the activity.

Understanding Behaviour

This approach to education emphasizes developing the ability to reflect and understand past and present individual behaviour in order to identify future actions. It is based on the concerns raised by Kahneman (2011) and Prentice (2014) about the link between moral judgement and moral behaviour and the understanding that we do not always act according to reason but mostly act on impulse. Therefore, understanding that we are not always as ethical as we think we are and how unconscious bias comes into play enables us to take control and behave responsibly. This approach particularly endorses experiential learning for the opportunity it provides the student in developing competencies such as reflective thinking skills (Kolb and Kolb 2005) and in promoting responsible action. Furthermore, various recently developed programmes encourage people not just to decide on intentions and make responsible decisions but to voice their values, speak up and behave accordingly. The example in Box 2.7 is part of a programme developed by Mary Gentile (2017) that empowers people to voice their values and thereby turn intention into action.

BOX 2.7   TEACHING CASE 3

Approach: Conative – action oriented

Technique: Experiential

Competencies: Reflective Practice, Action

Approach
This approach is based on the work of Mary Gentile (2017), 'Giving voice to values'. It enables people to understand what prevents them from speaking up and acting according to their values. It assumes an individual who understands their values, wants to act on them and voice them but often find obstacles to doing so. Students identify some of the conditions and cultural factors that make it easier for people to act according to their values and understand that they do have choices. The focus is therefore on reflection and developing actions rather than on decision making.

Subject Area

Students in a class focusing on different elements of communication, such as internal comms, advertising and sales are asked to consider how the manager and the junior employee can deal with unethical practices.

This topic is highly relevant to many of the students who are often on the receiving end of poor management and communications practices in their places of employment. Instead of posing an ethical dilemma, where cynical attitudes are often displayed, this activity helps them identify obstacles and then come up with ways to handle these challenges.

Activity

This activity is based on the work of Mary Gentile's 'Giving voice to values' work and her classroom exercise 'A tale of two stories'. This activity is divided into three parts: part 1 is a reflective exercise focused on personal experiences, identifying positive actions and outcomes. Part 2 uses the positive solution-based focus to make suggestions as to how to act in different scenarios of relevance to marketing communications and sales roles. Finally, part 3 summarizes the two activities by identifying what enables us to speak up or act upon our values when values conflict and we want to behave responsibly.

Part 1

Students start by working alone to reflect on the task below and then discuss their experiences in groups.

Recall a time in your work experience when your values conflicted with what you were expected to do and you spoke up and acted to resolve the conflict.

1. What did you do, and what was the impact?
2. What motivated you to speak up and act?
3. How satisfied are you? How would you like to have responded?
4. What would have made it easier to act or speak?
    a. Things within your control and things within the control of others.

Part 2

In a small group, students refer to one of the following case scenarios:

*   an employee suspects a manager to be behaving improperly or breaking the law;
*   morale is low amongst employees and complaints of short-handedness of staff are being lodged by customers;
*   a junior advertising executive is being directed by her managers to exaggerate claims;

- the sales targets are set very high, prompting some sales executives to over-promise and mislead their clients in order to make a sale;
- pressure is being exerted by top management to use market research respondent quotes or footage to publicize products or services.

Each group then discusses the questions below:
1. What obstacles do both manager and employee face to solve the problem?
2. What will make it easier to speak up and act?
3. What will the impact be of behaving according to values?

Part 3
- Students present their solutions to the rest of the class.
- Full class debrief summarizes the key obstacles and enablers to personal responsible behaviour.

Participants Take Away

- Ability to reflect on own behaviour.
- A format for devising action-based solutions to problems.
- Confidence to voice concerns and values

Evaluation
This type of reflective activity works best when students have been encouraged to reflect and have developed their reflective capacity in previous modules. As a result, reflective practice becomes a habit. It is important to emphasize that students are to work according to their values and what they think is responsible behaviour without having to debate what is considered right.

While the above examples identify a preferred method for each approach, this polarization of approaches and associated methods can be restrictive. Each of the above methods can be adapted to integrate different approaches and competencies. In particular, experiential learning is supported for the integration of learning with students' work and personal experiences to enable a more meaningful and relevant educational experience (Kolb and Kolb 2005). Hands-on experience of ethical issues and decision-making as part of a short-term or long-term activity appears to be a popular teaching strategy, irrespective of the philosophical and psychological approach to moral education (Beggs 2011). Furthermore, combining the use of case studies with role play and reflection can allow students to develop reasoned decision making, consider the impact of ethical behaviour on various stakeholders and reflect upon how they represent their values in various contexts.

Integrating Approaches

These diverse approaches to ethics education have resulted in a polarization between advocates of reasoning, values education, relationships and behavioural ethics (Tello et al. 2013). In practice, many ethics educators reveal their combined use, with a heavy focus on moral reasoning not solely to understand the role of duty and universal values but also to enable self-reflection, to question one's actions and examine diverse stakeholder positions. While some claim that each of these approaches require different methods and techniques of delivery, integration of ethics across the curriculum allows for a combination of methods and techniques to be used for different subjects and for different contexts. It allows the study of ethics and responsibility to move from a polarized view of its purpose and approach to combine 'developing cognitive abilities to apply ethical concepts to solutions ... developing affective elements of human and self-awareness, core values such as caring and empathy ... and the ability to reflect critically and thereby integrate cognitive and affective learning to focus on action and problem solving' (Tello et al. 2013: 108).

This is particularly achievable where ethics is not only just taught as one dedicated module but where responsible principles, values and criteria are integrated throughout the curriculum.

THE ROLE OF THE UNIVERSITY

Business ethics has grown in importance in the twenty-first century, with companies investing significant efforts into Corporate Social Responsibility (CSR), sustainable practices, and ethical reputation management. However, criticism of unethical practices in business and marketing and recent global scandals suggest that ethics education is not doing enough to develop ethics as integral to students' approach to business issues. More broadly, there is significant debate about the role that moral education occupies in our public institutions, schools and universities, with some calling for universities to take the lead and set the moral education agenda.

This chapter offers a proactive and practical approach to fulfil the call for change, to challenge the critics of business education and to take business at its word by applying the newly stated purpose of business to meet the needs of its stakeholders.

The key elements of this integrated approach are not new. There have been many calls for greater emphasis on ethics and responsibility from both the academic and business communities. Some claim that this is already taking place, often without ethics interventions being labelled as such (Peleg 2019). In reality, however, research reveals that many institutions overclaim their focus on ethics and responsibility and many at best offer elective courses in these areas (Rasche et al. 2013).

Challenges to implement such an approach often come from within, with faculty resistance identifying few proven long-term effects of business education, lack of expertise and training in ethics, an overcrowded curriculum and the values of academic freedom that until recently allowed faculty members to pursue their areas of expertise.

However, as with many meaningful changes to the curriculum, this approach can be delivered from the bottom up by individual champions that adapt their modules, share their practice with others and then lead the course team to consider necessary changes in structure. This can often be a more successful approach than drive from the top, which often just creates a mere tick-box exercise. A bottom-up approach can be supported and encouraged by the top, by demonstrating responsible values and leadership, enabling appropriate training, creating space and time to develop this approach, applauding and publicising genuine change. The course can then be promoted as an example innovation of good practice to be disseminated internally and externally.

The formalization of this stakeholder approach further supports the calls for institutions of higher education to take the lead and teach beyond the acquisition of knowledge for its own sake towards a responsible application and purpose of that knowledge, towards wisdom. 'Arguably, wisdom is at least as important as, or even more important than, sheer knowledge and intelligence. Thus, promoting the development of wisdom in schools represents a clear need and responsibility.' (Sternberg et al. 2007: 145).

REFERENCES

Abend, G. (2013) The origins of business ethics in American universities, 1902–1936, *Business Ethics Quarterly*, 23(2), pp. 171–205.

American Marketing Association (2013) Marketing (definition). Accessed 18 October 2017 at: https://www.ama.org/AboutAMA/Pages/Definition-of-Marketing.aspx.

Aristotle (c325 BC [2008]) Nicomachean ethics. In J. Cottingham (ed.), *Western Philosophy: An Anthology*. 2nd edn. Oxford: Blackwell Publishing, pp. 492–5.

Austin, L. and Toth, E. (2011) Exploring ethics education in global public relations curricula: Analysis of international curricula descriptions and interviews with public relations educators, *Public Relations Review*, 37, pp. 506–512.

Barnett, R. (1990) *The Idea of Higher Education*. Buckingham: The Society for Research into Higher Education & Open University Press.

Beggs, J.M. (2011) Seamless integration of ethics, *Marketing Education Review*, 21(1), pp. 49–56.

Bok, D. (1982) *Beyond the Ivory Tower: Social Responsibilities of the Modern University*. Cambridge, MA: Harvard University Press.

Breaugh, J.A. and Starke, M. (2000) Research on employee recruitment: So many studies, so many remaining questions, *Journal of Management*, 26(3), 405–34.

Business Round Table (2019) Business roundtable redefines the purpose of a corporation to promote 'an economy that serves all Americans'. Accessed September 2019 at: https://www.businessroundtable.org/business-roundtable-redefines-the-purpose -of-a-corporation-to-promote-an-economy-that-serves-all-americans.

Conduit, J., Matanda, M.J. and Mavondo, F.T. (2014) Balancing the act: The implications of jointly pursuing internal customer orientation and external customer orientation. *Journal of Marketing Management*, 30(13–14), pp. 1320–52.

Cone Communications (2015) *2015 Cone Communication millennial CSR study*. Accessed 15 November 2017 at: http://www.conecomm.com/research-blog/2015 -cone-communications-millennial-csr-study.

Davis, P. (2016) 'Retrieving the co-operative value-based leadership model of Terry Thomas', *Journal of Business Ethics*, 135(3), pp. 557–68.

Deloitte (2016) The 2016 millennial survey: Winning over the next generation of leaders. Accessed 10 October 2017 at: https://www2.deloitte.com/content/ dam/Deloitte/global/Documents/About-Deloitte/gx-millenial-survey-2016-exec -summary.pdf.

Edelman PLC (2020) Edelman Trust Barometer 2020. Accessed March 2020 at: https:// www.edelman.com/trust/2020-trust-barometer

Elkington, J. (1998) Accounting for the triple bottom line, *Measuring Business Excellence*, 2(3), pp. 18–22.

Emmet, D. (1979) *The Moral Prism*. London: Macmillan.

Fischbach, S. and Conner, S.L. (2016) Empathy and interpersonal mentalizing in ethics education: An exercise with graphic novels, *Journal for Advancement of Marketing Education*, 24, pp. 88–94.

FleishmanHillard Fishburn (2019) Leading with impact: UK authenticity gap report 2019. Accessed April 2020 at: https://fhflondon.co.uk/2019/07/leading-with-impact -fleishmanhillard-fishburn-launches-2019-authenticity-gap-report/.

Freeman, C. (1984). Prometheus unbound, *Futures*, 16(5), 494–507.

Gentile, M.C. (2017) Giving voice to values: A pedagogy for behavioural ethics, *Journal of Management Education*, 41(4), pp. 469–79.

Ghoshal, S. (2005) Bad management theories are destroying good management practices, *Academy of Management Learning & Education*, 4(1), pp. 75–91.

Gilligan, C. (1982) *In a Different Voice: Psychological Theory and Women's Development*, Boston, MA: Harvard University Press.

Godfrey, P.C., Merrill, C.B. and Hansen, J.M. (2009) The relationship between corporate social responsibility and shareholder value: An empirical test of the risk management hypothesis. *Strategic Management*, 30(4), 425–45.

Greenley, G.E., Hooley, G.J., Broderick, A.J. and Rudd, J.M. (2004). Strategic planning differences among multiple stakeholder orientation profiles. *Journal of Strategic Marketing*, 12(3), pp. 163–82.

Habert, T. and Ingulli, E. (2012) *Law and Ethics in the Business Environment*. 7th edn. Boston, MA: Cengage Learning.

Henisz, W.J., Dorobantu, S. and Nartey, L.J. (2014) Spinning gold: The financial returns to stakeholder engagement. *Strategic Management Journal*, 35(12), 1727–48.

Herrington, C. and Weaven, S. (2007) Does marketing attract less ethical students? An assessment of the moral reasoning ability of undergraduate marketing students, *Journal of Marketing Education*, 29(2), 154–63.

Jagger, S., Siala, H. and Sloan, D. (2016) It's all in the game: A 3D learning model for business ethics, *Journal of Business Ethics*, 137(2), pp. 383–403.

Jensen, T., Sandstrom, J. and Helin, S. (2009) Corporate codes of ethics and the bending of moral space, *Organisation*, 16(4), pp. 529–45.

Jost, J. (2014) Is ethics the saviour of branding? *Ethical Corporation*. Accessed 16 November 2017 at: http://www.ethicalcorp.com/business-strategy/ethics-saviour-branding.

Kahneman, D. (2011) *Thinking, Fast and Slow*. New York: Farrar, Straus and Giroux.

Kant, I. (1785[2008]) Groundwork of the metaphysics of morals. In J. Cottingham (ed.), *Western Philosophy: An Anthology*. 2nd edn. Oxford: Blackwell Publishing, pp. 506–512.

Kaplan, R.S.W. (2017) Internal marketing and internal branding in the 21st century organization, *IUP Journal of Brand Management*, 14(2), pp. 7–22.

Kenny, B. and Lincoln, L. (2015) Ethics cases: Do they elicit different levels of ethical reasoning? *Journal of Academic Ethics*, 33(3), 259–75.

Kirman, J. (2016) Behavioural interviewing as part of values-based recruitment for postgraduate community nursing programmes, *Community Practitioner*, 89(9), pp. 42–7.

Kohlberg, I. and Turiel, E. (1971) Moral development and moral education. In G.S. Lesser (ed.), *Psychology and Educational Practice*. Glenview, IL: Scott, Foresman & Company, pp. 410–65.

Kolb, A.Y. and Kolb, D.A. (2005) Learning styles and learning spaces: Enhancing experiential learning in higher education, *Academy of Management Learning & Education*, 4(2), pp. 193–212.

Levine, S.J. (2015) The law and the 'spirit of the law' in legal ethics, *Journal of Professional Law*, 1.

MacFarlane, B. (1995) Business ethics: Too little, too late, *Education & Training*, 37(5), pp. 32–6.

MacFarlane, B. and Perkins, A. (1999) Reconceptualising corporate strategy in business and management education, *Education and Training*, 41(1), pp. 20–26.

Maignon, I., Ferrrell, O.C. and Ferrell, L. (2005) A stakeholder model for implementing social responsibility in marketing, *European Journal of Marketing*, 39(9/10), pp. 956–1219.

Matchett, N.J. (2008) Ethics across the curriculum, *New Directions for Higher Education*, 142(Summer), pp. 25–38.

Maxwell, N. (2007) From knowledge to wisdom: The need for an academic revolution. *London Review of Education*, 5(2), pp. 97–115.

McGlone, T., Spain, J.W. and McGlone, V. (2011) Corporate social responsibility and the millennials, *Journal of Education for Business*, 86(4), pp. 195–200.

Merriam Webster (2020) Stay woke. Accessed March 2020 at: https://www.merriam-webster.com/words-at-play/woke-meaning-origin.

Michaelson, C. (2016) A novel approach to business ethics education: Exploring how to live and work in the 21st century, *Academy of Management Learning & Education*, 15(3), pp. 588–606.

Murphy, P.E., Laczniak, G.R. and Harris, F. (2016) *Ethics in Marketing: International Cases*. New York, NY: Routledge.

Nelson, J., Smith, L.B. and Hunt, C.S. (2014) The migration toward ethical decision making as a core course into the b-school: Instructional strategies and approaches for consideration, *Journal of Education for Business*, 89(1), pp. 49–56.

Paul, P. (2019) A gap analysis of teaching marketing ethics: Desired versus current state, *Journal of Education for Business*, 94(7), 460–70.

Peleg, A. (2019) Early-career marketing practitioner experiences of ethics: Implications for ethics education. Thesis, London South Bank University School of Business.

Peppas, S.C. and Diskin, B.A. (2001) College courses in ethics: Do they really make a difference? *International Journal of Educational Management*, 15(7), pp. 347–53.

Prentice, R. (2014) Teaching behavioural ethics, *Journal of Legal Studies Education*, 31(2), pp. 325–65.

Rasche, A., Gilbert, D.U. and Schedel, I. (2013) Cross-disciplinary ethics education in MBA programs: Rhetoric or reality? *Academy of Management Learning & Education*, 12(1), pp. 71–85.

Rawls. J. (1972[2008]) A theory of justice. In J. Cottingham (ed.), *Western Philosophy, an Anthology*. 2nd edn. Oxford: Blackwell Publishing, pp. 534–40.

Sternberg, R.J., Reznitskaya, A. and Jarvin, L. (2007) Teaching for wisdom: What matters is not just what students know but how they use it. *The London Review of Education*, 5(2), pp. 143–58.

Sundheim, D. and Starr, K. (2020) Making stakeholder capitalism a reality, *Harvard Business Review*, 22 January.

Syed Alwi, S.F., Muhammad Ali, S. and Nguyen, B. (2017) The importance of ethics in branding: Mediating effects of ethical branding on company reputation and brand loyalty, *Business Ethics Quarterly*, 27(3), pp. 393–422.

Tello, G., Swanson, D., Floyd, L. and Caldwell, C. (2013) Transformative learning: A new model for business ethics education. *Journal of Multidisciplinary Research*, 5(1), pp. 105–120.

Trevino, L.K., Weaver, G.R. and Brown, M.E. (2008) It's lovely at the top: Hierarchical levels, identities, and perceptions of organizational ethics, *Business Ethics Quarterly*, 18(2), pp. 233–52.

Tveit, A.D. and Sunde, A.L. (2016) How different insights from a variety of theories might help ethical decision-making in educational counselling, *Interchange: A Quarterly Review of Education*, 47(2), pp. 121–32.

Vos, L. and Page, S. (2020). Marketization, performative environments and the impact of organisational climate on teaching practice in Business Schools. *Academy of Management, Learning and Education*, 19(1): 59–80.

Warren, R.C. (1995) Practical reason in practice: Reflections on a business ethics course, *Education & Training*, 37(6), pp. 14–22.

Weber, J. (2013) Advances in graduate marketing curriculum: Paying attention to ethical, social and sustainability issues, *Journal of Marketing Education*, 35(2), pp. 85–94.

APPENDIX A

This example highlights key areas where alignment of ethics, responsibility and business success can serve as guiding considerations throughout a module through the content delivery and the student-based activity of planning and execution of a public relations plan.

BOX 2.8   INTEGRATING ETHICS AND RESPONSIBILITY IN A LEVEL 5 OR 6 PR MODULE

The marketing communications field is often in the spotlight for unethical practices and irresponsible communication. A public relations module is therefore a useful example of how to integrate ethics and responsibility into the curriculum with a view to teaching for a more responsible approach to PR, through the development of the subject knowledge and practice. From 2004 to 2015 I developed and taught the PR modules at undergraduate and post-graduate levels at London South Bank University. I present here a version of that module, further developed to fully integrate ethics and social responsibility.

In developing this module, I was aware of the poor reputation of the Public Relations discipline and so from week one students were tasked with ensuring that ethical issues were considered when developing PR activities. As mentioned previously, I found a passion for discussion of these issues but a great deal of cynicism when it came to consideration of the ethical nature of PR and of CSR initiatives, in particular. What I suggest here is designed to present a proactive approach to PR and responsibility that not only develops a consciousness of ethical challenges in PR but tries to find synergies between PR, ethics and responsibility. Particularly useful for this approach is the practical experiential nature of this module that requires strategic and practical planning and the execution of PR-based activities. This allows for the development of responsible decision making, development of ethical sensitivity and behaviour.

Introduction to Public Relations: Agenda Setting
1. to create and to identify the key principles that the PR profession holds itself to;
2. to define the principles of PR that the students will use when devising and executing PR plans that they will be working on throughout the semester.

Introduction

- When introducing PR, I present professional definitions of PR from various sources and identify the key words that drive the purpose of PR. Definitions: 'Public relations is a strategic communication process that builds mutually beneficial relationships between organizations and their publics.' Key Words: Reputation management, public image, communications, relationships, publics, mutual benefit.
- In particular, I present the theory behind PR that suggests synergies between trust, reputation and the PR Role.
- I ask the students to compare these definitions with their own perceptions of Public Relations. I show them excerpts from two films that reveal both positive and negative practice in PR. This raises awareness of the ethical challenges that face PR practitioners and invites the students to discuss those challenges.

Workshops

- In the related workshops students are given examples of PR campaigns and identify the key PR activities and what they are trying to achieve.
- Key words produced are often: informing, educating, persuading, introducing change, re-branding, product introduction, crisis management, image building, reputation building and management, communications, stakeholders/publics, build relationships, maintaining goodwill, create understanding, influencing the public image of the organization, managing interpretation of messages.
- Students are also asked to identify the public perceptions of PR and their own personal definitions. This usually elicits more negative terminology such as propaganda, spin, lying, greenwashing, amongst others. I ask them to identify activities that might fit into these categories, either from examples in *PRWeek* or from examples that they know about.
- The formal definitions of PR are then scrutinized to see how far their responses and key words fit the formal PR definitions.
- What follows is a discussion of the thin line between what PR aims to be and its more negative public perception. Students are asked to differentiate between PR and propaganda with the aim of creating their own definition of what PR is trying achieve, that is both realistic and responsible. This definition will then serve as principles or values that will guide the students as they develop, manage and execute a PR campaign throughout the module.
- The purpose is to develop principles together with the students that will set the tone of the module and guide the students when considering the elements of PR and how to plan and carry out PR activities. Throughout

the module when putting together a PR plan and executing PR activities they will justify their plans and activities and assess their potential success according to those principles that combine building reputation, developing positive relationships, managing stakeholder relationships and behaving responsibly.

In the following weeks as the module focuses on the different elements of building a PR campaign these principles will be at the core of their discussions and planning.

Media Relations

- We debate what makes something newsworthy. Tools of communication with the media: press releases and Twitter feeds are analysed to understand how to create newsworthy copy, the role of truth and spin. The trade-off between making a story newsworthy and responsible.
- We consider how to develop relationships with journalists and other media influencers. Here the synergies between truth, trust, credibility, developing long-term relationships and building reputation can be studied through case studies or film.
- Finally, students review examples of communications with the press, such as press releases, and in writing workshops develop those tools for their group campaigns, always considering the underlying principles they have set.

The Role of Influencers

- We consider the role of individual influencers on social media, such as bloggers, vloggers, and the ethical concerns regarding their influence and power in shaping views. Students are asked to review blogs/vlogs and influencers on social media, assess their value and impact as PR tools and identify ethical issues that compromise their usage as a responsible comms tool. Examples from *PRWeek* and case studies highlight controversial uses of influencers discussed.
- As part of the PR campaign that students develop they are required to devise the content of these materials, execute them, justify their use to fulfil the goals and principles set out in week one and recommend responsible engagement with these types of influencers.

Promoting CSR

- Examples of CSR as part of an integrated strategy across the organization are compared with examples where CSR appears to be used solely as a promotional tool.

- Through analysis of case studies, students are required to consider when it is appropriate to promote elements of an organization's CSR campaign, the pros and cons of doing so.
- For those wishing to create a CSR activity uniquely to promote their organizations they will be tasked to consider the criteria that make a CSR campaign more than just a publicity tool but an activity that integrates the CSR strategy and behaviour across the organization.

Internal Relations

- The synergies between internal relations, employee satisfaction and brand reputation are familiar to many students who combine work and study and as demonstrated in academic research (Conduit et al. 2014; Kaplan, 2017). Generating a personal discussion of experiences of employee/management relations can be a useful way to reflect on this link.
- This allows students to consider the various communications tools used in their place of work, what works and what does not. Alternative internal communications tools are suggested and considered. Finally, the internal communications tools are applied to the group PR campaigns.
- The Voicing Values approach (Gentile, 2017) suggested previously can also be used to develop an action-based approach to internal communications that develops transparent internal communications, employee satisfaction and positive engagement with their brand.

Tools to Develop these Activities
Throughout the module I use a variety of tools to enable the students to understand the theory and practice of PR and to plan and execute a campaign, whilst constantly reviewing the ethical issues that arise and how they might affect the key goal of reputation.

- Experiential learning: Each week students apply their learning about the PR tools to a live group project. This form of experiential learning where students learn by doing over a 12-week period, allows for the application of theory and general practice to a live case. It enables the development of specific PR skills such as researching, planning, writing etc. and the opportunity to reflect on the ethical issues that arise and justify and evaluate the achievement of their goals and values.
- Cases and examples from *PRWeek*: To maintain a current and practical focus on PR, cases and articles from *PRWeek* are of particular importance. Each week students read news items and cases from this journal related to the weekly topic to stimulate discussion. They often use examples from *PRWeek* to guide the planning of their PR project. Mini cases

are also used to highlight current issues and concerns and to encourage a range of practical activities that can be applied to their projects.

• Film: Film can also be very useful to facilitate this discussion. For example: *Jerry Maguire, Jersey Girl, Phone Booth, People I Know* and *Thank you for Smoking* all identify important issues that can elicit discussion about the nature and goal of PR and the public perception of PR. Film and story-telling are particularly useful to allow students to understand and empathize with different characters and points of view, thus enabling reflection. Choosing short clips from one or two of these movies can be tools that create engagement during lectures, and where the library gives the students access to these films they can be used in preparation for a particular lecture or seminar and a link made available on the virtual learning environment (VLE).

3. Teaching marketing theory and critical thinking

Caroline Tynan and Teresa Heath

INTRODUCTION

Nurturing the next generation of competent and informed marketing professionals requires that marketing academics engage in developing both students' knowledge of their discipline and their critical thinking skills. Achieving one of these without the other will not provide a solid base for the career development of our students. Understanding marketing only at the level of checklists would consign those graduates to an endless round of repeating the same processes regardless of the changing environment, changing understandings in the discipline, or moral requirements of their profession. Alternatively, fostering critical thinking skills without an understanding of the theory underpinning marketing and the development of the discipline would lead to ill-informed decisions. We need marketing professionals who are capable of analysing the assumptions, practices and discourses of both its discipline and practice. In an increasingly 'ambiguous, uncertain, fast-changing, and complex marketplace' (Reibstein et al. 2009: 1), we also require marketing practitioners and academics who can not only analyse, but also provide creative solutions to marketing problems identified by managers, consumers and society. So, to educate reflexive practitioners and future scholars, we need to address both the development of theoretical understandings and critical thinking skills.

In agreement with Wilkie and Moore (1999: 198), we were drawn to marketing because we found it to be 'among the most stimulating, complex and intellectually challenging of academic areas in a university setting'. This is still clearer when we apply a critical lens to marketing's scholarship and its practice. This challenge is rooted in the combination of disciplines that inform marketing, the wide range of paradigmatic understandings that are accepted within it, and also to its grounding in human behaviour. Marketing's ever more complex environment, and, crucially, the dramatic challenges caused by the current COVID-19 pandemic, exacerbate the urgency of developing professionals capable of making informed decisions, based on sound knowledge, and with a firm basis of critical thought and moral awareness. However, a brief review of popular undergraduate marketing texts still suggests the promulgation of a 'theory-light' reflection of this complexity, which fails to interlink phenomena in a deeper sense (Gummesson 2002), and offers a relentlessly positive presentation of the virtues of a seemingly universally applicable discipline. Such overly positive and self-legitimising rhetoric discourages criticism (Hackley 2003), reflexivity and imagination. This perspective also overlooks the negative effects of marketing systems, and offers oversimplified representations of the difficulties inherent in analysing and understanding the complex, previously unthinkable contexts in which businesses now operate, and in arriving at sound marketing decisions as a marketing practitioner today. Such texts very rarely encourage students to challenge the status quo, to question the various effects of marketing on consumers, business or society, or to critically evaluate its consequences. To address this technocratic perspective (Catterall et al. 2002) and facilitate students' in-depth understanding, we need to teach marketing theory in ways that engage students, promote participation and nurture intellectual curiosity to seek new ways of thinking about, and doing, marketing.

This is a demanding set of goals given that our students come from a wide variety of different cultural and linguistic backgrounds where their undergraduate education may privilege various outcomes involving recall, descriptive skills, and problem solving. Financially driven recruiting, primarily by English-speaking universities in the UK and USA, has led to large multinational student cohorts on many marketing modules. This role as 'cash cows' for many Western universities (Contu 2017) has produced unintended consequences. In this rush to globalisation (Bradshaw and Tadajewski 2011), little consideration appears to have been given to the needs of students who plan to return and practise marketing in different parts of the globe, ranging from affluent Gulf states and rapidly developing Asian nations to countries impoverished by suffering war and disruption. Neither has much thought been given to the needs of the societies that sponsor them (Bradshaw and Tadajewski 2011). For us, it is problematic that a discipline which aims to meet others' needs is delivered in a way which fails to consider the context-specific needs of many of its students who hail from parts of the world where society's requirements and marketing practice are shaped by a substantially different environment to that which we experience in the UK.

This chapter is based on our experience of teaching a Masters-level module entitled Critical Marketing. The module was grounded in a consideration of theory and its role in marketing. The four learning aims of the module are: first, to develop a critical understanding of the main theoretical debates in a range of historical, current and emerging marketing areas and contexts; secondly, to critically analyse assumptions, concepts and effects of marketing from the perspectives of different agents; thirdly, to develop a broad and critical understanding of the discipline and of related ethical and sustainable considerations; and, finally, to critically review academic contributions to the discipline and present a carefully argued case. The introductory section on marketing theory aims to explore the concepts of theory and marketing theory and to analyse their value and usefulness. Within this, we discuss the perceptions of the value of practitioner-oriented research and finally introduce the importance of adopting a societal viewpoint to understand marketing theory. To achieve this, we utilise the practice of critical thinking and embed an understanding of its processes through a number of exercises. We consider this essential for students to be able to engage with and benefit from the experience.

ON DEFINING AND TEACHING THEORY

As Tellis (2017: 3) states, a 'good theory is just a simple explanation for a phenomenon'. Persuading students of the importance of theory and stimulating them to engage critically with it are not, however, easy challenges. Many may see theory as too complex, uninteresting, or irrelevant to their planned careers as marketing practitioners. Endorsing a critical, theoretical pedagogy to teaching marketing raises yet further difficulties. Students may view critical approaches as labour intensive and intellectually challenging (Tregear et al. 2007), and some may feel defensive or anxious about questioning their established ideas (Gray 2007; Spicer et al. 2009; Heath et al. 2019). Thus, we seek to facilitate a participative classroom environment where students feel included, reassured, and valued for sharing their experiences and views.

In keeping with the above approach, we encourage students to recognise that the significance of critical thinking skills extends beyond their value in understanding theory and contributing to knowledge creation. Critical thinking is one of four fundamental competencies for twenty-first-century learning (Scott 2015), and represents a highly sought set of skills in job candidates (Plummer 2019), which employers believe will grow in importance over the next five years (Whiting 2020). Critical thinking is 'the intellectually disciplined process of actively and skilfully conceptualising, applying, analysing, synthesizing, and/or evaluating information gathered from, or generated by, observation, experience, reflection, reasoning, or communication, as a guide to belief and action' (Scriven and Paul 1987: 1). It requires self-discipline and personal commitment to self-improvement and entails skills of problem solving and communication (Paul and Elder 2006). In general, to participate in and learn from the module, we expect students to engage with the material thoughtfully, to form and articulate their own opinions, to develop creative insights and imaginative, justified solutions, and to engage in informed discussion with peers and educators. We also encourage students to strive to attain the good scholarship qualities of 'clarity, precision, accuracy, relevance, depth, breadth, logicalness, significance, and fairness', which are an inherent part of developing the skills of critical thinking (Paul and Elder 2013: 32). We aim to foster in our students the practice of examining received truths, which Brookfield refers to as 'reflective scepticism' (1987: 21), so that they do not unquestioningly accept that some statement or argument is true because it has been offered by an authoritative source or refuse to challenge the status quo because 'That's just the way things are'. Discussing with students the importance of critical thinking skills and outlining their nature and attributes provides a foundation for discussing theory.

Although the term 'theory' may sound intimidating, people have a constant drive to find explanations and, in some way, 'theorise' (Davidoff et al. 2015). One way of illustrating this is to lay out different phenomena to students and ask their views on what has caused them. They are likely to bring different explanations and assumptions to the table and, in doing so, to consider the relevance of theorising (and theories) to provide meaning and make sense of the world.

Then, we need to consider the nature and importance of theory, as well as to explore the specific situation of theory in marketing. One way of first involving students in the topic of theory is to ask them to complete the exercise in Box 3.1, which explores their knowledge of particular, important theories and implicitly considers how these theories have significantly changed the world. This helps to build students' confidence and to engage them with complex topics in a participative environment. Issues that can be drawn from this exercise include an examination of the science and evidence that underpin the theories and also how the new understandings from these theories have effected change.

BOX 3.1   LEARNING ACTIVITY 1

This activity asks students to discuss the theories they are familiar with which in their opinion have changed the world. Theories which have been typically raised for discussion include: Darwin's Theory of Evolution, Copernicus on Heliocentrism, Einstein's Theories of Special and General Relativity, Plate Tectonics by Wegner and Wilson, Freud's Theory of Personality, and Quantum Theory developed by Niels Bohr and Max Planck. Having listed the theories raised, we ask students to outline the theories drawing out the evidence that supports them, consider why they were impactful and to discuss the changes they have wrought. Drawing on these ideas we enable a discussion that highlights the varied nature, domains and impact of the theories in order to emphasise the importance of theory in our lived world.

Following this practical insight into the importance and widespread applicability of specific theories, we discuss and review the nature of theory.

BOX 3.2 LEARNING ACTIVITY 2

Having explored students' suggestions of world-changing theories and subsequently discussed the nature and the changes brought by these theories, we ask students in groups of two or three to discuss the question 'what is theory?'. Then they share their views with each other and with the class about what constitutes theory and we use this as a basis for defining theory.

The word 'theory', and its derivatives, such as 'theorise' and 'theoretical', are not always understood or used in similar ways by different scholars, so there is often confusion about their meaning, nature and processes. Students' understandings of theory, as well as those of their teachers, depend largely on their worldviews. All research is conceived, designed and shaped by the researcher's understanding of the world (Tadajewski 2014) through assumptions concerning what constitutes knowledge and appropriate ways to create it in social sciences. Some view reality to be objective, tangible and observable and so can be measured, whilst others emphasise the socially constructed nature of reality (or realities), which requires interpretation to determine meaning and the implications of such understandings (Hudson and Ozanne 1988).

Etymologically, theory derives from the Greek word for spectator 'theōríā', which can be translated as 'contemplation, conjecture, a looking at, things looked at' (Chambers Dictionary of Etymology 2008: 1132). So, from this root, we understand the term to be about observing, thinking and conjecturing. Thus, we can explain the essence of theory as: careful examination of events or behaviours; developing and organising our ideas about the relationships between what we have observed; and then extending this understanding to create an explanation for, or a 'story' about, a new situation.

As Maclaran and Stevens (2008: 347) explain, a theory is essentially 'an organized way to think about a topic'. Where we need stories to make sense of, and to navigate the world (Monbiot 2018), theories provide us with helpful narratives, illuminating how and why things happen (Saren 2016). The concept of theory is insightfully described by Baumol (1957: 414) as a 'structure which describes the workings and interrelations of the various aspects of some phenomenon' offering 'systematic explanation'. In exploring this issue in the classroom, we often make reference to our favourite fictional detectives including Sherlock Holmes, Colombo and Saga Norén to show

how they develop their theories about who the murderer must be, based on their investigation, asking many questions and relating what they learn about people, motives, events and timelines to reach a solution. In an everyday sense we may use the term 'theory' to mean speculation about, or contemplation of, something (Baker 1995). Students often consider with amusement the 'theories' they may have to explain events in their everyday lives.

In an academic environment, the meaning of theory is more nuanced, often obscured by a practice-distant stance, unnecessarily complex language and sometimes used as a source of intimidation against practitioners and other academics (Maclaran and Stevens 2008). Saren (2016: 32) explains how theory can be described as 'a set of propositions or an abstract conceptualization of the relationship between entities' or 'a general principle that is used to explain or predict facts or events' (see also Maclaran et al. 2010). As well as considering the nature and outcomes of theory, we cannot ignore the processes by which it is developed. Theories should include a precise definition of the meanings of any terms used and clarify the conditions or assumptions under which it will hold (Baker 1995). In this sense they may comprise a 'statement of the principles' on which a subject is based (Hornby 1980: 1330). Discussing passages from Rawls' *Theory of Justice* with students helps to elucidate how theories can lay out a set of principles and illuminate relationships between concepts (in this case between freedom, equity and a just society).

Bringing these ideas together, a theory can be described as a set of testable and related ideas that explain particular phenomena. In a seminal paper, Alderson and Cox (1948: 137) take a broader view when they define theory as 'the general or abstract principles underlying the body of facts which comprise this field'. Within disciplines, relevant bodies of theory are built up as researchers study phenomena by applying their unique lens (Saren 2016: 26); a viewpoint which is achieved through the employment of the discourse, extant theory, methods and approaches of their subject.

The position of theories is not immutable; they can evolve as new information emerges, and they can be contested. For example, the 'miasma theory' which was popular through the Middle Ages, held that diseases such as cholera, malaria or the black death were caused by a miasma (or bad air). It was believed that people became ill by inhaling poisonous vapour which was infected through exposure to corrupting matter (Science Museum 2019). Hundreds of years later in the nineteenth century, the theory was finally displaced by the discovery of germs and the development of germ theory which states that disease is spread by micro-organisms (ibid.). More recently, on 23 September 2011, Reuters published a news item that subatomic particles apparently travelling 'faster than light' could force a rethink about how the cosmos works and threaten Einstein's theory (Evans 2011). In the article, Reuters' Robert Evans (2011) reported 'Sub-atomic particles apparently traveling faster than light could force a major rethink of theories about how the cosmos works and even allow dreams of time travel and extra dimensions.' However, when further tested, the claims made by international physicists at CERN (in French, 'Conseil Européen pour la Recherche Nucléaire') contesting Einstein's theory did not disprove it. So rather than allowing us to send information into the past and perhaps even enjoy time travel to the past, this new data turned out to be an artefact of experimental error. This notwithstanding, examples such as these highlight how important it is that theories are constantly challenged and tested against current data to verify their relevance and validity.

BOX 3.3   LEARNING ACTIVITY 3

When do you think you will use theory in the future? This exercise aims to help students engage with the relevance of theory to their own lives. First suggestions are usually from an academic perspective when students propose using theory to complete an assignment, a project or their dissertation. Further probing and possibly specific questioning should help students to consider the use of theory in a work context, for example to solve a new marketing problem at work, or when making consumption decisions.

Grand, Mid-range and Applied Theories

It is helpful for students to understand that not all theories are the same and that they differ in levels of abstraction, scope, degree of integration, and distance from practice. This understanding supports students in their evaluation of research articles and is a theme that is returned to in discussions of proposed theoretical contributions in research projects and dissertations. At the highest levels of abstraction, the grand or general theories of marketing state fundamental premises about the domain and have a wide applicability across the discipline. These broad theories operate at high levels of abstraction, are integrative in unifying more focused theories and 'provide the foundations for understanding and explanation' (Brodie and Peters 2020: 416). Examples of grand theory include Bagozzi's (1975) general theory of '*marketing as exchange*' and Vargo and Lusch's (2004) '*service dominant logic*' theory. Such overarching theories provide conceptual overview and perspective but the level of abstraction makes them difficult to test (Brodie et al. 2011).

Mid-range theory is an intermediate body of theory that acts as a bridge between the highly abstract grand theory on one hand and applied theory based on empirical investigation on the other (Brodie and Peters 2020), and can inform both (Vargo and Lusch 2017). A mid-range theory does not have grand theory's integrative capability, is more specific and more narrowly framed than grand theory and therefore explains fewer phenomena. Operating in specific contexts, it provides links between the high level of abstraction of grand theory and empirical findings. Brodie et al. (2011) offer a helpful discussion of how mid-range theory links grand service dominant logic theory and empirical evidence on marketing practices, using the example of the theorising process used to develop the mid-range theory of '*actor engagement*'.

Applied theory in marketing addresses practice issues within specialist areas of the discipline and provides insights from the marketplace. It frequently includes theories which originate in other subject areas (Burton 2005) like psychology, but which have proved useful in marketing such as Ajzen's (1991) '*theory of planned behaviour*', widely adopted in the subfield of consumer behaviour. Theories-in-use are a particular form of applied theory which also adopts a bottom-up approach (Burton 2005). It recognises that consumers, managers and public policy officials use theory in their everyday lives (Brodie and Peters 2020). Researchers examine topics from the perspective of the individuals who are close to the problem under investigation, by eliciting their mental models concerning the phenomenon under investigation and then co-creating theory with them (Zeithaml et al. 2020). Kohli and Jaworski's (1990) theory of '*marketing orientation*' employs a theory-in-use approach (ibid.).

THEORY IN MARKETING

In order to discuss marketing meaningfully, and develop an understanding of the discipline's theory, we need to define our terms of reference and understand its historical evolution (Saren 2016; Tadajewski 2014; Yadav 2017). Baker (2005: 1) reminds us that we should not 'neglect or overlook hard-won lessons from the past' as to do so will simply consign us to repeating them. In quoting Isaac Newton's famous observation 'If I can see further it is because I am standing on the shoulders of giants', Baker highlights the process by which knowledge is built. He then raises the 'principle of cumulativity' (2005: 3) and commends researchers to take advantage and learn from reviewing the work of scholars who have preceded them. In the light of this scholarly process, it is also important that marketing theory is recognised and understood as timebound and therefore an artefact of the thinking, context and environment at the time it was produced.

Our definition of marketing and its boundaries is a platform upon which marketing theory is grounded. Definitions of marketing have proliferated and changed substantially over the years as 'marketing as a phenomenon has changed' (Grönroos 2006: 395). Simply stated, we often conceive marketing as the practice of identifying customer needs by creating and delivering appropriate offerings profitably. The earliest formal definition of marketing, adopted by the AMA in 1935, explicates it as a business activity that directs the flow of goods and services from producers to consumers, placing particular emphasis on distribution-related aspects of marketing (Wilkie and Moore 2007). Around 1985 the one-way process from firm to customer was reconsidered; marketing management issues, the 4Ps, and the notion of mutually satisfying exchange relationships between firm and customer were introduced by the AMA as follows '[Marketing is] the process of planning and executing the conception, pricing, promotion, and distribution of ideas, goods and services to create exchanges that satisfy individual and organizational objectives' (Wilkie and Moore 2007; AMA 2008). A more explicit consideration of value and relationships was included in the 2004 AMA definition (Ellis et al. 2011), based on research addressing customer value, relationship marketing and service dominant logic (Grönroos 2006).

This framing of marketing definitions upon the business process was noted by Wilkie and Moore when they observed that the focus of the discipline was 'squarely upon firms, markets and household consumers' (1999: 198). In focusing attention on the business and the firm it allowed many in the discipline to ignore the wider societal ramifications of marketing (Wilkie and Moore 2006, 2007) in its cultural and geopolitical contexts and thus limiting its true scope. While there is general agreement that marketing should be relevant to managers (Kumar 2015), this singular concentration on business transactions served to hinder the scrutiny from within marketing of major public policy and societal problems associated with the discipline and the unintended consequences thereof. In 2007 the AMA introduced the most recent form of its official definition of marketing, which is 'Marketing is the activity, set of institutions, and processes for creating, communicating, delivering, and exchanging offerings that have value for customers, clients, partners, and society at large' (AMA 2008), explicitly acknowledging that marketing has a role in providing value not just to customers but also to society at large. The definition was greeted with some scepticism and it is still questionable as to whether this viewpoint is widely held. Tadajewski and Brownlie (2008: 8) note the importance of it not being merely 'window dressing', while 'we continue business as usual'. However, these broadening perspectives have been reflected in the widening domain of marketing theorising which now unequivocally embraces a macro, societal perspective (Kotler 2011; Peattie and Peattie 2009). In order to support this through our teaching, we adopt Dehler et al.'s (2001: 500) recommendation that we engage in deep analysis which evaluates the influence of the ideological, political and social contexts on the roots and emergence of the discipline and 'the way it shapes human beings and society'. This enables us to recognise the complexity of marketing's environment and the ambiguous and contradictory nature of many discourses within marketing.

It also underpins our commitment to encourage students to understand the discipline of marketing in its societal context and recognise both its benefits and problems. In concert with this broadening understanding of the domain of marketing, it is important to recognise that there is now a widespread acceptance that marketing can be employed with a transformative effect to improve individual, organisational, social and environmental well-being (Bolton 2020).

What Constitutes Theory in Marketing?

The ongoing debate about what constitutes theory within marketing is driven by the philosophical perspective of researchers (Maclaran et al. 2010; Saren 2010; Tadajewski 2014) and dependent upon the context of the behaviours and events studied. It is an important issue for students, as it forms the foundation for understanding research methodology and their personal, research worldview. It also resolves confusion about the criteria that will be employed to judge their own research as presented in a dissertation or project. According to the viewpoint adopted, marketing can be judged as being 'either theory-rich or theory impoverished' (Burton 2005: 9). On one hand, the historically dominant positivistic approach (Saren 2010), which adopts a scientific perspective, is exemplified by Hunt (1983) who states very stringent criteria regarding what constitutes theory in marketing. These comprise the requirement for a systematically defined set of statements, law-like generalisations and empirically testable propositions. Examining the marketing theories through the lens of resource-advantage theory, Hunt (2011) identified five factors that contribute to success. These include addressing important issues in both macromarketing and micromarketing; having high explanatory and predictive power; respecting literature from other disciplines; being published in non-marketing journals; and having normative implications for marketing. On the other hand, interpretivists highlight how marketing is a social process that deals with human endeavour. Accordingly, theory is inductively generated through a sense-making process using data collected by embedded researchers within the social context. Viewed as a social process, marketing cannot be studied and measured by importing the criteria of theory from the natural sciences (Gummesson 2001). Thus, interpretivist researchers argue that Hunt's criteria and similar measures are 'inappropriate vehicles for theory construction in marketing' (Burton 2005: 10).

BOX 3.4 LEARNING ACTIVITY 4

In this activity we ask students working in small groups to list the marketing theories with which they are familiar. In a feedback and discussions session we collect and collate this list, discuss which of the suggestions meet the criteria of being a theory, and support students in identifying the underpinnings of the theories they have suggested.

THE CASE FOR THEORY IN MARKETING

Slow theoretical progress in marketing has been a matter of concern for many years (e.g., Alderson and Cox 1948; Burton 2005; MacInnis 2011; Schlegelmilch 2011). Informed by historical reflection, theory provides a nuanced and contextual understanding of phenomena. Researchers can use this theoretical platform and build upon the contributions of earlier scholars (Tadajewski and Jones 2014) to advance the discipline. The development of theory is needed for other reasons, including: providing a formal structure for learning (Halbert 1965); supporting practitioners in the face of unprecedented market and technological changes (Moorman et al. 2019); addressing the decline of marketing's academic and organisational influence (Bolton 2020; Key et al. 2020); and building academic status (Saren 2016). A greater theoretical focus should help to combat an anti-intellectual image that has affected both marketing and marketing scholars (Burton 2005). While marketing scholars are seen as 'magpies', constantly borrowing from other areas (Baker 1995), much less frequently are they cited by colleagues outside their field (Clark et al. 2014). Attention to theory may also prevent a certain 'amnesia' in marketing scholarship, where our theoretical heritage may be ignored, dismissed or re-packaged as novel work (Tadajewski and Saren 2008).

There is a longstanding *theory versus practice* divide in the discipline's research (Cornelissen and Lock 2005). On the one end of the spectrum, Holbrook (1995) argues that marketing academics should be independent of practitioners and produce theory-driven research that is unconstrained by commercial pressures. Using a metaphor of household pets, Holbrook (1995) controversially compares applied researchers to dogs, who do their master's bidding and are eager to please, and 'pure academic researchers' to cats, who love academic freedom and refuse to 'fetch obediently the data' (p. 645). Others, as Burton (2005) conveys, are happy for the field to be light on theory, arguing that, as an applied discipline, marketing should be chiefly concerned with producing useful knowledge for business. Accordingly, authors like Rossiter (2001) and Piercy (2006) argue for a much closer relationship with practitioners. The middle ground in the debate, which sees academic and practitioner research as complementary (Brinberg and Hirschman 1986), is exemplified by Gummesson (2002), who sees the benefit of having both practitioner-focused research to support marketing managers and basic research which takes time, may not yield the anticipated benefits, but has the ability to generate change. In a similar vein, Levy (2002: 303) eschews the lack of support for theory in marketing as a 'foolish "know-nothing" anti-intellectual attitude' that fails to comprehend that the practical value of basic research may not be immediate.

In light of the above, the question of why theory matters within marketing (Burton 2005) is likely to provoke vigorous discussion in the classroom. We usually start this point by asking students to argue the case for (or *against*) theory in marketing. Students rarely argue against it, although this may be them savvily judging what lecturers in a marketing theory class want to hear. Their response in support of theory does, in any case, often show an appreciation of how theory organises understanding, offers meaning and sets a platform on which knowledge is constructed.

In supporting knowledge creation, theory has a crucial role in guiding research. Being researchers ourselves enables us to attest to the usefulness of theory by pointing to specific examples where theory has illuminated our understanding. This includes the utility of '*service dominant logic*' theory (Vargo and Lusch 2004) in understanding value co-creation in the luxury market (Tynan et al. 2010), and the usefulness of Weiner's (1986) '*attributional theory of motivation and emotion*' to illuminate self-gift giving (Faure and Mick 1993; Heath et al. 2015). Similarly, students comprehend that there can be immediate, practical value to theory (Gummesson 2001; Keleman and Bansal 2002; Rotfeld 2014; Saren 2016), which is especially important for an applied discipline like marketing (Kumar 2015). Discussing with students how theory can inform advertising (Reese et al. 2020), and showing them real examples raises engagement in what might otherwise be a dry discussion.

Our students are going to work in a world in which an unprecedented quantity of data is available. To make informed decisions they need both numbers and explanations, and, thus, their access to big data increases, rather than decreases, the need for theory (Wise and Shaffer 2015). Indeed, facts are silent (Baumol 1957) and necessitate good theories to inform their analysis (Saren 2016). Numbers can only guide strategy if one can find meaningful patterns within them, and theory offers context and the conditions for such patterns to emerge (Gummesson 2002). In particular, big-data researchers need theories to decide which variables they should include in a model, and which of these should be considered a causal pathway and which a confounder (Wise and Shaffer 2015). Furthermore, theories are needed to judge which results are important, what they mean, how much they can be generalised and what should be done about them (ibid.). Theories that can explain and predict a phenomenon accurately can reduce uncertainty and therefore aid decision making (Rotfeld 2014). Given the unprecedented scale of disruption in business environments, understanding of theory and its uses is going to be more important than ever. Businesses require employees capable of critically drawing on sound knowledge to predict scenarios and anticipate new solutions to the challenges and dilemmas they face. A notable recent example would be managers deciding how to react to a single case of COVID-19 amongst the workers of a factory before clear rules had been set by governments.

The famous artist, engineer and architect, Leonardo da Vinci, offered a helpful quotation that highlights the link between theory and practice when he said, 'He who loves practice without theory is like the sailor who boards ship without a rudder and compass and never knows where he may cast' (Kline 1972: 224). Discussing this metaphor with students provides a pause for reflection. It helps them to consider how theory may act like a compass to provide the navigation necessary to find the course we want, and like a rudder to steer the way to our planned destination. Importantly, it also offers a starting point for discussion about the extent to which a particular theory 'points them in the right direction'. Theories are, after all, 'nothing more than social constructions' (Thiel et al. 2018: 2) and, in this sense, any theory provides *one* of many possible ways of looking into a phenomenon. Thus, students may begin to consider the need to interrogate, or be suspicious (Maclaran and Stevens, 2008) of theories, when they favour some over others in their interpretation and construction of the social world.

BOX 3.5   LEARNING ACTIVITY 5

We use this exercise to encourage learners to consider why we need theory and consider the importance of challenging the status quo. We offer a number of examples (see some suggestions below) and ask students to try to devise additional examples of people who have challenged the status quo with theory and later to argue the case for (or against) theory in marketing. The statement that precedes all is: WE WOULD STILL BELIEVE:

- That the Earth is the centre of the universe and sun goes around the world ... if Copernicus had not questioned the Church's word and done his own research and published it in a little handwritten book in 1514.
- That objects in outer space behave entirely differently from those on Earth ... if Isaac Newton had not accurately described both with his law of universal gravitation in 1687.

- That species of organisms were unchanged since the beginning of time … if Charles Darwin had not proposed (and carefully collected support for) the theory of evolution by means of natural selection in 1859.
- That outbreaks of diseases were caused by air pollution … if Louis Pasteur and Robert Koch (amongst others) had not developed and tested the germ theory of disease in the late nineteenth century. (In this case the 'we' that would still believe should perhaps be limited to Europeans, since theories of person-to-person contagion were commonly accepted by ancient Indian and the Medieval Islamic scholars.)
- That the continents had always been in their current positions on the Earth … if Alfred Wegener had not started the move towards plate tectonics (the theory that the large parts of the Earth's crust move relative to others, afloat on a layer of magma, or molten rock) in 1912. This was only widely accepted in the 1950s when the weight of evidence became overwhelming.

The conclusion we seek to draw through the discussion is that challenging the status quo is not a negative thing to work towards but a necessary first stage of improving on what has gone before.

CAUTION WITH THEORY

A theory is a story describing a phenomenon, and can be powerful and illuminating, but may also be dangerous when mistaken, ill intended, or wrongly applied. For all their benefits, any theory must be taken with a pinch of salt. From the infamous racial theories conjured by the Nazis to the more recent conspiracy theories denying the severity (or existence) of a world pandemic, history is full of dramatic examples illuminating the perils of certain narratives. In an academic environment, theory, and the concepts that surround it, are also far from being neutral or value free (Tadajewski 2018). Theoretical discourses are built on their authors' assumptions and they are, thus, often laden with implicit support for hegemonic value systems or beliefs (Maclaran and Stevens 2008). They can broaden our minds but equally bind our views in ways that that may go unnoticed (Maclaran and Stevens 2008; Tadajewski 2018). Discourses that prevail often reflect and reinforce mainstream agendas, where citing the 'right' scholarship favours acceptance and ensures the persistence of the status quo. In this vicious cycle, certain topics, seen as marginal for publication or simply unfashionable, may be disfavoured, or simply forgotten, regardless of their important social impact (e.g. on poverty, social inequality, racial issues, etc) and so remain hidden, unseen and unconsidered. As Hutton and Heath (2020) argue, what one chooses to research and how one does so require 'bold decisions about issues that are often easier to evade than to confront'. The same applies to our teaching and we believe it is our responsibility to foster in students such a critical mindset towards theory.

Insights from critical marketing studies (e.g., Tadajewski and Brownlie 2008; Tadajewski 2018) and their commitment to 'denaturalization' (Fournier and Grey 2000) help students to appreciate that theoretical discourses are historically contingent and socially constructed, and require thoughtful inquiry. This should help them to grow more aware of the contradictions underlying the rhetoric of mainstream texts, which legitimise and normalise marketing as something 'benign and beyond question' (Hackley 2003: 1326). This reduces the 'disservice' (Tadajewski 2016: 1522) that we would otherwise do to our students by representing marketing theory (and its practice) in overly positive terms while ignoring a series of uncomfortable issues raised within it. As students gain understanding that marketing and its theory are open to transformation and grow confidence to challenge others' arguments, they can start imagining new possibilities for marketing.

IN CONCLUSION

Theory offers an organised way of thinking about phenomena, which then helps one to comprehend, explain, and hopefully predict, how and why things happen. The proficient use of marketing theory requires the student to understand the language of the discipline, critically engage with the various discourses recognising strengths and weaknesses in methods and approach, and be familiar with the concepts they are using to form new insights. Marketing theory is useful to enable academics to create new knowledge, which helps us to support practitioners in making decisions in a complex and mutable environment (Moorman et al. 2019). It can also help us arrest the decline and improve the *status* of the discipline. An ever-increasing body of theory concerned with marketing systems effects on the well-being of individuals, society and the planet shines a hopeful light on a transformative agenda.

However, if it is to illuminate examples from practice, deepen our understanding of the function of marketing as a whole, and guide behaviour, theory needs to be engaged with using a critical and enquiring mind. In the face of growing threats to sustainability, which are currently dramatically worsened by the social and economic crisis created by the COVID-19 pandemic, this is particularly important. We must rekindle calls to re-examine the theory and practice of marketing (e.g., Kotler 2011; Davies et al. 2020), and apply similar transformative efforts in our classrooms. Decades of grave threats to sustainability were not enough for us to really tackle the topic of consumption reduction in marketing scholarship for this did not sit comfortably with accepted theory and practice (Peattie and Peattie 2009). Dramatically, we appreciate now how demand stimulation is far less important than other concerns, such as equitable distribution (Key et al. 2020). Honest and reliable content marketing and social marketing are amongst topics and areas whose importance was brought to the fore by the pandemic (Key et al. 2020).

With Key et al. (2020), we argue that disciplines progress by creating knowledge useful to society. As we have discussed above, for a great part of its existence, scholarship in marketing has been driven by its applied roots and focus on a view of the marketing system that privileged what researchers perceived to be the interests of practitioners, even though these same practitioners may have rarely considered the scholarship relevant to their work. Academic marketing throughout this era largely ignored any negative outcomes for consumers, the environment and society. How marketing as a discipline rises to current challenges and serves society will dictate, to a great extent, the respect and reputation that it will receive. For our scholarship to be considered relevant by a wide variety of stakeholders, it needs to be meaningful and intelligible. We need to observe and tackle issues that matter, to create meaningful frameworks and theoretical contributions, and to communicate those in ways that are comprehensible and engaging to those affected by the phenomena we study (Key et al. 2020; MacInnis et al. 2020). Our impact upon practice will always be limited if we write nothing that anyone outside academia wants to read.

Crucially, it is also our role, as marketing educators, to nurture students' enquiring minds with critical skills as well as curiosity to know about, and question, theory, so that they can dare to imagine beyond what we chose to share with them. In time, we hope that as academics and practitioners our students will learn to develop new marketing knowledge which takes a societal perspective, an ethical stance, emphasises fairness and justice for all individuals and utilises its transformative potential for improving wellbeing.

REFERENCES

Ajzen, I. (1991), 'The theory of planned behavior', *Organizational Behavior and Human Decision Processes*, 50 (2), 179–211.

Alderson, W. and R. Cox (1948), 'Towards a theory of marketing', *Journal of Marketing*, 13 (2), 137–52.

AMA (2008), Press release: The American Marketing Association releases new definition for Marketing, accessed 1 February 2018 at https://www.prweb.com/releases/definition/for_marketing/prweb621321.htm

Bagozzi, R. (1975), 'Marketing as exchange', *Journal of Marketing*, 39 (4), 32–9.

Baker, M.J. (1995), *Marketing: Theory and Practice*, London: Macmillan.

Baker, M.J. (2005), 'Marketing is marketing – everywhere!', *Vikalpa*, 30 (3), 1–9.

Baumol, W.J. (1957), 'On the role of marketing theory', *Journal of Marketing*, 21 (4), 413–18.

Bolton, R.N. (2020), 'First steps to creating high impact theory in marketing', *AMS Review*, 10, 172–8.

Bradshaw, A. and M. Tadajewski (2011), 'Macromarketing roundtable commentary – the export of marketing education', *Journal of Macromarketing*, 31 (3), 312–21.

Brinberg, D. and E.C. Hirschman (1986), 'Multiple orientations for the conduct of marketing research: An analysis of the academic/practitioner distinction', *Journal of Marketing*, 50 (4), 161–73.

Brodie, R.J. and L.D. Peters (2020), 'New directions for service research: Refreshing the process of theorizing to increase contribution', *Journal of Services Marketing*, 34 (3), 415–28.

Brodie, R.J., M. Saren and J. Pels (2011), 'Theorizing about the service dominant logic: The bridging role of middle range theory', *Marketing Theory*, 11 (1), 75–91.

Brookfield, S. (1987), *Developing Critical Thinkers: Challenging Adults to Explore Alternative Ways of Thinking and Acting*, San Francisco, CA: Jossey Bass.

Burton, D. (2005), 'Marketing theory matters', *British Journal of Management*, 16 (1), 5–18.

Catterall, M., P. Maclaran and L. Stevens (2002), 'Critical reflection in the marketing curriculum', *Journal of Marketing Education*, 24 (3), 184–92.

Chambers Dictionary of Etymology (2008), *Chambers Dictionary of Etymology*, Edinburgh: Chambers.

Clark, T., T.M. Key, M. Hodis and D. Rajaratnam (2014), 'The intellectual ecology of mainstream marketing research: An inquiry into the place of marketing in the family of business disciplines', *Journal of the Academy of Marketing Science*, 42 (3), 223–41.

Contu, A. (2017), 'Time to take on greed: Why business schools must engage in intellectual activism', *The Guardian*, 17 January, accessed 23 January 2021 at www .theguardian.com/higher-education-network/2017/jan/17/taking-on-greed-business -schools-must-engage-in-intellectual-activism.

Cornelissen, J.P. and A.R. Lock (2005), 'The uses of marketing theory: Constructs, research propositions, and managerial implications', *Marketing Theory*, 5 (2), 165–84.

Davidoff, F., M. Dixon-Woods, L. Leviton and S. Michie (2015), 'Demystifying theory and its use in improvement', *BMJ Quality & Safety*, 24, 228–38.

Davies, I., C. Oates, C. Tynan, M. Carrigan, K. Casey, T. Heath, C. Henninger et al. (2020), 'Seeking sustainable futures in marketing and consumer research', *European Journal of Marketing*, 54 (11), 2911–39.

Dehler, G.E., M.A. Welsh and M.W. Lewis (2001), 'Critical pedagogy in the "new paradigm"', *Management Learning*, 32 (4), 493–511.

Ellis, N., J. Fitchett, M. Higgins, G. Jack, M. Lim, M. Saren and M. Tadajewski (2011), *Marketing – A Critical Textbook*. London: Sage Publications.

Evans, R. (2011), "Faster than light" particles threaten Einstein, accessed 23 January 2021 at https://www.reuters.com/article/us-science-light-idUSTRE78L4 FH20110923

Faure, C. and D.G. Mick (1993), 'Self-gifts through the lens of attribution theory', *Advances in Consumer Research*, 20 (1), 553–6.

Fournier, V. and C. Grey (2000), 'At the critical moment: Conditions and prospects for critical management studies', *Human Relations*, 53 (1), 7–32.

Gray, D.E. (2007), 'Facilitating management learning: Developing critical reflection through reflective tools', *Management Learning*, 38 (5), 495–517.

Grönroos, C. (2006), 'On defining marketing: Finding a new roadmap for marketing', *Marketing Theory*, 6 (4), 395–417.

Gummesson, E. (2001), 'Are current research approaches in marketing leading us astray?', *Marketing Theory*, 1 (1), 27–48.

Gummesson, E. (2002), 'Practical value of adequate marketing management theory', *European Journal of Marketing*, 36 (3), 325–49.

Hackley, C. (2003), '"We are all customers now..." rhetorical strategy and ideological control in marketing management texts', *Journal of Management Studies*, 40 (5), 1325–52.

Halbert, M. (1965), *The Meaning and Sources of Marketing Theory*, New York: McGraw-Hill.

Heath, T., L. O'Malley and C. Tynan (2019), 'Imagining a different voice: A critical and caring approach to management education', *Management Learning*, 50 (4), 427–48.

Heath, T., C. Tynan and C. Ennew (2015), 'Accounts of self-gift giving: Nature, contexts and emotions', *European Journal of Marketing*, 49 (7/8), 1067–86.

Holbrook, M. (1995), 'The four faces of commodification in the development of marketing knowledge', *Journal of Marketing Management*, 11 (7), 641–54.

Hornby, A.S. (1980), *Oxford Advanced Learner's Dictionary of Current English*, 4th edn, Oxford: Oxford University Press.

Hudson, L.A. and J.L. Ozanne (1988), 'Alternative ways of seeking knowledge in consumer research', *Journal of Consumer Research*, 14 (4), 508–521.

Hunt, S.D. (1983), *Marketing Theory: The Philosophy of Marketing Science*, Homewood, IL: Irwin.

Hunt, S.D. (2011), 'Developing successful theories in marketing: Insights from resource-advantage theory', *AMS Review*, 1 (2), 72–84.

Hutton, M. and T. Heath (2020), 'Researching on the edge: Emancipatory praxis for social justice', *European Journal of Marketing*, 54 (11), 2697–721.

Kelemen, M. and T. Bansal (2002), 'The conventions of management research and their relevance to management practice', *British Journal of Management*, 13 (2), 97–108.

Key, T.M., T. Clark, O.C. Ferrell, D.W. Stewart and L. Pitt (2020), 'Marketing's theoretical and conceptual value proposition: Opportunities to address marketing's influence', *AMS Review*, 10 (3), 151–67.

Kline, M. (1972), *Mathematical Thought from Ancient to Modern Times*, Oxford: Oxford University Press.

Kohli, A.K. and B.J. Jaworski (1990), 'Market orientation: The construct, research propositions, and managerial implications', *Journal of Marketing*, 54 (2), 1–18.

Kotler, P. (2011), 'Reinventing marketing to manage the environmental imperative', *Journal of Marketing*, 75 (4), 132–5.

Kumar, V. (2015), 'Evolution of marketing as a discipline: What has happened and what to look out for', *Journal of Marketing*, 79 (1), 1–9.

Levy, S. (2002), 'Revisiting the marketing domain', *European Journal of Marketing*, 36 (3), 299–304.

MacInnis, D.J. (2011), 'A framework for conceptual contributions in marketing', *Journal of Marketing*, 75 (4), 136–54.

MacInnis, D.J., V.G. Morwitz, S. Botti, D.L. Hoffman, R.V. Kozinetz, D.R. Lehmann, J.G. Lynch and C. Pechmann (2020), 'Creating boundary-breaking, marketing-relevant consumer research', *Journal of Marketing*, 84 (2), 1–23.

Maclaran, P. and L. Stevens (2008), 'Thinking through theory: Materialising the oppositional imagination', in M. Tadajewski and D. Brownlie (eds), *Critical Marketing: Issues in Contemporary Marketing*, Chichester, UK: John Wiley & Sons, pp. 345–61.

Maclaran, P., M. Saren, B. Stern and M. Tadajewski (2010), 'Introduction', in P. Maclaran, M. Saren, B. Stern and M. Tadajewski (eds), *Handbook of Marketing Theory*, London: Sage Publications, pp. 1–24.

Monbiot, G. (2018), *Out of the Wreckage – A New Politics for an Age of Crisis*, London: Verso.

Moorman, C., H.J. van Heerde, C.P. Moreau and R.W. Palmatier (2019), 'Challenging the boundaries of marketing', *Journal of Marketing*, 83 (5), 1–4.

Paul, R. and L. Elder (2006), *The Miniature Guide to Critical Thinking: Concepts and Tools*, Dillon Beach, CA: Foundation for Critical Thinking.

Paul, R. and L. Elder (2013), 'Critical thinking: Intellectual standards essential to reasoning well within every domain of human thought, Part Two', *Journal of Developmental Education*, 37 (1), 32–6.

Peattie, K. and S. Peattie (2009), 'Social marketing: A pathway to consumption reduction?', *Journal of Business Research*, 62 (2), 260–68.

Piercy, N. (2006), 'The trouble with marketing research is marketing researchers', *International Journal of Market Research*, 48 (3), 253–4.

Plummer, M. (2019), *A Short Guide to Building Your Team's Critical Thinking Skills*, accessed 23 January 2021 at https://hbr.org/2019/10/a-short-guide-to-building-your -teams-critical-thinking-skills.

Reese, P.P., K. Glanz, A. Shah, A. Mussell, S. Levsky, L. Shuda, J. Shults and J.B. Kessler (2020), 'A randomized trial of theory-informed appeals for organ donor registration using internet advertisements', *Kidney International Reports*, 5 (12), 2238–45.

Reibstein, D.J., G. Day and J. Wind (2009), 'Is marketing academia losing its way?', *Journal of Marketing*, 73 (4), 1–3.

Rossiter, J.R. (2001), 'What is marketing knowledge?: Stage I: forms of marketing knowledge', *Marketing Theory*, 1 (1), 9–26.

Rotfeld, H. (2014), 'The pragmatic importance of theory for marketing practice', *Journal of Consumer Marketing*, 31 (4), 322–7.

Saren, M. (2010), 'Marketing theory', in M.J. Baker and M. Saren (eds), *Marketing Theory: A Student Text*, 2nd edn, London: Sage, pp. 26–50.

Saren, M. (2016), 'Marketing theory', in M.J. Baker and M. Saren (eds), *Marketing Theory – A Student textbook*, 3rd edn, London: Sage Publications, pp. 31–59.

Schlegelmilch, B.B. (2011), 'Commentary on "Developing successful theories in marketing: insights from resource-advantage theory"', *AMS Review*, 1 (2), 85–9.

Science Museum (2019), 'Cholera in Victorian London', accessed 23 January 2019 at www.sciencemuseum.org.uk/objects-and-stories/medicine/cholera-victorian -london.

Scott, C.L. (2015), 'The futures of learning 2: What kind of learning for the 21st century?', ERF Working Paper No. 14, Paris: UNESCO Education Research and Foresight, accessed 23 January 2021 at https://unesdoc.unesco.org/ark:/48223/ pf0000242996.

Scriven, M. and R. Paul (1987), 'Critical thinking as defined by the National Council for Excellence in Critical Thinking – 1987', accessed 23 January 2021 at www .criticalthinking.org/pages/defining-critical-thinking/766.

Spicer, A., M. Alvesson and K. Kärreman (2009), 'Critical performativity: The unfinished business of critical management studies', *Human Relations*, 62 (4), 537–60.

Tadajewski, M. (2014), 'Paradigm debates and marketing theory, thought and practice, *Journal of Historical Research in Marketing*, 6 (3), 303–30.

Tadajewski, M. (2016), 'Relevance, responsibility, critical performativity, testimony and positive marketing: Contributing to marketing theory, thought and practice', *Journal of Marketing Management*, 32 (17/18), 1513–36.

Tadajewski, M. (2018), 'Critical reflections on the marketing concept and consumer sovereignty', in M. Tadajewski, M. Higgins, J. Denegri-Knott and R. Varman (eds), *The Routledge Companion to Critical Marketing Studies*, London: Routledge, pp. 196–224.

Tadajewski, M. and D. Brownlie (2008), 'Critical marketing: A limit attitude', in M. Tadajewski and D. Brownlie (eds), *Critical Marketing – Issues in Contemporary Marketing*, Chichester: John Wiley and Sons, pp. 1–28.

Tadajewski, M. and D.B. Jones (2014), 'Historical research in marketing theory and practice: A review essay', *Journal of Marketing Management*, 30 (11/12), 1239–91.

Tadajewski, M. and M. Saren (2008), 'The past is a foreign country: Amnesia and marketing theory', *Marketing Theory*, 8 (4), 323–38.

Tellis, G.J. (2017), 'Interesting and impactful research: On phenomena, theory, and writing', *Journal of the Academy of Marketing Science*, 45, 1–6.

Thiel, A., K. Seiberth and J. Mayer (2018), 'Why does theory matter? Reflections on an apparently self-evident question in sport sociology', *European Journal for Sport and Society*, 15 (1), 1–4.

Tregear, A., S. Kuznesof and M. Brennan (2007), 'Critical approaches in undergraduate marketing teaching: Investigating students' perceptions', *Journal of Marketing Management*, 23 (5/6), 411–24.

Tynan, C., S. McKechnie and C. Chhuon (2010), 'Co-creating value for luxury brands', *Journal of Business Research*, 63 (11), 1156–63.

Vargo, S.L. and R.F. Lusch (2004), 'Evolving to a new dominant logic for marketing', *Journal of Marketing*, 8 (1), 1–17.

Vargo, S.L. and R.F. Lusch (2017), 'Service-dominant logic 2025', *International Journal of Research in Marketing*, 34 (1), 46–67.

Weiner, B. (1986), *An Attributional Theory of Motivation and Emotion*, New York: Springer-Verlag.

Whiting, K. (2020), 'These are the top 10 job skills of tomorrow – and how long it takes to learn them', accessed on 23 January 2021 at www.weforum.org/agenda/2020/10/top-10-work-skills-of-tomorrow-how-long-it-takes-to-learn-them/.

Wilkie, W.L. and E.S. Moore (1999), 'Marketing's contribution to society', *Journal of Marketing*, 63 (4), 196–218.

Wilkie, W.L. and E.S. Moore (2006), 'Macromarketing as a pillar of marketing thought', *Journal of Macromarketing*, 26 (2), 224–32.

Wilkie, W.L. and E.S. Moore (2007), 'What does the definition of marketing tell us about ourselves?', *Journal of Public Policy and Marketing*, 26 (2), 269–76.

Wise, A.F. and D.W. Shaffer (2015), 'Why theory matters more than ever in the age of big data', *Journal of Learning Analytics*, 2 (2), 5–13.

Yadav, M.S. (2017), 'Disciplinary memory and theory development', *AMS Review*, 7 (1/2), 1–3.

Zeithaml, V.A., B.J. Jaworski, A.K. Kohli, K.R. Tuli, W. Ulaga and G. Zaltman (2020), 'A theories-in-use approach to building marketing theory', *Journal of Marketing*, 84 (1), 32–51.

4. The marketing curriculum

Michael Harker and Andrew Paddison

INTRODUCTION

What is a curriculum? The Oxford English Dictionary tells us that curriculum entered into usage from Latin, and originally from the verb *currere* – to run/ to proceed – with the original meaning being 'a running, course, career' (Etymology Online). Within education, the term has a near 500-year history, being first applied within degrees offered in logic and philosophy. Charmingly this originator, the French humanist and logician Pierre de la Ramée, was also known as an educational reformer. Within these courses of study, students received a basic foundation in philosophy, before moving on to studying words through rhetoric, logic and the formal grammar of Latin or Greek; or numbers, moving towards geometry, physics and ethics.

In English, Glasgow University applied the term to its courses of study in 1633 (Oxford English Dictionary) and whilst plenty of differences exist between the myriad of definitions presented since then, from within and without educational literature, the essence of shared meaning is there. A curriculum is a whole, an entire programme of study. It is also a journey, with a beginning and an end, where the end is dependent on a foundational beginning.

The great bulk of educational research is on pre-university education, with particular focus on primary over secondary education. We must be aware then, that many if not most claims made about the value, structure and purpose of curricula emerge from a body of work in which empirical research is a small minority and that takes as its focus children that are much younger than university students. These are situations that are more holistic and integrated, where tuition is provided by professionally trained staff with a teaching focus – all factors which reduce the relevance and applicability of most of this research to the HE sector.

Do universities then have curricula within programmes of study? Naturally, the answer is *sometimes*. Certain disciplines, such as medicine, engineering and natural sciences – perhaps law – have more established systems of curricula, and are perhaps more naturally predisposed by educational culture, established traditions and particular discipline characteristics to have curricula (Koch, 1997).

What commonalities are there where curricula can be seen to clearly exist, perhaps commonalities that could be considered as criteria? Here are five. First, there are clear foundations, a starting point – such as essential mathematics, or an understanding of the parts or the chemistry of the human body – upon which other knowledge and skills are to be based. Secondly, there is a hierarchy of knowledge, within which a rational and practical approach can be taken in respect of building and implementing a curriculum – which from the point of view of a student will be their journey, and that of the staff as being means and methods of teaching and applying pedagogy. Thirdly, the curriculum will be made finite, limited and specific by there being pretty clear (if imperfect) dividing lines between what the subject is, and what it is not – 'this is chemistry, that is biology'. Fourthly, the specific destinations and results of these journeys will be understood and accepted by the involved parties – 'this makes you a structural engineer, this makes you a doctor' – they will have an answer to the 'what is this for?' question. Importantly, knowledge and skills will be assessible readily. Fifth and finally, a student having reached the end of the curriculum journey will be seen as a credible and qualified new entrant into a fairly specific profession – by themselves and their institution, by professional bodies and employers, and by the state and wider society itself (Koch, 1997; Wellman, 2017).

The presence and viability of curricula are less obvious in other fields, perhaps because one or more of the above criteria are not met. Do Art Schools have curricula? Certainly there is training in basic techniques, and structured study of the history of art, but later study is far more self-directed, individual, and unique work is only assessible in highly subjective ways, as conforming to some standard is not what art is about. How about a traditional discipline such as history or a modern social science? Are curricula more present where a discipline is usually faculty wide – such as engineering – and less present when it is departmentally, or sub-departmentally located? That is, is the curriculum whole and complete on its own within the discipline, or does it require input from outside?

So, are there curricula in marketing? What is their nature and purpose? Are they a good thing (Ackermann and Hu, 2011)? Is there standardisation between institutions? What does a curriculum-journey in marketing produce and look like from the perspectives of staff and students? Is a/the marketing curriculum whole and complete on its own within the discipline, or does it require input from outside? Further, how are they being impacted upon by broader social and societal changes, and what changes is this causing? Finally, what shapes and structures and intentions should exist for the marketing curricula of the future (Wellman, 2017)?

RESEARCH ON MARKETING CURRICULA

Relevant literature is very highly concentrated in just a handful of journals and is essentially absent from many of the most prestigious. It isn't surprising that specific topics are more often present within journals covering and specialising in that domain, but the distribution does seem to present prima facie evidence that marketing education generally, and curriculum-related topics in particular are not treated as having equal significance with many other arguably far less significant and relevant studies, or the many commentaries on obscura. As is typically and unhelpfully the case, literature has a predominantly Anglosphere focus.

At the time of writing, literature on the subject is concentrated very heavily around a limited number of anxieties in respect of deficiencies of and within the curriculum. These anxieties cluster around metrics and numeracy (LeClair, 2018; Spiller and Tuten, 2015; Weathers and Aragón, 2019), and their diminishing presence within the curriculum, and the refocusing of core marketing activities around digital means of implementation (Atwong, 2015; Kim and Freberg, 2017; Crittenden and Peterson, 2019).

Table 4.1 outlines 29 publications containing data about marketing curricula. These were found via a literature search that sought work on marketing and business education with a curriculum/programme or class concept focus. This represents just a small fraction of the curriculum-related literature, the great majority of which constructs, designs and idealises curriculum-related aspects, stances and perspectives without engaging in anything more than a theoretical or abstract line of reasoning.

In respect of method, there are four broad categories: personal reflections on a recent implementation; surveys of one or more groups; analysis of collated documents and online information; and, interviews with stakeholders. Of these, by far the most common are surveys and document analysis, with 13 and 12 examples respectively. In regard to respondent groups, and noting that some projects used mixed methods or polled multiple categories of respondent, five papers drew heavily on personal reflections after a class had been implemented, more than the mere three which engaged with colleagues at other institutions. Student opinion was only sought by seven, and the leading groups were document sets and employers/professionals, with 12 and 11 respectively. Of the papers found, only one reported on the involvement of a professional body or sector-organisation, and that was the AASCB. No CIM, no AMA or AM, no MRS, no DMA. Whilst such bodies are sometimes asked to look over already produced curricula/class outlines, there seems little to no evidence from the US/UK that they are proactively integrated into the curriculum building process. Arguably they are passively involved, with their own internally

Table 4.1   *Marketing curriculum research papers*

Authors	Method	Sample/Respondents	Key theme	Categories
Bacon, 2017	Survey	864 marketing professionals		Replication, Opinions of employers/professionals
Brennan and Vos, 2013	Experiment – pre- and post-class experience Survey	76 UG students	Numeracy skills	Report on implementation, single class, specific skills, opinions of students
Brocato et al., 2015	Content analysis of course syllabi	90 syllabi from 65 US Business Schools	Content and pedagogy in Social Media classes	Review of current marketing curricula
Centeno et al., 2008	Collation of publicly available documents Survey	60 programmes at 45 UK institutions 129 PGT students from five UK institutions	Teaching–practitioner divide	Review of current marketing curricula
Cheng et al., 2016	Interviews	10 SME owners and 20 UG students	Employability	Opinions of employers/professionals, opinions of students
Di Gregorio et al., 2019	Content analysis of job adverts Survey	359 job adverts from 5 EU countries 1562 marketing professionals in 5 EU countries	Employer/professional desired skills	Opinions of employers/professionals
Elam and Spotts, 2004	Project orientated coursework review/Survey	53 students in 12 coursework groups from 3 programmes in the US	Marketing Management skills development	Report on implementation, single class, opinions of students
Finch et al., 2013	Survey	253 marketing professionals	Matching curriculum to practice	Opinions of employers/professionals
Fowler et al., 2019	Content analysis of marketing-related periodicals Survey	2 periodicals for 15 issues 66 UG and MBA students at a single US institution	Information literacy	Specific skills, opinions of students
Freberg and Kim, 2018	Interviews	20 US marketing professionals1	Social Media practice	Opinions of employers/professionals

Authors	Method	Sample/Respondents	Key theme	Categories
Harker et al., 2016	Collation of publicly available information and class documentation interviews	1582 classes within 542 programmes at French Grande Ecoles 6 programme managers	Classes taught	Replication, review of current marketing curricula, opinions of academics
Harker, 2015	Collation of publicly available information and class documentation	66 UK institutions	Classes taught	Review of current marketing curricula
Harrigan and Hulbert, 2011	Interviews	70 UK marketing professionals	Employer/professional desired skills	Report on implementation
Hartley et al., 2019	Panel Survey	11,609 marketing majors from panel of 442,250 US post-18 students	Skill changes for current marketing students	Opinions of students
Kim and Freberg, 2017	Interviews	20 US marketing professionals1	Social Media practice	Opinions of employers/professionals
Langan et al., 2019	Content Analysis of programme documentation	529 US websites	Digital marketing integrated across curriculum	Review of current marketing curricula
Liu and Burns, 2018	Text-mining, Survey	400 marketing job adverts, 1,000,000 tweets on Marketing Analytics, 13 syllabi, 33 business executives	Relevant and meaningful content for an analytics course	Report on Course design, single class, review of curricula
McDaniel and Hise, 1984	Survey	236 US CEOs	Importance of marketing activities	Opinions of employers/professionals
Nicholls and Hair, 2016	Survey	111 Business School Deans and Marketing Dept Chairs in US [41/70]	Efforts in regard to teaching ethics and sustainability	Programme-wide implementation

Authors	Method	Sample/Respondents	Key theme	Categories
Oksiutycz and Azionya, 2017	Class redesign reflection	One class in South Africa	Marketing Communications	[African¹]
Parker, 2014	Programme design reflection	One new programme	Developing a new curriculum	Report on implementation
Pharr and Morris, 1997	Content Analysis of programme syllabi	14 US institutions	Matching with sector body guidelines	Review of current marketing curricula
Pilling et al., 2012	Class redesign reflection/ survey	40 students	Metrics related skills	Report on implementation, single class
Rohm et al., 2019	Class redesign reflection	One programme in US	Digital Marketing practice	Report on implementation
Schlee and Harich, 2010	Content analysis	500 job adverts	Employer/professional desired skills	Opinions of employers/professionals
Stringfellow et al., 2006	Collation of publicly available documents Interviews	28 UK institutions 15 marketing professionals from West Scotland	Classes taught	Review of current marketing curricula
Vriens et al., 2019	Survey	148 alumni from one US institution	Matching curriculum to practice	Opinions of employers/professionals
Wellman, 2017	Content analysis Interviews	375 job adverts 19 recent graduates, 15 marketing academics, 15 marketing professionals	Evaluating the marketing curriculum	Opinions of employers/professionals, opinions of graduates
Wilson et al., 2018	Class redesign reflection	One class in US	Marketing analytics skills	Report on implementation

Note: 1. These samples are the same interviewees.

produced curricula for their own professional awards being available for co-option by higher education institutions. France does better (Harker et al., 2016), with local industry bodies heavily involved, and current professionals directly engaged in teaching.

In respect of scope, 15 took a sector-wide perspective, and seven focused on a single topic – like MarComs or social media – and just three took a position overviewing a programme/curriculum. Given that a curriculum only really exists in a whole programme, if at all, does this suggest that too much scholarship has either a too-tight, or too-loose focus? Additionally, the extant research has – like so many other areas of marketing scholarship – a disproportionate concentration in the US and then the UK. Of the sample, only three papers reported from elsewhere: Oksiutycz and Azionya (2017) from South Africa, Di Gregorio et al. (2019) from around the EU and Harker et al. (2016) from France. In the wider marketing curriculum literature, the spread is a little better, but not by much. What is the Asian marketing curriculum?

A good proportion of the single class focused research, and that of the sector-wide research listed above has at its centre social media and the idea of 'digital' skills and knowledge. Given the rate of change in professional practice, to what degree can university classes keep pace?

And what are those components? Stringfellow et al. (2006) investigated sets of marketing classes offered at 28 institutions. These offerings were divided into core, standard and peripheral offerings in respect of the proportion of sample institutions that offered them. The core offerings, provided by more than 75 per cent of the sample were: Marketing Principles, Marketing Research, Marketing Communications and Strategic Marketing. The standard offerings, provided by 50–75 per cent of the sample were: International Marketing, Consumer Behaviour, Product/brand Marketing, Services Marketing, Retail Marketing, B2B Marketing, E-Marketing. Of the core, the absence of Consumer Behaviour is perhaps most striking. Earlier, the lack of a hierarchy – or clear route through – knowledge in marketing was noted, but Consumer Behaviour is an obvious continuation point, after the breadth and foundations of Marketing Principles. Considered together, those classes pass a smell-test as representing a fairly well-developed curriculum. Those class titles however, are merely the labels on a tin. What is in the tins? Further, how have things been changing in more recent years – what are the vectors?

Current Provision

The Academy of Marketing recently sponsored a project to try and answer these questions. Data collection produced a list of 481 classes[1] provided within one or more marketing-related programmes provided by 41 UKHEIs (see

Table 4.2   Subjects by levels and credits in the UK marketing offering

Subject	Offered	Institutions	Year breakdown (where known)								Total credit breakdown (where known)					Total
	%	N=41	1	1–2	2	2–3	3	3–4	4	Total	10	15	20	30	>30	
Principles	100	41	37	0	4	0	0	0	0	41	2	12	15	2	0	31
MarComs	83	34	2	0	7	10	8	0	2	29	3	5	7	2	9	26
Consumer Behavior	83	34	4	0	20	1	7	0	2	34	4	9	12	3	2	30
Market Research	80	33	2	2	12	2	6	1	1	26	2	6	11	2	3	24
Strategic Marketing/Marketing Management	76	31	0	0	5	6	16	2	1	30	4	6	6	4	8	28
International Marketing	66	27	1	0	3	1	17	1	3	26	3	5	10	1	3	22
Digital	56	23	1	0	10	0	11	1	0	23	1	6	10	2	1	20
Services Marketing	54	22	0	0	5	0	11	1	1	18	4	5	5	1	3	18
Critical/Contemporary	44	18	1	0	4	1	11	0	1	18	1	3	6	3	2	15
Product/Brand Marketing	41	17	1	0	6	0	6	0	1	14	2	4	4	1	1	12
Dissertation/Project	41	17	2	0	0	0	11	0	4	17	0	2	1	5	8	16
CRM	24	10	0	0	4	0	4	0	1	9	0	3	5	0	0	8
Retail Marketing	22	9	0	0	3	0	4	0	1	8	2	2	2	0	0	6
Professional Practice	22	9	0	0	2	2	4	0	0	8	1	1	3	1	2	8
B2B Marketing	17	7	0	0	1	0	5	0	0	6	1	2	3	0	0	6
Sales Management	12	5	0	0	2	0	3	0	0	5	0	1	3	0	0	4

Table 4.2). As part of data collection, documents such as programme and/or specific class outlines were also collected. Some institutions were not willing to share that level of detail, most often citing 'commercial sensitivity' as a reason not to, as though saying: 'We teach services marketing. No one must know!'.

These classes were categorised into 16 groups, imperfectly reproducing the Stringfellow et al. (2006) schema which derived 17. Thirteen classes could be fairly assigned to two categories, based on information available – such as the 'Marketing Planning and Research' and 'Research and Planning for Marketing' at Northumbria and Nottingham Trent respectively and 'Branding and Advertising' at City, London. A number of institutions had multiple versions of the same class for administrative/programme reasons, or for exchange students only. These were considered as one class.

Figure 4.1 compares these categories, with the 28 institutions of Stringfellow et al. (2006) compared against the 41 of this project. Each list is ranked by the percentage of institutions within the samples that offered at least one class in that category. Observers will be struck by both notable similarities and differences.

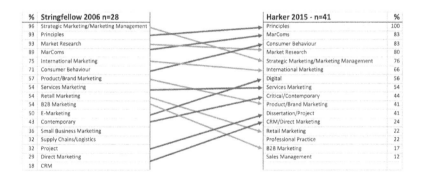

%	Stringfellow 2006 n=28	Harker 2015 - n=41	%
96	Strategic Marketing/Marketing Management	Principles	100
93	Principles	MarComs	83
93	Market Research	Consumer Behaviour	83
89	MarComs	Market Research	80
75	International Marketing	Strategic Marketing/Marketing Management	76
71	Consumer Behaviour	International Marketing	66
57	Product/Brand Marketing	Digital	56
54	Services Marketing	Services Marketing	54
54	Retail Marketing	Critical/Contemporary	44
54	B2B Marketing	Product/Brand Marketing	41
50	E-Marketing	Dissertation/Project	41
43	Contemporary	CRM/Direct Marketing	24
36	Small Business Marketing	Retail Marketing	22
32	Supply Chains/Logistics	Professional Practice	22
32	Project	B2B Marketing	17
29	Direct Marketing	Sales Management	12
18	CRM		

Figure 4.1   Trends in subject prevalence

Unsurprisingly, an introductory class in marketing is near the top of both lists, and Marketing Communications and Marketing Research remain at the top. Strategic Marketing/Marketing Management has dropped substantially, as has Product/Brand Marketing. International Marketing and B2B and Retailing have crashed. CRM and Direct Marketing have combined less than synergistically and Services Marketing remains static.

Which categories have risen? Project work with a client, or a specifically marketing-based dissertation are more prevalent, and as will be noted soon, the final years of a number of programmes are substantially filled by one or both of those. Consumer Behaviour is more widespread, as are classes taking a critical stance and/or those focused on contemporary issues around marketing in society – ethics classes subsumed here. E-Marketing rises, being re-labelled as Digital. The rise isn't substantial, perhaps evidence that as Stringfellow et al. (2006) predicted, digital and social media skills have entered into being the default situation of Consumer Behaviour, Marketing Research and of course Marketing Communications, making a separate and distinct class less necessary. A similar argument could be made for International Marketing. This can be called *subsumption*, and is an issue that seems particularly strong with marketing classes – where there are so many 'debatable lands' between topics.

Are there generalities observable in those rises and falls? Perhaps. Classes that might be expected to typically include substantial elements of numeracy, analysis and strategic level planning and organisational management are down, as are classes more directly related to basic practice, such as Product and Brand Management, and especially B2B. There was next to no evidence of pricing appearing anywhere, and only a very limited amount for logistics and distribution. Hard is down, soft is up. The aggregate vector is away from being trained to practise as a marketer, and towards being educated about and becoming able to critically appraise marketing's role in society. Is that vector desirable? Is it one that current and future students would wish if they were aware of it? Perhaps not.

Whilst not definitive, the data does suggest that there is far less marketing in a marketing degree than there was. The gap is covered by non-marketing classes within a wider faculty – most obviously a Business School.

To examine programmes across institutions is to discover that whilst there is quite a lot of standardisation, there is also a significant amount of variation. That is not to claim that either standardisation or distinctive variation are of themselves good objectives to have. As a fundamental example, Scottish programmes are typically four years, and whilst some of the rest-of-the-UK programmes are as well, a majority are three years. Therefore, programmes are split into their first year, intermediate year/s and final year. Two programmes with the same name at different institutions might contain a radically different number and mix of classes, despite being covered by the same institutionally selected UCAS code.

That being said, the standardised UK credit structure of 120 credits per year, and credits per class (where known) allows insight into marketing's prevalence within a programme/structure: 30 credits is a quarter, 20 a sixth and 15 an eighth of a study-year. This project therefore also profiled the classes by credit weightings and by programme year, so as to specify patterns in sequence and significance. Stringfellow et al. (2006) broke their roster of class-categories into three: Core – offered by more than 75 per cent; Standard, offered by more than 50 per cent; and Peripheral, offered by less than 50 per cent. We retain the classification names, but change the divides to 66 per cent and 33 per cent.

The Core Marketing Curriculum therefore has five constituents: Principles; MarComs; Consumer Behaviour; Market Research; and Strategic Marketing/ Marketing Management.

Marketing Principles was offered by all of the sample institutions. Indeed, at the time of data collection this was the only class offered by Said at Oxford and Judge at Cambridge. Only four institutions didn't offer this in the first year of a programme, providing it in the second year – perhaps as an outcome of a common first year or as service teaching for other departments? Some institutions broke even the start of the journey into more than one chunk, perhaps as an administrative requirement to have what were effectively year-long courses split into semester-long halves – as at Lincoln and Plymouth. Where credits were indicated, this class was typically 15 or 20 credits. Almost always, this was the only marketing class in that programme-year, meaning that between three-quarters and seven-eighths of study were not marketing specific in the first third of the programme. As can be envisaged, these classes present a breadth of material to very large numbers, with specific topics generally getting no more than two lectures and usually just one with a quite limited amount of supporting reading, students being inculcated with basic concepts, processes and vocabulary. An issue made clear in numerous class outlines is that the class was at one and the same time meant to provide a foundation for future study of the discipline and to be complete in and of itself for those not continuing. A difficult trick to pull off.

Marketing Communications has a unique feature to the data relating to its time/year position. Other class-categories were almost always present in one year of a specific programme, with the topic usually being contained within a single class. This was not the case for MarComs, which was very often split between the second and third year of a programme and over more than one class. More institutions provided more than 30 credits (in fact, the spread here was 40–120 credits – Brighton–Kingston) than did those offering fewer than 20. That is about double the credits for the Principles or Consumer Behaviour classes. Unsurprisingly, the typical content of these classes was built around the Integrated Marketing Communications (IMC) concept, with each element being dealt with in turn between bookends of the need to integrate communications and the requirement of a strategically coherent communications plan. Also notable was that this was where a lot of the subsumed topics from what had been separate Digital classes were ending up. In some cases, this was clearly a recent and/or unhappy hybrid.

Consumer Behaviour was typically a second class in a programme after Principles and is very likely to be in the first semester of a second year. As a set of topics, it is highly contained, with institutions offering more than one class and/or more than 20 credits, being exceptional – NTU and Strathclyde offering the most at 40 credits over two years. Content-wise, many focused on very traditional topics such as customer decision making and psychology and segmentation and targeting. Also present were more recent topics such as consumer activism, consumer tribalism, sustainability and other ethical issues – indeed, on many programmes this class seemed to be the home for ethics and discussion of them.

Market Research was quite often twinned with Consumer Behaviour in a second year, and also generally contained within a single class, with 19 of 26 instances being of 20 credits or fewer. Notable in the documents reviewed from institutions was the scarcity of assessment involving primary data collection, focus instead being given to the process of market research and its aims and ambitions (Nunan and Di Domenico, 2019). A focus on the abstract rather than the practical. Research ethics were common as a focus, and there was some evidence that the primacy of online/social media-related MR activities was reflected in teaching, if less often in assessment. Surprisingly absent was anything over and above rudimentary analytical skills development, and training in the use of a statistical package – even Excel – was pretty rare. Within the heart of what should be numeracy and analytical development, students aren't getting much, with the balance of what is taught being qualitative only. There is an evolution in the skill sets and preferences of younger generations of academics. Wilson et al. (2019) examined Marketing PhD theses from the last 40 years and found a longitudinal switch *to* a strong majority of qualitative research and *from* a strong majority of quantitative research. It would be surprising if that trend had not impacted upon the teaching and class design by those newer cohorts.

Finally, in the Core there is Strategic Management/Marketing Management. Usually a final year class but sometimes split over two classes in the penultimate and final year. Provision-weighting was pretty split within the sample, with more than half containing it within 20 or fewer credits and 40 per cent 30 or more – 40 being typical and 60 at Hull. To compare the Principles Class outlines and those of this category was to see a quite significant overlap, something which is perhaps not helpful, useful or efficient. Marketing planning as a process, and the use of case studies were widely prevalent. This was the home for much of what little there was on pricing and distribution.

The Standard offering contains International Marketing, Digital Marketing, Services Marketing, Critical/Contemporary, Product and Brand Marketing and Dissertations and Project classes.

International Marketing, like Digital, is a category that appears to have suffered from subsumption into other classes. Most likely, an international/ global perspective is now the default. This could be a category in danger, as many areas are ripe for further transitioning into Consumer Behaviour, IMC,

Digital, Marketing Management and so on. What is intrinsically and specifically International only? This was typically being provided as a third/final year single class and very commonly at 20 credits or fewer.

On the face of it, the fact that only just over half of the sample offered a Digital marketing class seems surprising. Again, subsumption seems to be the key issue. Content and topics used to populate such classes have at an equal or greater rate to incorporation been sucked into other classes as online/social becomes the norm. Given that, is this a category of class that would survive? If decisions were made objectively, perhaps not, but how comfortable would you feel – against student expectation – stating publicly that your programme contained no Digital Marketing class (Crittenden and Crittenden, 2015)? These classes were offered in the penultimate and final year and almost always at 20 credits or fewer.

Services Marketing is offered at the same proportion of the sample as Digital. As a category there is surely more inherent and contextual strength here, with services representing the bulk of the UK economy – as is true for many other developed nations – and career paths for marketing graduates in combination with a deep and wide literature and theoretical base (Juaneda-Ayensa et al., 2019). This is mostly a final year single class, averaging 15–20 credits.

Classes focused on assessing marketing in a Critical and Contemporary manner grew in number. This is the home for a lot of marketing as sociology/ anthropology, and also much of the discussion on ethics and the role of companies within society – especially sustainability (Akrivou and Bradbury-Huang, 2015; Bridges and Wilhelm, 2008). Is this very much a focus on the studying of the impacts of marketing, rather than training to practise as a marketer? Arguably it could be about training marketers to be aware of and sensitive to context of operations within cultures and societies. There is room for both within a full curriculum, but where should the balance be? This is typically a final year single class, averaging 20 credits.

Product and Brand management classes are typically second or final year classes, averaging 15 credits as a single class within a programme. Within the limited supplementary documentation there is some evidence of the balance very much being towards the branding here. NPD content is marginal at best.

Unsurprisingly, Dissertation/Project classes are for the final year of study, often as capstones to the programme. If this project had collected Business School-wide class lists and documents, we'd see a lot more of them. Dissertations are on the classic line of contextual and theoretical summaries before the collection and interpretation of primary data. Arguably this may make up some of the numeracy deficit of the rest of the programme, but it would be better if that were integrated throughout, rather than at the end. Project-based classes typically involved working with a local organisation on a particular issue and presenting and reporting back to current professionals alongside academic staff. These classes occupied at least 30 credits of the final year and usually 40–60. Many programmes offered both.

The Peripheral categories classes are those offered by less than a third of sampled institutions. Those low percentages and incomplete profiles make generalised comments difficult: CRM and Relationship Marketing, Retail Marketing, Professional Practice, B2B and Sales Management.

CRM and Relationship Marketing classes have suffered multi-directional subsumption. Elements of these classes are now in Consumer Behaviour, Digital, MarComs and Services classes. As with what were E-Marketing and International classes, the position has moved from being separate and distinct to being default. Marketing is about relationships and networks, off and online. These classes are second or final year, and always 20 credits or fewer.

Retailing has suffered badly in popularity, provision falling by more than half between our two samples. This is a vocationally orientated area, so why is it suffering? Some speculations: it is perhaps deeply unfashionable, and continued poor news about the retail sector may be putting off students, and the academy is no longer getting a stream of new recruits with retail experience. These are single classes, offered in the penultimate or final year. All six examples were 20 credits or fewer, averaging 15.

Professional Practice classes are a new entrant to the list, being classes with a clear and specific focus on elements of practice (Cheng et al., 2016; Kelley and Bridges, 2005). Examples include marketing-related law, marketing within a new business, and skills in respect of continuous personal development as a professional marketer. On the face of it, the rise of this category of classes seems a good thing, but should these issues be siloed rather than programme-wide? These are classes in the second or final year, with some institutions using them as a spine after a Principles class. They are relatively credit heavy, most often 20 or more credits – albeit with only a limited sample of eight.

B2B is the discipline focus that has suffered even more badly than Retail. Fully two-thirds of provision has gone in the nine years between data collection for these two projects. There is some subsumption away into Strategic Marketing and Services and a split via Sales Management. These topics are unfashionable, suffering from student interest quite strongly focused on Consumer Behaviour, and Digital. Additionally, they suffer from a reduced number of recruits in the academy with personal/professional experience. Given the split of the economy over B2C and B2B jobs, this is troubling. A single, final year class of 20 credits or fewer.

Finally, we have Sales Management, an emergent class from the Harker (2015) sample not present in Stringfellow et al. (2006). This is only a very small sub-sample, which for what it's worth indicates single classes of 20 credits or fewer, usually in the final year.

Table 4.3   *A generalised (median) marketing curriculum*

Level of Programme	Core		Standard		Peripheral	
	Subject	Credits	Subject	Credits	Subject	Credits
First	Principals	20				
Intermediate	Consumer Behaviour	20	Digital Marketing	20	Professional Practice	20
	MarComs	20	Product and Brand Marketing	15		
	Market Research	20				
Final	Strategic Marketing and Management	20	International Marketing	20	CRM	20
			Services Marketing	20	Retail	15
			Critical and Contemporary	20	B2B Marketing	15
			Dissertation and Project	60	Sales Management	20

What other observations might be made? First, there is very little in the way of specialisation, with most institutions taking a broad approach. Loughborough has a lot of depth to retailing, and Gloucestershire for communications, but outside those exceptions there is a lot of genericism and not much depth. Most of the time, a subject gets a single class. Most programmes employ some form of capstone – a more significant and challenging project or dissertation – as an end to the curriculum as delivered. What isn't there that should be? Not much on supply chains – subsumed into other subjects or dropping out entirely. Pricing is also absent, and NPD is heavily under-represented. Outside tourism/heritage within Services, and a smattering of new-business marketing classes, there isn't much at all that could be said to be sector-specific.

Whilst far from perfect, the data available can be used to generate a typical or genericised undergraduate curriculum. This has been done by taking the median positions for both year of programme and credit weighting for each subject and can be seen in Table 4.3. To accommodate that some programmes are four rather than three years, 'intermediate' sometimes refers to years 2–3, rather than just a second year.

What reflections can be made on this? Perhaps most important is the proportion of a programme that is – or even can be – marketing teaching. The breakdown of credits means that the Core is only 100 out of 360. The Standard components offer another 155 and the Peripheral only 90 more, meaning that only one in three offer marketing teaching to cover more than two-thirds of a complete programme. Also, subjects most directly related to being a professional marketer are heavily focused in the final year and in the Peripheral offering, meaning most students will miss out on most of what is surely already too limited. Can the glass be instead considered half full? Perhaps – the biggest credit gap is the first year of the programme. Here students are typically taking a wide spread of classes from inside and outside a Business School. It is difficult to argue that is bad or inappropriate. Most programmes are fairly flexible in respect of class selection for intermediate and especially final years – that being the case, students minded to fill out their credits with marketing teaching are able to do so at most institutions.

ANSWERING THE QUESTIONS

Earlier, a number of questions were raised.

There are marketing curricula. They have paths and structures. What they are not is entire unto themselves – even the departments offering the greatest spread of teaching are substantially reliant on external teaching to fill out a programme and round out intended skill and knowledge sets, and marketing is very likely to be a minority within the credit structure. There is a degree of commonality – if not standardisation – between institutions. The purpose of these programmes and supporting curricula is less clear. Looked at from a safe distance, it could reasonably be said that they might educate and train for communications and brand management generally, and social media management specifically, but many other professional marketing careers are unsupported. This is education and training for a proportion of the careers available only. If current and prospective (or past) students were told that, how would they respond?

In respect of nature, the ability to interpret marketing events and practices critically has validity as something to impart (Dahl et al., 2018; De Los Reyes Jr et al., 2017; Fotaki and Prasad, 2015), but is that really something an employer would value as strongly as good analytical skills, or the ability to construct and implement a marketing plan? The academy is losing for actuarial reasons colleagues with substantial professional careers across industry and gaining new entrants who tend to have only experienced the educational conveyor belt prior to a university post.

So, how could things be made better?

Enhancing the Marketing Curriculum through Signature Pedagogy, Problem-Based Learning and Professional Certification

When framing curriculum concepts at the outset of the chapter, a number of theoretical parameters were identified. Ultimately, a curriculum, irrespective of its disciplinary base, needs to be structured around a sense of consistency that allows the learners to have some certainty as to its content as well as the impression, and reality, that the curriculum enables the learner to embark upon a journey to a destination they want to arrive at. That is, will the degree equip the learner to perform at the requisite level in their chosen profession? To ascertain whether this is so, the significance of shared meaning should also be stressed. In effect, is there commonality and does a resultant sense of confidence ensue in terms of one's professional preparedness? An overarching and instructive feature, which reiterates earlier discussion, is that project work and professional practice are categories within marketing curricula that are both emergent and growing. It is appropriate that professional preparedness should be increasingly at the fore.

We have therefore three suggestions in respect of enhancing the marketing curriculum. Two are examples of pedagogical phenomena and current practice in curriculum redesign, selected to show how classes can be improved through redesign in a manner applicable regardless of specific class topic, and the third is a call to make more deliberate connections between HE classes and professional training as a means to creating professional preparedness.

Consider the latter strategy first. Already many universities seek to align some of their taught marketing modules with professional body requirements in order to provide students with credit towards a professional qualification, such as the Chartered Institute of Marketing Foundation Certificate in Professional Marketing. A brief review of the scope and content of this certificate shows a strong match with many Principles of Marketing classes. The same can be said for a good higher education Market Research class and the MRS Certificate in Market Research from the Market Research Society. Those are just two examples from the number of comparisons between HE classes and professional certificates that exist. University marketing departments need to keep track of changing professional body requirements so as to support students to achieve professional qualifications. This brings many benefits. The curriculum is more directly relevant to practice through the discipline of the certifications and the contribution to meeting the curriculum naturally allows more and better input from current professionals. In terms of employability, the graduate can point to industry-relevant knowledge and skills, often supported by professional body certification.

Turning to pedagogical phenomena and current practice in curriculum redesign. First, the embracing of Signature Pedagogy (SP) as a structuring mechanism will be used to frame pedagogical change and curriculum relevance. Secondly, the utilisation of Problem-Based Learning (PBL) will show how the redesign of a class's curriculum enabled the reconfigured class to offer learners more. Common to both of these examples is an emphasis upon how current practice can be improved, in terms of the throughput and outcome, with the consequent worth of the degree then being more tangible and apparent as a function of its improved robustness and rigour.

A recurrent and underpinning prerequisite between both examples is the significance of three curriculum characteristics: disciplinary substance and curriculum appropriateness; learner engagement; and eventual benefit.

Curriculum (re)design and the manner in which this is thought through by those involved in teaching undergraduate programmes in marketing, and tasked with the responsibility of (re)shaping them, can be explored through the lens of Signature Pedagogies (Shulman, 2005). Shulman defined SPs as characterising teaching forms distinct to that discipline. Abel (2009) views them as the means through which the text, thought and practice of the respective profession is conveyed – that is, how disciplinary knowledge translates into professional education.

Very broadly, SPs are the types of teaching that act as an organising mechanism and, thereby, a guide as to how future practitioners should best be educated for their professions. From the perspective of to-be graduates of marketing programmes, are two criteria fulfilled? First, is this programme undertaken as preparedness for their professional life and, secondly, does the rigour and criticality of their cognate subject befit its status as a profession? The first is a clear yes, whilst the short answer for the second is also yes, with a longer answer bringing in the highly variant career paths for marketers, and the number of roles where marketing is a component but not the whole of the profession.

Therefore, the concept and use of SP has value in marketing education. An intrinsic feature of SP is the continual emphasis that it places upon viewing the pedagogical experience as one which blends a recognisable suite of teaching forms that enables learning together with the professional needs and values of the discipline. Instead of viewing teaching, and its forms, simply as the basis of imparting knowledge, this reflects that the discipline in question is a form of professional education that accords balance across the facets of thinking, performing and demonstrating integrity.

Structurally, SP can be sub-divided into three components: surface structures associated with thinking; deep structures centred on skills and 'performing'; and implicit structures that place an accent upon the requisite moral beliefs and attitudes that enable professionals to act with integrity. 'Surface' refers to the acts of teaching that develop the 'habits of the head' in terms of one's mind, the second (deep) deals with imparting and dealing with the 'habits of the hand' in the sense of one's skills, whilst the third (implicit) revolves around the 'habits of the heart' centred on morals, beliefs and values in so far as they relate to anticipated professional life.

Conceptualised sequentially across the undergraduate journey, the first year can be seen as an introductory underpinning, the intermediate year/s one/s of application and the final year being one where a more critical stance is injected. Across all years, it suggests a curriculum that is ever deepening, but one which is layered in terms of the accumulation of the three sub-components required for professional life.

Within the domain of the *surface structures*, there is recognition that the orthodoxy of the marketing mix, whilst widely practised and previously proven, is increasingly outdated and not 'fit for purpose'. Its limitations reside chiefly in its linear and, by default, compartmentalised nature. It is a child of the 1950s and US retail after all. To correct this, there are instances where the class curriculum has been improved through activities and case studies that show the 'bigger picture'. Rather than the understanding of the marketing mix being accumulated in siloed portions, a sense of holism is possible if the inter-linkages across the mix elements are drawn out. A lack of a holistic curriculum was earlier identified as a key issue and a common failure in the building of marketing curricula.

Across the entirety of the curriculum, the rapidity and intensity of change impacting upon marketing and marketing practice has the scope to render marketing classes and the content of them progressively obsolete. The implication for marketing graduates is unambiguous and fairly stark, namely that the content of their degrees will in time be superseded and become steadily less relevant to their continued practice. A teaching mechanism to limit and slow this is to incorporate concepts of resilience and adaptability into the syllabus through more and better engagement with current practitioners/employers to demonstrate that seemingly abstract concepts underpin professional activities, and that recruitment into their organisations has a preference for graduates with the wherewithal to be critical, to absorb new concepts quickly and to be selective when applying them. In short, the possession of concept knowledge, at any point in time, is secondary but necessary to the ability to acquire, master and apply new concept knowledge iteratively.

Another related pedagogical and curriculum feature centres on engendering a greater sense amongst marketers of their professional worth and contribution. As was highlighted earlier there are significant issues and anxieties around numeracy and particularly a real or perceived sense of inadequacy as to how numerically competent marketing graduates are. This can be tackled in the content and the pitch of the teaching. It is important to make a distinction between the two: content and pitch. The former relates, for example, to what components of numeracy, such as the ability to interpret marketing data within a spreadsheet, need to be imparted, whilst the pitch corresponds to what the role of the marketer is. In this case, their role is chiefly one of interpretation rather than formulation. By pitching and calibrating the marketer's role proportionately, the intention is to show that numerical skill, in this case the understanding and use of data, is one to embrace rather than one to be over-whelmed by.

Given the practical and applied nature of marketing, curriculum content should be more imbued with a sense of, first, closeness to those who are current practitioners and, secondly, a sense of work readiness. The role of marketing practitioners is integral to this. A guest lecture is a single point, weak and isolated. Significantly better value than merely varying the class format and delivery on one occasion can and should be found by spreading out the intensity, duration and significance of these interactions. For example, utilising and developing the guest lecturer's insights and perspective as an initiator of student research into topics and situations within an assessment framework. Rather than the transmission of the subject being through the prism of theory, it affords the students the ability to capture the realities of, and the attendant complexities within, marketing decisions that are rarely dichotomous and unambiguous. Through such an approach, a greater sense of curiosity can be generated, whilst overly prescriptive approaches that circumscribe thinking can be avoided. In short, some of the creativity stems from what the student produces – passive becomes active; apart becomes together.

Through the metaphorical use of the 'habits of the hand' term, the significance of skills is explicit within a Signature Pedagogy's *deep structures*. An integral aspect and outcome are the transference of skills together with a shared understanding, if not consensus, as to how this can be enabled. Instead of skills being either assumed or engaged with seamlessly, the structuring of an undergraduate curriculum can acknowledge and seek to counter ambivalence or reticence in embracing the repertoire of skills that professional marketers should possess – such as the commonplace student fear of activities and classes requiring good numeracy. A second example of this is networking. Recognising that this is a soft skill that has to be nurtured subtly and incrementally, rather than overtly and directly, networking can be blended within a programme in a way that involves rather than dissuades the student base. A simple implementation of this would be encouragement and support in building up a profile and network on professional social media platforms like LinkedIn, or events where students in earlier years meet students in later years and/or recent graduates. Thereby, a sense of the benefits of networking can be conveyed. In instances where networking is viewed as a skill that has to be developed, if not relished, the furtherance of this can be done intuitively in an almost unseen and generally incremental manner. Not only does this approach at embedding networking help to build confidence, with this being another manifestation of resilience as noted previously, but it also achieves this in a peer-to-peer context that lends a sense of authenticity. As such, skills development and reinforcement, as a key curriculum component, originates (partially) from interactions amongst the student base rather than the conduit being in the form of a speaker-to-student transmission.

Rather than dealing with skills in an identikit and standardised manner, a more nuanced and granular approach is to tailor the skills auditing (and subsequent delivery) to the specific needs of learners. By doing so, any skills acquisition stems from what the learner is seeking rather than there being any impression, warranted or not, that the content and direction of the skills is being foisted and imposed. A critical component enabling this more student-led rather than purely interventionist approach is that the skills audit, within the auspices of a Professional Practice class, elicits from the students what skills require improvement. Reflecting the truism that curricula should be concerned with the destination, in the sense that it seeks to develop one, and that it leads one on a journey of heightened credibility, there needs to be a focus upon softer, yet indispensable, skills. As an accompaniment to the harder and more factual bases of disciplinary knowledge, an emphasis upon aspects such as negotiation and the interpretation of body language would play a contributory role in shaping graduates with a more holistic perspective.

The third and final component revolves around *implicit structures*, namely the morals, beliefs and values that provide a foundational element to one's future professionalism. Sequentially, the prior acquisition of knowledge together with the furtherance of one's skills coalesce into the qualities and mores that are intrinsic to a profession. This is akin to the journey that is so embedded within abstract discussions of curricula. Here, stress is placed upon achieving professional preparedness and serving, in effect, a moral apprenticeship. To achieve this, there needs to be a candid review of the challenges encountered by marketing professionals. An example would be the legitimate and pressing questions of sustainability, or of labour conditions at suppliers, or in the use and abuse of data harvested by social media platforms. As noted earlier, a more critical and questioning stance is more appropriate for the latter stages of the journey as the ability to discuss this question fully, together with all its ramifications, is contingent upon a certain baseline of knowledge and absorption of skills.

Alongside this coverage of the somewhat darker side of the subject and sector, which should not be minimised or downplayed, the more positive aspects can be accentuated. As such, the professional preparedness transitions from a mere rhetorical notion into one that learners resonate and connect with.

An Example of Curriculum (Re)Design: Utilising PBL in Export Marketing

Utilising PBL theory, this vignette will outline how one of the authors redesigned a class. Within PBL, there are three stages (Barrows, 1984): the identification and clarification of a problem; the undertaking of research to answer this; and, finally, a summation of this learning journey that has yielded new knowledge.

For any class revision, there are a series of considerations. First, theoretical rigour has to be maintained. Secondly, the teaching experience has to interest students. Concomitantly, the culmination of the teaching experience, in the form of an assignment as a learning outcome, reflects the fact that students will, irrespective of any sense of engagement, still be looking for the class content to prepare them in getting a grade. In short, there must be substance, engagement and eventual benefit.

As a teaching approach, PBL accords with constructivist theory (Ryan, 1997). Concepts of constructivism place an emphasis on learning being viewed through the learner's mindset (Stewart, 2013). As such, the acquisition and expression of knowledge should demonstrate originality rather than simply being one of regurgitating facts. Exemplifying this, Rhem (1998) highlighted how PBL progresses beyond the collection of facts to a situation where one is constructing one's own meaning.

Contextually, Export Marketing was an elective. In summary the aim and associated learning objectives were to critically explore the export marketing process. Logically, the class progressed from understanding why an organisation would wish to start exporting, the extent to which they were in a state of readiness, how they could best achieve this in terms of the strategic direction taken and, finally, what operational marketing tactics they would deploy. In essence, this class looked at the exporting marketing journey from an organisational perspective and in accordance with Norman and Schmidt (1992) the scenarios are actual rather than notional.

Crucially, this futurist perspective shaped the class. The problem, subsequent tasks and exercises, and, finally, assessment template were on organisations that were envisaging exporting. By focusing on a future scenario, the problem could be framed as one where a definitive solution or outcome did not necessarily exist. To achieve this, each teaching session presented a series of problems, with these being accompanied by tasks and partially self-directed exercises. Initially, the strategic problem was why an organisation wanted to start exporting, with this opening problem, corresponding with the first stage of Barrows (1984), articulating why the remainder of the exporting journey should be pursued.

When developing PBL, attention needs to be focused on the role of the facilitators, the manner in which learners interact both with the former as well as with one another, and, finally, how both parties function within a structured series of session-specific problems culminating in the learning being articulated through an assessment. This structuration of PBL manifests itself through the distinct stages of definition, knowledge-gap identification, information collection and suggesting outcomes (Smith, 2005).

Across the session-specific problem, material was accessed from a range of sources: academic, practitioner and governmental. Some of these sources were provided by the facilitator, with others being the responsibility of the learners. By the end of the final session-specific problem, the students had made use of academic sources (journal articles), newspaper websites focusing on export matters, financial services companies' export guidance websites, YouTube videos on exporting 'best practice' and export promotion websites that form the basis of a role play.

Across the session-specific problems, there were common features. First, the problems were outlined. Secondly, the students were expected to research these scenarios and use these insights as a basis for discussion. At the next lecture session, a nominated spokesperson from each group presented their insights. Following each teaching session, the facilitator synthesised these outputs on a discussion forum. Not only does this provide an information depository for students, but it was also reflective of an iterative process (Stepien and Gallagher, 1993) whereby one's observations and interpretations may evolve.

Instead of being factual, PBL assessment needs to be demonstrative of the learning journey that the individual undertakes. By focusing on their insights and knowledge (De Graff and Kolmos, 2002), this assignment centred on the export marketing journey of a prospective exporter. By rationalising the initial strategic and tactical decisions that an exporter makes, the focus is by definition seeking to solve a problem – as the endpoint should be a more favourable competitive position. Once the initial problems have been framed as questions, the sub-questions for the assignment filter down explicitly. The learning from the session-specific group discussions, the class discussions and the facilitator discussion board summaries all contributed to this end.

CONCLUSION

As has been shown, research into curricula is not usually proximate or supportive of efforts to improve marketing education. The amount of relevant evidence-based work is too low and too many intended contributions are too abstract or too irrelevant to the realities of large-scale provision to have much value. Nevertheless, marketing curricula exist and are in need of support and development, better to support the needs of all involved, whether institutions, instructors, students or employers. Key anxieties exist, most notably in the development of analysis/numeracy and in the impact of rapidly developing technologies and cultures in making too much current provision ineffective at best and nearly obsolete at worst.

The collation and interpretation of data on provision shows the strengths and weaknesses of what is offered in the UK. There are signs of adaptation towards more modern needs, but also extinctions in respect of key topics and skills caused at least in part by a changing academy no longer being able to support them – by inclination or absence of experience. There is too much of a production-orientation, and this has in turn kept holistic integration elusive, even where sought.

There are key objectives for those who seek to improve marketing education provision through curriculum development. First – and perhaps most importantly – that there is effort to make the curriculum feed powerfully into what is taught, rather than what can be easily or conveniently taught becoming the criteria of curriculum coverage. This is especially true of topics which are suffering from (amongst other things) the evolution of the academy caused by new-entrant cohorts and their skill-sets, or an aging class that is the protected pet of a senior colleague. Secondly, the curriculum should be purposeful, useful and pragmatic, with the learning transferable to a professional context and if possible to other disciplines. Thirdly, a curriculum should be able to recognise the importance of skills furtherance and intensification, with an emphasis on professional preparedness, and this might be most efficiently done by making connections with appropriate options for professional certification and by incorporating more input from current professionals. Fourthly, that sufficient attention is given to making individual classes sit within integrated programmes with respect to coverage of skills and topics and concepts – especially at the early stages. Fifth and finally, that some means of curriculum improvement are general across subjects – such as the making of pedagogic strategies like PBL and SP, and that others must be identified on a class by class basis – and that this will vary in difficulty from the easy and trivial to the complex and hard. Good luck to all!

NOTE

1. Class here is used as a synonym for the also common terms of module and unit.

REFERENCES

Abel, C.F. 2009. Toward a signature pedagogy for public administration, *Journal of Public Affairs Education*, *15*(2), pp. 145–60.

Ackerman, D.S. and Hu, J. 2011. Effect of type of curriculum on educational outcomes and motivation among marketing students with different learning styles. *Journal of Marketing Education*, *33*(3), pp. 273–84.

Akrivou, K. and Bradbury-Huang, H. 2015. Educating integrated catalysts: Transforming business schools toward ethics and sustainability. *Academy of Management Learning & Education*, *14*(2), pp. 222–40.

Atwong, C.T. 2015. A social media practicum: An action-learning approach to social media marketing and analytics. *Marketing Education Review*, *25*(1), pp. 27–31.

Bacon, D.R. 2017. Revisiting the relationship between marketing education and marketing career success. *Journal of Marketing Education*, *39*(2), pp. 109–123.

Barrows, H.S. 1984. A specific problem-based, self-directed learning method designed to teach medical problem-solving skills, and enhance knowledge retention and recall. In H.G. Schmidt and M.L. DeVolder (eds), *Tutorials in Problem-based Learning: A New Direction in Teaching the Health Professions*, Maastricht: Van Gorcum, pp. 16–32.

Brennan, R. and Vos, L. 2013. Effects of participation in a simulation game on marketing students' numeracy and financial skills. *Journal of Marketing Education*, *35*(3), pp. 259–70.

Bridges, C.M. and Wilhelm, W.B. 2008. Going beyond green: The 'why and how' of integrating sustainability into the marketing curriculum. *Journal of Marketing Education*, *30*(1), pp. 33–46.

Brocato, E.D., White, N.J., Bartkus, K. and Brocato, A.A. 2015. Social media and marketing education: A review of current practices in curriculum development. *Journal of Marketing Education*, *37*(2), pp. 76–87.

Centeno, E., Harker, M.J., Ibrahim, E.B. and Wang, L.W. 2008. What is postgraduate marketing education for? Observations from the UK. *European Business Review*, *20*(6), pp. 547–66.

Cheng, R., Lourenço, F. and Resnick, S. 2016. Educating graduates for marketing in SMEs. *Journal of Small Business and Enterprise Development*, *23*(2), pp. 495–513.

Crittenden, V.L. and Crittenden, W.F. 2015. Digital and social media marketing in business education: Implications for student engagement. *Journal of Marketing Education*, *37*(3).

Crittenden, V.L. and Peterson, R.A. 2019. Digital disruption: The transdisciplinary future of marketing education. *Journal of Marketing Education*, *41*(1).

Dahl, A.J., Peltier, J.W. and Schibrowsky, J.A. 2018. Critical thinking and reflective learning in the marketing education literature: A historical perspective and future research needs. *Journal of Marketing Education*, *40*(2), pp. 101–116.

De Graff, E. and Kolmos, A. 2002. Characteristics of problem-based learning. *International Journal of Engineering Education*, *8*(1), pp. 657–62.

De Los Reyes Jr, G., Kim, T.W. and Weaver, G.R. 2017. Teaching ethics in business schools: A conversation on disciplinary differences, academic provincialism, and the case for integrated pedagogy. *Academy of Management Learning & Education*, *16*(2), pp. 314–36.

Di Gregorio, A., Maggioni, I., Mauri, C. and Mazzucchelli, A. 2019. Employability skills for future marketing professionals. *European Management Journal*, *37*(3), pp. 251–8.

Elam, E.L. and Spotts, H.E. 2004. Achieving marketing curriculum integration: A live case study approach. *Journal of Marketing Education*, *26*(1), pp. 50–65.

Finch, D., Nadeau, J. and O'Reilly, N. 2013. The future of marketing education: A practitioner's perspective. *Journal of Marketing Education*, *35*(1), pp. 54–67.

Fotaki, M. and Prasad, A., 2015. Questioning neoliberal capitalism and economic inequality in business schools. *Academy of Management Learning & Education*, *14*(4), pp. 556–75.

Fowler, K., Thomas, V.L. and Saenger, C. 2019. Enhancing students' marketing information literacy. *Marketing Education Review*, *29*(1), pp. 52–64.

Freberg, K. and Kim, C.M. 2018. Social media education: Industry leader recommendations for curriculum and faculty competencies. *Journalism & Mass Communication
Educator, 73*(4), pp. 379–91.

Harker, M.J. 2015. UK undergraduate marketing education, Internal Report for the
Academy of Marketing.

Harker, M.J., Caemmerer, B. and Hynes, N. 2016. Management education by the French
Grandes Ecoles de Commerce: Past, present, and an uncertain future. *Academy of
Management Learning & Education, 15*(3), pp. 549–68.

Harrigan, P. and Hulbert, B. 2011. How can marketing academics serve marketing
practice? The new marketing DNA as a model for marketing education. *Journal of
Marketing Education, 33*(3), pp. 253–72.

Hartley, P., Routon, P.W. and Torres, L. 2019. The skills marketing majors believe they
acquire: Evidence from a national survey. *Journal of Marketing Education, 41*(3),
pp. 202–214.

Juaneda-Ayensa, E., Olarte-Pascual, C., San Emeterio, M.C. and Pelegrín-Borondo,
J. 2019. Developing new 'Professionals': Service learning in marketing as an
opportunity to innovate in higher education. *Studies in Educational Evaluation, 60*,
pp.163–9.

Kelley, C.A. and Bridges, C. 2005. Introducing professional and career development skills in the marketing curriculum. *Journal of Marketing Education, 27*(3),
pp. 212–18.

Kim, C. and Freberg, K. 2017. The state of social media curriculum: Exploring professional expectations of pedagogy and practices to equip the next generation of
professionals. *Journal of Public Relations Education, 2*(2).

Koch, A.J. 1997. Marketing curriculum: Designing its new logic and structure. *Journal
of Marketing Education, 19*(3), pp. 2–16.

Langan, R., Cowley, S. and Nguyen, C. 2019. The state of digital marketing in
academia: An examination of marketing curriculum's response to digital disruption. *Journal of Marketing Education, 41*(1), pp. 32–46.

LeClair, D. 2018. Integrating business analytics in the marketing curriculum: Eight
recommendations. *Marketing Education Review, 28*(1), pp. 6–13.

Liu, X. and Burns, A.C. 2018. Designing a marketing analytics course for the digital
age. *Marketing Education Review, 28*(1), pp. 28–40.

McDaniel, S.W. and Hise, R.T. 1984. Shaping the marketing curriculum: The CEO
perspective. *Journal of Marketing Education, 6*(2), pp. 27–32.

Nicholls, J. and Hair, J.F. 2016. An exploratory study of ethics, CSR and sustainability
education in graduate/undergraduate business schools: Specifically in the marketing
curriculum. In K. Plangger (ed.), *Thriving in a New World Economy* (pp. 243–6).
Cham: Springer.

Norman, G.R. and Schmidt, H.G. 1992. The psychological basis of problem-based
learning: A review of the evidence, *Academic Medicine, 67*(9), pp. 557–65.

Nunan, D. and Di Domenico, M. 2019. Rethinking the market research curriculum. *International Journal of Market Research, 61*(1), pp. 22–32.

Oksiutycz, A. and Azionya, C. 2017. Using action research for curriculum development
and improving the learning experience: A case study. *South African Journal of
Higher Education, 31*(3), pp.193–208.

Parker, B.J. 2014. Innovating the marketing curriculum: Establishing an academic
major in internet marketing. *Atlantic Marketing Journal, 3*(2), p. 13.

Pharr, S. and Morris, L.J. 1997. The fourth-generation marketing curriculum: Meeting
AACSB's guidelines. *Journal of Marketing Education, 19*(3), pp. 31–43.

Pilling, B.K., Rigdon, E.E. and Brightman, H.J. 2012. Building a metrics-enabled marketing curriculum: The cornerstone course. *Journal of Marketing Education, 34*(2), pp. 179–93.

Rhem, J. 1998. Problem-based learning: An introduction, *The National Teaching & Learning Forum,* 8(1).

Rohm, A.J., Stefl, M. and Saint Clair, J. 2019. Time for a marketing curriculum overhaul: Developing a digital-first approach. *Journal of Marketing Education, 41*(1), pp. 47–59.

Ryan, G. 1997. Ensuring that students develop an adequate and well-structured knowledge base. In D. Boud and G.I. Feletti (eds), *The Challenge of Problem-based Learning,* London: Kogan Page, pp. 125–36.

Schlee, P.R. and Harich, K.R. 2010. Knowledge and skill requirements for marketing jobs in the 21st century. *Journal of Marketing Education, 32*(3), pp. 341–52.

Shulman, L.S. 2005. Signature pedagogies in the professions. *Daedalus,* 134(3), pp. 52–9.

Smith, G.F. 2005. Problem-based learning: Can it improve managerial thinking?, *Journal of Management Education, 29*(2), pp. 357–78.

Spiller, L. and Tuten, T. 2015. Integrating metrics across the marketing curriculum: The digital and social media opportunity. *Journal of Marketing Education, 37*(2), pp. 114–26.

Stepien, W. and Gallagher, S. 1993. Problem-based learning: As authentic as it gets, *Educational Leadership, 50*(7), pp. 25–9.

Stewart, M. 2013. Understanding learning: Theories and critique. In L. Hunt and D. Chalmers, *University Teaching in Focus,* Oxford: Routledge.

Stringfellow, L., Ennis, S., Brennan, R. and Harker, M.J. 2006. Mind the gap: The relevance of marketing education to marketing practice. *Marketing Intelligence & Planning, 24*(3), pp. 245–56.

Vriens, M., Brokaw, S., Rademaker, D. and Verhulst, R. 2019. The marketing research curriculum: Closing the practitioner–academic gaps. *International Journal of Market Research, 61*(5), pp. 492–501.

Weathers, D. and Aragón, O. 2019. Integrating analytics into marketing curricula: Challenges and effective practices for developing six critical competencies. *Marketing Education Review, 29*(4), pp. 266–82.

Wellman, N., 2017. *Are Marketing Degrees Fit for Purpose?* Doctoral dissertation, Cardiff Metropolitan University.

Wilson, E.J., McCabe, C. and Smith, R.S. 2018. Curriculum innovation for marketing analytics. *Marketing Education Review, 28*(1), pp. 52–66.

Wilson, J., Harker, M.J. and Murdy, S. 2019. Appraising research methods training for marketing, Internal Report for the Academy of Marketing.

5. Integrating learning with marketing simulations

Lynn Vos

Marketing degree programmes are generally structured as a set of discrete courses covering various branches of marketing knowledge such as consumer behaviour, marketing communications, market research, and strategic marketing, among others. During their programmes, students take courses in other business-related subjects such as economics and statistics and, often, courses from other disciplines including the humanities and/or natural sciences. As educators, we often assume that students are integrating what they have learned in one course with the ideas presented in another. For example, when students take strategic marketing, we assume they have a good grounding in the basics of marketing as well as some knowledge about budgeting from their first course in accounting and finance.

Our own experiences as educators, however, generally support the research that students have a very challenging time transferring knowledge in one setting to another. For example, studies from the neuroscience of education by Bransford et al. (2000) have demonstrated that for successful transfer of knowledge to take place, a number of prior and current conditions must exist: the student must have adequately mastered and not simply memorised the original concept(s); had adequate time to learn and process the old and new information; received regular tutor feedback and engaged in 'deliberate practice' (p. 59) including monitoring and reflecting on their learning approaches. Furthermore, the more the original content was context-specific, the more the student would find it difficult to transfer the knowledge to new contexts (Bransford et al., 2000). For example, learning about budgeting where only general business examples are used can make it difficult for students to transfer this learning to a marketing context. Thus, as educators we need to provide opportunities for students to meet these learning conditions and also carefully scaffold that learning so students have many opportunities to practise both their understanding and the application of marketing concepts.

The ability to integrate knowledge across the curriculum is not only important for a deeper understanding of marketing but also because this skill will be required in their professional lives, particularly as they progress and take on more challenging tasks in what is a rapidly changing and developing profession, not to mention one that is becoming increasingly multi-disciplinary in its application. Indeed, the marketing literature has had much to say in the past two decades about how the profession is changing. Thus, researchers have argued from a growing weight of evidence that graduates are not meeting the expectations of employers, that marketing careers are more complex, more technology oriented, have uncertain tenures, and are characterised by knowledge that is growing exponentially but, given the vast number of information sources and formats, in a fragmented manner (e.g. Kedia and Mukerjee, 1999; Ackerman et al., 2003, Crittenden and Crittenden, 2015; Rohm et al., 2018). For example, in 2002 Catterall, Maclaran and Stevens portrayed the modern marketing environment as offering little career stability, where knowledge and technology were advancing rapidly, and where globalisation had led to greater economic, social and political instability – all of which increase the complexity of problems and decision-making. In these circumstances, they argued, students needed the skills and aptitudes to manage change, to solve difficult problems, to think cross-functionally, to reason critically and to make sound judgements. Yet, despite the wealth of literature related to the importance of developing these skills, Catterall et al. (2002) contended that management and marketing educators had not sufficiently adapted what and how they teach, still emphasising the 'how to' of practice above the knowledge and skills needed for a more complex world:

> management education subscribes to an instrumental view of knowledge whereby the educators' task is to proffer a variety of models and techniques that equip managers with useful knowledge [to manage. But this emphasis on the] 'how to' of marketing management fails to meet the needs of managers who work in the increasingly uncertain and complex world ... characterized by ambiguity, uncertainty, diversity, disorganization, rapid change, the erosion of traditional divisions, questioning of received truths, and the undermining of established forms of expert knowledge (pp. 185–6).

While almost two decades old now, this article still resonates in the classroom where curriculum remains broken into modules where students have limited opportunities to consolidate what they have learned or to focus on the bigger picture associated with management decision-making in all its complexity.

The marketing profession continues to become more multi-disciplinary and marketers are more and more called upon to work with those in other specialised fields, such as information technology, data analytics, psychology and finance, given the complexity of operating across global markets in an increasingly digital world. To deal with problems that are often ill-structured, require knowledge from other disciplines, and are difficult to demarcate and contextualise, Catterall et al. (2002) call for students to have greater 'cross-functional thinking skills'; Pappas (2004) for 'meta-cognitive skills'; Spiro et al. (1988) for greater 'cognitive flexibility' and Perkins and Salomon (1992) for more sophisticated 'transfer of learning' skills, all of which help the student skilfully to weave prior learning from a range of different contexts with new ideas.

Research into how to develop these skills comes from many areas within education, one being a theory of learning that has the 'integration of learning' or IOL as its specific objective. Barber (2009), who has done much to advance the field, contends that when problems are complex and ambiguous, managers need to draw upon multiple areas of knowledge and skills, 'from multiple sources and experiences; applying theory to practice [across] various settings; utilizing diverse and even contradictory points of view; ... [and understand] issues and positions contextually' (p. 6). The American Association of Colleges and Universities (AAC&U) and the Carnegie Foundation for the Advancement of Teaching have supported this contention, warning that most college and university education remains highly fragmented and does not prepare students for the complex decision-making they will encounter (Huber and Hutchings, 2008). As Barber (2009) has argued, graduates who can make connections between 'disparate information and meaningfully synthesise concepts [will be] better prepared for success in the ... evolving knowledge economy of the 21st century' (p. 1). Building on earlier work by the AAC&U and the Carnegie Foundation, Barber (2009) developed the umbrella term 'integration practices' to mean the structures, learning, strategies and activities that span at least three ways of making connections: the ability to make connections across multiple contexts (intercontextuality), across ideas within a discipline (intradisciplinarity) and across domains and disciplines (interdisciplinarity).

Marketing educators do of course expose students to material and assessments that require integration and indeed the marketing education literature provides many examples of ways in which courses or programmes can be made more integrative (e.g. DeConinck and Steiner, 1999; Elam and Spotts, 2004; Craciun and Corrigan, 2010; Rohm et al., 2018). Most of these examples demonstrate Barber's (2009) integration practices even though they do not use his terms. For example, when students complete a client project (e.g. Elam and Spotts, 2004), they are operating, according to Barber's (2009) definition, intercontextually (context of the classroom and context of the client's workplace). To propose solutions to clients' problems, the students need to gain a deep understanding of their operations, culture and current approaches to marketing and link this knowledge with ideas, theories and frameworks learned in more than one marketing course (intradisciplinarity), and apply accounting and finance principles learned in another course or elements of data analysis learned in statistics, thus adding the elements of interdisciplinarity. The benefits of integrative learning experiences are highlighted by Elam and Spotts (2004) who provide evidence that marketing students will gain a deeper level of understanding of new material (by linking new material with previously learned information); better retention (as students rehearse old material to link it with new ideas); and, in working cross-functionally across a range of activities, gain professional experience. However, they and others who champion integrative activities do not explore the challenges associated with their use in the classroom.

A number of factors affect transfer and integration (Bransford et al., 2000). Huber et al. (2007) also argue that the ability to integrate ideas successfully is a relatively sophisticated skill and students need many opportunities for both guided and unguided practice during their university education. However, given that higher education tends towards compartmentalisation where programmes are made up of stand-alone courses that often appear as independent subjects, '[f]aculty should be intentional and explicit about opening the doors to broader integration' (Barber, 2014, p. 12) of subjects and content. Barber notes however that 'research has found that there is a lack of mentors or guides involved in students' integration [of learning as] there are few instances in [the research] that show involvement or influence of faculty members or educational administrators in this process' (Barber, 2014, p. 13).

In addition to mentors, Huber et al. (2007) propose that the curriculum be redesigned to include specific opportunities and guidance for integration. They suggest adding in curricular 'enriching activities' (p. 48) or what Kuh (2008) calls 'high impact practices', such as internships, cross-disciplinary courses, final year projects/dissertations, among other initiatives. They also recommend experiential learning activities such as simulations that allow students to make connections between theory and practice and between ideas learned in other contexts and disciplines.

Indeed, *simulation games* offer great potential for integrating learning from across the marketing curriculum (intradisciplinarity) and from other business subjects such as accounting and finance, operations management, data analytics and human resources (interdisciplinarity). Marketing educational games offer a simulated competitive environment in which rival teams make regular decisions; the decisions provide the inputs to a software package that produces management information (such as profit & loss statements, demand levels and sales to target markets) which then provides the basis for the next round of decision-making. Simulations are a form of active learning that imitate certain aspects of the business world that are otherwise hard to bring to the classroom such as working to deadlines, generally in teams, to make concrete decisions under competitive conditions, and then have students live with the consequences of those decisions (Gosen et al., 2000; Vos and Brennan, 2010). One could argue, therefore, that simulations are also intercontextual (academic and (simulated) work settings). As Hertel and Millis (2002) note: 'Simulations constitute a powerful tool for learning. They allow teachers simultaneously to integrate multiple teaching objectives in a single process. They motivate students, provide opportunities for active participation to promote deep learning, develop interactive and communication skills, and link knowledge and theory to application.'

Games require students to integrate concepts successfully within their own discipline and to think cross-functionally (Chakravorty and Franza, 2005). In a marketing simulation, student teams manage a division or small firm that produces a product such as mobile phones (Simbrand©) or jeans (MyMarketingExperience©). Teams work with and integrate marketing concepts, theories and decision areas such as segmentation, targeting, positioning, branding, product development, sales, pricing, distribution, promotion, and service quality, among others. They also make decisions that require the application and understanding of financial concepts (setting budgets, interpreting profit and loss statements), human resources (hiring, training and remunerating staff), and production and operations (forecasting, setting production levels and logistics). To integrate the various decision areas effectively, students undertake financial calculations, make forecasts, estimate demand and review market and competitor research, and link theory to practice – all of which involve trade-offs and managing constraints (e.g. fluctuations in the market environment; competitors' actions). In general, game designers are attempting to create an environment that mimics a relatively complex decision-making environment and, as Goosen et al. (2001) note: 'The assumption is that through the manipulation of multiple decision elements, and through an analysis of how their decisions in one area interact with and affect those in other areas, students will come to have a better understanding of the totality of marketing management' (p. 26).

In addition, simulation games require students to integrate skills and emotions. Students not only come to have a better understanding of how marketing decision areas interact and work together but also develop important personal and transferable skills:

> One ... aspect of simulation gaming that sets it apart from most contemporary academic disciplines is that their design, playing, and debriefing require synthesis ... [they] call for integration of faculties on the part of the players. In games, intellect ... control of emotions, and social skills are all activated in an integrated, purpose-driven way. (Hofstede et al., 2010, pp. 829–30).

Students generally start out with a poor grasp of the decision-making environment and limited ability to transfer or apply what they have learned in other courses. However, over the six to eight weeks that most educators run the simulation, students' understanding, the sophistication by which they integrate decision areas, and their ability to apply theory to practice generally improves, as does their ability to reflect critically on prior decisions. Where the educator applies specific pedagogic principles, this learning and development can be advanced.

Various decisions made by the tutor can further enhance the learning and integration of learning that takes place in a simulation. Following an overview of the various kinds of simulation games available in marketing, the remainder of this chapter will explore ways to enhance the learning from simulations, including ways to overcome some of the challenges that may arise so as to enhance the possibilities for integration of learning and the student experience.

MARKETING SIMULATION GAMES: AN OVERVIEW

Simulation games have become more sophisticated over time, with some now moving closer to the interfaces of other multi-player online games (e.g. Practice Marketing, McGraw Hill; Marketplace Live). The variety of available games means that educators can use them at different stages of the programme (Faria et al., 2009). *Introductory marketing games* provide students with insights into basic marketing concepts such as the seven P's of marketing and how they are best developed and integrated to meet the needs of a particular target market. Introductory games help students to differentiate between strategic and tactical decision-making and the majority of games come with measures of both financial and marketing performance; for example, financial statements, brand loyalty and stock management appear in MyMarketingExperience by Pearson. While some educators use them in the first year, experience has shown that they are better in later classes after the students have a foundation in core marketing concepts and processes as well as an introduction to accounting and finance. Thus, the second semester of year one is recommended; even better, in year two.

More sophisticated games that are best used in *strategy courses*, final undergraduate levels and Master's level include Markstrat by Stratx and Cesim Simbrand, for example. These games involve more detailed and complex financial analysis and marketing decision-making, thus they are more effective learning tools when students have studied strategic decision-making, analysis of business performance and potentially, production and operations courses. Finally, there are *specialist games* focusing on particular aspects of marketing such as branding, digital marketing, services marketing, sales, entrepreneurship, international marketing and B2B marketing. Overall, opportunities exist for tutors of many different marketing subjects and at different levels to engage students with an active learning tool that gives them regular practice in integrating their learning from across the curriculum, thus allowing them to grasp marketing decision-making in most, if not all, of its complexity.

Games can be integrated into an existing course, such as strategic marketing, or taught as a separate simulation course. Given that most games are designed with a series of decision-making periods, generally set up as quarterly business reporting cycles, tutors can choose to run each period weekly for the length of the game, perhaps using most of the seminar time for the simulation, thus making it ideal for a flipped-classroom learning strategy where most of the face-to-face learning involves student-centred active learning. The average number of decision-making periods across marketing simulations is eight, but the author has found that seven is generally sufficient for students to address all of the learning outcomes before losing interest. Some tutors, particularly those teaching senior level or postgraduate, choose a more intensive approach such as running the simulation over two days, generally over a weekend. The latter framework is best suited when the simulation is being used as a capstone experience for students who have already had some business experience or are in the later stages of their degree. In terms of weekly decision-making, tutors often set aside one or two hours in class each week for students to review the results of their previous decisions, consider their next moves and receive individualised feedback. The latter is absolutely critical for a deep learning experience, more of which will be discussed below under pedagogic principles for enhancing integration and learning with simulations. Students submit their weekly or periodic decisions by a deadline set by the tutor. The time should be the same each week or after a set number of hours for an intensive course. Almost immediately after the deadline, the game algorithm provides teams with results and students can begin their analysis for the next round of decisions.

Most games allow the educator to make adjustments to the level of complexity. Students can begin with a basic level of the game and over time the tutor can add additional decision areas. For example, in one popular game, tutors can change the operating conditions (e.g. economic conditions, demand levels, stage in the product life cycle), thus requiring students to rethink their current strategies and tactics under dynamic conditions.

Potential Learning Outcomes

When well set up and managed by the tutor, simulation games allow students to achieve the learning outcomes outlined in Table 5.1. Many others could be added, but these are the core outcomes of most games.

Table 5.1   Potential learning outcomes from simulation games

---

• How to undertake marketing planning, implementation and control.

• How the external macro and micro environments affect operating conditions and decision-making over time.

• The importance of constantly monitoring the external environment to anticipate and plan for changing conditions.

• The value of regular, good and timely information for improved decision-making. The value of using, buying and interpreting marketing research to improve decision-making and find new opportunities.

• How to interpret research on the environment, competitors and target markets to improve decision-making.

• The differences between strategic and tactical decision-making.

• Setting objectives, monitoring whether they are being achieved and adjusting them under different conditions.

• How critical it is to make decisions with the target market's needs, characteristics and expectations in mind.

• The significant and often difficult to predict effects that competitors can have on a company's fortunes.

• Using key performance indicators, both marketing and finance based.

• Interpreting and analysing financial and market data.

• Relationships between prices, costs, sales and contribution.

• Setting up and working within a budget.

• Calculating final prices given dealer margins, competitor pricing, customer expectations and company positioning.

• Setting brand values and monitoring brand metrics (loyalty, image, awareness).

• The relationships between and the need to carefully integrate product, price, promotional and distribution decisions.

• Costs associated with product, pricing, promotion and distribution strategies and how decisions affect outcomes.

• The interdependence of functional areas within an organisation such as marketing, finance/accounting, production, operations and human resources.

• How organisations make decisions within a competitive context and with finite resources, thus requiring trade-offs.

• Application of positioning principles and how positioning affects strategic choices (and vice versa).

• The dynamic nature of marketing decision-making wherein markets, operating conditions, competitor actions and customer expectations can change, thus requiring adaptations in strategy and tactics.

• The iterative process that is strategic marketing decision-making (not the step-by-step approach generally taught in class). The importance of effective team working and communication.

DECISION-MAKING ENVIRONMENTS

As noted above, games come in different levels of complexity. At the core of most games, however, are four features:

- The ability for students to work through the steps in strategic decision-making (environmental analysis, determining strategic direction and objectives, segmentation and targeting, positioning, branding, the integration of marketing tactics, implementation and evaluation);
- Key performance indicators and metrics that allow for understanding and analysis;
- A dynamic operating environment with available marketing research but also the need for participants to adjust their strategies to changing conditions;
- Allowing students to move from a round by round operational and often reactive decision-making approach to a more strategic and anticipatory approach to decisions.

Table 5.2 outlines the typical decision areas and features within most marketing simulation games.

Students generally begin the simulation feeling overwhelmed by the amount of information and what is expected of them in terms of the number and types of decisions to be made and how to interpret the results and metrics. Each round, they have an opportunity to revise their decisions, but the decision types remain the same until the tutor decides to increase the complexity by adding additional information, changing the operating environment and/or increasing the number of decisions to be made. All of this can be carefully controlled such that students are being challenged sufficiently to maintain their interest while at the same time allowing for some mastery of core concepts.

Practice is one pedagogic principle that is built into games. In order to enhance the learning from games, the tutor can include others from a framework known as authentic assessment (see for example: Newmann et al., 1995; Newmann et al., 1996; Gulikers et al., 2006; Rule, 2006; Ashford-Rowe et al., 2014; Vos, 2015; Lincoln and Cassidy, 2018; Villarroel et al., 2018). In addition to other principles, authentic assessment supports and provides guidance on integrating prior and ongoing learning and thus it offers a very useful framework for structuring the simulation course.

Authentic assessment principles and practices emerged out of the debates in the 1980s and early 1990s about standardised testing, its limitations in terms of learning (see for example: Frederiksen, 1984; Banta et al., 1996; Sambell et al., 2013) and the emerging research on the benefits of constructivist approaches to learning that advocate activities allowing students to construct meaning in

Table 5.2   Typical decision areas in marketing simulation games

Operational

Segmentation and positioning	Choose from 2 to 8 different customer segments who buy either directly or through channel members. Tailor aspects of the marketing mix to each segment such as product features, price, promotional tools and channel structure. May offer perceptual positioning maps. Generally games offer a range of positioning options such as broad low-cost approach, value pricing or higher priced, higher quality.
Product and product portfolio decisions	Choice to offer from 1 to 6 products, 1 or more at the beginning of the game with more available to offer as the game progresses. Configure product features based on segment and cost. Ability to add or reduce features over time. Generally, games have a product life cycle built into the algorithms – teams need to judge when the industry is reaching maturity and adjust their marketing accordingly. Allows for investment in research and development. Often allows for different after sales service packages to be added to each product.
Brand and branding decisions	Many games allow teams to choose brand names for their products and to specify brand values/characteristics for individual products. Some games use the term 'brand' while others use 'product'. Investments and decisions around a brand in one game are generally similar to investments and decisions in products in other games. May include key performance indicators around brand awareness, brand image and/or brand loyalty.
Pricing decisions	Will either be final consumer pricing or pricing to a channel member – either wholesale or retail depending on the game; need to calculate mark-ups and explore the relationship between price, sales revenue and profitability. Require students to understand the relationships between costs, competitor pricing, customer expectations, current market conditions and company strategy. Most offer promotional pricing including discounts, rebates or other forms. Differentiate between pricing strategies and pricing objectives.

Place and channel decisions.	May include 2 to 6 direct-to-customer, retail (physical and online stores); wholesale channels, depending on the game.
	Channel members use different margins depending on factors such as type of channel and level of service offered.
	Channel decisions are linked to segment characteristics, competitor offerings and cost.
	Ability to offer channel members various types of promotions.
	Opportunity to tailor the retail environment (place) depending on positioning and target market expectations.
	Supply chain and logistics decisions such as type of producer and transportation and warehousing costs (generally for unsold production).
	Use of discount channels (and lower profit margins) when all goods have not been sold.
Promotional decisions	Ability to set different promotional options for each product/brand.
	A range of promotional methods available including advertising (online and offline), direct marketing, sales promotions (to final customer and to channel members), corporate advertising, public relations, sales force and sales force incentives.
	Often include decisions about choice of media, message source (e.g. celebrity), message type and promotional objectives.
	Using the principles of Integrated Marketing Communications.
	Cost vs. benefits of promotional expenditure.
	Impact of promotional decisions on brand metrics and sales revenue.
	Carry-over effect of promotion on future periods.
Sales Force	May include the need to select how many sales people, their compensation and selling approach, and what training to offer.
	Assessing sales people's effectiveness.
	Sales force may sell direct to customer or via retailers/wholesalers.
	Hiring and firing sales people and associated costs.
	Giving sales people the ability to offer promotional pricing and other incentives to channel members.
Production	Teams set production levels based on analysis of demand, operating conditions and other factors.
	Generally allow a margin for under- or over-production before a team is charged extra.
	Include warehousing and/or inventory costs.
	May allow for stock buybacks, discount channels or disposal costs for excess inventory (at a cost).
	May allow for investment in increased plant capacity and/or new plant technology to allow for product upgrades or new products.
	Production process likely to have both fixed and variable costs.
Strategy and planning	

Planning and planning tools	May include business and marketing planning tools to allow for forecasting (see Budgeting and Forecasting below).
	May include cash flow planning.
	Generally allows students to think about their source of competitive advantage and conduct a SWOT analysis.
	Positioning tied to strategic decisions and strategy options.
	Documentation to help with each part of the planning process that includes strategic options such as 'broad, low-cost strategy' or 'focused differentiation strategy'.
Research – macro, micro environments including competitor data	May provide free market updates for each decision period with information on changes to the macro environment (some or all elements of the PEST), customer needs and other factors.
	Allows teams to purchase a range of market research reports such as market share and sales reports for all teams, market analysis, sales by segment, customer preferences, reports from focus groups on product tests, conjoint analysis and perceptual maps, among others.
	Offers competitor data, some free and others at a cost.
	Operating conditions including the macro environment can change either with tutor input or as the game progresses.
Financial decisions, budgeting and forecasting.	Budgets may be fixed each period or vary depending on performance in the previous round (all tend to provide a minimum budget regardless of performance).
	May provide budgeting and forecasting spreadsheets where teams can enter products by segment, associated costs, production levels research and development spending and/or after-sales service costs (e.g. warranty).
	Allow for the creation of pro forma income statements, cash flow and/or balance sheets, production schedules among others.
	With budgeting software, teams can change their decisions as many times as they like before making the final decision.
	Generally includes both fixed and variable costs. Fixed costs may change during the game based on team decisions (e.g. investing in new plant) or due to inflation. Variable costs may change depending on sales, marketing tactics, competitor tactics, changes to the market environment and/or production levels. The exact changes to costs are not generally known to teams until after they have their results.
	Some games allow students to save money for future decisions (i.e. not spend their entire budget each period).
	Some games allow teams to raise money through short-term borrowing, selling assets (equity or debt instruments) selling inventory or investing cash.

Metrics and performance indicators	Most games offer a range of metrics to help with analysis of results and decision-making. Include from 4 to 45 metrics, some of which may only be viewed by the tutor. Generally include an income or contribution statement each period; some have balance sheets, market share and positioning reports. Among the metrics available are financial statements, team position with respect to competitors (measured on a range of metrics), operating profit, market share, segments served, products and product features, portfolio analysis, stock management, demand and supply, marketing metrics (e.g. brand awareness, image, loyalty, promotional effectiveness, sales to target market, distribution effectiveness), dealer ratings, effectiveness of R&D spending. Some of these metrics may only be available for purchase. Allows for basic to highly sophisticated financial and marketing effectiveness analyses. More sophisticated games include conjoint, regression and shareholder value analyses.
Research and development, investments and longer-term perspectives.	Many games allow teams to invest in research and development (R&D) to upgrade current products, reduce current features or introduce new products to meet changing customer needs, address a changing product life cycle or market conditions and to remain competitive. Effect of investment in R&D generally occurs over more than one period, thus requiring students to consider the effect of their decisions over the longer term. Other expenditures are also viewed from an investment and longer-term perspective. These may include decisions about technology, capacity, inventory, financial investments (e.g. investing cash, purchasing bonds) and marketing investments (e.g. promotion, new product development).
Variable game features	
Decision periods	Between 1 and 10 decision periods, with each decision representing either a quarter or a financial year.
Levels of complexity	Many games have levels of complexity. The tutor may set the initial level with the opportunity to raise the levels over time.
Changes to the decision-making environment	Most games have built-in changes to aspects of the operating and decision-making environment that come into effect over the duration of the game such as changes to the economy or the product life cycle. As noted above, many games allow tutors to make some changes to the operating environment to make the game more or less challenging depending on the student cohort or to demonstrate the impact of certain events (e.g. recession, maturity phase) on decision-making and results.

Competitive framework	Most games allow teams to compete against each other, with some allowing students or teams to compete against the game itself.
Assessments	Many games offer built-in assessments such as multiple-choice questions or short answer questions.
	Most games provide guidance to students on key concepts and decision areas; some also provide guidance on how to write up business, marketing and financial plans, how to prepare a presentation for a Board of Directors. In some cases specific marking rubrics are included.
	Some games offer assessment of team performance, leadership and peer evaluation tools and provide guidance to the tutor on how to grade them.

their own terms rather than memorising existing material for a test (Biggs, 1996, 2003). Over time, as further research has demonstrated their value, the principles have evolved and other principles and practices added and validated (see for example: Fook and Sidhu, 2010; Swaffield, 2011; Villarroel et al., 2018). Rather than being a specific type of assessment, authentic assessment is a way to structure *all* of the learning and activities within a course, including the means by which students will be assessed for grades. The principles and practices work particularly well in structuring an effective simulation course. While there are many conceptualisations of authentic assessment, most researchers advocate for the core principles outlined in Table 5.3. Each will be discussed in relation to the simulation course. Table 5.3 outlines the main principles of authentic assessment practice.

Table 5.3   Principles of authentic assessment

1. The applied nature and/or real-world/work world value of the assessment task;
2. Students perform or create a product as the output;
3. Developmental opportunities with formative assessment and regular feedback;
4. Challenge and complexity of tasks and issues of transfer;
5. Sufficient and varied activities/assessments to make up the whole;
6. Known criteria and assessment literacy;
7. Opportunities for reflection;
8. Interaction and collaboration.

The Applied Nature and/or 'Work World' Value of the Task

Motivation to learn is increased when students are involved in active and applied learning tasks that can also be of value to them in a professional setting (Sambell et al., 2013). Simulations are designed to allow students actively to experience marketing decision-making in as close to a work-world setting as possible but without the same level of risk. Tutors can help students to see the value of their learning from a simulation by augmenting the game with lessons and cases from industry to demonstrate the challenges marketers face. YouTube is a good source of short marketing case studies. Often, they are delivered by academics or respected marketing specialists. For example, The London Business Forum interview with Howard Schultz, former CEO of Starbucks, discusses how the company adapted during the financial crisis (2008–2012) by recreating the store experience for customers and going back to core brand values so as to differentiate the company from other coffee retailers and survive a difficult period. The lessons to be learned include the importance of focusing on a few concrete and unique values or aspects of the organisation that set it apart from competitors and how these values can be conveyed in brand communications, both consistently and in an integrated fashion.

Students Perform or Create a Product as Output

As noted above, authentic assessment developed from the debates and criticism of standardised testing (1980s–1990s) or what has since that time been called 'traditional assessment'. As Boud (1995) argued, too often 'assessment tasks are set to encourage a narrow instrumental approach to learning that emphasises the reproduction of what is presented, at the expense of critical thinking, deep understanding and independent activity' (p. 104). An outcome of this debate was a move into the foreground of constructivist approaches where learning is viewed as a 'process of active engagement through which learners construct meaning and new ideas, taking into account current and previous knowledge' (Vos, 2015, p. 39). Learning is not 'imposed' but takes place within active learning situations set within particular contexts where students assume more control and build their own understanding through practice. In these settings, the goal is to create a more complete, complex and integrated understanding over time by adding more elements to be learned and integrated, thus requiring more critical thinking and deep learning if the student is to master the evolving, multi-element problem or context. To support the learning, tutors need to scaffold new information carefully so that students are not overwhelmed or become confused or demoralised.

Challenge and Complexity of Tasks and Issues of Transfer

Simulations are generally designed to allow for increasing complexity and/or adding decision-making elements each period. For example, in one simulation students begin by selecting characteristics of the target markets they wish to serve. Lessons about segmentation are embedded into this set of decisions.

Students must ensure that their chosen segments are accessible, measurable and substantial enough to allow their company to be profitable. However, by choosing too many criteria for the segment (e.g. age, income, stage in the adoption process, loyalty level, among others), students find that their chosen segments become too small, thus teaching them the importance of making trade-offs between which criteria to select and which to leave out. More importantly, as the game progresses, students begin to see how their segmentation decisions are affecting profitability. In addition, as new decisions bring in other areas of marketing, they begin to see how an integrated set of decisions (e.g. product features, pricing, choice of retail locations and various promotional decisions) needs to be tailored to their target market characteristics if they are to increase customer satisfaction and profitability. In this particular game, the results from each decision round include measures of customer satisfaction, brand awareness, and sales to target markets. These quarterly metrics can be used to interpret the effectiveness of both targeting and marketing mix decisions.

Thus, following authentic assessment principles, games provide a scaffolded level of complexity as new elements are added each round and, in some games, where tutors can add greater complexity over the course of the simulation. There are also ongoing opportunities for practising and coming to terms with prior elements introduced in earlier rounds, such as the importance of meeting target markets needs and expectations, setting the appropriate level of production under a given operating environment (e.g. growth or slow-down) and for a chosen positioning strategy (e.g. volume-based, lower quality vs profitability-based, higher quality).

Since the simulation gives teams the opportunity to make a series of up to 10 decisions (as noted above, seven is recommended) with each decision round requiring students to revisit and refine prior decisions while also adding new elements, there are ongoing opportunities for practising key concepts and processes. In higher education we often underestimate the value of practice in learning. We give students one or more assessments during the semester often without giving them multiple opportunities to practise that which is being assessed and yet we know both from research and experience that practice, and in particular 'deliberate practice' is essential to skill development (e.g. Ericsson et al., 1993; Anderson, 1996; Bransford et al., 2000; Campitelli and Gobet, 2011; Ericsson and Pool, 2016). As noted, simulations have built-in iterative processes that allow students to practise making the same decisions each week, with additional decision areas being added in by the game and/or by the tutor. In most marketing simulations, students make product, pricing, distribution and promotional decisions each decision round, although they may begin making decisions in one part of the marketing mix before moving on to others in upcoming rounds. Students can choose to make the same decisions as previously or adjust one or more of the decision areas. In the early stages of the game students may not be able to identify how their specific decisions led to the outcomes they receive after submission, but by making similar decisions each week, and with tutor feedback, they begin to see the relationship between their choices, how their outcomes are based not upon the results of a single decision made (e.g. price) but based on an integrated set of decisions within a competitive environment affected by external factors.

Suggestions for summative assessment of learning from the game are provided below, but the author recommends that students should not be given grades for their performance on key metrics (e.g. level of profit, market share, brand loyalty) or from their ranking in terms of profitability at the end of the game. In the author's experience this puts too much emphasis on the competitive aspect of the game and not enough on the learning that is taking place. It can also lead to early demoralisation and loss of interest in the game amongst teams who are not performing well. Furthermore, just because a team is highly profitable or has high market share does not mean that members truly understand the reasons for their success. As noted, they may attribute it to only one or two of their decision areas and not see how all of the factors work together. Winning teams can be awarded a certificate or another non-graded recognition of their achievement in order to provide some acknowledgement of their decision-making successes.

Note that even if grades are not awarded for achieving top scores on one or more metrics, students still play the game competitively and seek to 'win'. This competitive element presents both benefits and challenges. In terms of benefits, wanting to be the top team promotes motivation, engagement with the game and learning. In terms of challenges, teams that consistently score lower than others can become demotivated and disengaged or, as noted above, focus on single tactics such as reducing price as a way to improve their position. Given the competitive nature of the game, emotions can run high and given the complexity involved with integrating decision areas successfully to achieve good scores, students can begin to feel negative emotions and stress that the tutor needs to manage. Thus, tutors should monitor the stress and motivation levels amongst students and sense when these factors are becoming detrimental to learning. However, bringing teams who have not been performing well back into the learning can be difficult. One approach that has some positive outcomes is to remind the students that those who have faced the most challenges generally achieve the most learning overall and thus will have much to discuss in a final graded assignment that asks them to reflect on their learning. Another approach is to set out non-graded awards for a range of successes such as achieving the highest mark share, the greatest overall improvement during the game, best at meeting target market needs, strongest brand loyalty and other important measures of marketing success and to congratulate each team on their achievement in a class setting. Each week, during the class-wide component of the debriefing session, the tutor can point out which teams are achieving top scores on a range of metrics and also discuss why these metrics are important in marketing in the short and long run, thus including a larger number of teams in the 'winning' and 'achieving' categories.

Challenge can also keep students motivated. In selecting the game to use in their course, tutors can choose a simulation that allows for increasing complexity over time, for example by increasing the number and type of decisions to be made each round and by changing the economic conditions from growth to slow-down or recession. These changes are either built into the game itself or made by the tutor at a point when he or she feels the students can take on more complexity. In addition to maintaining motivation, these adjustments move the simulation closer to the reality of what students will experience in their marketing careers. Nevertheless, tutors need to manage the enhanced complexity and seek to balance keeping the students engaged while ensuring that the increasing complexity is not greater than the students' competence. Getting the right level of challenge and complexity for students is learned from experience but generally, the tutor will come to recognise or sense when the balance is right. To aid in getting the balance right, tutors are reminded of one of Chickering and Gamson's (1987) 'Seven principles of good practice in undergraduate education': communicating high expectations. Setting higher expectations enhances motivation to learn. Other researchers have considered the benefits of setting tasks that are challenging. Csikszentmihalyi (2008) for example demonstrated that learning motivation, affect, arousal and concentration are highest when the levels of challenge and skill are perceived to be about equal and when both are perceived as high. Alter et al. (2007) have also done numerous studies across a range of learning tasks on the benefits of providing more challenge. They find that learners assign their cognitive resources depending on the perceived difficulty of a task. By making the task more challenging than what students may be used to (what Alter et al. (2007) call disfluency), they tend to increase their effort to learn.

Simulations do expose students to many of the realities of decision-making at work with its complexities and ambiguities and the potential for multiple solutions and perspectives. Problem solving in these contexts requires higher order thinking skills such as analysis, evaluation, critical thinking and revising of previous decisions. Games help students to see that there are often no 'right or wrong' answers to problems and that even when decisions have been effective (in increasing sales or profitability for example), generally some trade-offs have had to be made given a changing external environment and competitors' decisions. Simulations also teach students that sometimes success is achieved without managers having a clear understanding of why, given that so many factors are at play. Thus, they are learning not only about the complexity of good decision-making but also ambiguity and uncertainty. This can make learning quite uncomfortable but again, helps to prepare them for the reality of outcomes from organisational decision-making.

Developmental Opportunities with Formative Assessment and Regular Feedback

The role of the tutor in helping students to improve their understanding and move towards higher levels of complexity is therefore critical, as is regular feedback on each team's decisions. While the game itself provides weekly formative feedback through metrics reports that are generated in the results stage, the depth of student understanding can be greatly enhanced with debriefing from the tutor.

Much has been written on the importance of tutor debriefing to individual teams after they have considered their results. Crookall (2010) goes as far as to say that the learning from simulations comes more from well constructed debriefing sessions than from the game itself. Guidance on how to enrich debriefing sessions comes from a range of studies (Crookall, 2010; Dieckmann et al., 2009; Fanning and Gaba, 2007; Kriz 2010; Peters and Vissers, 2004; Petranek, 2000; Rudolph et al., 2006). Among the recommendations is to continually help students make connections between the world of work and the game, between what they have learned in other courses and the game (intra- and interdisciplinary integration) and between the game and students' own experiences (intercontextual integration). Active discussions between the tutor and individual teams work best as the tutor can draw out students' understanding and experiences in the students' own words, thus allowing them to link theory to practice, become more self-reflective and to solidify what they have learned.

Debriefing and feedback work best when the tutor takes on a coaching role (Wolfe, 1997). Wolfe (1997) notes that '[h]ands on instructor involvement, coaching and debriefing are needed'. (Wolfe, 1997, p. 369). A coach 'takes a more active part in the simulation by playing the game along with the students and/or by encouraging them to stretch outside their comfort zones and by not telling them the "right" way to do things' (Vos, 2015). Kriz (2010) argues that debriefing should be done both with individual teams and with the class as a whole because all can benefit from the many different perspectives on what the results mean, the challenges teams are facing, and how they are addressing them. Petranek (2000) advocates for the benefits of written debriefing/reflection each round.

Debriefing and formative feedback along with active class discussion should occur after each decision round. Presenting the class with charts of current metrics from all teams such as operating profits, sales revenues, gross margins, expenses, market share, and/or brand loyalty is a good starting point. Or different metrics can be selected for sharing and discussion each week to remind students of their importance. For example, the tutor might share sales revenue, cost of sales and gross margin from all teams' results in order to discuss the importance of setting an appropriate margin and the relationship between sales revenue and strategic positioning (e.g. low-margin, high-volume approaches vs high-margin, lower-volume approaches with greater marketing support). Students can then be introduced to the link between strategic objectives, positioning and pricing strategy (e.g. maximising market share vs maximising current profit), to various pricing methods (e.g. mark-up pricing, perceived value pricing, going rate/competitor responsive pricing) and how to calculate mark-ups.

In these discussions, the tutor is revisiting students' prior learning, calling upon them to transfer their prior learning to the game and integrate that learning, thus providing an opportunity to identify gaps in knowledge that can make transfer difficult (Bransford et al., 2000). For example, students in lower level courses generally have difficulties interpreting financial results even though they have taken classes in accounting and finance. As noted above, transfer of knowledge is difficult when the prior learning was highly contextualised. Learners may not be able to easily apply their knowledge of financial statements viewed from an accounting perspective to that viewed from a marketing perspective. Thus, tutors can take the opportunity to provide exercises and activities to review the relationship between sales and demand, sales revenue and average prices (the price that goods are sold at in a game may not reflect the price set by the team as some goods may be sold in discount channels at lower prices), setting the sales margin to reflect positioning (e.g. a high volume retailer will set a lower price per unit than a luxury retailer but requires many more sales to make a profit), sales margin and cost of goods sold and other factors affecting operating profit. Students can be given exercises to calculate various ratios and then be asked to track them as the game progresses, knowing that they may be required to discuss these ratios in their end of game report or presentation.

As part of each week's debriefing, the tutor continually reminds students how the game is demonstrating that a successful marketing strategy requires the integration of marketing tools and tactics and that the results, whether good or not so good, are a reflection of this integration, not the outcome of any single decision made by the team. This is by no means an easy idea for students to come to terms with. At earlier stages in the game, they are often at a loss to explain their results, generally pointing to one or a few reasons only. Those with lower profits or operating losses will invariably turn to pricing as the answer to their problems. Despite their earlier decisions to, for example, use high end positioning and to invest in a product with additional features, their reflex is to turn to a single tool to improve their fortunes and it is invariably price. This very common response by students demonstrates that team members are not yet understanding the difference between strategy and tactics, how all of their decisions are acting as an integrated whole or the influence of external factors such as competitors' decisions or the operating environment on their results. Therefore, the tutor needs to step in and remind students of what is likely to occur if they simply lower the price (further alienate their target markets, earn less per unit sold and/or decreasing demand) and for them to think more deeply and broadly about what could be affecting their results.

It should be clear from the discussion above that the tutor needs to know the game well and to wear many hats during the simulation exercise. As Hofstede et al. (2010) argue, '[f]acilitating simulation games is a complicated, multifaceted skill and very hard to teach in any way other than by experience' (p. 837). As Vos (2015) noted, the tutor needs to be able 'to undertake and switch between the roles of motivator, coach, mediator of disputes, administrator, and when called upon, teacher' (p. 87) to ensure the smooth running of the game and the ongoing motivation and learning of students.

Sufficient and Varied Activities Make Up the Whole and Known Criteria and Assessment Literacy

Students benefit when they have many opportunities to learn the material through practice but also through different activities. The game itself already offers students a wide variety of activities as part of their learning and this can be enhanced with additional tasks related to understanding mark-ups, financial ratios, and branding, for example. In addition, as noted above, the tutor can use videos as well as short cases and lectures to explore theories and how marketing firms have managed difficulties arising from poor decision-making or a changing environment. The assessment choices are themselves additional activities to practise and extend student knowledge and understanding.

We have seen how simulations with their regular feedback via game results and tutor debriefing provide students with a great deal of formative feedback. How, therefore, should students be assessed for grades? In prior research with 35 simulation users in the UK, the author found that the most commonly used forms of simulation summative assessment are final group reports, individual reflective essays on learning from the simulation and final group presentations (often to a 'board of directors' made up of the tutor, supporting seminar tutors and perhaps guests from industry) (Vos, 2015). Tutors in the study also used interim summative assessments including multiple choice tests on game features (often provided by the game publisher), team presentations, weekly learning logs and short individual reflective pieces on students learning. Fewer than 10 per cent used peer assessment, but when done well, this can be a valuable learning opportunity for students. Interim peer assessment is recommended in addition to a final one, and as with all learning approaches, students should be coached in the value of peer assessment, how to undertake it constructively, as well as ways to use the findings to improve the participation and input of all members of a group. More discussion on peer assessment is provided in the section on interaction and collaboration.

Assessment should provide opportunities for students to demonstrate what they have learned but also to fill in any gaps in that learning. It should not simply be a 'test' of what they know. Reflective assessments are of this type, and reflection on learning is a core principle of authentic assessment (Herrington et al., 2010; Lombardi, 2007). It too will be discussed further below. However, another approach to assessing learning is to hold a group discussion forum where the tutor presents questions to the team as a whole based on each learning objective. The questions may be given in advance so the teams can prepare, but the students know that each and every member of the team is responsible for addressing the questions. This approach allows the teams to think about and explain areas where they performed well, as well as those where they were less effective, and be asked to give reasons for both outcomes. Where they have had poor results, students can be asked to speculate on what they could have done to improve the outcome, what factors outside their control may have played a part and what they might do to buffer their company in future rounds. A 20-minute forum is recommended, but it could be longer depending on the tutor's available assessment time. Each student should then be required to write a response to a question from the forum where the tutor felt they did not respond very well or in sufficient depth. This approach allows for individual assessment in addition to a group assessment component. Thus, even if some students come to the final assessment with only some understanding of the learning outcomes, the forum approach will give them an opportunity to revisit concepts and ideas for deeper learning.

A key principle of authentic assessment is assessment literacy – in other words prior to undertaking and submitting the work, students should have a very good idea of how they are going to be assessed. Simply providing a rubric and going over it with students is insufficient given that a major and real challenge for students is understanding what their tutor is looking for, what he or she will put emphasis on and/or the depth of discussion required. For each assessment that a student undertakes with a different tutor, these questions are being considered. Every tutor is different and assessment generally has subjective components (even multiple choice tests have elements of subjectivity given how statements are phrased). The tutor has tacit knowledge of his or her expectations (Gulikers et al., 2004), often not even explicit to themselves until the assignments come in. Thus, Price et al. (2011) ask tutors to help students become more 'assessment literate'. As noted, this goes beyond simply going over the criteria to be graded to include assignments from pre-vious years (without grades) – weak, good and excellent. Give students class time to review one or more from each category along with a grading rubric and ask them to assign what they believe is an appropriate grade before discussing with others how and why they arrived at their decision (see also Rust et al., 2003). Price et al. (2011) note that following the application of this approach in their own classes, it was extended to the entire business school such that all first year students were given this opportunity on more than one occasion. The overall result was improved work from the students in both years one and two (the length of the research study) and higher grades.

Enhancing assessment literacy through using exemplars of prior simulation assessment has worked very well in the author's experience. Given the range of learning that has taken place across the simulation course and given that different members of the team may have undertaken alternative tasks over the course of the game (e.g. one student analyses the financial statements; others focus on other metrics and decision-making) by the end, each individual is likely to have learned some aspects of the game in more depth, potentially at the expense of other aspects. Ideally, each student should achieve all of the learning outcomes in the simulation course and thus some individual assessment is recommended. In order that all students are prepared for the assessment, exemplars from previous years can show the depth and breadth of knowledge and learning that is expected.

Reflection

One common form of assessment with simulations is the reflective report in which the student or students look back on a range of decision areas and results, consider what they learned from those activities/outcomes and then show their understanding further by explaining what they could have or should have done to improve their outcomes. During any reflective exercise, students are exploring what they have done or learned in order to make new connections, form new understandings, but also to identify weak or missing links in knowledge or skills. In addition to the cognitive-structuring benefits of reflection, it allows students to fill in any gaps in their learning.

Thus reflection on learning should involve some demonstration of what the student knows now that they did not know before, provide an opportunity to address gaps in their learning that were not fully addressed in the activity, plus a discussion of the challenges they faced in the learning process, how they did or did not overcome them and what this means for future learning situations. During this process, a student is exploring not only knowledge gained, but the way in which they approached their learning or their 'metacognition'. Boud et al. (1985), among others, have researched the value of 'metacognitive' thinking processes, also known as 'thinking about one's thinking processes'. Such an analysis of one's approach to learning and thinking can help students identify any weaknesses and strengths and how they might approach learning in the future. The student is not reflecting on content so much as how they approached decision-making and analysis in the game.

Experts in both reflection and metacognitive thinking caution that these practices do not come naturally and students should be coached in how to undertake both effectively; there are some excellent resources available for tutors such as those by Moon (1999, 2004) and Kramarski et al. (2002). Given the strong evidence for the effectiveness of reflection in contributing to deep learning, students should be given opportunities to learn these skills. Self-reflection can be developed during debriefing sessions where all team members are present and the tutor can ask questions that require them to consider why they made certain decisions, the outcome of these decisions, and the factors that led to these results. As noted, the key element of coaching in these discussions is helping the students to understand that, more often than not, a single decision (e.g. price or positioning choice) did not lead to their results. Students should be encouraged to consider how their decisions acted as an integrated whole and also that despite making very good decisions, competition and external factors are also likely to have influenced their results.

Interaction and Collaboration

When students are asked what they have learned from the simulation, working effectively in a team comes up surprisingly often in addition to other marketing and business-related knowledge and skills. From the perspective of authentic assessment, many work-related tasks take place in teams and therefore learning should reflect that (Reeves and Okey, 1996; Herrington and Herrington, 2006). More importantly are the insights students gain from others' ideas, knowledge and approaches to learning. Research on social-constructivist approaches to learning point to the value of collaborative discussions in helping students move towards greater levels of understanding and performance (Biggs, 1996, 2003; Vygotsky, 1978; Lave and Wenger, 1991). Team members can also motivate each other to perform at higher levels and group discussions can uncover answers to problems that a single individual may not have arrived at or taken much longer to grasp. Groups generally bring together a diverse range of skills, thus those with greater knowledge and skill in one area (e.g. understanding and working with financial statements; an understanding of segmentation) can help to improve the understanding and skills of others. Furthermore, in being called upon by team members to articulate their reasons for suggesting a particular decision, a student is able to clarify his or her own thoughts.

Ideally, of course, the tutor seeks to ensure that every member of the team has grasped each of the learning outcomes from the simulation, including the importance of integrating all decisions to meet the needs of the target market while meeting financial and marketing goals. However, students approach the simulation differently and some are less motivated than others. Often the author has watched students not participating in group discussions, and instead looking at their phones or simply sitting in silence. Student demotivation can occur because they haven't taken the time to really understand the simulation and the reasons behind their weekly results, thus they are left behind. Or, they are having trouble grasping certain aspects of the game while others in their group are doing so more quickly.

Therefore, as with reflection and metacognition it is important to begin the simulation by providing guidelines on how to work effectively as a team. More time should be put into this than the reader might think and it should be revisited regularly throughout the simulation. Boud et al.'s (2014) edited work on peer learning provides valuable insights and tips on how to improve learning within teams. They also provide guidelines in building peer assessment into the course as an additional supporting mechanism to enhance team performance. The work by Kayes et al. (2005) on developing team effectiveness is also very helpful as is the shorter work on peer assessment by McDonald (2015). In his article on debriefing, Kriz (2010) also gives many tips for improving group functioning in simulations.

In the author's experience, team size should not exceed four students. Three also works well. Smaller teams increase the likelihood that all members will contribute to the decision-making and analysis of results, thus enhancing the opportunity for all students to learn deeply from the simulation experience.

SUMMARY

Simulations offer one of the greatest opportunities for students to integrate their learning from across the marketing and business curriculum, thus enhancing their learning while also allowing them to gain insights into the challenges of marketing practice. The disparate nature of most curriculum design today leaves students with few opportunities to bring their learning together in a coherent way, and they can leave higher education without a clear sense of the realities of their profession as a complex interplay of marketing and business functions affected by ever-changing external forces and competitor actions. Simulation games can be run in stand-alone courses or as part of a strategic marketing or specialist marketing course given that so many games are now available for different levels and subject areas. When structured using authentic assessment principles, simulations offer excellent opportunities to enhance the learning experience for students, to encourage deep learning and to provide a fun and competitive alternative to standard classroom activities. This chapter has made the argument that students need more opportunities to integrate their learning and simulations are among the best learning tools for this purpose. When applying authentic assessment principles to the structure and management of the course, students can also develop analysis, problem solving, reflection, team work and other important skills valued by employers and have the opportunity for weekly practice of these skills leading to a higher level of understanding and greater likelihood that they can apply what they have learned in a work situation.

REFERENCES

Ackerman, D.S., Gross, B.L. and Perner, L. (2003). Instructor, student, and employer perceptions on preparing marketing students for changing business landscapes. *Journal of Marketing Education*, 25(1): 46–56.
Alter, A.L., Oppenheimer, D.M., Epley, N. and Eyre, R.N. (2007). Overcoming intuition: Metacognitive difficulty activates analytic reasoning. *Journal of Experimental Psychology*, 136(4): 569–76.
Anderson, J.R. (1996). ACT: A simple theory of complex cognition. *American Psychologist*, 51(4): 355–68.
Ashford-Rowe, K., Herrington, J. and Brown, C. (2014). Establishing the critical elements that determine authentic assessment. *Assessment and Evaluation in Higher Education*, 39(2): 205–22.
Banta, T.W., Lund, J.P., Black, K.E. and Oblander, F.W. (eds) (1996). *Assessment in Practice: Putting Principles to Work on College Campuses*. San Francisco, CA: Jossey-Bass.
Barber, J.P. (2009). Integration of learning: Meaning making for undergraduates through connection, application, and synthesis. PhD Thesis University of Michigan. Available at: http://bit.ly/1P80z5d.
Barber, J.P. (2014). Integration of learning model: How college students integrate learning. *New Directions for Higher Education*, 2014(165): 7–17.
Biggs, J. (2003). *Teaching for Quality Learning at University*, 2nd edn. Buckingham: Open University Press.
Biggs, J.B. (1996). Enhancing teaching through constructive alignment. *Higher Education*, 32: 347–64.
Boud, D. (1995). Assessment and learning: Contradictory or complementary. In P. Knight (ed.), *Assessment for Learning in Higher Education*, London: Kogan Page.
Boud, D., Cohen, R. and Sampson, J. (2014). *Peer Learning in Higher Education: Learning From and With Each Other*. Abingdon: Routledge.
Boud, D., Keogh, R. and Walker, D. (eds) (1985). *Reflection: Turning Experience into Learning*. Abingdon: Routledge.
Bransford, J.D., Brown, A.L. and Cocking, R.R. (eds) (2000). *How People Learn: Brain, Mind, Experience and School*, 2nd edn. Washington, DC: National Academies Press.
Campitelli, G. and Gobet, F. (2011). Deliberate practice: Necessary but not sufficient. *Current Directions in Psychological Science*, 20(5): 280–85.
Catterall, M., Maclaran, P. and Stevens, L. (2002). Critical reflection in the marketing curriculum. *Journal of Marketing Education*, 24(3): 184–92.

Chakravorty, S.S. and Franza, R.M. (2005). Enhancing cross-functional decision making: A simulation approach. *Decision Sciences Journal of Innovative Education*, 3(2): 331–7.

Chickering, A.W. and Gamson, Z.F. (1987). Seven principles for good practice in undergraduate education. *The Wingspread Journal*, 1–10.

Craciun, G. and Corrigan, H.B. (2010). An integrative experiential learning project in the undergraduate branding course: Creating a marketing department brochure. *Journal of Marketing Education*, 32(2): 116–17.

Crittenden, V. and Crittenden, W. (2015). Digital and social media marketing in business education: Implications for the marketing curriculum. *Journal of Marketing Education*, (37): 71–5.

Crookall, D. (2010). Serious games, debriefing, and simulation/gaming as a discipline. *Simulation & Gaming*, 41(6): 898–920.

Csikszentmihalyi, M. (1996). Motivation and creativity: Toward a synthesis of structural and energistic approaches to cognition. *New Ideas in Psychology*, 6(2): 159–76.

Csikszentmihalyi, M. (2008). *Flow: The Psychology of Optimal Experience.* New York: Harper Perennial Modern Classics.

DeConinck, J. and Steiner, T. (1999). Developing an integrated finance and marketing MBA core course. *Journal of Marketing Education*, 21(1): 44–50.

Dieckmann, P., Molin Friss, S., Lippert, A. and Ostergaard, D. (2009). The art and science of debriefing in simulation: Ideal and practice. *Medical Teacher*, 31(7): 287–94.

Elam, E.L.R. and Spotts, H.E. (2004). Achieving marketing curriculum integration: A live case study approach. *Journal of Marketing Education*, 26(1): 50–65.

Ericsson, A. and Pool, R. (2016). *Peak: Secrets from the New Science of Expertise.* New York: Eamon Dolan/Houghton Mifflin Harcourt.

Ericsson, K.A., Krampe, R.T. and Tesch-Romer, C. (1993). The role of deliberate practice in the acquisition of expert performance. *Psychological Review*, 100(3): 363–406.

Fanning, R.M. and Gaba, D.M. (2007). The role of debriefing in simulation-based learning. *Simulation in Healthcare*, 2(2): 115–25.

Faria, A.J., Hutchinson, D., Wellington, W.J. and Gold, S. (2009). Developments in business gaming: A review of the past 40 years. *Simulation & Gaming*, 40(4): 464–87.

Fook, C.Y. and Sidhu, G.K. (2010). Authentic assessment and pedagogical strategies in higher education. *Journal of Social Sciences*, 6(2): 153–61.

Frederiksen, N. (1984). The real test bias: Influences of testing on teaching and learning. *American Psychologist*, 39(3): 193–202.

Goosen, K., Jensen, R. and Wells, R. (2001). Purpose and learning benefits of simulations: A design and development perspective. *Simulation & Gaming*, 32(1): 21–39.

Gosen, J.J., Washbush, J. and Scott, T. (2000). Initial data on a test bank assessing total enterprise simulation learning. *Developments in Business Simulation and Experiential Learning*, 27: 166–71.

Gulikers, J.T.M., Bastiaens, T.J. and Kirschner, P.A. (2004). A five-dimensional framework for authentic assessment. *Educational Technology Research and Development*, 52(3): 67–86.

Gulikers, J.T.M., Bastiaens, T.J. and Kirschner, P.A. (2006). Student perceptions of assessment authenticity: Study approaches and learning outcome. *Studies in Educational Evaluation*, 32(4): 381–400.

Herrington, J. and Herrington, A. (2006). Authentic conditions for authentic assessment: Aligning task and assessment. In A. Bunker and I. Vardi (eds), *Research and Development in Higher Education* (Vol. 29, pp. 146e151). Milperra: HERDSA.

Herrington, J., Reeves, T.C. and Oliver, R. (2010). *A Guide to Authentic E-learning*. London: Routledge.

Hertel, J.P. and Millis B.J. (2002). *Using Simulations to Promote Learning in Higher Education: An Introduction*. Sterling, VA: Stylus Publishing.

Hofstede, G.J., de Caluwe, L. and Peters, V. (2010). Why simulation games work: In search of the active substance: A synthesis. *Simulation & Gaming*, 41(6): 824–23.

Huber, M.T. and Hutchings, P. (2008). Integrative learning. *Peer Review*, 10(4): 31.

Huber, M.T., Hutchings, P., Gale, R., Miller, R. and Breen, M. (2007). Leading initiatives for integrative learning. *Liberal Education*, 93(2): 46–51.

Kayes, A.B., Kayes, D.C. and Kolb, D.A. (2005). Developing teams using the Kolb team learning experience. *Simulation & Gaming*, 36(3): 355–63.

Kedia, B., and Mukerjee, D. (1999). Global managers: Developing a mindset for global competitiveness. *Journal of World Business*, 34: 230–51.

Kramarski, B., Mevarech, Z.R. and Arami, M. (2002). The effects of metacognitive instruction solving mathematical authentic tasks. *Educational Studies in Mathematics*, 49(2): 225–50.

Kriz, W.C. (2010). A systemic-constructivist approach to the facilitation and debriefing of simulations and games. *Simulation Gaming*, 41(5): 663–80.

Kuh, G.D. (2008). Why integration and engagement are essential to effective educational practice in the twenty-first century. *Peer Review*, 10(4): 27–8.

Lave, J. and Wenger, E. (1991). *Situated Learning: Legitimate Peripheral Participation*. Cambridge: Cambridge University Press.

Lincoln, T.J. and Casidy, R. (2018). Authentic assessment in business education: Its effects on student satisfaction and promoting behaviour. *Studies in Higher Education*, 43(3): 401–415.

Lombardi, M. (2007). Authentic learning for the 21st century: An overview. Paper 1: 2007. EDUCAUSE Learning Initiative. Accessed 1 March 2017 at https://net .educause.edu/ir/library/pdf/ELI3009.pdf.

McDonald, B. (2015). *Peer Assessment that Works: A Guide for Teachers*. Lanham, MD: Rowman and Littlefield Publishers.

Moon, J.A. (1999). *Reflection in Learning and Professional Development: Theory and Practice*. London: Kogan Page.

Moon, J.A. (2004). *A Handbook of Reflective and Experiential Learning: Theory and Practice*. Abingdon: Routledge.

Newmann, F.M., Marks, H.M. and Gamoran, A. (1996). Authentic pedagogy and student performance. *American Journal of Education*, 104(4): 280–312.

Newmann, F.M., Secada, W. and Wehlage, G. (1995). *A Guide to Authentic Instruction and Assessment: Vision, Standards and Scoring*. Alexandria, VA: ASCD.

Pappas, E. (2004). Teaching thinking and problem solving in the university curriculum: A rationale. Proceedings (juried) of the 2004 American Society for Engineering Education (ASEE) Southeastern Section Meeting, Auburn University, April. Available at http://www.jmu.edu/ihot/.

Perkins, D. and Salomon, G. (1992). A model for transfer of learning. In P. Peterson, R. Teirney, E. Baker and B. McGaw (eds), *International Encyclopedia of Education*, 2nd edn. Oxford: Pergamon Press.

Peters, V.A.M. and Vissers, G.A.N. (2004). A simple classification model for debriefing simulation games. *Simulation and Gaming*, 35(1): 70–84.

Petranek, C.G. (2000). Written debriefing: The next vital step in learning with simulations. *Simulations & Gaming*, 31(1): 108–118.

Price, M., Carroll, J., O'Donovan, B. and Rust, C. (2011). If I was going there, I wouldn't start from here: A critical commentary on current assessment practice. *Assessment and Evaluation in Higher Education*, 36(4): 479–92.

Reeves, T.C. and Okey, J.R. (1996). Alternative assessment for constructivist learning environments. In B.G. Wilson (ed.), *Constructivist Learning Environments: Case Studies in Instructional Design* (pp. 191–202). Englewood Cliffs, NJ: Educational Technology.

Rohm, A.J., Stefl, M. and Saint Clair, J. (2018). Time for a marketing curriculum overhaul: Developing a digital-first approach. *Journal of Marketing Education*, 41(1): 47–59.

Rudolph, J.W., Simon, R., Dufresne, R.G. and Raemer, D. (2006). There is no such thing as 'non-judgemental' debriefing: A theory and method for debriefing with good judgement. *Simulation in Healthcare*, 1(1): 49–55.

Rule, A.C. (2006). The components of authentic learning. *The Journal of Authentic Learning*, 3(1): 1–10.

Rust, C., Price, M. and O'Donovan, B. (2003). Improving students' learning by developing their understanding of assessment criteria and process. *Assessment & Evaluation in Higher Education*, 28(2): 147–64.

Sambell, K., McDowell, L. and Montgomery, C. (2013). *Assessment for Learning in Higher Education*. Abingdon: Routledge

Spiro, R.J., Coulson, R.L., Feltovich, P.J. and Anderson, D.K. (1988). Cognitive flexibility theory: Advanced knowledge acquisition in ill-structured domains. In *Proceedings of the 10th Annual Conference of the Cognitive Science Society* (pp. 375–83). Hillsdale, NJ: Lawrence Erlbaum.

Swaffield, S. (2011). Getting to the heart of authentic Assessment for Learning. *Assessment in Education: Principles, Policy & Practice*, 18(4): 433–49.

Villarroel, V., Bloxham, D.B., Bruna, C. and Herrera-Seda, C. (2018). Authentic assessment: Creating a blueprint for course design. *Assessment & Evaluation in Higher Education*, 43(5): 840–54.

Vos, L. (2015). Simulation games in business and marketing: How educators assess their students. *International Journal of Management Education*, 13(1): 57–74.

Vos, L. and Brennan, R. (2010). Marketing simulation games: Student and lecturer perspectives. *Marketing Intelligence and Planning*, 28(7): 882–97.

Vygotsky, L.S. (1978). *Mind in Society: The Development of Higher Psychological Processes*. Cambridge, MA: Harvard University Press.

Wolfe, J. (1997). The effectiveness of business games in strategic management course work. *Simulation and Gaming*, 28(4): 360–76.

6. Teaching consumer behaviour

Andrew Corcoran

INTRODUCTION

With marketing being the organisational leadership of the buyer–seller relationship, much of what we teach will necessarily be biased towards an organisational point of view. However, if we are truly to maintain the ethos of the marketing profession then it is crucial to see this relationship from the consumer's perspective. Knowing our customers' needs and their experiences of trying to meet these needs helps marketers to understand the choices before them of how to deploy the full marketing mix effectively and efficiently.

As teachers of marketing practice it is important to communicate the multi-disciplinary nature of consumer behaviour. Saad (2018) demonstrated the diversity of approaches to the subject with some examples:

- Clinical Psychology: Are there demographic variables that best predict who is likely to succumb to compulsive buying, eating disorders, pornographic addiction, or pathological gambling?
- Public Policy: Policy responses to marketing actions and consumption behaviours (e.g. the banning of smoking or alcohol advertising, or the drive to improve exercise and diet to reduce obesity).
- Sociology: The processes by which opinion leaders, and influencers diffuse new consumer fads in a social circle; attract followers and thus promote specific brands/products.
- Medicine: Exploring how many non-communicable diseases are rooted in poor consumer choices (e.g. diet, lifestyle, addictions).
- Neurosciences: Examining the neural activation patterns of consumers when they are exposed to rational versus emotional ad appeals.

Consumer behaviour is something that we have all engaged in consistently over a long period because we are all consumers. We buy products that include groceries, clothes and computers. We purchase services ranging from bank accounts to university education. However, we also know that consumers are different from one another. We eat different foods, buy different clothes, use different computers. Moreover, even the same consumer can make different decisions depending on the situation. So how are we to construct coherent marketing strategies? In this chapter we will examine how and why consumers behave in the ways that they do. Such an understanding helps marketers to identify what individuals want, how they want to be spoken to, and how the behaviour of consumers can be influenced in certain situations. Even though this chapter will also provide a decision-making process within which we will structure the key theories and models, it is important to understand that the decisions that consumers make vary based both on complexity and proximity. A marketer that appreciates this will both tailor and time their offerings to be 'just right'.

Whilst this chapter cannot deliver the full content of a module, it will guide you in some of the core models and techniques which would normally form the basis of any Consumer Behaviour or Marketing Psychology short programme of study. The key content is as follows:

- The Introduction sets the scene by considering what types of decisions we make, how these decisions contribute to our overall consumer experience, and how current trends in consumer behaviour may influence future marketing approaches.
- In the section on General Approaches to teaching Consumer Behaviour we will consider some of the principles of designing a programme of study to include a theoretical framework, learning objectives, and a delivery plan.
- The remaining sections systematically break down the overarching structure into its component parts to explore:
  - Identification and description of the core theory;
  - Ideas for how to engage students through illustration and discussion;
  - Suggestions for the assessment of learning.

Types of Decisions

When reflecting upon each of the decisions that we make daily we will notice that certain low value and frequently bought purchase decisions will feel automated, for example food purchases can be highly habitual, with certain preferences embedded in our memory. Sometimes we may not actively consider alternatives simply because we feel that we do not see a benefit in putting in the necessary time or thinking effort when we have other pressing matters to deal with. On the other hand, more complex and infrequent purchases (e.g. somewhere to live, a holiday or a car) will require more of a conscious effort on our part, mainly due to the potential financial risks and pleasurable benefits that they represent. These are referred to as Extended Problem-Solving activities. So, in summary:

- *Low Effort Decisions* often relate to low-cost products, frequently purchased, that are familiar to us. As a result, little thought or time is given to the purchase.
- *High Effort Decisions* often relate to more expensive products, infrequently purchased, that are unfamiliar to us. As a result, extensive thought or time is given to the purchase.

Levels of Decisions

Decision-making is not a static activity. Whilst it can seem as if a buyer can make an impulsive decision in a matter of seconds, the influences that lead to this decision may have accumulated over a significant period. The Hierarchy of Effects Model (Lavidge and Steiner, 2000) describes the stages in the influencing process that culminates with a purchase.

- *Awareness*: In a global and fragmented marketplace sellers need to work hard to get the buyers' attention. It is important to get the focal attention of the target consumers since they are the ones at which the marketing mix is principally aimed. Activities here may use all five of our basic physical senses – sight, hearing, touch, smell and taste – as appropriate, so that the recipient notices us.
- *Knowledge*: The recipient should have some understanding of what you are communicating. This level of familiarity, which may be based on a past use, current need or future aspiration, will act as a shortcut for your communications methods, both images and language, which retains their attention and allows further messages to permeate their consciousness to create favourable memories, creating the basis for future action.
- *Liking*: Here we aim to get the receiver to agree with statements and suggestions that we make about the goods we are encouraging them to use. This might relate to the relevance of the goods to the recipient's needs, or that the seller is a reputable supplier of these goods. In the consumer's mind this helps them to create a shortlist of potential goods or suppliers to meet their needs, whenever they might arise (which may not be immediately).
- *Preference*: With constant and intense competition from direct and substitute suppliers, buyers will have many additional factors to consider as they get closer to the purchase. No longer is the product of sole importance. We might consider price (given our budgetary constraints), availability (how quickly our need can be met in the required quantities), and consumer

service (such as a tailored delivery or after-sales support) to be of similar importance.

- *Conviction*: Pushing the consumer to move from an intention to buy the good from 'at some point in the future' to 'now' can be influenced by other marketing incentives such as 'buy-one-get-one-free', interest-free credit, limited edition, competitions, and vouchers, which can all provide the necessary stimulus to act with urgency.
- *Purchase*: Ease of payment terms create a 'frictionless' experience for consumers. When buying a more expensive item it is helpful if the seller can also provide additional services, sometimes through other organisations, and not have these as separate activities which might deter consumers. For example, if buying a new laptop computer, you would see the price for the device itself. If you needed cloud storage, external hard drive, peripherals (e.g. mouse, keyboard, printer, speakers), insurance for theft or breakdown, or credit terms to borrow the money and pay it back in instalments, then the provision of these in one convenient bundle might also convince you that you are getting a better overall deal.

The Importance of the Consumer Experience

When studying consumer behaviour, it is important to remember that our success as marketers is dependent upon the relationships that we build with our target consumers. Since marketing relationships are social in nature, including many logical and emotional exchanges and decisions in multiple contexts over a long period of time, then we must make some effort to plan for this complexity if they are to be both effective and efficient over a sustained period of time. For us to plan our efforts we need to understand what matters to consumers, and when and how it matters. In the first instance Watkinson (2012) identifies ten principles for ensuring superior consumer experiences which indicate that to be considered successful in the consumer's eyes our marketing efforts should endeavour to:

1. *Strongly reflect the consumer's identity*: Experiences that reinforce our self-image and resonate with our personal values leave us feeling good about our decisions, while those brands that clearly stand for something engender much stronger loyalty.
2. *Satisfy our higher objectives*: Wants and needs are derivative; it is satisfying the higher objective behind them that is the foundation on which great experiences are built.
3. *Leave nothing to chance*: To create consistent, smooth consumer journeys, every interaction needs to be considered, planned and designed.

4. *Set and then meet expectations*: Existing expectations, learnt behaviours and associations are the criteria that consumers use to judge an experience from the beginning.
5. *Be effortless*: Interactions that put fewer demands on the consumer, in time or effort, are more appealing. Few things generate more goodwill and repeat business than being effortless to deal with.
6. *Be stress free*: We all instinctively avoid stressful situations. Consumer experiences that eliminate confusion, uncertainty and anxiety reap the rewards, generating competitive advantage and loyalty.
7. *Indulge the senses:* From delicious food to relaxing music or a beautiful painting, we all actively seek sensory pleasure.
8. *Be socially engaging*: We more readily buy from a friend than a stranger. However, our position within a social group is also a powerful and private motivator. Those experiences that elevate our status are often the most highly valued.
9. *Put the consumer in control*: We want to do things in our own time and in our own way. We appreciate experiences that are flexible and leave us feeling in control.
10. *Consider the emotions*: Evaluating the emotional aspect of an experience brings often unconsidered issues to the surface and opens new ways to delight the consumer.

Consumer Journey Mapping

Whilst being mindful of these factors helps us to understand the overall relationship, it is only when we connect these feelings to tangible business operations that we can test and maximise how well we do what we do and how it translates into consumer benefits. For this purpose, we use the process of Consumer Journey Mapping, which helps the seller to understand the different 'touch points' in the relationship:

*   *Awareness* – first contact with the brand or organisation;
*   *Consideration* – the information provided to create a compelling case for choosing;
*   *Decision* – selection over its rivals and the clear setting of expectations;
*   *Delivery* – providing a quality product, on time, in full and within budget;
*   *Use* – the product or service does at least what it promises;
*   *Loyalty* – the customer is willing to repeat buy, or purchase other items from you;
*   *Advocacy* – promoting your product or organisation to friends and contacts.

The Consumer Journey Map will examine the step-by-step process of serving the consumer, connecting the organisation's actions to consumer needs and expectations, leading to an assessment of whether the organisation falls short of, or exceeds, these expectations. It is easy in this activity to lose sight of priorities, for example not all aspects of the journey are equally important to the overall consumer satisfaction, but poor service in an area may lead to poor feedback from the consumer which all too easily could lead to poor word of mouth, deterring other potential consumers. Consumer Journey Mapping takes account of detailed consumer feedback, normally in the form of a series of focus group activities, that explore transactional and emotional relationships in depth. They can be used to identify additional needs that were unserved by the organisation, or they can be used to create efficiencies by removing aspects of the product and service that consumers consider to be irrelevant or, in some cases, frustrating barriers to their experience. It is also helpful if the Consumer Journey Map is kept under regular review to account for the changes in consumer habits which may also be driven by the emergence of competing offerings, such as other suppliers offering improved products or processes, or technology changes which may render obsolete the traditional methods of buyer–seller interaction (e.g. social media, analytics, instant consumer feedback).

To illustrate this, you could develop a worked example on a whiteboard that first asks students to identify a high value purchase that they all have in common. A safe choice here might be a smartphone or a tablet/laptop. Alternatively, you could stimulate debate and insight by exploring their customer experience of their programme of study. Then, with the students, you can detail each of the contacts that they had with the organisation from first awareness of its products/services, all the way through to ongoing use (i.e. how well is the product/service meeting their expectations), whether they consider themselves loyal enough to make another purchase, and whether they would advise others to buy from the organisation. This breaking down of the journey into individual steps, exploring how expectations are set and met, offers great insight for students into the complexity of the marketing relationship.

Trends

To maintain a contemporary feel to students' teaching and learning we can ground our discussions in a guided examination of emerging trends, for example:

Complicated lives

• Consumers in recent years have witnessed a 'choice explosion' in which the range of choice in various markets has grown significantly. When considering groceries, we have not only our local shops but also large

out-of-town stores and online deliveries to choose from. When within a store, take a moment to consider how many different types of a specific product are on offer. Our ability to handle information has grown, but not at the same pace, and more choice has been shown to increase anxiety.
* Despite unprecedented affluence, consumers seem little happier. Their expectations are continually increasing, bringing with them greater complexity.

Sustainable worlds, sustainable consumption
Contemporary consumer culture is one that is dominated by ideas around abundance and excess. Much of marketing activity is aimed at selling goods and services that enhance people's sense of self. What happens if we try and step out of that system, try to consume less, and have a lifestyle less focused on buying things?

* Voluntary simplicity refers to consumer acts which refine their consumption towards ethical standards, thus consuming differently (rather than less).
* Mindful consumption considers the threats of climate change and resource scarcity. This has led to an increased effort toward self-sufficiency among consumers, for example increasing popularity of allotments in the UK; online auction sites; recycling sites.
* An ownerless economy is where consumers are starting to consider what they can live without and how they access goods and services. For many of these consumers, having goods and services is not critical but rather it is the experience that is important.

GENERAL APPROACHES TO TEACHING CONSUMER BEHAVIOUR

Consumer behaviour is a highly reflective subject to teach since all students come with the experience of being a consumer and consume a wide range of products such as food, clothing, entertainment and travel. However, many of these are routine, low-effort decisions. In order to explore the complex high-effort decisions we can ask them to consider the purchase of ICT equipment (e.g. smartphones, tablets, laptop PCs), vacations or accommodation. One purchase experience that unites both teachers and learners is their programme of study. This experience can be explored to take them back to their school/college experiences of first considering further or higher study. We can encourage them to explore the influences (e.g. personal, peer or family), how they were engaged by institutional communications, their enquiry and visiting day impressions, all the way through to the management of their application, enrolment, induction and their ongoing student experience.

The Consumer Decision Making Process (Blackwell et al., 2001) provides a helpful structure for the purposeful study of the phenomenon. It begins with the consumer realising that they feel dissatisfied, then taking active measures to gain information to help them to make and reflect upon their decision. We hope that a satisfying experience will lead to loyalty but must be wary of the damaging effects of a dissatisfying experience. However, the linear nature of the model can be misleading. For example, with low-effort decision-making, the consumer may not feel that there is a conscious effort to gain information and evaluate alternatives; they simply choose and buy based on their previous experiences. This automated or conditioned response has been built up over a significant period via the organisation's communication and processes, potentially leading to an intrinsic brand loyalty. This can create some interesting discussions with students when you probe them for why they prefer, for example, one snack or drink over another. They may respond that they 'just know' but this is clearly not true since they will have gone through a learning process to create these memories and attitudes. There is a significant 'lightbulb moment' once learners become fully aware of the range of messages, media and techniques that organisations use to condition the responses of consumers over a significant period. This realisation may lead to them feeling manipulated and exploited (for instance into being stimulated into buying goods that they do not really need) by marketers and is always an interesting ethical discussion to conclude the first teaching session. The stages of the model are:

- Need Recognition;
- Search for Information (both internally and externally);
- Pre-purchase Evaluation;
- Purchase and Consumption;
- Post-purchase Evaluation (leading either to Satisfaction or Dissatisfaction).

Learning Objectives

This chapter aims to provide guidance on suggested learning and teaching activities which are clearly founded on learning outcomes (Biggs, 1996; Biggs and Tang, 2007) to direct content and delivery as well as assessment breadth and method. Module learning outcomes are typically aligned with the six levels of cognitive ability in Bloom's revised taxonomy (Krathwohl, 2002). Stating how the intended learning outcomes will be assessed consequently provides transparency in terms of constructive alignment (Lawrence, 2019). This increases the validity of the methods of assessment as they align directly with the learning outcomes (Zacharis, 2010). Once these outcomes are established, their achievement is the responsibility of both the lecturer and learner in partnership, through the ongoing use of personal and group reflection on their purchase experiences. Accessing this rich supply of widely variable personal experience relies upon a discursive approach (Taylor, 2001) which allows us to dynamically adjust the balance of our teaching (focusing on some elements more than others) to enable it to be tailored to the needs of as many individuals in the group as possible. The following represents a typical set of learning outcomes that a tutor might use for their introduction to a consumer behaviour module:

Upon successful completion of this module, students will be able to:

- Apply consumer behaviour theory to the consumer experience context in industry.
- Demonstrate how as a marketer they can use their knowledge of Consumer Behaviour concepts to develop better marketing programmes and strategies to influence those behaviours.
- Analyse the trends in consumer behaviour and apply them to marketing in a practical context.
- Critically evaluate their own behaviours as consumers.

Delivery

A module with the learning outcomes listed above could fit within a wide range of general marketing or business management programmes. It can be delivered at levels 1–3 (i.e. undergraduate) or level 4 (i.e. postgraduate) and can be delivered over a single 10-week semester/term. It can also be taught as a two-week intensive block, but this gives very little time for external observation and individual reflection. Here is a suggested programme for a series of 90-minute or 2-hour lectures:

- *Lecture 1:* Module Introduction (to include staff introductions, 'ground rules', delivery and assessment plans, feedback) and an overview of the Consumer Decision Making Process model;
- *Lecture 2*: The Customer Experience Journey;
- *Lecture 3:* Need Recognition;
- *Lecture 4:* Search for Information;
- *Lecture 5:* Pre-purchase Evaluation;
- *Lecture 6:* Purchase and Consumption;
- *Lecture 7:* Post-purchase evaluation;
- *Lecture 8:* Divestment, satisfaction, and loyalty;
- *Lecture 9:* Dissatisfaction and misbehaviour;
- *Lecture 10:* Revision for the assessment.

Choosing the Core Textbook

There is a wide selection of guiding texts on the market, and their format can be similar given the established nature of the core concepts and theories. When selecting a recommended text, it is helpful to have:

- An accessible style with lots of visual examples;
- Short and long case studies;
- Extensive further reading;
- Access to a digital copy via the institution's online library;
- Online resources which include additional learning materials such as video and audio recordings;
- An author's blog which provides updates outside the publishing cycle.

Suggested texts are as follows:

- Evans, M., Jamal, A. and Foxall, G. (2009). *Consumer Behaviour*. 2nd edn. John Wiley & Sons.
- Solomon, M.R., Askegaard, S., Hogg, M.K. and Bamossy, G.J. (2019). *Consumer Behaviour – a European Perspective.* 7th edn. Pearson.
- Szmigin, I. and Piacentini, M. (2018). *Consumer Behaviour*. 2nd edn. Oxford University Press.

NEED RECOGNITION

Physiologist Walter Cannon (1932) coined the term 'homeostasis' to describe how complex organisms must maintain balance in their internal environment to lead a 'free and independent life' in the world beyond. Homeostasis occurs when we have a balance between our desires and items within our control. If there is an increase in our desires or a decrease in our resources, then our emotions will be out of balance leading to the conscious recognition of a need. The severity and urgency of resolving this need will determine how quickly we will act to resolve it in order to again experience a feeling of equilibrium, calm and satisfaction, no matter how temporary.

There is much debate about the role of marketers in the process of consumer need recognition. Do consumers come to the marketplace with already determined needs or can marketers stimulate the need for products and services? In class discussion can explore this question. Many students might argue that marketers are simply responding to existing needs that consumers freely identify for themselves. On the other hand, marketing has a significant role in *stimulating latent needs*. Such stimulation activity can take the form of simple reminders for consumers who are identified as loyal and repeat purchasers, for example by notifying them of special offers. On the other hand, it is also the responsibility of marketers to access new markets in order to drive the growth towards sustainability and profit for the organisation. This is where marketers can move onto potentially hazardous ethical grounds. After all, there is a significant difference between a need that is latent and just waiting to be stimulated by an insightful provider, versus a need that is artificial, or at the least exaggerated, which often plays on the consumer's need for social acceptance, and to be part of a desired group, sharing similar experiences which bond them together into a common identity. To understand what 'needs' are, we can access the work of Maslow (1943) and McGuire (1974).

Hierarchy of Needs (Maslow, 1943)

This theory comprises a five-tier model of human needs, often depicted as hierarchical levels. It proposes that needs lower down in the hierarchy must be satisfied before individuals can attend to needs higher up. When a need has been 'more or less' satisfied it will go away, and our activities become habitually directed towards meeting the next set of needs that we have yet to satisfy.

Physiological needs are the biological requirements for human survival – for example, air, food, drink, shelter, clothing, warmth, sleep – which are required for the human body to function optimally. Once an individual's basic physiological needs are satisfied, the needs for *safety* become relevant since people want to experience order, predictability and control in their lives. These needs can be fulfilled by the family and society (e.g. police, schools, medical care). Moving beyond the basic survival needs, Maslow recognised that humans are sociable by nature and need to feel a sense of *belongingness*. Interpersonal relationships satisfy the human need for friendship, intimacy, trust and acceptance, requiring the giving and receiving of affection. It will also encompass being part of a group (i.e. family, friends, work). Once relationships are established, Maslow claimed that our motivations move onto feelings of *esteem*, both for oneself (e.g. dignity, achievement, independence) and the desire for reputation or respect from others (e.g., status, prestige) within our groups. *Self-actualisation needs* refer to the realisation of a person's potential, self-fulfilment, seeking personal growth and peak experiences driven by the desire to accomplish everything that one can.

Drives and Motives (McGuire, 1974)

McGuire's work offers a differing, but in some ways complementary, perspective to that of Maslow. There is less of a linear determination and more of a broader consideration of the enviroment in which we live, work and have relationships. McGuire differentiated between Drives (i.e. 'must haves' or needs) and Motives (i.e. 'would like to haves' or wants):

- *Biogenic Drives*: such as hunger and thirst originate from our physiology.
- *Psychogenic Drives*: such as to achieve a certain status originate from our social and cultural environment and psychological make-up.
- *Cognitive Motives*: we are motivated to adapt to our environment and achieve a sense of meaning.
- *Affective Motives*: we are motivated to attain emotional goals and to achieve satisfying feeling states.

Student Engagement in the Learning Discussion

Here are some suggestions of how to engage students in an examination of the theory by utilising it in a practical fashion, which can then be critiqued through discussion.

Illustration and discussion

Students can easily reflect upon their own personal experience. Beginning with Low Effort Decision Making activities you may discuss frequent decisions such as food or travel choices. Students may consider that these decisions are automatic, or a 'no brainer', but you can help them to dig deeper to recognise their motives as they arise. Next you can move on to more complex High Effort Decision Making activities, which might include a smartphone or laptop purchase, university accommodation, choice of university, or a vacation. However, these student-driven examples will only explore parts of the Maslow and McGuire models, rarely the whole. To maximise coverage of the models I use their university journey with the basic needs met by institutional services, but the higher needs potential met by levels of learning. For example, we know that, for first years, study is not the main priority since they may be adjusting to living away from home for the first time and will be trying to establish new networks of friends and contacts. In the second-year, study starts to matter and in the final year all students are striving to achieve the highest possible degree classification to help them in the next stage of their career.

Assessment

1. Summarise your thoughts, for and against the statement: 'Marketing creates needs'
2. Using products or services of your choice describe:
    a. Hierarchy of needs (Maslow);
    b. Drives and motives (McGuire).

SEARCH FOR INFORMATION

For suggestions of how to meet our needs, our first resort may be to *internal search* by exploring our intrinsic knowledge or memories which have accumulated through exposure to information and our lived experience of either having previously used a product or observing someone who has. Should we not feel sufficiently well-informed to make a suitable decision, we will then revert to an *external search* utilising sources such as advertisements, friends and family, salespeople, store displays, and product reviews. The amount of external search is influenced by the following environmental characteristics:

- Market conditions: external search is greater when:
  - prices are high;
  - price differences between brands are large;
  - style and appearance are important;
  - the perceived difference between alternative product attributes is high.
- Product characteristics: external search is reduced when:
  - buying decision is complex;
  - information available is complex.

At a consumer level the following factors will influence the degree of external search which is likely to be undertaken:

- Personal determinants leading to more external search:
  - more open minded and self-confident;
  - better educated and higher income;
  - involvement with the product.
- Personal determinants leading to less external search:
  - greater market experience;
  - older;
  - limited ability to process information.

Getting the Buyer's Attention

Consumers exist within a noisy communications environment with a great deal of internal and external forces competing for their attention. Our complicated lives and the relationships that we maintain will vie for our attention with various product, brand and corporate messages that we are bombarded with through communications media that are both offline (e.g. logos, signs, leaflets, displays, TV, radio, newspapers/magazines, direct mail, salespeople) and online (e.g. text messages, pop-ups, banner adverts, email, social media). Our level of activity, in terms of the amount and types of environment that we expose ourselves to on a day-to-day basis, may lead to us being exposed to many thousands of advertising messages. No matter how dedicated and attentive we are it is impossible to process these messages in a meaningful manner so we consciously screen messages based on their relevance and familiarity to us. This creates a 'bottleneck' effect where sellers fight to win the buyer's focal attention, which gives them a significant opportunity to engage and create a relationship since these messages are processed by both sides of the brain and therefore are more likely to be retained in the memory. The degree to which people notice a stimulus that is within range of their sensory receptors which include sight (e.g. images, shapes, colours), sound (e.g. music, spoken word), taste (e.g. product sampling in grocery stores and restaurants), smell (e.g. bakeries in grocery stalls or fragrance counters in department stores), touch (e.g. garments to try on in clothing stores). By accessing the senses, we move beyond relying on the human capacity to know a fact, which has less power to motivate human behaviour than creating a feeling or an emotion which has a great deal more motivational power. Sensory communication also compensates for differences in learning styles amongst the target audience.

Creating Lasting Memories

Once the receiver has perceived the desired message it is then necessary to embed this into their memory, to create positive associations with the brand to assist with recall (i.e. when the consumer recognises a new need for the product) and a subsequent purchase. Since consumer behaviour is learned behaviour, it is beliefs, tastes, preferences and habits that strongly influence consumers' shopping, purchase and consumption behaviour. Learning deals with how we acquire new information, whereas memory is the internal recording of information or experiences and is related to our ability to store, retain, and subsequently recall information. Forgetting is our inability to retrieve previously stored information. This could be caused by many factors including the probability that the information was never encoded into long-term memory in the first place (encoding failure) or that, for some reason, we are unable to retrieve the information from long-term memory (retrieval failure).

Classical and Operant Conditioning are two important concepts that explore how stimuli or sensory input can be 'programmed' into an individual's behaviour to create a desired response. While both result in learning, the processes are quite different. Classical Conditioning associates an involuntary response to a stimulus whereas Operant Conditioning associates a voluntary behaviour and a consequence.

Classical Conditioning: In his famous experiment, Ivan Pavlov noticed dogs began to salivate in response to a tone after the sound had repeatedly been paired with presenting food. Pavlov quickly realised that this was a learned response and set out to investigate the conditioning process further. The classical conditioning process involves pairing a previously neutral stimulus (such as the sound of a bell) with an unconditioned stimulus (the taste of food). This unconditioned stimulus naturally and automatically triggers salivating as a response to the food, which is known as the unconditioned response. After associating the neutral stimulus and the unconditioned stimulus, the sound of the bell alone will start to evoke salivating as a response. The sound of the bell is now known as the conditioned stimulus and salivating in response to the bell is known as the conditioned response. Classical conditioning stimulates an involuntary response. In a marketing context we can apply these principles by pairing a brand simultaneously and repetitively with music or a celebrity so that each time the consumer thinks of the brand the positive feelings associated with that music or celebrity are aroused.

Operant Conditioning (or instrumental conditioning) focuses on using either reinforcement or punishment to increase or decrease a behaviour. Through this process, an association is formed between the behaviour and the consequences of that behaviour. Imagine that a trainer is trying to teach a dog to fetch a ball. When the dog successfully chases and picks up the ball, the dog receives praise as a reward. When the animal fails to retrieve the ball, the trainer withholds the praise. Eventually, the dog forms an association between his behaviour of fetching the ball and receiving the desired reward. Operant conditioning stimulates a voluntary response. An example of this in a marketing context would be when a supermarket offers a price reduction of 10 per cent off everything bought at the time of purchase to increase the possibility that consumers will repeat behaviour (i.e. extend their shop at the store).

Student Engagement in the Learning Discussion

Here are some suggestions of how to engage students in an examination of the theory by utilising it in a practical fashion, which can then be critiqued through discussion.

Illustration and discussion

Here you can have great fun by bringing a series of stimuli that can include music, logos, images (without text), and advertisements (print, radio and TV) and asking students what memories and associations they evoke. You could also ask students to identify their favourite brands and ask them to reflect upon the various sensory stimuli that make them feel this way. Lastly, with specific reference to operant/instrumental conditioning, you could stimulate a debate about situations in which punishment or reward might act as the more effective motivator in a purchase decision.

Assessment

1.   Choose one or more high-value purchases that you have recently made.
     a.   What internal search activity (referring to experience and knowledge)
          did you undertake?
     b.   What external search activity did you undertake?
2.   What did the companies do to ensure that you processed the information
     effectively and efficiently?

PRE-PURCHASE EVALUATION

At this stage we synthesise the form and urgency of our *needs* with the choice
and availability of feasible alternatives that were identified from our *search*
activities. In a crowded and overlapping marketplace this can be a highly
complex activity. For example, in the financial services market for credit
cards, personal loans and insurance, intermediaries exist to broker the services
of sellers with the needs of buyers (e.g. online price comparison websites).
When evaluating potential alternatives, the buyer will, unconsciously or
consciously, depending upon the level of decision-making effort required, go
through a formal decision-making process. Table 6.1 shows a worked example
based on my need for a regular supply of coffee throughout the working day,
to demonstrate how these factors interrelate:

1.   *Define the needs and weight them.* These needs change over time and
     with experience. Consumers consider fewer needs when evaluating low
     involvement products than high involvement ones. We may start with
     a long list of different needs which through the process of internal and
     external search we will narrow down based on perceived feasibility. Since
     not all needs are likely to be equally important, we may prioritise, or
     rank, some needs over others. Here we may apply non-compensatory and
     compensatory rules. Non-compensatory rules are when good performance
     on one need does not offset bad performance on another. In my example
     a low price for a cup of coffee would not compensate for a poor blend.
     Compensatory rules are when favourable ratings for one need offset
     unfavourable ratings for other needs. In my example this would occur as
     I would be happy to accept sub-standard food for a good blend of coffee.
2.   *Define the options to be considered* – which will emerge from a combina-
     tion of our internal and external search. This will not include all potential
     offerings but will comprise a shortlist of potential alternatives.
3.   *Determine the degree to which options meet their needs.* Using
     a Likert-based performance rating system where 1 = mostly unsuitable,

2 = partially unsuitable, 3 = neutral, 4 = partially suitable, 5 = mostly suitable we will score each option against each need.

4. *Select the option which will best meet their most important needs.* This will involve working across the rows, multiplying each weighting against each assessment to create a score. These scores are then added together to provide a final tally for each option. The highest number indicates the preferred choice.

Student Engagement in the Learning Discussion

Here are some suggestions of how to engage students in an examination of the theory by utilising it in a practical fashion which can then be critiqued through discussion.

Illustration and discussion

You could do a similar exercise with your students, either in groups or as individuals. Since the answers will always be different, a detailed discussion can be had about the choices that were made. It is helpful to compare approaches to meeting similar needs with the following questions for the group to discuss:

- Why did you choose these needs?
- What other needs did you ignore?
- Why did you ignore them?
- Why did you allocate these weightings?
- Why did you select these options?
- What other options did you ignore?
- Why did you ignore them?
- Was the result what you expected it to be?
- Would this result be consistent in all circumstances?

You may need to remind the group that needs are subjective so there is no such thing as a 'right' or 'wrong' answer. Some students may challenge the choices of others, which is OK, but this should be done in a respectful way to understand and compare the different rationales for decision-making. At the end of this discussion it is helpful to revisit the different choices, values and assessment, reinforcing the challenge to the marketer of serving the needs of diverse groups of consumers with different needs and values.

Assessment

Based on the above in-class discussion you can set an individual task for a student to undertake their own evaluation. This reflection/critical evaluation can be enhanced by challenging students to gain a deeper understanding of

Table 6.1   Worked example of a pre-purchase evaluation

Need	Weight	Option 1 Starbucks		Option 2 Costa		Option 3 Nero	
		Performance (1–5)	Score (weight × performance)	Performance (1–5)	Score (weight × performance)	Performance (1–5)	Score (weight × performance)
Blend	15%	4	60	3	45	5	75
Choice of flavours	5%	4	20	2	10	1	5
Size	20%	5	100	4	80	3	60
Food	5%	4	20	2	10	3	15
Price (cheaper is better)	10%	2	20	4	40	3	30
Availability (opening hours and proximity)	30%	2	60	5	150	3	90
Option to eat in or take out	15%	5	75	5	75	5	75
TOTAL	100%		355		410		350

their motives and drivers (see above) and in which ways the buyers have sought to influence their beliefs and attitudes (see above).

PURCHASE AND CONSUMPTION

This part of consumer decision-making is often skimmed over in books and lectures since it is treated as a natural culmination of the momentum that has been built in the preceding stages. If we return to consumer experience journey mapping, many consumers will see this as the core of their experience since it contains many of the principal 'touch points' in the relationship. It is also the stage at which they start to see a return on the investment of time, attention and money that they have invested in the process, to create the 'value' that they are seeking from the relationship. It is also important since it builds trust between buyer and seller, which, if managed well, will create future loyalty benefits for the seller.

Purchase Processes

Once the consumer has made the purchase decision, they will expect the subsequent fulfilment process to be as frictionless as possible (see above). At this point the following questions are likely to be on the buyer's mind:

*   *Availability*
    *   Are the goods I want in stock? If so, do they have the quantity I need? If not, when can I expect this to change? If there is no possibility of getting the goods I want can you suggest a suitable alternative?
    *   Can I buy online or offline to my own convenience?
    *   Can I try a sample before buying the product?
    *   Can I buy it alongside other complementary products?
*   *Delivery*
    *   Can I choose between collection or delivery?
    *   Can I click and collect?
    *   When can you deliver (date and time slot)?
    *   Where is the most convenient offline store?
    *   When is the offline store open?
*   *Payment*
    *   Cash;
    *   Card (debit, credit, store);
    *   App (e.g. PayPal or Apple Pay);
    *   Vouchers;
    *   Credit terms;
    *   Volume discounts.

- *Responsiveness to consumer contact*
  - How quickly are questions answered?
  - Confirmation of delivery arrangements;
  - Progress updates for delayed or time slot deliveries.
- *Returns*
  - Am I guaranteed a free of charge refund or replacement if the goods are faulty?
  - Can I cancel or return without penalty if I change my mind?

Consumption Experiences

During the consumption phase the focus of activity largely moves away from the seller since the product is now being utilised by the buyer or the consumer. The exception here is when after-sales support is required. When designing both the product and purchase experience it is important to remember that the customer is not just buying a physical 'thing' but that they will judge their overall experience based on the perceived value that they accrue from the decision. Considerations include:

When is it consumed?

- Proximity to the purchase:
  - Consumable products such as food could be consumed immediately (fast food, snacks, sandwiches), within 30 minutes (time to get to work or home) or within a week (kept in a cupboard, fridge or freezer). Each will have different packaging and transportation requirements to keep the goods fresh.
  - Durable goods such as computers or phones will be consumed over a longer period so reliability and support will be important.
  - Services such as insurance may never be used so it is the guarantee of usefulness should they need to be used.
- Timing:
  - Products will give different benefits at different times. Using the example of clothing, there will be different requirements for different types of activity (e.g. work, social, formal, sporting, leisure) and at different times of the year (e.g. winter versus summer).

Where is it consumed?

Single products may have multiple applications. For example, a car could be used to transport just you to university or work, your friends for a social event, transport clothes, books and furniture when you move to a new house or go home for the summer, or used to go on vacation. Each application will emphasise the importance of a different feature of the vehicle (i.e. comfort, economy, capacity).

How is it consumed?

Sticking with our car example we might use it for short trips, longer trips, or a mix. We could be travelling on motorways, city roads or small side streets.

How much is consumed?

Returning to our food example, restaurants offer a wide range of menu options to cater to different appetites. Heavy users can select multiple courses (i.e. starter, main and dessert) or optional side-dishes; moderate users may select a single course of a standard portion size; light users could select from the children's menu.

Student Engagement in the Learning Discussion

Here are some suggestions of how to engage students in an examination of the theory by utilising it in a practical fashion, which can then be critiqued through discussion.

Illustration and discussion

Discuss a range of products and services in different purchase and consumption scenarios. For example, we can talk about the experience of buying food. What factors would alter the perceived satisfaction in the following situations?

- Buying a pre-packed sandwich to eat on the move (e.g. Tesco, Sainsbury's);
- Buying a freshly made sandwich to eat on the move (e.g. Subway);
- Buying a fast food meal to eat on the move, in the restaurant or at home (e.g. McDonald's);
- Buying a pre-prepared meal that you will heat up later at home (e.g. Asda);
- Buying a fresh meal for delivery at home (e.g. pizza);
- Buying a meal in a restaurant, eating with family and friends for a special occasion;
- Buying ingredients for a meal that you will cook at home later and consume with family and friends.

Assessment

Consider a purchase and consumption experience:

- List the individual stages within the overall process;
- What were your expectations?

- How well did the seller meet those expectations?
- How did you feel as a result?
- Who is accountable (i.e. were your expectations unreasonable or did the seller fail in communication or delivery of their expectations?)
- How could this be a better experience?

POST-PURCHASE EVALUATION

We must accept that in the post-consumption phase consumer actions will vary significantly both in the nature, timing and degree of their response. For example, a satisfied consumer may take no action at all since their needs have been satisfied. On the other hand, they may be so delighted by their experience that they will become a loyal consumer, making repeat purchases for the same product on a regular basis and extending their purchases into other product categories supplied by the organisation. Ideally, they will also share their happy experiences with friends and relatives, encouraging them in turn to become loyal consumers of the organisation. The organisation should seek to do everything in its power to amplify the feelings of a satisfied consumer, offering a loyalty discount, benefits for referring their products and services, and liking or sharing their positive social media contributions. When it comes to dissatisfied consumers the opposite is true. Organisations should seek to understand and resolve issues quickly, making the necessary remedial action within the organisation to avoid a repeat that could jeopardise future loyalty and business growth. Besides issues of satisfaction and dissatisfaction, responsible organisations will also consider the way their goods are disposed of to maximise usefulness and value, avoid waste and minimise ecological damage.

Divestment

Technological advancements have led to shortened product life cycles for some products (e.g., mobile phones, computers, printers), which along with a desire to buy the latest model puts extra pressures on consumers to dispose of their old products. Disposal behaviour includes throwing away, recycling, selling/swapping, giving away or keeping it for an extended period.

Consumers throw away due to convenience or to make room for new products. However, some consumers are chronic keepers – they have a large pile of products (e.g., old PC monitors, cables) in their cupboards and spare rooms. Some may be kept for their nostalgic value or due to an emotional attachment (e.g., they remind them of a loved one); most of the other items are kept in the hope of using them some time in the future.

- Rethink your choices;

- Refuse single use;
- Reduce consumption;
- Reuse everything;
- Refurbish old stuff;
- Repair before you replace;
- Repurpose – be creative, invent;
- Recycle as a last option.

To develop this theme, you can ask students to consider their most recent purchases where a physical item has been received. For example, when buying a coffee do you make the choice to drink at the café using their cups, use a disposable take-away cup, or reusable mug that can be cleaned and stored: A similar discussion could be had regarding take away or fresh food packaging. Did learners make a conscious decision to cook fresh at home to avoid disposing of single-use packaging? To move the discussion away from disposal to re-use, students can discuss what happened to mobile phones, tablets, or laptops that they have previously owned.

Satisfaction and Loyalty

Our feelings of satisfaction are determined by the difference between pre-purchase expectations (belief about anticipated performance) and post-purchase beliefs (how well the product performed). Satisfaction occurs when the product's perceived performance exceeds consumer expectation. Dissatisfaction occurs when the product's performance falls short of the consumer's expectations. Consumers seek explanations for the causes of outcomes and according to Oliver (1993) feel satisfaction when they attribute favourable outcomes to themselves and negative outcomes to others. Furthermore Oliver (1997) identified that consumers feel satisfied when they perceive fair (i.e. equitable) treatment. It is generally understood, but inconsistently supported by empirical evidence, that consumer satisfaction leads to loyalty and all the effectiveness and efficiency gains that it creates for a seller. True relational interaction can be mutually rewarding and occurs when:

- Consumers feel an affinity with the organisation beyond mere repeat purchase;
- Consumers can feel 'known' to the organisation, not just as an anonymous consumer but akin to the personal interaction of restaurateur and regular consumer;
- Consumers often receive special treatment and extra pampering by the organisation;

- Consumers are likely to receive timely and relevant communications of offers that would be of interest to them at that moment.

A satisfying consumer experience, beyond individual loyalty, could also lead to those satisfied consumers becoming advocates for the seller through Word of Mouth (WOM) effect, which Arndt (1967) defines as 'oral person-to-person communication between a receiver and a communicator whom the receiver perceives as non-commercial, regarding a brand, product or service'. WOM influences purchase decisions since consumers consider it to be reliable and trustworthy as it is personal contacts who are providing a stamp of approval and social support for a purchase. The effectiveness of WOM is a function of its:

- *Independent Credibility*: recommendations made by consumers are generally perceived as being more credible and trustworthy than those stemming from commercial sources (Day, 1971; Silverman, 2001).
- *Information Tailoring*: the WOM channel is immediately bi-directional and interactive, which allows for a 'tailored' flow of information to the information seeker. This tailoring may involve reducing confusion, making clarifications or bringing the topic into context appropriate for the individual etc. (Gilly et al., 1998).
- *Experience Delivery*: before product purchase individuals may wish to try a product and gain low-risk real world experience of it. WOM facilitates this, enabling indirect experience to be obtained, by hearing about other people's experiences with the product; this reduces time and cost. Successful experience is likely to lead to purchase (Silverman, 2001).

Dissatisfaction and Misbehaviour

Dissatisfied consumers may seek to take action to assuage their sense of perceived grievance at the loss of a happy experience. The most immediate consequence of consumer dissatisfaction is complaining. This allows consumers to get rid of their anger and frustration. Consumers are likely to complain when:

- They attribute the blame to someone else;
- There are greater chances of redress;
- They have the time and confidence to complain;
- The experience is severe enough to cause damage;
- The reputation of the firm is high;
- There is a chance of redress.

In more serious cases of dissatisfaction there exists the potential for consumer misbehaviour, which Fullerton and Punj (2004) define as 'Behavioural acts by consumers which violate the generally accepted norms of conduct in consumption situations and thus disrupt the consumption order.' Examples of misbehaviour include:

- Abuse of services, such as 'bad behaviour' when travelling on aeroplanes or when on holiday;
- Use of environmentally damaging products such as cars, airline travel, fur garments, non-degradable fishing lines which can kill birds, guns to shoot wildlife;
- Disposal of products in an environmentally damaging manner;
- Buying from sellers that exploit child labour or other socially undesirable practices;
- Consumption of products we know will damage our health. At its extreme this can constitute addictive behaviours such as smoking, drug abuse, excessive eating, or alcoholism;
- Consumer boycotts of organisations that they feel are behaving irresponsibly (e.g. ecological pollution, unsafe work practices, employee exploitation);
- Illegal behaviour such as theft, shoplifting, buying products from black markets, bootlegging products from other countries to save taxes, purchasing counterfeit brands, downloading music/games over the internet without explicit permission, and identity theft.

Student Engagement in the Learning Discussion

Here are some suggestions of how to engage students in an examination of the theory by utilising it in a practical fashion, which can then be critiqued through discussion.

Illustration and discussion

A class discussion of satisfying and dissatisfying consumer experiences can explore a range of examples to test the theory. What is particularly interesting to explore is what degree of responsibility the consumer (i.e. the students) felt for their poor experience; the more reflective ones may put their response down to poorly stated needs or poor search for information in the initial stages. Secondly, students will no doubt have a wide range of colourful examples of consumer behaviour that they have directly experienced or have heard of. The motivation, method and effect (both on the seller and the consumer) of these events can be discussed in detail.

Assessment

1. What are your experiences of consumer misbehaviour?
2. What could the company have done to improve the consumer experience?
3. How far should a company go to completely satisfy every consumer, always?

CHAPTER SUMMARY

This chapter has given an overview of what Consumer Behaviour is and its relevance to us both as marketers, and as consumers ourselves. We have considered the varying complexity of decisions that we make throughout the pre-purchasing, purchasing and post-purchasing contexts and how the organisation can structure their understanding to maximise positive customer experiences, which should lead to loyalty. We used the Consumer Decision Making Process (Blackwell et al., 2001) as the theoretical model to frame how we explored the subject.

It is great fun to teach this subject given the rich source of contemporary experiences and attitudes to certain organisations and brands that we all have. Discussing these in the classroom leads to interesting debates that challenge the accepted models of behaviours. Also, students have a great opportunity to take away their learning and use it in the practice environment next time they make, or consider making, a purchase. Why did they act in the way that they did? Would they change anything? How could the seller have done better? Each of these questions underlines the students' reflective practice.

REFERENCES

Arndt, J. (1967). Role of product-related conversations in the diffusion of a new product. *Journal of Marketing Research*, 4(3), 291–5.

Biggs, J. (1996). Enhancing teaching through constructive alignment. *Higher Education*, 32, 347–64.

Biggs, J. and C. Tang (2007). *Teaching for Quality Learning at University*, 3rd edn, Maidenhead: Open University Press & McGraw-Hill Education.

Blackwell, R.D., Miniard, P.W. and Engel, J.F. (2001). *Consumer Behaviour*, 9th edn. Mason, OH: Southwestern.

Cannon, W.B. (1932). The wisdom of the body. *The British Medical Journal*, 2(3745), 713.

Day, G.S. (1971). Attitude change, media and word of mouth. *Journal of Advertising Research*, 11(6), 31–40.

Fullerton, R.A. and Punj, G. (2004). Repercussions of promoting an ideology of consumption: Consumer misbehavior. *Journal of Business Research*, 57(11), 1239–49.

Gilly, M.C., Graham, J.L., Wolfinbarger, M.F. and Yale, L.J. (1998). A dyadic study of interpersonal information search. *Journal of the Academy of Marketing Science*, 26, 83–100.

Krathwohl, D.R. (2002). A revision of Bloom's Taxonomy: An overview. *Theory into Practice*, 41(4), 212–18.

Lavidge, R.J. and Steiner, G.A. (2000). A model for predictive measurements of advertising effectiveness. *Advertising & Society Review*, 1(1).

Lawrence, J.E. (2019). Designing a unit assessment using constructive alignment. *International Journal of Teacher Education and Professional Development (IJTEPD)*, 2(1) Accessed 12 August 2021 at: https://www.igi-global.com/article/designing-a-unit-assessment-using-constructive-alignment/217457.

Maslow, A.H. (1943). A theory of human motivation. *Psychological Review*, 50(4), 370–96.

McGuire, W. (1974). Psychological motives and communication gratification. In J.F. Blumer and Katz (eds), *The Uses of Mass Communication: Current Perspectives on Gratification Research* (pp. 106–167). Beverly Hills, CA: Sage.

Oliver, R.L. (1993). Cognitive, affective and attribute base of the satisfaction response, *Journal of Consumer Research*, 20, December, pp. 418–30.

Oliver, R.L. (1997). *Satisfaction: A Behavioral Perspective on the Consumer*. New York, NY: Irwin/McGraw-Hill.

Saad, G. (2018). *Marketing is Life and Life is Marketing: I Consume Therefore I Am* [online]. Accessed 19 August 2020 at: https://www.psychologytoday.com/ca/blog/homo-consumericus/201805/marketing-is-life-and-life-is-marketing.

Silverman, G. (2001). *The Secrets of Word-of-mouth Marketing: How to Trigger Exponential Sales Through Runaway Word of Mouth*. New York, NY: AMACOM.

Solomon, M.R., Askegaard, S., Hogg, M.K. and Bamossy, G.J. (2019). *Consumer Behaviour: a European Perspective*. 7th edn. Harlow: Pearson.

Szmigin, I. and Piacentini, M. (2018). *Consumer Behaviour*. 2nd edn. Oxford: Oxford University Press.

Taylor, Stephanie (2001). Locating and conducting discourse analytic research. In M. Wetherell, S. Taylor and S.J. Yates (eds), *Discourse as Data. A Guide for Analysis*. London: SAGE.

Watkinson, M. (2012). *The Ten Principles Behind Great Consumer Experiences*. London: *Financial Times*.

Zacharis, N.Z. (2010). Innovative assessment for learning enhancement: Issues and practices. *Contemporary Issues in Education Research*, 3(1), 61–70.

7. Teaching marketing history

Ben Wooliscroft

INTRODUCTION

Anything that happened before a student was in high school is generally considered ancient history and as far from today as the wearing of togas. Reading some of the earlier writing on marketing might jar with our "enlightened" views, being set in the time of the author, the use of pronouns associated with gender roles may cause discussion. But there is much value in seeing how the market(ing) system operated in those times.

Often with less dominant major players and more competition markets were more efficient. At the same time, production often took place close to market, meaning that the benefits of employment flowed into the same society as the benefits of consumption. Personal and company taxes have also been much higher in most countries at times during the last century, including during times of high growth post WWII (Pickett and Wilkinson, 2010; Piketty, 2020). The key thing to impress on the students is that the current economic system, and its attendant policy settings, is not the only system that is beneficial to society or business.

There are many ways that a course on the history of marketing could be founded:

- Teaching an organised understanding of the history of marketing thought (based on a textbook);
- Teaching a body of knowledge (largely from journal and conference papers) or a philosophy of inquiry/approach (Jones and Shaw, 2002);
- Teaching the history of marketing practice, through case studies (Dash, 2011; Ferguson, 2008; Kurlansky, 2011; Mackay, 2012);
- Teaching the history of marketing in a particular context – product category, market, region (Witkowski, 2010, 2017).

Which of these approaches the lecturer, department or university chooses would depend on their students and their goal(s). The vast majority of students want a course that contributes to their value in the employment market and makes them better marketers and leaders of business. That is often in contrast to academic staff who favour critical thinking and lifelong learning as the goal of university education. How could that vocational focus relate to a course with both "history" and "theory" in the title? The first challenge in teaching this course is introducing students to the idea that critical thinking, the availability of multiple frameworks/theories and a grasp of the impact of history/the environment on marketing theory and practice will make them a better marketer (or citizen). The course described below achieves both the goals of staff and all but the most vocationally minded students.

Should students care about marketing history? Hunt (2011) argues that it can contribute to the development of marketing thought. It is my experience, teaching the history of marketing theory for two decades, that students learn theories from the history of marketing that add value to them and their organisations as they enter their careers, or undertake higher study. They arrive at their organisation with a wider understanding of markets and marketing and access to a lot more tools/frameworks to apply to problems they may face.

TEACHING MARKETING HISTORY: A COURSE

There is the history of marketing thought/theory and the history of marketing practice. Both are worthy of investigation. This illustrative course description uses a textbook to structure the body of marketing theory. That text is heavily supplemented by illustrations of marketing practice, counter-arguments and examples and a general approach of critical engagement with the material. It is presented below in modules that can be combined to fill the needs of the instructor. Some modules warrant considerable extra time (Functionalism for example is almost entirely new to the students), while others require less time (the Managerial School is essentially the undergraduate programme that the students will have completed).

A Textbook

Sheth et al. (1988), *Marketing Theory: Evolution and Evaluation*, is a rare book, but the history of marketing is not often taught. While there are other books on marketing history, they tend to heavy scholarship (e.g. Jones and Shaw, 2002; Tadajewski and Jones, 2007), to be too old to stimulate current students (e.g. Bartels, 1976a, 1976b). To students normally born after its publication date, the Sheth et al. (1988) textbook is dated, but that gives the class the opportunity to "update" the book in latter lessons. The major benefit of using *Marketing Theory: Evolution and Evaluation* is its framework that spaces the topics out and provides a (post hoc) set of schools of thought in marketing.

There are other analyses of the history of marketing theory and allocation of authors, and their work, to schools of thought (e.g. Hollander et al., 2005; Shaw and Jones, 2005). But none of those provide the semester-friendly four categories of theories, presented in a two by two matrix, that Sheth et al. (1988) provide. The four categories are too convenient and the inter-active/non-interactive distinction is not nearly as strong as the economic/ non-economic (basis of thought) dimension, but it is useful for organisation and gives the instructor and students manageable "chunks" of focused material.

One word of caution about this textbook is that it scores each of the schools of thought. It is worth discussing the scoring system: what attributes do we as a discipline require from our theories or frameworks? There are many attrib-utes that might be considered necessary for a theory in marketing. Sheth et al.'s (1988) discussion of theory as structure, specification, testability, empirical support, richness and simplicity as attributes to judge the schools of thought is useful to start a conversation. During that conversation, the scores given by Sheth et al. (1988) are not likely to survive critical reflection, and discussing the issues with the scores provides an opportunity to role model critical think-ing and reject any idea that textbooks are beyond question.

Each of the schools of thought presented below have been post hoc cate-gorised. The schools have a starting date and a period of focus, but none of the schools have left the business school entirely. Some of them have left the marketing department and are now in separate departments. Logistics, for example, is often taught outside of the marketing department. The regional school is now seen in Geographical Information Systems departments and courses, rarely in marketing departments. Bringing these theories and frame-works back to marketing provides students with additional opportunities to improve business and new ways of seeing/understanding the marketing/market phenomena.

Along with the textbook, students are also provided with a reading list (see the Appendix).

What is (and was) Marketing?

- What is marketing (as the students currently understand it)?
- How long have humans been marketing?
- What is a theory?
- What are examples of marketing theories with which the students are familiar?

The first topic inevitably results in a student, or multiple students, parroting the AMA definition from the year that they sat the introductory marketing paper. The definition is rarely understood or examined and this is a useful point at which to break it down. It is also a good opportunity to introduce different perspectives on what marketing is and its purpose.

Early writers such as Breyer (1934, p. 192) saw systems at the centre of the marketing problem and marketing as the centre of the system of provision:

> Marketing is not primarily a means of garnering profits for individuals. It is, in the larger, more vital sense, an economic instrument used to accomplish indispensable social ends. Under a system of division of labor there must be some vehicle to move the surplus production of specialists to deficit areas if society is to support itself. This is the social objective of marketing.

How long have we been marketing, when the textbooks' earliest references are the start of the twentieth century? It doesn't take long to separate the discipline of marketing, and its associated theories, from the practice of marketing and trade. There are examples of trade in the earliest of human artefacts:

- The Beaker people, originally thought to have migrated through Europe on the basis of grave goods, are now understood to have traded across an increasingly large part of Europe.
- Romans were practitioners of conspicuous consumption through their highly stratified clothing, should they have the rank to be allowed to do so.
- Pompeii has preserved advertisements for branded traders and producers of goods and service providers.
- Egyptians transported branded sarcophagi through the Mediterranean.

Marketing was then, and remains, a provisioning technology necessary for the standard of living and quality of life of citizens in our society. Throughout the following sections of the course students receive a richer understanding of how marketing provides economic efficiencies and contributes to societal well-being. There is also ample opportunity to discuss examples of inefficient behaviours and the negative impacts of marketing.

Many students are reluctant to engage in a discussion of theory, wishing to focus on the practice of marketing. Discussing what a theory is and its relationship to practice is useful to break down the artificial divide between theory and practice. The suggestion that marketing "practice" happens without a theory/hypothesis regarding the outcome is generally quickly dispatched and the false divide between theory and practice, academic and real world, etc. disappears, or reduces.

The final question above, in light of the discussion that has preceded it, results in a lengthy list of theories that students are familiar with and a recognition that they have been studying marketing theory already.

Introduction to the Course and the Textbook's Five Questions

Sheth et al. (1988) provide five questions to structure reading of the textbook, also applying to developments in marketing theory beyond the scope of the textbook.

1.   Is marketing an art or a science?
2.   What is, or should be, the dominant perspective in marketing?
3.   What is/are the proper domain(s) of marketing?
4.   What is the relationship between marketing and society?
5.   Do we need a theory of marketing?

These questions provide an opportunity for lively debate. The questioning of fundamental terms has, in some cases, been uncomfortable for students.

For the first question students need to explicate what art and science are. A third category, technology, is generally discovered during this discussion. The relationship between professions like medicine and engineering and technology frequently lead to students feeling more positive about their chosen discipline. It is clear that we can find examples of marketing as an art, as a technology and as an application of the scientific method.

Very few students have considered that there might be any other dominant perspective in marketing than profit maximisation/increase. This discussion allows careful reflection and expansion of their views. It allows students to look at the following schools of marketing with a more critical approach.

The question regarding domains of marketing, those areas of exchange to which marketing can be applied, is really only of historical interest. Students have grown up in a world where everything is marketed – there are no boundaries to the application of marketing techniques. Sandel (2000) makes a strong case for the limits of markets, things which should not be for sale. That does not negate the fact that some of those things that should not be for sale are for sale. Or, that marketing is applied to areas that might be beyond our comfort zone, or cultural norms.

Students are interested that this was not the case in the past; marketing was limited in its application. But the domains of marketing debate largely took place in the 1970s, which is considered distant history to today's undergraduate students, being before they were born.

The relationship between marketing and society often stimulates a lively debate, but the question is redundant once students realise that marketing is not separate from society, but an institution within it. The question is then rephrased as what form of marketing, as an institution, society should allow.

Students are less sure about the need for a theory of marketing. "Shouldn't we just be doing it?" The distinction between theory and practice is a useful discussion, discussed above. Which practices do we undertake without an idea (theory) about the outcome? Students typically don't think of this causal proposition as theory and a useful discussion follows, particularly if the scientific method is discussed and applied to practice.

The Commodity School – What Should We Do with Different Types of Goods? (1920–)

Some of the earliest writing in American marketing concerned itself with how we should treat different types of shopping goods. There are a number of variations of the theme of emergency, convenience and shopping goods as categories, but the central theme remains the same. How involved is the customer in the act of shopping and/or with the good being purchased?

Reflecting on this School through the lens of retail layout, supermarkets or American pharmacies works well, and allows students to see that the theories in this school are very much in use today. The theories make explicit where in the store different goods should be provided.

The Functional School – What Do Marketers Do? (1912–)

The history of the Functional School predates the 4Ps and includes significantly longer lists of functions that are undertaken by marketers. These longer lists encourage students to go well beyond the simplistic 4Ps framework with which they are almost certainly familiar. The dangers of siloing different functions and the poverty of theories that include multiple functions is a useful outcome of reviewing this material. Ryan (1935) found 52 different functions of marketers in their review of the functional literature.

Much of this material has flowed into the managerial school and students are familiar with that through the 4 (or more) Ps (or As, etc.). Understanding the richer history of marketing functions leads to a better understanding of what marketers do.

The Regional School – Where Should We Do Things? (1931–)

Very little attention is paid in the modern curriculum as to where marketing "happens". The Regional School exposes students to rich material on modelling where retail, and by extension wholesale and manufacturing, should be situated relative to customers. Reilly's (1929) Law of Retail Gravitation provides a gentle mathematical introduction and the opportunity to discuss the nature of these types of models (attractors and costs associated with destinations).

A discussion of the current use of these models by major chains and their importance to customer acquisition is helpful. The frameworks that underpin these models can be extended to supply chains, with differences in the cost of travel and/or labour leading to very different solutions. This approach to marketing provides students with value to employers above and beyond a typical marketing graduate.

The Institutional School – What Institutions Do We Need for Markets (and Marketing) to Function? (1910s–)

Farmer (1967, p. 1) wrote in the *Journal of Marketing*, "For the past 6,000 years the field of marketing has been thought of as made up of fast-buck artists, con-men, wheeler-dealers, and shoddy-goods distributors."

In a reaction to a surge in the unpopularity of marketing, and particularly "middlemen", during the 1910s and 1930s the institutional school sought to demonstrate the economic efficiency and value generation of the channel. As consumers moved from living close to production, where prices were low, to urban areas where prices felt "inflated", middlemen were often blamed for these increases in prices.

This school focused on how the number of exchange negotiations, the costs of searching, and so on are reduced through the use of middlemen and thus time and place utility are provided. Middlemen have been castigated throughout history as profiting without providing value and this discussion overturns those prejudices. Marketers provide value to consumers through distribution, but do a poor job of communicating that value creation. The marketing of marketing is a topic that students frequently engage with, including personal experiences of being looked down upon because of their choice of discipline.

Bringing the institutional school to current days allows students to see that e-commerce is still required to provide time and space utility, while the costs of searching have reduced (if the firm/product being searched is available on the search platform). The particular case of digital products (music, TV/movie downloads) may appear to be etherial, but they require servers, cellphone towers, fibre optic cables and are frequently affected by geographic restrictions – the world wide web is not so wide. A more mature understanding of the differences between e-commerce and bricks and mortar arises from studying the institutions necessary for getting products into the hands of customers.

The Functionalist School – What Would a Theory of Marketing Look Like? (1948–1965)

Unique to this taxonomy of marketing theory, Functionalism is almost entirely the work of one individual, Wroe Alderson. Alderson's contributions to marketing should elevate him to the status of our Newton or Einstein, but he has been largely forgotten. His first major textbook, *Marketing Behavior and*

Executive Action (Alderson, 1957), starts with a discussion of the philosophy of science and a justification for the flavour of systems thinking that Alderson uses to generate his theories, many of which culminate in his broader theory of functionalism. Alderson gave us many theories that have value, including the Law of Exchange, transvections for channel efficiency analysis that goes beyond any one firm, hedonomics (a call for the study of consumption after purchase), and so on. All of which are posited in a theory of marketing that starts from an assumption of perfectly heterogeneous demand and supply in markets.

Law of Exchange

> Given that x is an element of the assortment $A1$ and y is an element of the assortment $A2$, x is exchangeable for y if, and only if, these three conditions hold:
> (a) x is different from y;
> (b)   The potency of the assortment $A1$ is increased by dropping x and adding y;
> (c)   The potency of the assortment $A2$ is increased by adding x and dropping y (Alderson, 2006, p. 255).

Reading Alderson is somewhat like opening Pandora's box; once you have seen the richness of his theories, developed through a systems approach, it is hard to stop thinking of marketing in that way. But Alderson remains a challenging author asking more of his readers than most. More than any other marketing author he is in need of a translation to make his theories available to an undergraduate audience. Alderson and Cox (1948) provides a thought provoking introduction to how a theory of marketing might be formed, borrowing from various social science disciplines and combining them under the umbrella of social systems. Students might notice how little progress we've made towards a theory of marketing since this proposal in 1948.

1959 – The Ford Foundation and Carnegie Corporation Reports into Business Education

This is not included in Sheth et al. (1988) as a school of thought, but is important context for the change in marketing.

In 1959 two major reports into business education in the USA were released (Gordon and Howell, 1959; Pierson, 1959). They were designed to address the perception that business education, and research, was of poor quality. The insights from hard sciences and a mathematical approach could be brought to business education. This was during the height of the Cold War and the Space Race, during which time science was deified. Books such as *What Ivan Knows that Johnny Doesn't* (Trace, 1961) stoked fear that the USA, and allies, were falling behind in educating their youth. Tadajewski (2006, 2009) has brought a critical perspective to these changes that students would benefit from reading.

The Ford Foundation went further and brought young business faculty to Harvard for a year's education in mathematics as it might be applied to business. Those faculty included Philip Kotler, Frank Bass and other leading thinkers in marketing during the 1960s. Regional training followed this year in an attempt to redirect business education and research. The Managerial School and the Buyer Behaviour School, in their original form, show a clear connection to these reviews and made the goal of making marketing, and other business disciplines, more effective.

The Managerial School – How Do We Sell More? (1950s–)

In many ways all marketing has been managerial in approach, but this school sets out to sell more units. It may be that more units are sold because of products being designed for customers, that the products are better positioned relative to other brands, that the right segment(s) of potential customers are being targeted, and so on. The Managerial School sets out to be better at marketing, in terms of increasing sales, increasing market share and profit maximisation.

It is in this school that marketing frameworks that students will be most familiar with are covered:

- Marketing Myopia (Levitt, 1960);
- The Marketing Concept;
- Segmentation, targeting and positioning;
- Sustainable competitive advantage;
- Pricing policies;
- The product lifecycle (students are often reluctant to give up this framework when confronted with the circular nature of its use as a strategic tool);
- BCG, Ansoff, etc. matrices.

Applying the tools developed through the shift to "scientific" marketing was very effective and consumption boomed, particularly in the USA. The post-World War II years saw rising standards of living, following the austerity experienced during and immediately after the war. This was coupled with the advent of new media, with novel advertising. The early years of TV advertising saw sales conversions that are almost beyond belief today, far removed from our over-exposed and jaded modern media consumers.

The Buyer Behaviour School – How Do We Get Them to Buy More? (1950s–)

It is rare that we'd think of buyer behaviour in the last 40 years. We, as a discipline, have moved beyond the act of buying to a focus on consumption. The Buyer Behaviour School was concerned with buying. It sought to answer the question, "how do we get (potential) customers to buy?". The focus on (potential) customer characteristics that lead to purchase, personality research, Freudian approaches to customer motivation, and so on exposes students to material that they are very unlikely to have encountered. Dichter's (1964) theories regarding Freudian motivation to consume sports cars, packet cakes, and so on are likely to entertain students.

Students are more likely to be familiar with Consumer Behaviour and its extension to Consumer Culture, where the focus is on studying and understanding consumption including the act of purchase. The story of a group of young scholars making the consumer behaviour odyssey, supported by the Academy of Marketing Science, highlights the change in focus (Belk et al., 1989). Whether consumer behaviour/culture research has relevance to business now is a matter for discussion. Many consumer behaviour/culture scholars would not see their purpose as informing business in any form. But there remain a large number of advertising or persuasion papers in the *Journal of Consumer Research*, the home of consumer behaviour research.

The Activist School – Who is Unhappy with Marketing, and Why? (Largely During Times of Economic or Social Stress)

That Sheth et al. (1988) chose to include this school is likely to be related to the desire for a balanced two by two matrix with three schools per cell. It is highly relevant to students of marketing to be familiar with the history of criticism of marketing and consumption. Very few of the articles or books cited in this section are published in marketing journals or for a marketing audience. This is the conscience of marketing – highlighting our failures.

Sheth et al. (1988) provide a very US-centric review of the critique of marketing, with Galbraith (1958) *The Affluent Society*, Carson (1962) *Silent Spring*, Nader (1965) *Unsafe at Any Speed* and Vance Packard's popular books (1958, 1959, 1960) *The Hidden Persuaders*, *The Status Seekers* and *The Wastemakers* highlighting US consumption issues, but with wider implications. Extending the critique of marketing to the region of instruction brings alive the long history of resisting business, cooperatives, unions, political parties and legislation all featuring in the narrative to avoid the excesses of business.

Books, such as that by Klein (2000), demonstrate that this discussion is anything but concluded. Business will continue to be questioned and one of the responsibilities of marketers is to ensure that they are operating in a manner that will not invite those questions.

It might be argued that the critical marketing school has its heritage in these publications that are critical of business, marketing and in some cases markets.

The Macromarketing School – What Are the Bigger Questions about Marketing and Markets? (1960s–)

What is macromarketing? Macromarketing is the only school of thought that has a society that has members, the Macromarketing Society, Inc.. The School/ Society has a very wide interest in marketing, markets and society and their interactions. The only exception to this interest is "how do I sell more X?" Papers received by the conference, or the *Journal of Macromarketing* with managerial implications are generally considered to be in the wrong place.

The works of Fisk (1961, 1967) and Layton (2007, 2009, 2011, 2014) form the basis of the canon of macromarketing texts with their basis in systems thinking, building on the work of Cox and Alderson (1950); Alderson (1957, 1965); Wooliscroft (2007); Boulding (1956) and Von Bertalanffy (1968) among others.

Macromarketing is in many ways a matter of scale, moving beyond micro-marketing's focus on the:

* single firm to customer relationship/interaction/exchange/communication;
* single firm to single firm relationship/interaction/exchange/communication.

Micromarketing shares some of the *ceteris paribus* assumptions or simplifica-tions of economics. Macromarketing looks at the more complex interactions between multiple firms, industries, customers and governments, with all the associated difficulties.

The vast majority of micromarketing theory and practice is fully committed to ignoring externalities in the catholic manner in which macromarketing considers them. Macromarketing is the discipline where externalities are most frequently discussed and solutions are proposed (Mundt, 1993; Mundt and Houston, 1996, 2010). While there is clearly work still to be done in this area – externalities remain ubiquitous and have great impact – macromarketing scholars are those with the head start in this area (Padela et al., 2020).

Both the decisions and philosophy of business (Mitchell et al., 2010) and consumers (Wooliscroft et al., 2014) are considered by macromarketers. It is not enough to blame the ills of the world on either consumer sovereignty (Birmingham, 1968) or evil business (Klein, 2000). Nor is the consumer without blame and the business always virtuous in the manner that Henry Ford (cited in Sinclair, 1962, p. 369) suggested when he stated that, "There is something sacred about big business. Anything which is economically right is morally right."

Macromarketing authors such as Mitchell et al. (2010) challenge this view and provide a vision for a more socially responsible business model.

The Organizational Dynamics School – How Do Firms Work? (1960s–)

Does the Organizational Dynamics School belong in marketing theory? A descendent of the Institutional School of thought, with an evolved theoretical base, it is relevant to marketing as a provisioning technology.

The majority of the research in the Organizational Dynamics School is found in management texts and journals, concerning itself with relationships in the channel, power, cooperation and conflict. If students have been exposed to this material it is likely in a business-to-business marketing course or during their management studies.

This school is useful to get students thinking about the shape and nature of markets and the balance of cooperation and competition, vertically and horizontally in markets. The importance of vertical cooperation, for efficient transactions, harks back to the work of Alderson (1965) considering the channel as an organised behaviour system.

The Systems School – How Do the Parts Interact? (Building on Functionalism 1960s–)

Building on the work of Von Bertalanffy (1971), Boulding (1956), Ackoff and Emery (1972), Churchman et al. (1957), Forrester (1969, 1971) and the work of Alderson and Cox (1948) and Alderson (1957, 1965) discussed above in the Functionalist School, the Systems School of marketing represents a philosophy of science and a collection of methods applied to the phenomena of marketing, business and markets. Sheth et al. (1988) provide the criteria for dynamic open systems from Katz and Kahn (1966). Students see that businesses, channels and industries are systems. That doesn't make controlling them easier, in fact it introduces them to wicked problems (Churchman, 1967).

Once students accept, if they do, the systems perspective, it is hard to consider marketing problems in a reductionist manner again. But systems research does not come without challenges. Where systems are bounded, how much information is required, the many interactions that should be considered, and so on all lead to difficult, and lengthy, research projects. Simulation software has improved and computing power is no longer a problem, so systems research methods are becoming more available to researchers. Those considering research in systems should consider the work of Layton (2007, 2009, 2011, 2014), Layton and Duffy (2018), and Shapiro and Layton (2019), who have made major contributions to understanding markets and marketing through a system's lens.

There are clear connections between Functionalism, Systems and Macromarketing as schools of thought and it may be appropriate to consider them together, but the focus of macromarketing remains at a different level and the focus of systems is the methods and philosophy of science brought to the study of the central phenomena.

Ultimately the systems approach offers students insight and influence, but not control (other approaches might pretend to offer control, but not deliver) over the focal system. It can be unsettling for students to realise how little any one player/firm/system is able to control their destiny.

The Social Exchange School – Why Do We Exchange? (1970s–)

This school builds on Alderson (1957) and his Law of Exchange extending it to second order value creation. It is largely the work of Bagozzi (1974, 1975, 1978) with significant contributions from Hunt (1983). Is it a separate school of thought in marketing? That question is likely to lead to useful discussion. What is marketing without exchange? Where does the boundary of that exchange finish?

As a basis for any theory of marketing, the social exchange school is foundational, but insufficient to give us a theory. Students do appreciate the contrast from zero sum exchanges provided by economics and marketing as value generating, contributing to society's overall well-being, which (not always) enables marketing students to feel more positive about their discipline and its place in the world.

Reflecting on the Schools

At the end of reviewing the above schools students are asked to place the schools on a timeline (roughly 1900–1988) and then add the relationship between the different schools. It becomes quickly apparent that Alderson (1957) holds a central, if largely forgotten, role in the development of marketing theory.

The impact of world wars, depressions, the Cold War and the space race, can be seen as focuses of change in marketing theory on that timeline. Marketing students frequently do not have a sound background in twentieth-century history and may require help with locating these events. The question that follows is how significant events in our times will impact marketing theory development; Trump and the post-truth era, COVID and a change to travel, distance and international borders, among many others.

Newer Schools – What Happened Since 1988

After touring the, largely American, history of marketing theory, students are invited to consider what schools of thought have arisen post-1988. The list, generally, includes:

• Marketing Science (Winer and Neslin, 2014);
• Relationship marketing (El-Ansary, 2005; Grönroos, 1995; Morgan and Hunt, 1994);
• E-marketing/digital marketing (Robins, 2000);
• Services marketing (Zeithaml et al., 1985);
• etc.

It is a good opportunity to give students Hunt (2020), one of our leading scholars' reflections on the discipline's theory development. Where do we need new theory? Which new contexts are merely that, different contexts with the same fundamental human behaviour – online vs. offline decisions is an example of a context where students may feel that behaviour is different. Is it really different, or just in a different context? Early twentieth-century business was convinced that catalogue shopping would fundamentally change shopping, then the telephone and, still later, the arrival of television. Has the internet changed human behaviour, or just adjusted the costs of search, decreased distance (in some directions) and cemented power in a few major players' hands?

During the course, assessment is challenging. While topics change, a first essay topic I have set more than once is "Write an Essay on Marketing". Requiring students to define their question and answer it might seem easy at first, but it is seen as the most difficult assessment students have undertaken. Opportunity is given for students to trial both their topic and their argument with staff, using the Socratic method to develop the assignment. Given the challenging nature of this assessment it is not weighted heavily, allowing students to learn from their first attempt at high-level critical thought.

The second assessment is normally a presentation, individual or in groups, that connects marketing history to the future of marketing. These presentations are based around emerging topics such as artificial intelligence and marketing or relocalisation. Students are given the opportunity to propose their own topics for this assignment. A written report attached to the presentation can help students to raise the standard of the content of the presentation. This presentation is done without PowerPoint or other digital presentation platforms.

Since removing PowerPoint from the course the standard of content has risen noticeably.

At the end of this course, students have been exposed to a much wider understanding of marketing and its contributions to society. They have many frameworks to bring to problems and are able to engage critically with current marketing fashions. They are better marketers and better citizens.

REFERENCES

Ackoff, R. and Emery, F.E. (eds) (1972). *On Purposeful Systems*. Chicago, IL: Aldine Atherton.

Alderson, W. (1957). *Marketing Behavior and Executive Action: A Functionalist Approach to Marketing*. Homewood, IL: Richard D. Irwin.

Alderson, W. (1965). *Dynamic Marketing Behavior: A Functionalist Theory of Marketing*. Homewood, IL: Richard D. Irwin.

Alderson, W. (2006). The heterogeneous market and the organized behavior system. In B. Wooliscroft, R.D. Tamilia and S.J. Shapiro (eds), *A Twenty-First Century Guide to Aldersonian Marketing Thought*, pp. 205–233. New York: Springer.

Alderson, W. and Cox, R. (1948). Towards a theory of marketing. *Journal of Marketing*, 13(October): 137–52.

Bagozzi, R. (1974). Marketing as an organized behavioral system of exchange. *Journal of Marketing*, 38(4): 77–81.

Bagozzi, R.P. (1975). Marketing as exchange. *Journal of Marketing*, 39(4): 32–9.

Bagozzi, R.P. (1978). Marketing as exchange: A theory of transactions in the marketplace. *American Behavioral Scientist*, 21(4): 535–56.

Bartels, R. (1976a). *The Development of Marketing Thought*. 2nd edn. Homewood, IL: Richard D. Irwin.

Bartels, R. (1976b). *The History of Marketing Thought*. Columbus, OH: Grid Inc., 2nd edn, originally published as *The Development of Marketing Thought* in 1962.

Belk, R.W., Wallendorf, M. and Sherry, J.F. (1989). The sacred and the profane in consumer behavior: Theodicy on the odyssey. *The Journal of Consumer Research*, 16(1): 1–38.

Birmingham, R.L. (1968). The consumer as king: The economics of precarious sovereignty. *Case Western Reserve Law Review*, 20(2): 354–77.

Boulding, K.E. (1956). General systems theory: The skeleton of science. *Management Science*, 2(April): 197–208.

Breyer, R.F. (1934). *The Marketing Institution*. New York: McGraw-Hill.

Carson, R. (1962). *Silent Spring*. Boston, MA: Houghton Mifflin

Churchman, C.W. (1967). Guest editorial: Wicked problems. *Management Science*, 14(4): B141–B142.

Churchman, C.W., Ackoff, R.L. and Arnoff, E.L. (1957). *Introduction to Operations Research*. New York: John Wiley and Sons.

Cox, R. and Alderson, W. (eds) (1950). *Theory in Marketing*. Homewood, IL: Richard D. Irwin.

Dash, M. (2011). *Tulipomania: The Story of the World's Most Coveted Flower and the Extraordinary Passions it Aroused*. Hachette.

Dichter, E. (1964). *Handbook of Consumer Motivations: The Psychology of the World of Objects*. New York: McGraw-Hill Book Company.

El-Ansary, A.I. (2005). Relationship marketing management: A school in the history of marketing thought. *Journal of Relationship Marketing*, 4(1–2): 43–56.

Farmer, R.N. (1967). Would you want your daughter to marry a marketing man?. *Journal of Marketing*, 31(1): 1–3.

Ferguson, N. (2008). *The Ascent of Money: A Financial History of the World*. New York: Penguin.

Fisk, G. (1961). The general systems approach to the study of marketing. In W.D. Stevens (ed.), *The Social Responsibilities of Marketing*, pp. 207–211. Chicago, IL: American Marketing Association.

Fisk, G. (1967). *Marketing Systems: An Introductory Analysis*. New York: Harper & Row.

Forrester, J. (1969). *Urban Dynamics*. Cambridge, MA: MIT Press.

Forrester, J.W. (1971). *World Dynamics*. Cambridge, MA: Wright-Allen Press.

Galbraith, J.K. (1958). *The Affluent Society*. Cambridge: The Riverside Press.

Gordon, R.A. and Howell, J.E. (1959). *Higher Education for Business*. New York: Columbia University Press.

Grönroos, C. (1995). Relationship marketing: The strategy continuum. *Journal of the Academy of Marketing Science*, 23(4): 252–4.

Hollander, S., Rassuli, K., Jones, D. and Dix, L. (2005). Periodization in marketing history. *Journal of Macromarketing*, 25(1): 32.

Hunt, S.D. (1983). General theories and the fundamental explanada of marketing. *Journal of Marketing*, 47(Fall): 9–17.

Hunt, S.D. (2011). On the intersection of marketing history and marketing theory. *Marketing Theory*, 11(4): 483–9.

Hunt, S.D. (2020). Indigenous theory development in marketing: The foundational premises approach. *AMS Review*, 10: 8–17.

Jones, D.B. and Shaw, E.H. (2002). A history of marketing thought. *Handbook of Marketing*, pp. 39–65.

Katz, D. and Kahn, R.L. (1966). *The Social Psychology of Organizations*. New York: John Wiley & Sons.

Klein, N. (2000). *No Logo: No Space, No Choice, No Jobs*. New York: Picador.

Kurlansky, M. (2011). *Salt*. London: Random House.

Layton, R. (2007). Marketing systems: A core macromarketing concept. *Journal of Macromarketing*, 27(3): 227–42.

Layton, R. and Duffy, S.M. (2018). Path dependency in marketing systems: Where history matters and the future casts a shadow. *Journal of Macromarketing*, 38(4): 400–414.

Layton, R.A. (2009). On economic growth, marketing systems, and the quality of life. *Journal of Macromarketing*, 29(4): 349–62.

Layton, R.A. (2011). Towards a theory of marketing systems. *European Journal of Marketing*, 45(1/2): 259–76.

Layton, R.A. (2014). Formation, growth, and adaptive change in marketing systems. *Journal of Macromarketing*, 35(3): 302–319.

Levitt, T. (1960). Marketing myopia. *Harvard Business Review*, 38(July–August): 24–47.

Mackay, C. (2012). *Extraordinary Popular Delusions and the Madness of Crowds*. Simon and Schuster.

Mitchell, R., Wooliscroft, B. and Higham, J. (2010). Sustainable market orientation: A new approach to managing marketing strategy orientation. *Journal of Macromarketing*, 30(2): 160–70.

Morgan, R. and Hunt, S. (1994). The commitment-trust theory of relationship marketing. *Journal of Marketing*, 58(3): 20–38.

Mundt, J. (1993). Externalities: Uncalculated outcomes of exchange. *Journal of Macromarketing*, 13(2): 46–53.

Mundt, J. and Houston, F.S. (1996). Externalities and the calculation of exchange outcomes. *Journal of Macromarketing*, 16(1): 73–88.

Mundt, J. and Houston, F.S. (2010). Ubiquitous externalities: Characteristics, climate, and implications for post-acquisition behaviors. *Journal of Macromarketing*, 30(3): 254–69.

Nader, R. (1965). *Unsafe at Any Speed: The Designed-in Dangers of the American Automobile*. New York: Grossman.

Packard, V. (1958). *The Hidden Persuaders*. New York: Pocket Books.

Packard, V. (1959). *The Status Seekers*. New York: The David McKay Company.

Packard, V. (1960). *The Wastemakers*. New York: The David McKay Company.

Padela, S.M.F., Wooliscroft, B., and Ganglmair-Wooliscroft, A. (2020). Brand externalities: A taxonomy. *Journal of Macromarketing*, forthcoming.

Pickett, K. and Wilkinson, R. (2010). *The Spirit Level: Why Equality is Better for Everyone*. London: Penguin.

Pierson, F.C. (1959). *The Education of American Businessmen. A Study of University-College Programs in Business Administration*. New York: McGraw-Hill Book Company.

Piketty, T. (2020). *Capital and Ideology*. Cambridge, MA: Harvard University Press.

Reilly, W.J. (1929). *Methods for the Study of Retail Relationships*. Austin, TX: University of Texas at Austin.

Robins, F. (2000). The e-marketing mix. *The Marketing Review*, 1(2): 249–74.

Ryan, F.W. (1935). Functional concepts in market distribution. *Harvard Business Review*, 13(January): 205–24.

Sandel, M.J. (2000). What money can't buy: The moral limits of markets. *Tanner Lectures on Human Values*, 21: 87–122.

Shapiro, S.J. and Layton, R. (eds) (2019). Marketing systems: The evolution of a concept over time. Sage Publications. Virtual Special Issue of the *Journal of Macromarketing*.

Shaw, E. and Jones, D. (2005). A history of schools of marketing thought. *Marketing Theory*, 5(3): 239–81.

Sheth, J.N., Gardner, D.M. and Garrett, D.E. (1988). *Marketing Theory: Evolution and Evaluation*. New York: John Wiley and Sons.

Sinclair, A. (1962). *Prohibition, the Era of Excess*. With an introduction by Richard Hofstadter. Boston, MA: Little, Brown.

Tadajewski, M. (2006). The ordering of marketing theory: The influence of McCarthyism and the Cold War. *Marketing Theory*, 6(2): 163–99.

Tadajewski, M. (2009). The foundations of relationship marketing: Reciprocity and trade relations. *Marketing Theory*, 9(1): 9–38.

Tadajewski, M. and Jones, B. (eds) (2007). *History of Marketing Thought*, vol. Two. London: Sage Publications.

Trace, Jr, A.S. (1961). *What Ivan Knows that Johnny Doesn't*. New York: Random House.

Von Bertalanffy, L. (1968). *General Systems Theory: Foundations, Development, Applications*. New York: George Braziller.

Von Bertalanffy, L. (1971). *General Theory of Systems: Application to Psychology*. Essays in Semiotics.

Winer, R.S. and Neslin, S.A. (2014). *The History of Marketing Science*. Singapore: World Scientific.

Witkowski, T. (2010). A brief history of frugality discourses in the United States. *Consumption Markets & Culture*, 13(3): 235–58.

Witkowski, T.H. (2017). *A History of American Consumption: Threads of Meaning, Gender, and Resistance*. Abingdon: Routledge.

Wooliscroft, B. (2007). Wroe Alderson: A life. In M. Tadajewski and B. Jones (eds), *History of Marketing Thought*, vol. Two. London: Sage Publications.

Wooliscroft, B., Ganglmair-Wooliscroft, A. and Noone, A. (2014). A hierarchy of ethical behavior: The case of New Zealand. *Journal of Macromarketing*, 34(1): 57–72.

Zeithaml, V.A., Parasuraman, A. and Berry, L.L. (1985). Problems and strategies in services marketing. *Journal of Marketing*, 49(2): 33–46.

APPENDIX: A READING LIST

No reading list is complete, but the following references have engaged students and broadened their perspective on what marketing is and can be.

Achrol, R. (1991). Evolution of the marketing organization: New forms for turbulent environments. *Journal of Marketing*, 55: 77–93.

Ahuvia, A. and Friedman, D. (1998). Income, consumption and subjective well-being: Toward a composite macromarketing model. *Journal of Macromarketing*, 18(2): 153–68.

Alderson, W. (1957). *Marketing Behavior and Executive Action: A Functionalist Approach to Marketing*. Homewood, IL: Richard D. Irwin.

Alderson, W. (1958). The analytical framework for marketing. In D.J. Duncan (ed.), *Proceedings: Conference of Marketing Teachers from Far Western States*, pp. 15–28, Berkeley, CA: University of California.

Alderson, W. (1965). *Dynamic Marketing Behavior: A Functionalist Theory of Marketing*. Homewood, IL: Richard D. Irwin.

Alderson, W. and Cox, R. (1948). Towards a theory of marketing. *Journal of Marketing*, 13(October): 137–52.

Anderson, P.F. (1983). Marketing, scientific progress, and scientific method. *Journal of Marketing*, 47(Fall): 18–31.

Arndt, J. (1978). How broad should the marketing concept be? *Journal of Marketing*, 42: 101–103.

Arndt, J. (1985). On making marketing science more scientific: Role of orientations, paradigms, metaphors & puzzle solving. *Journal of Marketing*, 49: 11–23.

Bagozzi, R.P. (1975). Marketing as exchange. *Journal of Marketing*, 39(4): 32–9.

Barksdale, H.C. (1980). Wroe Alderson's contributions to marketing theory. In C. Lamb and P. Dunne (eds), *Theoretical Developments in Marketing*, pp. 1–3. Chicago, IL: American Marketing Association.

Bartels, R. (1951). Can marketing be a science? *Journal of Marketing*, 15(January): 319–28.

Bartels, R. and Jenkins, R.L. (1977). Macromarketing. *Journal of Marketing*, 41: 17–20.

Baumol, W.J. (1957). On the role of marketing theory. *Journal of Marketing*, 21(April): 413–18.

Baumgartner, H. (2002). Toward a personology of the consumer. *Journal of Consumer Research*, 29(2): 286–92.

Belk, R. (1988). Possessions and the extended self. *Journal of Consumer Research*, 15: 139–68.

Bell, S.J., Whitwell, G.J. and Lukas, B.A. (2002). Schools of thought in organisational learning. *Journal of the Academy of Marketing Science*, 30(1): 70–86.

Bond, P.F. and Corey, R.J. (1998). Moral reflections in marketing. *Journal of Macromarketing*, 18(2): 104–114.

Breyer, R.F. (1934). *The Marketing Institution*. New York: McGraw-Hill.

Brown, S. (2004). Theodore Levitt: The ultimate writing machine. *Marketing Theory*, 4(3): 209–238.

Brown, S.W. and Fisk, R. (eds) (1984). *Marketing Theory: Distinguished Contributions*. New York: John Wiley & Sons.

Brown, S., Webster Jr, F., Steenkamp, J., Wilkie, W., Sheth, J., Sisodia, R., Kerin, R. et al. (2005). Marketing renaissance: Opportunities and imperatives for improving marketing thought, practice, and infrastructure. *Journal of Marketing*, 69(4): 1–25.

Brownlie, D., Saren, M., Wensley, R. and Wittington, R. (1999). *Rethinking Marketing: Towards Critical Marketing Accountings*. London: Sage Publications.

Burawoy, M. (2004). Public sociologies: Contradictions, dilemmas, and possibilities. *Social Forces*, 82(4): 1603–618.

Burton, D. (2005). Marketing theory matters. *British Journal of Management*, 16(1): 5–18.

Buzzell, R.D. (1963). Is marketing a science? *Harvard Business Review*, 41(January–February): 32–36, 39–40, 166, 168, 170.

Carsky, M.L., Dickinson, R.A. and Canedy, C. (1998). The evolution of quality in consumer goods. *Journal of Macromarketing*, 18(2): 132–43.

Carson, R. (1962). *Silent Spring*. Boston, MA: Houghton Mifflin.

Chalmers, A.F. (1999). *What is this Thing Called Science?* 3rd edn, St Lucia: University of Queensland Press.

Cova, B. and Cova, V. (2002). Tribal marketing. The tribalisation of society and its impact on the conduct of marketing. *European Journal of Marketing*, 36(5/6): 595–620.

Day, G.S. and Wensley, R. (1983). Marketing theory with a strategic orientation. *Journal of Marketing*, 47(Fall): 79–89.

Ehrenberg, A.S.C. (1964). Estimating the proportion of loyal buyers. *Journal of Marketing Research*, 1(1): 56–9.

Ehrenberg, A.S.C. (1995). Empirical generalisations, theory, and method. *Marketing Science*, 14(3): G20–G28.

Enis, B.M., Cox, K.K. and Mokwa, M.P. (eds) (1990). *Marketing Classics*, 8th edn. Upper Saddle River, NJ: Prentice Hall.

Farmer, R.N. (1967). Would you want your daughter to marry a marketing-man? *Journal of Marketing*, 31(January): 1–3.

Farmer, R.N. (1987). Would you want your granddaughter to marry a Taiwanese marketing man? *Journal of Marketing*, 51(October): 111–16.

Fisk, G. (1971). *New Essays in Marketing Theory*. Boston, MA: Allyn & Bacon.

Fornell, C. (1992). A national customer satisfaction barometer: The Swedish experience. *Journal of Marketing*, 56(January): 6–21.

Fornell, C., Johnson, M.D., Anderson, E.W., Cha, J. and Bryant, B.E. (1996). The American Customer Satisfaction Index: Nature, purpose, and findings. *Journal of Marketing*, 60(October): 7–18.

French, J.R.P.J. and Raven, B. (1959). The bases of social power. In D. Cartwright (ed.), *Studies in Social Power*, pp. 150–67. Ann Arbor, MI: Institute for Social Research.

Fullerton, R. (1988). How modern is modern marketing? Marketing's evolution & the myth of the "production era". *Journal of Marketing*, 53: 108–125.

Galbraith, J.K. (1958). *The Affluent Society*. Cambridge: The Riverside Press.

Gummesson, E. (1997a). Relationship marketing as a paradigm shift: Some conclusions from the 30R Approach. *Management Decision*, 35(4): 267–72.

Gummesson, E. (1997b). Relationship marketing: The emperor's new clothes or a paradigm shift? *Marketing and Research Today*, 25(1): 53–60.

Hirschman, E.C. and Holbrook, M.B. (1992). *Postmodern Consumer Research*. Newbury Park, CA: Sage Publications.

Holbrook, M.B. and Hulbert, J.M. (2002). Elegy on the death of marketing: Never send to know why we have come to bury marketing but ask what you can do for your country churchyard. *European Journal of Marketing*, 36(5/6): 706–732.

Hunt, S.D. (1976). The nature and scope of marketing. *Journal of Marketing*, 40(July): 17–28.

Hunt, S.D. (1991). *Modern Marketing Theory: Critical Issues in the Philosophy of Marketing Science*. Cincinnati, OH: South-Western Publishing.

Hunt, S.D. (1992). For reason and realism in marketing. *Journal of Marketing*, 56(April): 89–102.

Hunt, S.D. (1993). Objectivity in marketing theory and research. *Journal of Marketing*, 57(April): 76–91.

Hunt, S.D. (1997). Evolutionary economics, endogenous growth models, and resource-advantage theory. *Eastern Economic Journal*, 23(4).

Hunt, S.D. and Burnett, J.J. (1982). The macromarketing/micromarketing dichotomy: A taxonomical model. *Journal of Marketing*, 46(Summer): 11–26.

Hunt, S.D. and Chonko, L.B. (1984). Marketing and Machiavellianism. *Journal of Marketing*, 48(Summer): 30–42.

Hunt, S.D. and Morgan, R.M. (1996). The resource-advantage theory of competition: Dynamics, path dependencies, and evolutionary dimensions. *Journal of Marketing*, 60(October): 107–114.

Hunt, S.D. and Morgan, R.M. (1997). Resource-advantage theory: A snake swallowing its tail or a general theory of competition? *Journal of Marketing*, 61(October): 74–82.

Hunt, S.D. and Vitell, S. (1986). A general theory of marketing ethics. *Journal of Macromarketing*, 6: 5–16 .

Hunt, S.D., Muncy, J.A. and Ray, N.M. (1981). Alderson's general theory of marketing: A formalization. In B.M. Enis and K.J. Roering (eds), *Review of Marketing*, pp. 267–72. Chicago, IL: American Marketing Association.

Ivens, B.S. and Blois, K.J. (2004). Relational exchange norms in marketing: A critical review of MacNeil's contribution. *Marketing Theory*, 4(3): 239–63.

Jaworski, B.J. and Kohli, A.K. (1993). Market orientation: Antecedents and consequences. *Journal of Marketing*, 57(3): 53–71.

Jones, D.G.B. and Monieson, D.D. (1990). Early development of the philosophy of marketing thought. *Journal of Marketing*, 54(January): 102–113.

Kohli, A.K. and Jaworski, B.J. (1990). Market orientation: The construct, research propositions, and managerial implications. *Journal of Marketing*, 54(2): 1–18.

Kotler, P. (1972). A generic concept of marketing. *Journal of Marketing*, 36(April): 46–54.

Lawson, R. and Wooliscroft, B. (2004). Human nature and the marketing concept. *Marketing Theory*, 4(4): 311–26.

Leong, S.M. (1985). Metatheory and metamethodology in marketing: A Lakatosian reconstruction. *Journal of Marketing*, 49(Fall): 23–40.

Levitt, T. (1960). Marketing myopia. *Harvard Business Review*, 38: 45–56.

Levy, S.J. and Luedicke, M.K. (2013). From marketing ideology to branding ideology. *Journal of Macromarketing*, 33(1).

Luck, D.J. (1969). Broadening the concept of marketing – Too far. *Journal of Marketing*, 33(July): 53–63.

Macchiette, B. and Roy, A. (2001). *Taking Sides: Clashing Views on Controversial Issues in Marketing*. New York: McGraw Hill.

McVey, P. (1960). Are channels of distribution what the textbooks say? *Journal of Marketing*, 24(3): 61–5.

Mitchell, R., Wooliscroft, B. and Higham, J. (2010). Sustainable market orientation – A new approach to managing marketing strategy orientation. *Journal of Macromarketing*, 30(2): 160–70.

Murphy, P.E. and Enis, B.M. (1986). Classifying products strategically. *Journal of Marketing*, 50: 24–42.

Nader, R. (1965). *Unsafe at Any Speed: The Designed-in Dangers of the American Automobile.* New York: Grossman Publishers.

Narver, J.C. and Slater, S.F. (1990). The effect of a market orientation on business profitability. *Journal of Marketing*, 54(4): 20–35.

Peter, J.P. (1992). Realism or relativism for marketing theory and research: A comment on Hunt's "scientific realism". *Journal of Marketing*, 56(April): 72–9.

Peter, J.P. and Olson, J.C. (1983). Is science marketing? *Journal of Marketing*, 47(Fall): 111–25.

Reidenbach, R.E. and Robin, D.P. (1988). Some initial steps toward improving the measurement of ethical evaluations of marketing activities. *Journal of Business Ethics*, 7(11): 871–9.

Schwartz, G. (1963). *Development of Marketing Theory*. Cincinnati, OH: South-Western Publishing.

Sheth, J.N. and Sisodia, R.S. (1999). Revisiting marketing's lawlike generalizations. *The Journal of the Academy of Marketing Science*, 27(1): 71–87.

Sheth, J.N., Gardner, D.M. and Garrett, D.E. (1988). *Marketing Theory: Evolution and Evaluation.* New York: John Wiley and Sons.

Shrivastava, S. and Kale, S.H. (2003). Philosophising on the elusiveness of relationship marketing theory in consumer markets: A case for reassessing ontological and epistemological assumptions. *Australasian Marketing Journal*, 11(3): 61–71.

Smithee, A.B. and Lee, T. (2004). Future directions in marketing knowledge: A panoramic perspective from Hollywood. *Journal of Business & Industrial Marketing*, 19(2): 149–54.

Vakratsas, D. and Ambler, T. (1999). How advertising works: What do we really know? *Journal of Marketing*, 63: 26–43.

Varadarajan, P.R. (2003). From the Editor: Musings on relevance and rigor of scholarly research in marketing. *Journal of the Academy of Marketing Science*, 31(4): 368–76.

Vargo, S.L. and Lusch, R.F. (2004). Evolving to a new dominant logic for marketing. *Journal of Marketing*, 68(January): 1–17.

Walle, A.H. (2002). *Exotic Visions In Marketing Theory and Practice.* Westport, CT: Quorum.

Waterschoot, W.V. and den Bulte, C.V. (1992). The 4P classification of the marketing mix revisited. *Journal of Marketing*, 56: 83–93.

Webster, F. (1992). The changing role of marketing in the corporation. *Journal of Marketing*, 56(4): 1–17.

Wedel, M. and Kamakura, W. (2002). Editors' introduction: Special Issue on market segmentation. *International Journal of Research in Marketing*, 19(3): 181–303.

Wells, W.D. (1993). Discovery-oriented consumer research. *Journal of Consumer Research*, 19(4): 489–504.

Wilkie, W.L. and Moore, E.S. (1999). Marketing's contributions to society. *Journal of Marketing*, 63(Special Issue): 198–218.

Williamson, O. (1975). *Markets and Hierarchies.* Glencoe, IL: The Free Press.

Wooliscroft, B. (2003). Wroe Alderson's contribution to marketing theory through his textbooks. *Journal of the Academy of Marketing Science*, 31(4): 481–5.

Wooliscroft, B. (2011). Marketing theory as history. *Marketing Theory*, 11(4): 499–501.

Wooliscroft, B., Tamilia, R. and Shapiro, S.J. (eds) (2006). *A Twenty-first Century Guide to Aldersonian Marketing Thought*. New York: Springer.

Zaltman, G. and Bonoma, T. (1979). The lack of heresy in marketing. In O.C. Ferrell, S.W. Brown and C.W. Lamb, Jr (eds), *Conceptual and Theoretical Developments in Marketing*, pp. 474–84. Chicago, IL: American Marketing Association.

Zaltman, G., LeMasters, K. and Heffring, M.P. (1982). *Theory Construction in Marketing: Some Thoughts on Thinking*. New York: John Wiley & Sons.

Zif, J. (1980). A managerial approach to macromarketing. *Journal of Marketing*, 44: 36–45.

Zinkhan, G.M. and Hirschheim, R. (1992). Truth in marketing theory and research: An alternative perspective. *Journal of Marketing*, 56(April): 80–88.

8.   Teaching business-to-business marketing

Ross Brennan

Consumption is the sole end and purpose of all production; and the interest of the producer ought to be attended to only so far as it may be necessary for promoting that of the consumer. The maxim is so perfectly self-evident that it would be absurd to attempt to prove it.

Extract from: *The Wealth of Nations: An Inquiry into the Nature and Causes of the Wealth of Nations*, by Adam Smith, available at https://scholarsbank.uoregon.edu/xmlui/handle/1794/782.

INTRODUCTION

The editor of one of the most important academic journals in the field of business-to-business marketing has written that: 'there is a long-standing history in academia of B-to-B as an outcast ... despite business marketing's prevalence' (Lichtenthal, 2007, p. 2), and elsewhere in this book Harker and Paddison (Chapter 4, this volume) present data suggesting that business-to-business marketing is declining in popularity as a component of marketing degrees in the UK. I had previously expressed a similar sentiment at the annual conference of the UK's Academy of Marketing: 'Business-to-business marketing seems to be both ubiquitous and unloved' (Brennan, 2000), although ubiquitous now sounds hollow given Harker and Paddison's findings. More recently the prominent business-to-business scholar and Research Director of the Institute for the Study of Business Markets at Penn State University, Gary Lilien, has opined that business marketing is of extraordinary economic importance but has been somewhat neglected by the marketing academy: 'B2B marketing is highly relevant and important but is underrepresented in academia' (Lilien, 2016, p. 9). Lilien (2016, p. 9) goes on to provide an insight into the origins of this problem, namely that: 'business markets are not overt, mostly taking place out of sight of casual observers'. This represents the first issue facing business-to-business marketing educators when they teach the subject to students who have no prior relevant experience, which usually means the great majority of students studying marketing at a business school. Marketing students are used to the idea, however misguided, that introspection from their perspective as consumers will provide them with some help in understanding marketing. No doubt many marketing educators trade on this belief by using examples from well-known consumer brands to ease students into the subject, and possibly by echoing the students' belief that experience as a consumer yields some useful insight into marketing. Whether such an educational approach is legitimate or not, it is not of much help to the business-to-business educator. Students without experience in a business-to-business context have little or no useful introspection to bring to bear. Under these circumstances the educator may choose a 'shallow end approach' or a 'deep end approach'. The 'shallow end approach' is to point to the contingent circumstances where business-to-business can be readily linked to consumer marketing; for example, where a fashion buyer for a major retailer seeks to buy the right jeans and trainers to match expected consumer preferences for the next selling season. The 'deep end approach' goes in a different direction, pointing to the many contingent circumstances where business-to-business marketing looks nothing like consumer marketing; for example, where a substantial team of professionals from an IT vendor works alongside a complementary team from a manufacturing organisation over an extended period to deliver an enhanced logistics and inventory control system. Issues such as these that face the business-to-business marketing educator are addressed in this chapter, with the contingent nature of business-to-business marketing a thread that runs throughout.

The chapter is organised into five sections. The practical significance and distinctiveness of business-to-business marketing are addressed first, and then in the second section there is an appraisal of several important and distinctive theoretical ideas that permeate business-to-business marketing thinking. Following this, the third section is devoted to an appraisal of the IMP approach to business markets. Some challenges that this approach, the most important coherent body of intellectual work in the business marketing field, poses to the educator are examined. The fourth section examines the specific ethical issues that are found in business markets and presents ideas for introducing ethical issues in the classroom and, in particular, ideas for convincing students of the significance of this topic. Finally, and in lieu of a conclusion, in the final section I have simply collected a few handy tips based on my own experience of teaching business-to-business marketing.

PRACTICAL DISTINCTIVENESS OF BUSINESS-TO-BUSINESS MARKETING

Various methods have been used to explain the importance of business-to-business, or industrial[1], marketing in the business school curriculum. Thirty years ago Lichtenthal and Butaney (1991) estimated that over half of business school graduates in the United States started their careers in the business-to-business sector. More recently, Lilien (2016) asserted that business-to-business and business-to-consumer marketing were roughly equal in terms of the economic value of transactions. Authors of textbooks in the business-to-business field naturally feel the need to emphasise the economic significance of economic activity falling within the scope of business marketing. Thus, Blythe and Zimmerman (2005, p. 8) claim that 'the B2B market is far larger than the consumer market'. Similarly, Hutt and Speh (2010, p. 4) assert that 'Business marketers serve the largest market of all: The dollar volume of transactions in the industrial or business market significantly exceeds that of the ultimate consumer market ... More than 50 per cent of all business school graduates join firms that compete directly in the business market.' It is worth pondering for a moment over these assertions that the business market significantly exceeds the consumer market in financial terms. In one sense, namely in terms of the total amount of sales revenue generated in business and consumer markets, this seems logically sound. The components of a final consumer good are traded many times between firms before the finished product is sold to the consumer (this is indeed the point that Blythe and Zimmerman, cited above, make – the example they use is all of the components that go into the production of a hair dryer). In another sense, however, it seems implausible to argue that the value of the business-to-business transactions needed to bring a product to the final consumer market may exceed the value of the final sale to the consumer. Surely the value captured in the final sale to the consumer must exceed the value of all the preceding (business-to-business) transactions, if all the intermediaries in the chain are to make a profit and stay in business? To students it may seem like a logical conundrum: on the one hand, it is obvious that the total sales revenue generated in business-to-business transactions must exceed that in consumer transactions, and on the other hand the final consumer transaction is where all the value created in the business-to-business chain is finally captured. The solution to this conundrum lies in the distinction between sales revenue and value-added. Value-added at each stage in the production process is the difference between the selling price and the cost of all inputs. Logically, while the total amount of business-to-business sales revenue in an economy will exceed consumer sales revenue, the total amount of value-added in business-to-business transactions will be slightly less than the final consumer market value. At the macroeconomic level, this distinction differentiates the familiar Gross Domestic Product (GDP) measure of national income from the less familiar, and much larger, Gross Output (GO) measure. GDP is a value-added measure of economic activity; GO is a measure of total economic activity. If the business-to-business marketing educator wants to introduce the importance of business markets using this kind of logic, then it is necessary to ensure that students understand the distinction between sales revenue and value-added.

Perhaps a simpler method of justifying the importance of business marketing, and one likely to be appreciated more immediately by students, is to focus on the major global brands that are largely or entirely business-to-business. Hutt and Speh (2010) mention brands such as Cisco, Caterpillar, GE, Intel and 3M. According to Interbrand (https://www.interbrand.com/best-brands/best-global-brands/2019/ranking/), these brands were all in the top 100 global best brands in 2019, with Intel placed 13th, Cisco 15th, GE 19th, 3M 64th, and Caterpillar 76th. For example, Interbrand values the Cisco brand at $35.6 billion.[2] Other prominent business-to-business brands found in the Interbrand top 100 include Oracle (18th), SAP (20th), Accenture (31st), Salesforce (70th) and LinkedIn (98th). For the business-to-business educator, the fact that many students will have only a hazy idea, or perhaps no idea at all, of what these companies do, can provide an intriguing way to engage the students' curiosity:

> So, there is this company called Cisco that had sales revenues of $51.9 billion in 2019 and has a brand valuation of $35.6 billion; they employ around 80,000 people, who are generally highly qualified and well-paid; they deliver products that are essential to the Internet and central to the development of big new technologies like the Internet of Things ... and all of this is business-to-business. You can find out about the marketing side of their business by looking at their customer case histories at https://www.cisco.com/c/en/us/about/case-studies-customer-success-stories.html.

Additionally, one can point out that several of the top B2B brands found in the Interbrand list are themselves deeply involved in the business-to-business marketing process. For example, sales, marketing and CRM solutions are major parts of the business activity of SAP, Oracle, Salesforce and LinkedIn.

These two methods of justifying business-to-business marketing as a legitimate, independent topic in the curriculum, and as an important topic of study for students might be summarised as *scale* and *glamour*. Because most business-to-business marketing activity is invisible to the general public, it is possible to imagine that it is relatively small, compared to consumer marketing. This is not the case; the scale of economic activity and of sales, marketing and related jobs attributable to B2B is substantial. Similarly, B2B marketers develop and manage some of the world's biggest brand names (the *glamour* dimension). However, a third aspect in delineating business-to-business marketing is its distinctiveness, meaning the degree to which it can be differentiated from other forms of marketing. Often, this means differentiation from marketing to consumers. The intellectual legitimacy of making a dichotomous distinction between business (industrial) and consumer marketing was questioned in an influential article by Fern and Brown (1984). It is worth noting that this article was published prior to the widespread dissemination of the ideas of the IMP Group and makes no reference to the IMP body of work, which is arguably the most substantial, coherent and original body of business-to-business research extant. The IMP approach to business markets and marketing is examined later in the chapter. I have argued elsewhere that it is futile to look for essential (intrinsic, absolute) differences between business and consumer marketing (Brennan, 2012), but that the contingent differences are so substantial that it makes sense to think of them as separate subjects in the curriculum. The next section looks at several contingency frameworks that can be used to differentiate marketing approaches within the business marketing sphere.

THEORETICAL DISTINCTIVENESS OF BUSINESS-TO-BUSINESS MARKETING

At the most fundamental level, business-to-business marketing is differentiated from consumer marketing by the nature of the transactions involved. Several core concepts can be used to bring home the distinctive nature of business markets and marketing to students: the transvection (Alderson, 1965; Alderson and Martin, 1965), derived demand (Marshall, 1920; Parkin and King, 1995), and the threefold (market structure/ buying behaviour/ marketing practice) classification of market distinctiveness (Brennan et al., 2017). According to Alderson and Martin (1965, pp. 122–3): 'The marketing process is the continuous operation of transforming conglomerate resources as they occur in nature into meaningful assortments in the hands of consumers ... the transvection comprises all prior action necessary to produce this final result, going all the way back to conglomerate resources'. From this perspective, business-to-business marketing can be explained as an essential part of the process of creating successful transvections. This insight can be particularly useful for students who may struggle at first to understand the close linkages between business marketing, purchasing and supply chain management; all these functions are intrinsically involved with transvections. Throughout the transvection, many transactions take place that involve derived demand. Derived demand arises where the demand for a good or service arises from its use in a production or service-delivery process: 'A derived demand is a demand for an input not for its own sake but in order to use it in the production of goods and services' (Parkin and King, 1995, p. 378); 'Unlike consumers' demands for goods and services ... factor demands are derived demands: they depend on, and are derived from, the firm's level of output and the cost of inputs' (Pindyck and Rubinfeld, 2001, p. 502).

A point of possible confusion here is that many things that companies purchase are not used directly in production or service delivery processes. For example, auditing services provided by an accounting firm to ensure that the business complies with all necessary financial reporting laws and standards are clearly not a direct input to the production or service-delivery process. Nevertheless, the demand for auditing services is a derived demand; the business only needs to purchase auditing services as an essential support for its productive activities.

A useful, related concept to derived demand and the transvection is the notion of upstream and downstream business activities. This concept, while intuitively obvious to business practitioners, may initially seem obscure to those students who lack business experience. The educator can help by tracing the concept to its roots in the metaphor of a river system, since in the metaphorical context of the river it is clear that upstream means 'nearer to the source' and downstream means 'nearer to the ocean', and it is equally clear that upstream and downstream are relative terms (what is upstream or downstream depends on your own location). By analogy, upstream business activities are those that are closer to raw material markets (what Alderson and Martin (1965) call conglomerate resources), downstream activities are closer to the final consumer, and whether a business activity is upstream or downstream is relative to your own position in the supply chain (or transvection). Any scope for confusion in understanding the concept of derived demand can be minimised using the concepts upstream and downstream. Upstream and downstream activities are linked in a chain of derived demand. All transactions that facilitate transactions further downstream exhibit derived demand. The end of the chain of derived demand arrives with a sale to a final consumer, which is defined as direct demand. Business-to-business marketing is concerned with derived demand.

Brennan et al. (2017) suggest that the distinctiveness of business markets and marketing can be understood in terms of a hierarchical classification scheme. At the most fundamental level, business markets exhibit particular market structure characteristics (for example, there is often high concentration of demand, meaning that a few buyers have considerable buying power). At the intermediate level, business buying behaviour exhibits specific characteristics (for example, transaction values are often high and the buying process is often complex, involving professionals from a range of business functions). As a consequence of differences at the level of market structure and buying behaviour, the marketing practices of business-to-business firms are often distinctive. For example, in those business markets where demand is highly concentrated, transaction values are high and the buying process is complex, one finds uniquely business-to-business marketing practices. A characteristic marketing approach in such circumstances is the key account management strategy (Abratt and Kelly, 2002; Ivens et al., 2018). Using this approach a marketing organisation appoints a key account manager (or team) to develop a specific marketing strategy for the individual key customer account, to coordinate all of the business activities undertaken for and with the customer, to act as an advocate for the customer seeking to align the firm with the customer's business strategy, and to adapt the firm's business processes to match those of the customer (Brennan and Canning, 2002; Brennan et al., 2003).

From an educational perspective, the key point of the market structure/ buying behaviour/ marketing practice approach to distinguishing business marketing is to emphasise that superficial differences in marketing practices are an insufficient way of defining business-to-business markets and marketing. The marketing practices employed in a certain market, whether a business market or a consumer market, follow logically from the buying behaviour characteristics of customers and the underlying structure of the market. For example, the key account management strategy is frequently used by business-to-business marketers because conditions favouring this strategy, such as highly concentrated demand, powerful buyers and complex buying processes, are frequently found in business markets. In business markets where demand is widely dispersed, buyers have little buying power and the buying process is simple, key account strategy makes no sense. This suggests that business-to-business marketing can, and perhaps should, be conceptualised within a contingency framework. Such a proposition makes a lot of intuitive sense and has received considerable support in the academic literature. Intuitively, the field of business-to-business marketing has to encompass circumstances from the global market for commercial aircraft engines, where giant suppliers such as Rolls-Royce and GE face giant customers such as Boeing and Airbus, to the local market for commercial decorating services, where a small business decorator may visit a DIY superstore to buy what is needed for today's job. A number of contingency frameworks have been suggested. Jackson (1985) proposed that business customers could be divided into the categories 'always a share' (from whom some business can always be won by offering the right selling proposition) and 'lost for good' (who seek stability through lasting supplier relationships). Different marketing strategies are required for the two categories of customer. Notably, Jackson observed that a relational marketing strategy seeking to build long-term relationships of trust by making substantial customer-specific investments would be entirely mistaken with customers in the 'always a share' category. Even though this is a very simple contingency framework, students can have trouble in understanding Jackson's conclusions. For example, they may imagine that working to deepen the relationship with the customer is appropriate in all marketing circumstances since intuition tends to suggest that a closer relationship with the customer is always a desirable marketing objective.

To help students grasp the point, it can be useful to introduce another contingency framework, that of Krapfel et al. (1991), and the related concept of coopetition (Bengtsson and Kock, 2014; Lacoste, 2012). Bengtsson and

Kock (2014, p. 180) consider that coopetition is an intrinsically paradoxical concept that can be defined in different ways, but that has the general meaning of 'simultaneous cooperation and competition between firms' and that it 'has become an integral part of many companies' daily agenda' (here they are referring to business-to-business companies). In the Krapfel et al. (1991) two-by-two framework, the degree of cooperation and competition within a supplier–customer marketing relationship is represented by the concept of 'interest commonality', the extent to which the supplier and customer have compatible economic goals. Because of the paradoxical nature of the concepts of interest commonality and coopetition they may be considered potential threshold concepts in business-to-business marketing education (Meyer et al., 2010). Threshold concepts are often 'troublesome' but, when mastered, they bring about a qualitative and irreversible improvement in the student's understanding. In the field of marketing, considered as a generic discipline, probably the most basic 'fact' that students learn is that marketing is concerned with satisfying customer needs and wants (Diamantopoulos and Hart, 1993; Jaworski and Kohli, 1993; Kohli and Jaworski, 1990). It is consequently 'troublesome' to encounter the idea that a marketing organisation may choose to refrain from actions that would increase customer satisfaction, and even take actions that damage the interests of a customer. Yet, as Bengtsson and Kock (2014) observe, such circumstances are encountered frequently in business markets. A simple example that makes the point for students addicted to their smartphone is that, in recent years, Apple has relied on Samsung for the supply of OLED displays for the iPhone; for Samsung, Apple is simultaneously a customer and a competitor. The complete contingency framework suggested by Krapfel et al. (1991) comprises four quadrants: the rival (high relationship value, low interest commonality); the friend (low relationship value, high interest commonality); the acquaintance (low relationship value, low interest commonality); and, the partner (high relationship value, high interest commonality). It is only in the last of these four cases that classic relationship-deepening marketing strategies, such as key account management, can be used without reservation. The other cases call for alternative approaches.

To conclude this brief discussion of contingency frameworks and their relevance to business marketing practice and education, it is helpful to appraise Day's (2000) conception of the 'relationship spectrum' for its potential usefulness as a pedagogic tool. The basis for the relationship spectrum lies in similar arguments to those discussed in the preceding paragraph:

> … a strategy of investing in or building close relationships is neither appropriate nor necessary for every market, customer, or company. Some customers want nothing more than the timely exchange of the product or service with a minimum of hassles.

And because close relations are resource intensive, not every customer is worth the effort.' (Day, 2000, p. 24)

Furthermore, argues Day (2000), the development of deep relationships with customers creates a sustainable competitive advantage in part because it is difficult, and therefore the development of a relationship-building capability is not a strategy that all firms should pursue. The relationship spectrum is the conceptual tool that Day proposes as the basis for evaluating when more, or less, relational marketing strategies are appropriate. Since this is a 'spectrum', there are in principle an infinite number of positions along the relationship spectrum. For presentational purposes Day divides this infinite spectrum into three categories: transactional exchange, value-adding exchange, and collaborative exchange. Transactional exchange involves 'the timely exchange of standard products at competitive prices', in value-adding exchange 'the focus of the firm shifts from getting customer to keeping customers', and collaborative exchange features 'very close information, social, and process linkages, and mutual commitments made in expectation of long-run benefits' (Day, 2000, pp. 24–5). While the relationship spectrum may be considered a generic marketing concept, it is also clear that it has specific usefulness in business-to-business marketing and the pedagogy of this field. Day (2000) makes it clear that marketing strategies of collaboration and bonding, associated with the collaborative exchange end of the relationship spectrum, are particularly relevant to business-to-business markets. More generally, while most or perhaps all consumer transactions fall within the transactional and value-adding exchange categories (since it is difficult to conceive of true collaborative exchange occurring between a consumer and a firm), the entire range of the relationship spectrum is relevant in business-to-business markets. Business-to-business exchanges range from the most anonymous of all, such as the purchase of industrial commodities at prevailing spot market prices, through to the most complex and collaborative major projects, such as the design and implementation of a global communications system by an IT/telecommunications vendor for a multinational financial services firm. Towards the collaborative exchange end of the relationship spectrum business marketers have to develop 'a superior market-relating capability' (Day, 2000, p. 26), and Hutt and Speh (2007) emphasise the cross-functional processes involved in such business activities. They propose that developing cross-functional management competencies should be at the core of business-to-business marketing education (Hutt and Speh, 2007).

IMP AND INDUSTRIAL NETWORKS

The body of research carried out by members of the IMP (Industrial Marketing & Purchasing) Group constitutes arguably the single largest coherent contribution to knowledge in the field of business-to-business marketing. From an educational point of view, it is very convenient that a large amount of this research is available in the public domain, since many papers from the Group's conferences and several major book-length works are freely available at www .impgroup.org. After a brief introduction to some of the main ideas of the IMP perspective there follows a discussion of some relevant pedagogical issues.

The first international IMP study (IMP1) was published as 'International Marketing and Purchasing of Industrial Goods: An Interaction Approach' (Håkansson, 1982). The conceptual origins of IMP research lie in inter-organisational theory, new institutional economics and the 'distribution systems perspective' in marketing research. The central features of the IMP interaction approach (Håkansson, 1982) are that the relationship rather than the discrete transaction is the appropriate unit of analysis in business markets; that both the buyer and the seller are active participants in the interaction process; that there is considerable stability of relationship structures in business markets; and, that buying and selling are similar processes that should be studied simultaneously. The IMP Interaction Model comprises the buying and selling parties to the relationship (each sub-divided into the individual and the organisational level), the interaction environment (e.g. market structure), the relationship atmosphere (power-dependence; conflict–cooperation; closeness–distance; mutual expectations), and the elements and processes of interaction (short-term exchange episodes and long-term relationship processes).

Considerable attention has been paid to the question of whether or not the process of relationship development can usefully be analysed in terms of a life-cycle, or 'stages', or 'states' (Ford, 1980; Kaunonen, 2010). The related topic of relationship portfolios has also attracted considerable attention from IMP researchers (Zolkiewski and Turnbull, 2002).

Håkansson and Snehota (1995) expounded industrial network theory, an important development in IMP thinking. The relationship unit of analysis is not abandoned, and it is emphasised that structural elements of relationships (continuity, complexity, symmetry and informality) and process elements (adaptations, cooperation–conflict, social interaction and routinisation) remain of interest and important. However, the influence of one relationship on another takes centre stage, with chain dependencies between relationships resulting in 'a form of organization we have chosen to qualify as a network' (Håkansson and Snehota, 1995, p. 19). Change in one relationship can propagate through the network of interconnected relationships, and the network 'form of organization' is a rather curious one that has neither a centre nor boundaries. Relationships are conceptualised to have three layers, and each business relationship can be characterised in terms of the relative importance and the complexity of each of the three layers. These three layers are the elements of the best-known conceptual framework to emerge from Håkansson and Snehota (1995): the AAR (activities, actors, resources) model. The relationships within an industrial network can be analysed in terms of the links between their activities, the ties between their resources, and the bonds between their actors. Alongside the AAR model, which Håkansson and Snehota (1995) deemed the 'substance' of the relationship, they also proposed three 'functions' for the relationship: the function for the dyad, the function for the individual firms, and the function for third parties (i.e. the function within the wider network of which the relationship is a part).

Work has continued within the IMP Group to refine and elaborate upon the concepts that were first expounded in detail in the 1980s and 1990s. For example, Ford and colleagues (2008) revisited the fundamental concept of interaction, and several researchers have continued to explore the concept of relationship atmosphere (examples: Blois and Ryan, 2010; Sutton-Brady, 2001). Prominent new strands of research that have emerged more recently include the question of whether strategic action is possible in networks and if so, how (Baraldi et al., 2007; Ford and Mouzas, 2007; Mouzas, 2001); the idea of network pictures – managers' subjective representations of their relevant business environment (Naude et al., 2004); and the transferability of the basic IMP conceptual frameworks across cultures, with particular reference to Chinese culture (Jansson et al., 2007; Kriz and Fang, 2000).

Turning to the pedagogical challenges raised by the IMP perspective, Aramo-Immonen et al. (2020) show that it is a common occurrence, when IMP ideas are discussed in the academic literature, to focus on the superficial rather than on the ontological basis for those ideas. Thus, IMP ideas are often presented as simply supporting the superficial idea that relationships and networks are important in business markets, rather than as a profound challenge to neo-classical orthodoxy and the managerial paradigm in marketing. An important question for the business-to-business educator is the extent to which one should encourage students to investigate these more profound ideas. At the simplistic level, IMP studies simply confirm the taken-for-granted assumption that relationships matter in business markets. However, at a deeper level the IMP approach challenges assumptions about the fundamental organisation of business and economic activity. At this level, the IMP approach seeks to replace the 'markets, firms and competition' view of economic activity with a 'networks, relationships and interaction' view. Of course, this can be a difficult concept to convey to students, since the 'markets, firms and competition' view is generally taken-for-granted as the way economic activity is, in fact, organised, rather than as a view, a perspective, or a paradigm. The educator must decide whether their students are willing to countenance the ideas that an alternative paradigm is feasible, and that the 'networks, relationships and interaction' view is a reasonable alternative paradigm of business and economic activity. At the core of the IMP approach is the idea that business-to-business 'markets' are better conceptualised as networks, so that 'marketing management' is better conceptualised as processes of managing relationships and 'marketing strategy' as seeking improved network positioning. The bold educator can go down this route supported by important work written by prominent IMP theoreticians (see Ford et al., 2002; Ford et al., 2003; Håkansson et al., 2009), while the less bold educator may augment a more conventional curriculum by suggesting that managing relationships and networks is also an important function of the business-to-business marketer. In addition to the educator's personal preference (or bravery), the decision is likely to be influenced by the intellectual environment of the school in which the educator works and the philosophical position of those with authority over the wider curriculum. For example, if marketing is primarily perceived as a subordinate discipline concerned largely with communications, then the scope to introduce an alternative paradigm of economic activity in the business marketing course will be limited. However, in schools that take a broader perspective on marketing, whether that is primarily managerial (emphasising that marketing has a key role to play in designing and delivering the firm's strategy) or critical, there will be greater scope to teach the deeper principles that lie behind the IMP perspective.

TEACHING BUSINESS-TO-BUSINESS MARKETING ETHICS

The Hunt/Vitell theory (or model) of marketing ethics is a useful place to start any classroom discussion of ethical decision-making in marketing (Hunt and Laverie, 2004; Hunt and Vitell, 1986, 2006). This proposes that ethical decision-making is influenced by antecedents that include personal factors such as religion and personal values, and environmental factors that can be classified as the organisational, professional and industry environment, and the cultural environment. These factors influence the circumstances under which an individual perceives an ethical problem to exist, and how the individual perceives alternative decisions and their consequences. Then the core of the theory proposes that ethical judgement is a function of a deontological evaluation and a teleological evaluation, or $EJ=f(DE, TE)$, as it is summarised by Hunt and Vitell (2006). The deontological evaluation is based on rules or norms (for example, it is wrong to lie), and the teleological evaluation is based on the evaluation of the likely outcome of the decision (for example, a utilitarian analysis focuses on the net benefits and costs to everyone affected). However, Hunt and Vitell (2006) emphasise that the theory does not imply that individuals use any complex, explicit calculus to arrive at their judgement: 'Instead, we propose, people actually go through an informal process for which the formula is an idealized, formalized representation.' (Hunt and Vitell, 2006, p. 145).

Certain characteristic marketing ethical dilemmas are less likely to be encountered in the business-to-business context, and others are more likely to be encountered. For example, ethical issues arising out of information asymmetries are commonly found in consumer markets because consumers are likely to be less knowledgeable than the provider/seller in many cases, such as medical or financial products and services (Emons, 1997; Grierson and Brennan, 2017). Similar issues may arise in business-to-business transactions where there is a substantial difference in size between the buying and selling organisation, such as in the case of a large firm selling to small or sole trader businesses. In these circumstances the selling firm has the information resources of management specialists to draw on, while the micro-business may have little more information than that available to a consumer. However, there are many circumstances in business-to-business markets where the information available to, and the expertise of, the buying organisation matches or exceeds that of the selling organisation. Even early models of organisational buying behaviour emphasised that the 'buying centre' would include people with a range of professional expertise (such as finance, purchasing and engineering professionals) combining their expertise in the buying decision process (Webster and Wind, 1972). More recent models that emphasise relational and network aspects of business-to-business exchange include information exchange as a core component (Turnbull et al., 1996; Wilson, 1996). This is not to argue that issues to do with information asymmetries do not exist or do not matter in business-to-business markets. Rather, the argument is that there can be no general presumption that the seller has an information advantage over the buyer.

A number of ethical dilemmas are characteristic of business-to-business markets. These arise particularly under conditions where demand is highly concentrated in the hands of a few powerful buyers, and conditions of small numbers exchange where:

> smaller numbers of participants in industrial exchanges make relationship with key exchange partners (either customers or suppliers) not only very important but also practically feasible. In other words, the exchange relationship involved in industrial marketing presents both problems and solutions: it reveals the insufficiency of the market mechanism, on the one hand, at the same time it introduces relationship (trust) as a supplement to the market mechanism, or even as a substitute for it (Fuan and Nicholls, 2000, p. 456).

The people involved in business relationships of this type get to know each other well by, for example, attending many of the same trade fairs, negotiating and delivering on contracts, and participating in explicit business social events such as lunches and client entertainment. Typical ethical issues that arise from such circumstances include excessive gift-giving, sharing of confidential information, bribery and corruption, and questions associated with cultural relativism and absolutism when substantial cultural differences are encountered. Cultural relativism may suggest that a certain business practice (such as giving a high-value gift) is 'right' in a local culture, but against this must be weighed the absolutism of many professional and corporate codes of conduct (and, indeed, legal instruments like the American Foreign Corrupt Practices Act) that generally insist that any gifts should be of no more than token value.

The educator may encounter students who are sceptical about the significance of ethical issues in the business-to-business marketing curriculum. On the one hand this may be because they hold to a strongly Friedmanite position (explicitly or implicitly); thus, do whatever you like so long as it is legal and benefits the business. On the other hand, it may be because they doubt that ethical issues arise very much in the normal conduct of business-to-business marketing; thus, the topic doesn't much matter because it is largely abstract and irrelevant to practice. Of course, one can use the substantial academic literature on ethical issues to seek to convince students of the importance of the topic, such as Fisher (2007) on gift-giving, Fulmer et al. (2009) on deception, and Hawkins et al. (2013) on opportunism. There is a perhaps even more substantial body of academic literature that emphasises the importance of understanding the culturally specific networks that may be relevant to business-to-business marketers, sales executives and key account managers, concerning guanxi (China), wasta (the Middle East), blat (Russia) and other culturally specific constructs (Abosag and Naudé, 2014; Hutchings and Weir, 2006; Smith et al., 2012; Velez-Calle et al., 2015). Those charged with designing and implementing strategies for business-to-business marketing are also often directly in contact with business partners from different cultures, must learn to handle the intricacies of cross-cultural negotiations, and often need to be educated in the cultural norms of their counterparts.

Despite all these excellent justifications for the study of ethics and culture in business-to-business marketing, there are always students who are likely to be more convinced by a few well-chosen examples than by a lengthy list of academic concepts and articles. A prominent recent example concerns the UK-based global industrial engineering firm Rolls-Royce Holdings plc. Having been investigated by the UK Serious Fraud Office, Rolls-Royce admitted to bribery and making corrupt payments in multiple countries during the period 1989 to 2013, behaviour that was described as 'egregious criminality over decades, involving countries around the world, making truly vast corrupt payments and, consequentially, even greater profits' by the presiding judge when the case was brought to court ('Serious Fraud Office v. Rolls-Royce plc/ Rolls-Royce Energy Systems, INC', 2017). Two excellent sources of further examples illustrating unethical and illegal behaviour in business-to-business markets are the UK Serious Fraud Office website (https://www.sfo.gov.uk/ our-cases/), and the US Securities and Exchange Commission website (https:// www.sec.gov/spotlight/fcpa/fcpa-cases.shtml). For example, the SEC website reported in December 2019 that: 'Ericsson – The multinational telecommunications company agreed to pay more than $1 billion to the SEC and DOJ to resolve charges that it violated the FCPA by engaging in a large-scale bribery scheme involving the use of sham consultants to secretly funnel money to government officials in multiple countries.' Another prominent example from the UK Serious Fraud Office in January 2020: 'Airbus SE agreed to pay a fine, disgorgement of profits and costs amounting to €991m here in the UK, and in total, €3.6bn as part the world's largest global resolution for bribery, involving authorities in France and the United States.' Even those students who are sceptical that ethical issues often arise in practice may be impressed by the line-up of charges against famous B2B names like Rolls-Royce, Ericsson and Airbus.

A FEW HANDY TIPS FOR TEACHING BUSINESS-TO-BUSINESS MARKETING

1. Examples, examples, examples. A point made at the start of this chapter is that most students are unfamiliar with business-to-business marketing and cannot bring prior experience to bear during the learning process. By providing a wide variety of different examples, particularly in the early stages, the educator can help students understand the complexities of business marketing theory and practice.

2. Corporate videos, often available at corporate websites and corporate YouTube channels, can serve a range of useful purposes on business marketing courses (examples: Air Products, https://www.youtube.com/user/ airproducts; ERIKS, https://www.youtube.com/user/ERIKSbv). First, they can show examples of the many contexts in which business marketing takes place; in many cases they will include technical language from a specific industry and demonstrate how important it is for the business marketer to become attuned to the technical vocabulary of the industry in order to design effective marketing communications. Second, they directly represent business-to-business marketing in practice; the video is almost always a marketing presentation and can be evaluated and critiqued by students from a professional marketing perspective. Third, they illustrate a part of what business marketers actually do; I frequently remind the class that the video was probably made by a specialist production agency,

possibly working for a marketing agency, which in turn was working for the client organisation: 'Every link in that chain is business-to-business marketing, and represents a possible career opportunity.'

3. At the start of the chapter I suggested that there was a 'shallow-end' and a 'deep end' approach to teaching business marketing. I imagine that the reader has identified my preference for the 'deep end' approach. While I can see the attraction of introducing students gently to the subject, since it might make the first few class sessions more straightforward, my preferred approach is to emphasize the distinctiveness of business marketing from the very start, usually by presenting a sequence of examples that make it obvious that we are far removed from the realm of consumer marketing. For example, what marketing processes are involved when Rolls-Royce negotiates with Boeing in connection with the design of a new aero engine for the next generation of airliner? Notice here the juxtaposition of well-known B2B brands, suggesting familiarity with a marketing problem that resists elementary marketing principles and requires a uniquely business marketing approach. My reasoning is that students, once introduced to the idea that business-to-business marketing can be considered in some ways to be just a different context in which to apply basic marketing principles (shallow-end approach), may cling to this even when, later, told that there are many circumstances where this is not true.

4. While enthusiasm and even exuberance in the classroom are valuable characteristics for all marketing educators (Lincoln, 2008), perhaps they are even more important for business-to-business marketing educators. You are teaching a subject that is called marketing, but that perhaps doesn't fit obviously and neatly into students' conceptions of what marketing is. As the introduction to the chapter mentioned, this is a subject that has been described by some of its strongest advocates as 'outcast' (Lichtenthal, 2007), 'unloved'(Brennan, 2000) and 'underrepresented' (Lilien, 2016). So, accentuate the positive. What a fabulous opportunity for students to learn interesting new theoretical concepts and to develop an understanding of a wide range of new marketing practices, with the possible pay-off of a well-remunerated, intellectually challenging career that might well involve working with people from many different professional and cultural backgrounds.

NOTES

1. The terms business-to-business marketing, business marketing, B2B marketing and industrial marketing are used interchangeably in this chapter.

2. This is Interbrand's valuation of the brand alone. It is quite distinct from the valuation of the company (e.g. stock market capitalisation or book value of assets). Information about Interbrand's valuation methods can be found at the Interbrand website.

REFERENCES

Abosag, I. and Naudé, P. (2014). Development of special forms of B2B relationships: Examining the role of interpersonal liking in developing Guanxi and Et-Moone relationships. *Industrial Marketing Management*, *43*(6), 887–96.

Abratt, R. and Kelly, P.M. (2002). Customer–supplier partnerships: Perceptions of a successful key account management program. *Industrial Marketing Management*, *31*(5), 467–76.

Alderson, W. (1965). *Dynamic Marketing Behavior: A Functionalist Theory of Marketing*. R.D. Irwin.

Alderson, W. and Martin, M.W. (1965). Toward a formal theory of transactions and transvections. *Journal of Marketing Research*, *2*(2), 117–27.

Aramo-Immonen, H., Carlborg, P., Hasche, N., Jussila, J., Kask, J., Linton, G., Mustafee, N. et al. (2020). Charting the reach and contribution of IMP literature in other disciplines: A bibliometric analysis. *Industrial Marketing Management*, 87, 47–62.

Baraldi, E., Brennan, R., Harrison, D., Tunisini, A. and Zolkiewski, J. (2007). Strategic thinking and the IMP approach: A comparative analysis. *Industrial Marketing Management*, *36*(7), 879–94.

Bengtsson, M. and Kock, S. (2014). Coopetition—Quo vadis? Past accomplishments and future challenges. *Industrial Marketing Management*, *43*(2), 180–88.

Blois, K. and Ryan, A.M. (2010). The changing nature of 'atmosphere' in B2B relationships. Paper presented at the 26th IMP Conference, Budapest.

Blythe, J. and Zimmerman, A.S. (2005). *Business-to-Business Marketing Management: A Global Perspective*. Cengage Learning EMEA.

Brennan, R. (2000). Whither business-to-business marketing education? Paper presented at the Academy of Marketing Conference, Derby.

Brennan, R. (2012). The industrial/consumer dichotomy in marketing: Can formal taxonomic thinking help? *Journal of Customer Behaviour*, *11*(4), 311–23.

Brennan, R. and Canning, L.E. (2002). Adaptation processes in supplier–customer relationships. *Journal of Customer Behaviour*, *1*(2), 117–44.

Brennan, R., Canning, L. and McDowell, R. (2017). *Business to Business Marketing* (4th edn). London: Sage.

Brennan, R., Turnbull, P.W. and Wilson, D.T. (2003). Dyadic adaptation in business markets. *European Journal of Marketing*, *37*(11), 1636–65.

Day, G.S. (2000). Managing market relationships. *Journal of the Academy of Marketing Science*, *28*(1), 24–30.

Diamantopoulos, A. and Hart, S. (1993). Linking market orientation and company performance: Preliminary evidence on Kohli and Jaworski's framework. *Journal of Strategic Marketing*, *1*(2), 93.

Emons, W. (1997). Credence goods and fraudulent experts. *The RAND Journal of Economics*, *28*(1), 107–119.

Fern, E.F. and Brown, J.R. (1984). The industrial/consumer marketing dichotomy: A case of insufficient justification. *Journal of Marketing*, *48*(2), 68–77.

Fisher, J. (2007). Business marketing and the ethics of gift giving. *Industrial Marketing Management*, *36*(1), 99–108.

Ford, D. (1980). The development of buyer–seller relationships in industrial markets. *European Journal of Marketing*, *14*(5/6), 339–54.

Ford, D. and Mouzas, S. (2007). Is there any hope? The idea of strategy in business networks. Paper presented at the 23rd IMP Conference, Manchester.

Ford, D., Gadde, L.-E., Håkansson, H. and Snehota, I. (2003). *Managing Business Relationships*. Chichester: John Wiley and Sons.

Ford, D., Gadde, L.-E., Håkannson, H., Snehota, I. and Waluszewski, A. (2008). Analysing business interaction. Paper presented at the 24th IMP Conference, Uppsala.

Ford, D., Berthon, P., Brown, S., Gadde, L.-E., Håkansson, H., Naude, P. et al. (2002). *The Business Marketing Course: Managing in Complex Networks*. Chichester: John Wiley and Sons.

Fuan, L. and Nicholls, J.A.F. (2000). Transactional or relationship marketing: Determinants of strategic choices. *Journal of Marketing Management*, *16*(5), 449–64.

Fulmer, I.S., Barry, B. and Long, D.A. (2009). Lying and smiling: Informational and emotional deception in negotiation. *Journal of Business Ethics*, *88*(4), 691–709.

Grierson, S. and Brennan, R. (2017). Referrals for new client acquisition in professional services. *Qualitative Market Research: An International Journal*, *20*(1), 28–42.

Håkansson, H. (ed.) (1982). *International Marketing and Purchasing of Industrial Goods*. Chichester: John Wiley and Sons.

Håkansson, H., and Snehota, I. (eds) (1995). *Developing Relationships in Business Markets*. London: Routledge.

Håkansson, H., Ford, D., Gadde, L.-E., Snehota, I. and Waluszewski, A. (2009). *Business in Networks*. Chichester: John Wiley and Sons.

Hawkins, T.G., Pohlen, T.L. and Prybutok, V.R. (2013). Buyer opportunism in business-to-business exchange. *Industrial Marketing Management*, *42*(8), 1266–78.

Hunt, S.D. and Laverie, D.A. (2004). Experiential learning and the Hunt-Vitell theory of ethics: Teaching marketing ethics by integrating theory and practice. *Marketing Education Review*, *14*(3), 1–14.

Hunt, S.D. and Vitell, S. (1986). A general theory of marketing ethics. *Journal of Macromarketing*, *6*(1), 5–16.

Hunt, S.D. and Vitell, S. (2006). The general theory of marketing ethics: A revision and three questions. *Journal of Macromarketing*, *26*(2), 143–53.

Hutchings, K. and Weir, D. (2006). Guanxi and wasta: A comparison. *Thunderbird International Business Review*, *48*(1), 141–56.

Hutt, M.D. and Speh, T.W. (2007). Undergraduate education: The implications of cross-functional relationship in business marketing – The skills of high-performing managers. *Journal of Business-to-Business Marketing*, *14*(1), 75–94.

Hutt, M.D. and Speh, T.W. (2010). *Business Marketing Management: B2B* (10th edn). Mason, OH: South Western, Cengage Learning.

Ivens, B.S., Leischnig, A., Pardo, C. and Niersbach, B. (2018). Key account management as a firm capability. *Industrial Marketing Management*, *74*, 39–49.

Jackson, B.B. (1985). Build customer relationships that last. *Harvard Business Review*, *12*, 120–28.

Jansson, H., Johanson, M. and Ramström, J. (2007). Institutions and business networks: A comparative analysis of the Chinese, Russian, and West European markets. *Industrial Marketing Management*, *36*, 955–67.

Jaworski, B.J. and Kohli, A.K. (1993). Market orientation: Antecedents and conse-quences. *Journal of Marketing*, *57*(3), 53–70.

Kaunonen, A. (2010). The development of industrial buyer–seller relationships in a Chinese context. Paper presented at the 26th IMP Conference, Budapest.

Kohli, A.K. and Jaworski, B.J. (1990). Market orientation: The construct, research propositions, and managerial implications. *Journal of Marketing*, *54*(2), 1–18.

Krapfel, R.E., Salmond, D. and Spekman, R. (1991). A strategic approach to managing buyer–seller relationships. *European Journal of Marketing*, *25*(9), 22–37.

Kriz, A. and Fang, T. (2000). Cross-cultural challenges to the IMP paradigm: Evidence from Chinese markets. Paper presented at the 16th IMP conference, Bath.

Lacoste, S. (2012). 'Vertical coopetition': The key account perspective. *Industrial Marketing Management*, *41*(4), 649–58.

Lichtenthal, J.D. (2007). Advocating business marketing education: Relevance and Rigor-uttered as one. *Journal of Business-to-Business Marketing*, *14*(1), 1–12.

Lichtenthal, J.D. and Butaney, G. (1991). Undergraduate industrial marketing: Content and methods. *Industrial Marketing Management*, *20*(3), 231–9.

Lilien, G.L. (2016). The B2B knowledge gap. *International Journal of Research in Marketing*, *33*(3), 543–56.

Lincoln, D.J. (2008). Drama in the classroom: How and why marketing educators can use nonverbal communication and enthusiasm to build student rapport. *Marketing Education Review*, *18*(3), 53–65.

Marshall, A. (1920). *Principles of Economics* (8th edn). London and Basingstoke: Macmillan.

Meyer, J., Land, R. and Baillie, C. (eds) (2010). *Threshold Concepts and Transformational Learning* (Vol. 42). Rotterdam: Sense Publishers.

Mouzas, S. (2001). Real mechanisms of strategic acting. Paper presented at the 17th IMP conference, Oslo.

Naude, P., Mouzas, S. and Henneberg, S. (2004). Network pictures – concepts and representation. Paper presented at the 20th IMP Conference, Copenhagen.

Parkin, M. and King, D. (1995). *Microeconomics*. Wokingham: Addison-Wesley.

Pindyck, R.S. and Rubinfeld, D.L. (2001). *Microeconomics*. Upper Saddle River, NJ: Prentice Hall.

Serious Fraud Office v. Rolls-Royce plc/Rolls-Royce Energy Systems, Inc. (2017). No. U20170036, Crown Court (Southwark) 2017.

Smith, P.B., Huang, H.J., Harb, C. and Torres, C. (2012). How distinctive are indige-nous ways of achieving influence? A comparative study of guanxi, wasta, jeitinho, and 'pulling strings'. *Journal of Cross-Cultural Psychology*, *43*(1), 135–50.

Sutton-Brady, C. (2001). Relationship atmosphere – The final chapter. Paper presented at the 17th IMP Conference, Oslo.

Turnbull, P.W., Ford, D. and Cunningham, M.T. (1996). Interaction, relationships and networks in business markets: An evolving perspective. *Journal of Business & Industrial Marketing*, *11*(3/4), 44–62.

Velez-Calle, A., Robledo-Ardila, C. and Rodriguez-Rios, J.D. (2015). On the influence of interpersonal relations on business practices in Latin America: A comparison with the Chinese guanxi and the Arab Wasta. *Thunderbird International Business Review*, *57*(4), 281–93.

Webster, F.E. and Wind, Y. (1972). A general model for understanding organizational buying behavior. *Journal of Marketing*, *36*(2), 12–19.

Wilson, E.J. (1996). Theory transitions in organizational buying behavior research. *Journal of Business & Industrial Marketing*, *11*(6), 7–19.

Zolkiewski, J. and Turnbull, P.W. (2002). Do relationship portfolios and networks provide the key to successful relationship management? *Journal of Business & Industrial Marketing, 17*(7), 575–97.

9. Why do students dislike research methods modules and what to do about it?

Barbara Czarnecka and Maria Rita Massaro

INTRODUCTION

University students at all levels and across a range of disciplines, including marketing and consumer behaviour, are increasingly required to understand and interpret research, as well as produce it. Marketing research has been rated by employers as one of the most important areas that students should have conceptual knowledge of (Di Gregorio et al., 2019; Vriens et al., 2019; Wilton, 2008). Despite the acknowledged importance of proficiency in marketing research, anecdotal and research evidence indicates that research methods is not an easy subject to teach and not an easy subject to learn (Stern and Tseng, 2002). Ideally, deans, course directors and lecturers would avoid teaching research methods or having it on their curriculum to avoid dealing with student dissatisfaction and complaints. However, we do live in a world that calls for data to be used as an evidence base, making research methods skills and knowledge paramount to working in marketing, if not to conduct primary research, then at least to evaluate the quality of commissioned research and correctly interpreting the results.

Teaching research methods is like trying to answer the 'chicken or egg' question: should we teach methods of research first or should we teach methods of data analysis first? Based on our interactions with researchers and educators, we have learnt that there are three perspectives on teaching research methods. Some researchers maintain that one cannot learn research methods without first learning how to analyse data. Others propose that learning research methods first is a prerequisite to learning data analysis. Yet others argue that the best solution is to learn both simultaneously, and then to practise and learn again. Whilst it is beyond the scope of this chapter to argue which perspective is more effective, we are of the opinion that research methods are best learnt by doing and practical instruction. In this chapter we discuss a number of topics which we believe could be useful for designing, preparing and delivering applied marketing research modules, namely: (1) existing literature on teaching research methods; (2) common challenges in teaching research methods; (3) the importance of teaching students how to analyse and evaluate existing research evidence; (4) big data and its importance in marketing research; (5) selected quantitative and qualitative research methods that could make teaching methods more accessible to students. We also discuss the importance of report writing and issues of ethics and responsibility in marketing research. Finally, we recommend a number of important readings that could constitute part of research methods courses for students of marketing. This chapter aims to serve as a general guide to those who teach or plan to teach research methods to undergraduate and postgraduate marketing students and is not meant to be exhaustive. It should be used alongside other 'standard' research methods textbooks.

WHAT RESEARCHERS SAY ABOUT TEACHING MARKETING RESEARCH: EXISTING LITERATURE ON TEACHING RESEARCH METHODS

Much has been written about teaching research methods in social sciences in general (Cvancara, 2017; Lewthwaite and Nind, 2016) and to marketing students specifically (Lassk and Mulki, 2018; Stern and Tseng, 2002). The importance of research skills to marketing specialists has never been more significant than now, when marketers are encouraged to make decisions that are informed by data and evidence (Thyroff, 2019; Vriens and Vidden, 2019). Researchers (e.g., Di Gregorio et al., 2019; Vriens et al., 2019) have studied what research skills employers find essential in graduates and found gaps between employers' expectations and graduates' abilities. This is partly due to how research methods is taught as a subject and partly due to the negative perceptions of research methods that students hold. However, teaching research methods has been described by many who study the pedagogies of this area as one of the most challenging tasks. In this section, we do not intend to provide a detailed literature review, but instead highlight selected solutions that we have come across in the literature on the subject.

Many point out the specific challenges that teaching research methods faces. Research methods courses (modules) are said to be the most intellectually demanding, and delivering them is challenging because methodological expertise is very fragmented and research methods content is evolving constantly (Lewthwaite and Nind, 2016). Most chapters or journal articles that propose solutions to overcome those challenges suggest that employing 'engaging' tasks (e.g. FitzPatrick et al., 2010; Wilson et al., 2009) or experiential learning (learning by doing and subsequent reflection) (Thyroff, 2019) are the keys to effective teaching, but what does it really mean? Groessler (2017) provides an excellent overview of specific approaches and specific ideas that may be used to teach research methods. We recommend that paper for all who search for ideas to incorporate them into their research methods modules.

To make research methods teaching engaging, Graham and Schuwerk (2017) proposed the use of *Undercover Boss* (a television series in which bosses go undercover to experience the employees' perspective) to illustrate the concepts, tools and process of qualitative research. Lassk and Mulki (2018) recommended the flipped classroom approach, in which team-based learning is applied, an approach recommended by many pedagogues (Chad, 2012). This student-centred approach, where small group exercises around a case study are given before the lecture and peer-to-peer interaction is encouraged, is also highly effective (Barraket, 2005).

To solve the problem of the fragmented methodological expertise of lecturers, team teaching is often proposed as an effective solution (Buckley, 1999). Team teaching involves a group of lecturers working purposefully, regularly and cooperatively, to help a group of students learn. The advantage of this approach is that the members of the teaching team are each expert on a specific research method. On the other hand, team teaching requires cooperation and coordination, and usually takes more time to implement.

In the following sections, we share our own suggestions (some tried and tested, others being ideas that we would like to implement in our teaching in the future) that helped us in supporting students to learn, understand and apply research methods to marketing problems.

COMMON CHALLENGES IN TEACHING RESEARCH METHODS

Focusing Too Much on Finding a 'Gap'

Our experience suggests that lecturers often start teaching students how to formulate a good research question by encouraging them to 'find a gap' in knowledge through analysis of existing literature. Whilst this approach may be appropriate for doctoral-level research in some cases, we argue that this is not a helpful approach in teaching students how to employ research methods to answer practical questions. Instead of focusing on 'finding the gap', students should be encouraged to come up with questions that help solve problems that marketers can encounter in practice. At undergraduate and postgraduate levels, this first step of research (i.e. coming up with a topic) should not focus on finding a gap and 'filling' the gap. The focus should be on learning how to answer questions and find solutions to problems by using data and doing research. Following on from this, it is important to demonstrate to students how to develop and state feasible and specific research questions. Hence, it is crucial that lecturers make students (and often themselves!) aware of the difference between academic and applied research. The classic academic approach to research involves 'finding a gap in knowledge and filling it', while the effective managerial approach to research involves identifying a management/marketing problem and gathering information to solve it. Our experience demonstrates that teaching research methods from the perspective of finding solutions to problems is more effective with undergraduate and postgraduate students than following the 'find the gap' perspective. It is indeed also more useful to students who will be in roles that focus on solving practical challenges, rather than building knowledge to fill gaps.

Specify the broad area of interest (for example, the impact of pricing on consumer behaviour)

Narrow down by looking at the component parts of this area (for example, the impact of price presentation on product choice)

Specify the research question by choosing components you want to focus on (for example, what is the impact of product packaging price presentation on product choice?)

Figure 9.1   Funnel approach to developing research questions

For undergraduate and postgraduate students who face working on a dissertation or a capstone project, it is often a challenge to specify a focused research question. Students often develop research questions that are too broad and find it difficult to narrow them down. Many sources offer advice on how to develop focused research questions (e.g. GMU, 2020). Based on those excellent resources and our own experience, we found that following the funnel approach (Figure 9.1) to developing research questions is helpful to students. Usually, students start with a very broad topic, for example, the role of pricing in consumer decision-making. They should be encouraged to unpack what those two variables consist of and what the variations of them are. For example, pricing may cover countless variations, including types of pricing, price presentation, and pricing of different product categories; and consumer decision-making consists of several stages each offering opportunities for investigation. Once the unpacking is done, students may start focusing their research question so that it is narrow enough and feasible to address in a given timescale. This funnel approach will work only if students devote their attention to reading published research studies (journal articles, market research reports, government research reports). We found that the biggest challenge in this process is overcoming students' reluctance to read recommended research papers and research reports. To help with this, lectures should carefully select research reports (be it in the form of journal articles or other research reports) that are approachable/easy to understand and gradually introduce more complex reports.

Teaching Without Providing Examples

Another common mistake is to teach research methods 'dry', that is without framing it as part of a practical/ applied problem. It is hard to believe, but many professors still do not teach or explain why a method is used, or how a particular method or set of data can help to answer a practical question or solve a pragmatic problem. The best solution is to support learning with practical examples that are worked through patiently. For example, if the lecture focuses on questionnaire design, a good method is to use an existing customer satisfaction survey or a survey that was used to collect data for market segmentation. Online survey platforms offer examples and templates of a wide variety of questionnaires – for example, Qualtrics offers a free account that comes with a number of questionnaire templates that could be used for teaching question-naire design (Qualtrics, n.d.). Another approach is to use existing databases (see Table 9.2 for examples of secondary data sources) which often provide access to questionnaires that were used to collect the data. For example, the European Commission's website is a good source of surveys used to examine consumers' attitudes in Europe (National questionnaires, n.d.).

Challenges of Teaching Quantitative Research Methods

Quantitative methods are usually viewed by students as more difficult than qualitative research methods because they include working with numbers. But that does not have to be the case. One way that pedagogues suggest this challenge can be addressed is to first choose a topic that students will find interesting, and a method that is easy to teach and understand. For example, quantitative content analysis of social media posts and images to count the number of certain words or appeals used in posts, images or users' comments, may be a good way to introduce students to simple quantitative methods. Another quantitative method that may be very enjoyable for students to participate in, and for lecturers to implement in a classroom setting, is an experiment. Our experience shows that simple experiments (testing effectiveness of two different designs of advertisements, or testing packaging concepts) can be easily implemented to show students fundamental principles of experimental design. The Economics Network, a website run by the University of Bristol and supported by a number of British universities, can serve as a good source of ideas for running experiments in a classroom (The Economics Network, 2020).

TEACHING TO REVIEW LITERATURE SYSTEMATICALLY: THE IMPORTANCE OF TEACHING STUDENTS HOW TO ANALYSE AND EVALUATE EXISTING RESEARCH EVIDENCE

Our combined experience of teaching research methods and supervising research projects (e.g. capstone projects and dissertations) at various levels (undergraduate, postgraduate taught and doctoral) suggests that teaching students how to review existing evidence in the form of literature on a particular topic is not often given enough attention. Students are often asked to review literature, but little guidance (beyond the general 'be more critical') is given on how to do it. We recommend that the principles of systematic narrative literature review should be stressed. Systematic narrative reviews provide a complete summary of the current literature relevant to a research question or a practical problem, and can be of significant use to marketing professionals. In many marketing roles, students will have to decide what existing evidence to review to analyse a practical problem they are facing, and they must understand the importance of systematic review of current literature, research reports or documents, in order to answer a particular question. Whilst there is no known framework specific to marketing that can guide the process of systematic review, lecturers can borrow from other fields and simplify frameworks such as PRISMA-P (e.g., Udall et al., 2020). Below we provide a simple framework that can be applied to systematically review literature, internal documents or research reports (Table 9.1). This framework can also be adapted to review internal documents or internal reports, in the context of a very pragmatic research problem.

Table 9.1   *Framework for systematic narrative literature/evidence review in marketing*

Criterion	Questions
Period that the review covers	What time period will the review cover?
Search terms used to identify studies	What search terms are used to identify studies? Which search engines are employed to search for sources?
Qualifying sources	Which sources qualify for the review?
Inclusion/exclusion criteria	On what basis are studies included or excluded from the review?
Author(s) of the study	Who conducted the study? What organisations are the authors associated with?
Research questions	Which research question(s) did it focus on?
Research methods	What methods were used in the study? What are the limitations of these methods? Were they appropriate for the stated research problem?
Sample	What are the sample characteristics? How large is the sample? How was the sample selected?
Findings	What do the findings say? Do they solve the stated problem?

BIG DATA AND ITS IMPORTANCE IN TEACHING AND PRACTISING MARKETING RESEARCH

Marketing specialists, especially those working in social media marketing or retail, will be faced with the challenge of working with large volumes of data. Whilst fields such as data science may be beyond the scope of standard research methods modules for marketing courses, it is important that students are exposed to those terms and are familiar with the concepts (Fayyad and Hamutcu, 2020). Analytics is a section of data analysis that focuses on the discovery, interpretation and communication of meaningful patterns in data. The data is usually available because technology allows organisations to collect data. For example, loyalty cards (such as the Tesco Clubcard) or social media platforms enable organisations to collect large volumes of data which are then used to discover patterns related to the selected behaviour(s). Marketing students should be at least familiar with some tools of analytics, such as Google Analytics, Clicky (https://clicky.com/), or Open Web Analytics (http://www.openwebanalytics.com/). There will be new analytics tools available at the time of publishing this book, but students should be familiar with one of them to understand what data is available and how it can be used to make decisions.

Each social media platform offers its own analytics tools, but marketers can also employ social media management platforms that help manage and track activity across several platforms. Social media management tools track and analyse how users interact with a company's social media profiles. At the time of preparing this chapter, the most used are Hootsuite and Sprout Social. More advanced research methods teaching could incorporate the use of application programming interfaces (APIs) to collect data from social media platforms or other online platforms.

Moreover, in the market research industry, the discussion around big data often includes social media data, and calls for an integration of quantitative and qualitative analysis to extract more meaningful information and provide a context to the interpretation of numbers (Ewing et al., 2016). Whilst analytics is important, a more qualitative approach to analysis of social media data is also needed. For example, one of the methods discussed below, social media listening, is a qualitative approach to observing what people say and how they behave on social media. We discuss the use of social media in research in one of the subsequent sections.

SELECTED QUANTITATIVE AND QUALITATIVE RESEARCH METHODS

How to Teach Statistics

Teaching statistics to marketing students is often challenging and many authors have suggested solutions before about how to teach statistics successfully to non-specialists (Mustafa, 1996; Smith and Martinez-Moyano, 2012). There are academic journals, such as the *Journal of Statistics Education*, devoted to providing research-underpinned advice on how to teach statistics to various groups. Many excellent papers (e.g. Sowey, 1995; Martin, 2003) provide numerous pieces of advice on how to make teaching statistics effective. Here, we do not want to repeat the recommendations of these pedagogists (who know more than us about teaching statistics), but would like to add three more approaches that we found useful in teaching statistics. As statistics is an inherent part of quantitative research methods, students who choose to specialise in such methods will also have to learn at least the basics of statistics.

First, we believe that engaging students with statistics reported in the media may be helpful in sparking their interest in learning the ropes behind those statistics. Statistics are reported everywhere in the news media, in management reports and in market research reports (Bell et al., 2019). For example, the recent COVID-19 pandemic can serve as an illustration of how important it is to understand how data are collected, reported and presented. Many other examples exist that instructors can tailor to their own context. Second, we would like to recommend specific textbooks that present statistics in a fun and straightforward way. Specifically, we recommend books by Professor Andy Field (https://www.discoveringstatistics.com/). Professor Field has authored a range of books that introduce and explain statistics, and the use of a number of statistical packages that we have used in our teaching (and learning!). Third, it is important that students learn how to use statistics packages, such as *SPSS*, *Mplus* or *R* (for those more advanced), or are at least aware that such tools exist.

As neither of the authors of this chapter is a trained statistician, we would like to refrain from making further recommendations on how to teach statistics and highly recommend the literature of those who are more able to do so. In addition, team teaching, which we have mentioned earlier in the chapter, is also a suitable solution for those lecturers who are not quantitative researchers.

Use of Secondary Data

The analysis of secondary data plays a vital role in marketing, for example, by supporting initial problem analysis or informing marketing models (Latta and Clark, 2016). Most marketing roles will involve analysing some kind of secondary data, be it sales figures or internal order documents, or previous research reports intended for a different purpose. Secondary data can include both quantitative and qualitative sources. Secondary data can be used in several ways: to demonstrate how research has been done previously, to demonstrate interesting relations between variables or to teach data analysis using publicly available data sets. Students should be able to evaluate the limitations of using secondary data and understand how such data can be used to support decision-making. The availability of publicly available secondary data creates numerous opportunities for research methods lecturers to teach students about the benefits and possible applications of such data. We give some examples of secondary data sources (Table 9.2) that can be used in teaching. Such data sets are a very good tool to teach students about study units, survey design, target population, sampling frame, sample size and response rate (Bell et al., 2019).

Table 9.2   *Examples of secondary data sources for use in teaching research methods*

The Australian Survey of Social Attitudes	https://www.acspri.org.au/aussa
Find open data	https://data.gov.uk/
Public Attitudes Tracker	https://www.gov.uk/government/collections/public-attitudes-tracking-survey
UK Data Service	https://ukdataservice.ac.uk/
Statistical data sets	https://www.gov.uk/government/statistical-data-sets
UK Data Archive	https://www.data-archive.ac.uk/
London Datastore	https://data.london.gov.uk/
Office for National Statistics (ONS)	https://www.ons.gov.uk/
WVS Database	http://www.worldvaluessurvey.org/
ICPSR	https://www.icpsr.umich.edu/web/pages/
QualiBank	https://discover.ukdataservice.ac.uk/QualiBank

Teaching Quantitative Research Methods

Quantitative research methods are usually employed in either descriptive or experimental designs. A descriptive study only establishes associations between variables; an experimental study aims to establish causality. One of the most well-known, and perhaps overused tools of quantitative research, is a questionnaire (Pew Research Center, 2020). Whilst ubiquitous, and many students admit to being exposed to such research as participants, this does not translate into the ability to design good questionnaires. Our experience with survey design teaching so far suggests that two approaches work very well: (1) ask students to bring along examples of questionnaires that they have come across; (2) expose them to a badly designed questionnaire as respondents. These two exercises allow students to evaluate the type of questions (open-ended versus closed-ended) and the structure of the questionnaire, as well as learn about common mistakes in survey design (overlapping categories for age, double-barrelled questions and imprecise response scales, to name just some).

Another quantitative method that could be incorporated into teaching is experiments. Experiments are often used to test the effectiveness of communication approaches (for example, to test how liked adverts are) or to ascertain how consumers react to price differences. Simple experiments can be performed in class, for example dividing students into control and experimental groups (ideally assigning the students randomly), exposing each to the control/experimental stimuli and measuring their responses. In fact, experiments are one of the easier methods to teach and can be planned as class activities, taking students through each stage of designing and reporting experiments (Harris, 2008). Materials (experimental stimuli and response scales can be sourced from published experimental studies (e.g. Kalliny et al., 2020; or Gunasti et al., 2020 are useful examples of experimental studies that can be replicated in a classroom setting); and from Open Science databases, such as the *Centre for Open Science* website (https://osf.io/) where lecturers can find data sets, experimental materials and questionnaires from previous studies.

Teaching Qualitative Research Methods

Qualitative research methods are an essential part of the marketing student's research toolbox. However, qualitative research methods and data analysis skills are often overlooked, or mentioned only superficially, when learning about research methods for marketing (Albinsson et al., 2018). Teaching qualitative methods to marketing students means that lecturers need to overcome students' prejudices and a series of challenges, namely: (a) changing the biased view of subjectivity; (b) changing the perception that qualitative research methods are easier than quantitative methods. Below we discuss those challenges and suggest some solutions that are based on our experience.

Most students will claim to know the difference between quantitative and qualitative research methods but their perceptions are often not supported by knowledge. One of the views held on the quantitative–qualitative divide is that the first is objective and the latter is subjective. Newcomers to research methods have a common misconception: believable and trustworthy research consists of and delivers numbers; all the rest is an art and purely subjective. Instead of trying to convince them of the opposite, or inviting them to join the centuries-old and never-ending discussion on qualitative versus quantitative (Ercikan and Roth, 2006), a successful approach for us was to provide real examples and exercises about the vital role that interpretation plays – even with numbers.

One tried and tested approach that we can recommend is to ask students to find examples of quantitative research results on any mainstream topic taken from two different newspapers (or websites, or magazines). For example, in the context of the UK, two newspapers that will present the same issue in most likely very different ways are *The Guardian* and the *Daily Mail*. Students can compare the interpretations of different journalists, and deconstruct the numbers and percentages, and the means of presentation. This is an excellent seminar activity. Students usually reach the conclusion that numbers and so-called 'objective' data can also be 'spun', that is, interpreted and presented in many different ways. Usually politicians are very productive in providing material for these discussions, so it will not be difficult to find relevant examples.

Even examples from pop culture domains can be a playful and engaging way to support this point. Inspiration for quotes can be taken from comics. There are plenty of examples in *The Manga Guide to Statistics* (Takahashi, 2008) or cartoons such as those featured in *The Cartoon Guide to Statistics* (Gonick and Smith, 2005). Quotes such as '31% of fatalities in car accidents happen because of alcohol. This means that 69% of death happens to those who are sober. So it is safer to drive when drunk' (quote adapted from Dylan Dog comics series) are an excellent example to use in class to encourage students to think about limitations and boundaries of numbers, and how interpretation of numbers can be very subjective. In our experience, such exercises were very effective in taking students toward deductive reasoning to conclude that numbers are not always unequivocally interpreted, because interpretation plays a role – even in statistics.

Demonstrating and discussing a range of response scales and scaling techniques, such as Likert scales or semantic differential scales, is also useful to demonstrate how quantitative measurement of latent variables can be very subjective. At first sight, the response scales appear as objective and immutable in students' eyes. We take a closer look together at proxies and scaling techniques used. At this stage, students usually identify the scales as hard and objective science. However, once students are invited to discuss what each point on these scales means to them, they often come to a conclusion that the categories 'strongly disagree' or 'strongly agree' may take on very different 'intensities'. In the context of marketing, customer satisfaction surveys can serve as an excellent example – does 'extremely satisfied' for one person mean the same to another person? These exercises teach students caution in approaching and relying on quantitative data derived from surveys in which such response scales are used.

Despite the firm and deep-rooted conviction that quantitative is superior to qualitative research, most students surprisingly opt for 'words' when selecting their methodology, so they choose qualitative research methods. This happens because qualitative design is believed to be easier, because it does not imply any mathematical skill set. This is the second important misconception that lecturers need to bring to students' attention: qualitative research is not easy and there is a huge amount of messiness to deal with. This recommendation is systematically neglected by students and we all end up reading about common mistakes: (a) difference between data and findings chapters, which are replicated in wordy and redundant discussion; (b) lack of transparency, such as when personal opinions are obscurely drawn from interviewees' answers and proposed as clearly emerging from data; (c) rushed writing up because students believe they can always 'waffle around' any finding based on qualitative research.

Therefore, a crucial point is to highlight to students that analysing qualitative datasets requires an interpretative skill set and follows a rigorous procedure, for which they must learn appropriate techniques. To support this point, it would be useful to run simple workshop exercises on thematic analysis. One way to do this would be to provide students with printed interview excerpts and ask groups of them to stick all the excerpts that have something in common on a single board (theme) and find a keyword which summarises the commonalities (code). Different groups of students will be likely to classify the excerpts in different ways and stick them on different boards. This is an effective visual approach to demonstrate that interpretation can vary, but if the analysis and classification process is made clear and explained, we should all reach the same or very similar conclusions (for more detailed description of such data analysis, please refer to Miles and Huberman, 1994). In other words, students need to be taught the meaning of 'rigour'. Coding of data is also applied in other contexts. For example, content analysis studies of advertising involve coders analysing and coding in order to identify advertising themes expressed through images or text. Whilst identifying such factors as gender of models featured in advertisements is mostly a very objective process, identifying cultural values, or emotions portrayed in advertisements is more subjective (e.g., Czarnecka and Mogaji, 2020; Czarnecka et al., 2018).

The key takeaways from these exercises are that the process is long, requires time, and it should be rigorous and systematic. This approach also allows lecturers to demonstrate the difference between data and interpretation of findings, and discussion.

Teaching Qualitative Research Methods in a Digital Era

Market researchers have adapted their methodological stance to the digital world and many of the conventional qualitative methods can also be applied online, together with new emergent approaches (Cluley et al., 2020). Online qualitative research, also called 'e-research', is 'an umbrella term to describe methodological traditions for using information and communication technology to study perceptions, experiences or behaviour through their verbal or visual expressions, action or writings' (Salmons, 2016). The advantages of doing e-research within marketing classes are numerous: (a) quick access to data – the opportunity to access information quickly; (b) marketing-focused research questions – the possibility to investigate research questions which are more marketing related, such as consumer perceptions, consumer sentiments, or customer complaints and satisfaction, but also to collect data on the company's storytelling, campaign evaluation, and (more generally) to gain market insights to inform marketing decisions or to gain competitive intelligence; (c) familiar environment – social media interfaces make the research process less tedious, and provide a context in which students are more keen and comfortable to work; (d) broader range of available data – at undergraduate level, especially, we discourage our students from undertaking primary research, as it is costly and time consuming; (e) variety of research techniques and design – data are collectable through social media, and netnographic studies, observational research, focus groups and in-depth interviews are all possible. An extended range and variety are also offered in terms of the type/format of data – not only text, but also photos, drawings, images, audio-visual presentations or podcasts, with a narrative or conversational structure for all of these in the same place.

Social Media Monitoring or Social Listening: Which One?

One example of digital research is social media research. Such research includes any type of research where data are collected through social media, which has the advantage of making a large volume of consumer data and user-generated content accessible to students. Promoting social media as a learning tool creates a more student-centric classroom (Greenhow, 2011), along with many other pedagogical benefits; moreover it is a great tool for doing online research. Two main approaches to social media research are through monitoring or listening. Even if they are often used interchangeably, they refer to different types of activities.

Social media monitoring is the act of monitoring social media platforms for information relevant to a given organisation (Hootsuite, 2020). This activity allows one to crawl (also referred to as trawling) social media to search for specific hashtags and words, to monitor the sentiment of a conversation around the brand, and to find out who is talking about the brand, how many times, how and why. The majority of the data that can be collected are qualitative, but some can also be quantitative. Social media listening, often labelled 'social listening' by market researchers, and recognised by academic researchers (Reid and Duffy, 2018), is defined as an approach that does not focus only on brand conversation, but analyses the conversations around an industry as a whole and any topic related to a brand (Sprout Social, n.d.). To sum up, social media monitoring is more reactive, while social listening is a proactive strategy, but both are suitable for collecting qualitative data in a simple and engaging way.

When teaching qualitative methods, social listening techniques and commercial social media monitoring tools can be used in combination with netnographic research to study consumer habits (Cheung and McColl-Kennedy, 2015; Harwood and Garry, 2015; Skålén et al., 2015), (see section on netnography). The advantage is that a netnographic approach can add richness and depth to the depth and scale of social media listening of mass consumer realities (Reid and Duffy, 2018). Social media monitoring and listening can be performed using social media Application Programming Interfaces (APIs).

In seminar classes or for workshops, instructors can simply let students use words, phrases and a brand name to search *Instagram* or *Twitter*, or to use Google Trends, Google Alerts or web crawlers. This is a basic search that can be done manually and is only possible on a small set of data, which nevertheless needs thematic coding from the students. When it comes to the analysis of larger datasets, and/or listening to and monitoring different platforms, social media listening tools are necessary. There are plenty of commercial tools, such as *Hootsuite, BuzzSumo, TweetDeck, Social Studio, Talkwalker, Socialbakers, Brand24* and *Brandwatch*, which support identifying social mentions and conversations around a specific topic or brand. If a social media listening tool subscription is not available, students can use the free trial version. Together with the advantages of gathering all the information in one place ready to be analysed, premium subscriptions can offer data analysis features such as thematic analysis, trend analysis and the creation of word clouds. Manual storage and coding of data can be done through Microsoft's Excel and OneNote, creating a local folder where files can be saved, but this is definitely old-fashioned and boring for students. In class, an NVivo add-on called NCapture (which can be installed free of charge on Google Chrome or Internet Explorer) can be employed to download web pages as PDFs or to store information downloaded from social networks to create a database. Some content or thematic analysis can be done manually by students. If available, *CAQDAS NVivo 12 Plus* allows the import and analysis of different types of qualitative documents, for example transcripts, videos, audios or images from interviews or focus groups, as well as data from the internet or social media such as YouTube. However, social media listening tools have an advantage over NVivo, as they offer the opportunity to track back the source of the social media post and enrich the dataset with information on individual community users.

There are a variety of possibilities among research methods which can be applicable in a social media context. For the scope of this chapter, we consider only those methods that might garner some more consensus and interest among marketing students. Of particular note, and in addition to social listening and social monitoring, are netnography and sentiment analysis.

How to Teach Netnography

The word 'netnography', a portmanteau of internet and ethnography, is used to study behavioural and cultural practices, languages, rituals, values and preferences of groups and individuals online. This is the 'intelligent adaptation' (Kozinets, 2015, p. 3) of the most traditional ethnography, combining specific sets of research practices, such as archival and online communication work, participation and observation, with new forms of digital and network data collection, analysis and representation (Kozinets, 2015). For teaching purposes at undergraduate level, a good way is to stage it in four steps which feature in any ethnographic research process (Kozinets, 2002): (1) select an appropriate online community; (2) gather and analyse the data in an ethical way; (3) ensure the correct interpretation; (4) triangulate the findings.

A further elaboration of the netnographic inquiry is made of twelve roughly temporal and interactive levels (Kozinets, 2015). However, within a taught research method module with time constraints, we found that presenting the entirety of the process was unmanageable. Secondly, being a reflective and interpretative approach, it is also complicated for students to master the technique in its entirety. Nevertheless, this research method is an excellent opportunity for students to learn aspects of ethnography, online research and content analysis. In class, a major focus is put on the selection of communities. We always invite students to reflect on the type of research question and unit of analysis they want to investigate. Sampling is key, and requires accuracy and rigour, even if we carry it out on social media. It is crucial that students understand the difference between two potential units of analysis: tribes and communities.

A brand community is a specialised, non-geographically bound community, based on a structured set of social relations among admirers of a brand (Muniz and O'Guinn, 2001). Tribes, despite having the same set of characteristics, do not have a brand focus, and if consumption is part of their activities they rarely consume brands and products without adding to them, blending them with their own lives and altering them – turning themselves into 'consumer tribes' (Canniford, 2011; Cova et al., 2007).

These two concepts can be used in class to help students refine their research question. While brand communities are the most popular term within marketing, tribes are more suitable when addressing broader research questions, looking at a product category rather than focusing on a brand. Students must make it clear that selecting a brand community means researching current and existing customers; opting for a tribe as a unit of analysis can provide answers about potential customers. Analysing the website *PurseForum* (https://forum .purseblog.com/), a tribe of passionate handbag fans, can address questions such as 'What are the rituals and the purchasing preferences/behaviours/ perceptions of bag consumers?' A brand community type of research question can sound like: 'How do people passionate about handbags perceive Louis Vuitton's new canvas bag?' A seminar exercise could be set up to identify a relevant community using search engines, or even hashtags and keywords on social media, taking the students toward a reflective discussion on research objectives and effective sampling.

Netnography is a very flexible method, so it offers opportunities for teaching, because data can be collected using a variety of forms (interviews, archives, journals, photos and audio-visual information) and it is a perfect method to apply to social media platforms. From the instructor's perspective, netnography is an effective example of a method that can be directly applied to *Facebook, Twitter, Instagram* and *Pinterest*, exploiting pedagogical advantages of carrying out online research. *NVivo* works perfectly with social media material (Wilk et al., 2019) through the *NCapture* feature. Apart from the synergies stemming from the technological aspects, there is research advocating the usage of a 'holistic' methodological approach (Reid and Duffy, 2018), which systematically combines netnographic techniques with social media listening tools. For example, netnographic field notes can be used to explain the social media listening data; a netnographic immersive cultural observation can help interpret social media results and overcome the limitations of quantitative social listening results. The netnographic approach allows access to consumption groups which are vital and valuable units of investigation for all our prospective marketers. Indeed, during their studies marketing students might have already learnt how to create and manage social communities, so it makes perfect sense to teach them how to research consumption groups and study their characteristics in order to gain considerable marketing insights. If we correctly frame the netnographic method as an addition to the student's employability skill set, this could even raise the interest and motivation of our audience toward research methods.

TEACHING REPORT WRITING AND ARTICULATION SKILLS

It is important for students to learn how to articulate, that is, to describe and explain how a given research project was carried out and what the data means. This step can only be successfully completed if students are comfortable with and proficient in the research skills they are using. Research reports should be focused (emphasising the important information), accurate (the report should not mislead the reader), clear (not confuse the reader) and concise (not waste the reader's time). As always, we recommend providing and working through examples of good and bad research reports of various types, such as students' papers, research articles and research reports (e.g. Mintel). Another approach that we found effective was to ask students to write an outline of a research report in the first class of the module, ask them to save it and then compare it to the research report they had to produce at the end of the module (the same exercise can be applied to teaching survey design). This allows them to see two things clearly: (1) their learning and progress in a module, and (2) the importance of learning and understanding research methods and data analysis, in order to be able to produce a research report.

THE IMPORTANCE OF TEACHING RESPONSIBILITY IN BUSINESS AND MANAGEMENT RESEARCH

Last but not least, business and management research, as well as research in fields such as psychology, has come under scrutiny for being irrelevant to societies and businesses (Losada et al., 2011). Many initiatives now try to encourage research that is responsible and thoughtful, carried out to benefit organisations, communities or societies (see, for example, the network *Responsible Research in Business and Management* (https://www.rrbm.network/). Whilst there is no doubt that applied research conducted by researchers in organisations is certainly useful to the organisations, we wonder what messages are delivered to students conducting their undergraduate and postgraduate dissertations. Students rarely go beyond the standard required ethics application, in which they have to consider the ethical aspects of the data collection stage, but they are not required to think about how their choices at that stage of their education contribute to businesses, organisations or societies. Ethical challenges are part of the everyday practice of doing marketing research. Hence, lecturers are responsible for teaching students about research ethics and research regulations.

CONCLUSION

If we had to conclude with only a few sentences to give a definitive piece of advice, it would be that successful research methods teaching relies on careful teaching preparation, which rests on the assumption that a student knows nothing about research methods. We think applying these principles to teaching research methods should yield positive results in students' understanding of methods and concepts, and lead to high levels of student satisfaction. As you do your teaching preparation, do not assume that students are aware of certain concepts. When structuring your work, realise that less is more – we found teaching fewer methods or concepts, but with greater attention, results in students understanding research methods better and their increased satisfaction with modules. Whilst we have shared a collection of our own eclectic experiences with teaching research methods, it is important to remember that a research methods curriculum should be designed to take students through the following structure of the marketing research process: (1) understanding business issues; (2) defining a marketing research problem; (3) designing marketing research; (4) analysing data and interpreting the results; (5) translating results into actions; (6) interacting effectively with clients. It is impossible to become an expert in all methodological approaches within a standard module that lasts one or two semesters. Therefore, we also recommend that students (after acquiring the basics of both qualitative and quantitative methods) should then specialise in selected methodological approaches and selected areas of marketing, for example, survey methods in the area of customer satisfaction or experiments in marketing communications.

RECOMMENDED READING

Belk, R.W. (ed.) (2006), *Handbook of Qualitative Research Methods in Marketing*. Cheltenham, UK and Northampton, MA, USA: Edward Elgar Publishing.

Bergstrom, C.T. and West, J.D. (2020), *Calling Bullshit: The Art of Skepticism in a Data-driven World*. New York: Random House.

Corti, L., Van den Eynden, V., Bishop, L. and Woollard, M. (2019), *Managing and Sharing Research Data: A Guide to Good Practice*. London: Sage Publications.

Field, A. (2013), *Discovering Statistics Using IBM SPSS Statistics*. London: SAGE Publications.

Hall, R. (2020), *Mixing Methods in Social Research: Qualitative, Quantitative and Combined Methods*. London: SAGE Publications.

Spiegelhalter, D. (2019), *The Art of Statistics: Learning from Data*. Penguin.

Wilson, A. (2018), *Marketing Research*. Macmillan International Higher Education.

REFERENCES

Albinsson, P.A., Barnes-McEntee, W., Markos, E. and Peterson, M. (2018), Teaching qualitative research methods. In 2018 Conference Proceedings *Back to the Future: Revisiting the Foundations of Marketing. Society for Marketing Advances*, West Palm Beach, FL, October–November.

Barraket, J. (2005), Teaching research method using a student-centred approach? Critical reflections on practice. *Journal of University Teaching and Learning Practice*, 2(2). Accessed 12 August, 2021 at https://files.eric.ed.gov/fulltext/EJ1059434.pdf.

Bell, A., Hartman, T., Piekut, A., Rae, A. and Taylor, M. (2019), *Making Sense of Data in the Media*. London: Sage Publications.

Buckley, F.J. (1999), *Team Teaching: What, Why, and How?* London: Sage Publications.

Canniford, R. (2011), How to manage consumer tribes. *Journal of Strategic Marketing*, 19(7), 591–606.

Chad, P. (2012), The use of team-based learning as an approach to increased engagement and learning for marketing students: A case study. *Journal of Marketing Education*, 34(2), 128–39.

Cheung, L. and McColl-Kennedy, J.R. (2015), Resource integration in liminal periods: Transitioning to transformative service. *Journal of Services Marketing*, 29(6/7), 485–97.

Cluley, R., Green, W. and Owen, R. (2020), The changing role of the marketing researcher in the age of digital technology: Practitioner perspectives on the digitization of marketing research. *International Journal of Market Research*, 62(1), 27–42.

Cova, B., Kozinets, R.V. and Shankar, A. (2007), *Consumer Tribes*. Abingdon: Routledge.

Cvancara, K.E. (2017), Optimizing how we teach research methods. *Communication Teacher*, 31(1), 35–40.

Czarnecka, B. and Mogaji, E. (2020), How are we tempted into debt? Emotional appeals in loan advertisements in UK newspapers. *International Journal of Bank Marketing*, 38(3), 756–76.

Czarnecka, B., Brennan, R. and Keles, S. (2018), Cultural meaning, advertising, and national culture: A four-country study. *Journal of Global Marketing*, 31(1), 4–17.

Di Gregorio, A., Maggioni, I., Mauri, C. and Mazzucchelli, A. (2019), Employability skills for future marketing professionals. *European Management Journal*, 37(3), 251–8.

Ercikan, K. and Roth, W.M. (2006), Constructing data. In C. Conrad and R. Serlin (eds), *Sage Handbook for Research in Education: Engaging Ideas and Enriching Inquiry* (pp. 451–75). Thousand Oaks, CA: Sage.

Ewing, T., Owens, J. and Cassidy, F. (2016), Integrated not isolated: How to improve customer insight by embracing social media data. London: IPA Social Works.

Fayyad, U. and Hamutcu, H. (2020), Analytics and data science standardization and assessment framework. *Harvard Data Science Review*, accessed 1 July 2020 at https://doi.org/10.1162/99608f92.1a99e67a.

FitzPatrick, M., Davey, J. and van Oostrom, M. (2010), Getting personal with marketing research: A first year teaching innovation. A Practice Report. *The International Journal of the First Year in Higher Education*, 1(1), 84–90.

GMU (2020), How to write a research question. Accessed 25 June 2020 at https://writingcenter.gmu.edu/guides/how-to-write-a-research-question.

Gonick, L. and Smith, W. (2005), *The Cartoon Guide to Statistics*. Collins Reference Publication.

Graham, L. and Schuwerk, T.J. (2017), Teaching qualitative research methods using 'Undercover Boss'. *Communication Teacher*, 31(1), 11–15.

Greenhow, C. (2011), Youth, learning, and social media. *Journal of Educational Computing Research*, 45(2), 139–46.

Groessler, A. (2017), Teaching research methods: An occasional paper. Accessed 24 May 2020 at https://itali.uq.edu.au/files/1294/Discussion-paper-Teaching-Research%20Methods.pdf.

Gunasti, K., Kara, S., Ross Jr, W.T. and Duclos, R. (2020), How language affects consumers' processing of numerical cues. *Journal of Consumer Behaviour*. DOI: https://doi.org/10.1002/cb.1876.

Harris, P. (2008), *Designing and Reporting Experiments in Psychology*. Maidenhead: McGraw-Hill Education.

Harwood, T. and Garry, T. (2015), An investigation into gamification as a customer engagement experience environment. *Journal of Services Marketing*, 29(6/7), 533–46.

Hootsuite (2020) 15 of the best social media monitoring tools to save you time. Accessed 24 May 2002 https://blog.hootsuite.com/social-media-monitoring-tools/.

Kalliny, M., Ghanem, S., Shaner, M., Boyle, B. and Mueller, B. (2020), Capitalizing on faith: A cross-cultural examination of consumer responses to the use of religious symbols in advertising. *Journal of Global Marketing*, 33(3), 158–76.

Kozinets, R.V. (2002), The field behind the screen: Using netnography for marketing research in online communities. *Journal of Marketing Research*, 39(1), 61–72.

Kozinets, R.V. (2015), *Netnography: Redefined*. 2nd edn. London: Sage Publications.

Lassk, F.G. and Mulki J. (2018), Flipping the marketing research classroom: Teaching with team-based learning: An abstract. In P. Rossi and N. Krey (eds), *Marketing Transformation: Marketing Practice in an Ever Changing World*. AMSWMC 2017.

Developments in Marketing Science: Proceedings of the Academy of Marketing Science. Cham: Springer.

Latta, M. and Clark, M. (2016), Maximising the value of a pharmaceutical line extension using discrete choice modelling, secondary data and market segmentation. *Applied Marketing Analytics*, 2(1), 84–91.

Lewthwaite, S. and Nind, M. (2016), Teaching research methods in the social sciences: Expert perspectives on pedagogy and practice. *British Journal of Educational Studies*, 64(4), 413–30.

Losada, C., Martell, J. and Losano, J.M. (2011), Responsible business education: Not a question of curriculum but a raison d'être for business schools. Business schools and their contribution to society. *Central European Business Review*, 1(2), 163–74.

Martin, M.A. (2003), 'It's Like… You Know': The use of analogies and heuristics in teaching introductory statistical methods. *Journal of Statistics Education*, 11(2).

Miles, M.B. and Huberman, A.M. (1994), *Qualitative Data Analysis: An Expanded Sourcebook*. London: Sage Publications.

Muniz, A.M. and O'Guinn, T.C. (2001), Brand community. *Journal of Consumer Research*, 27(4), 412–32.

Mustafa, R.Y. (1996), The challenge of teaching statistics to non-specialists. *Journal of Statistics Education*, 4(1).

National questionnaires (n.d.), National questionnaires. Accessed 31 October 2020 at https://ec.europa.eu/info/business-economy-euro/indicators-statistics/economic-databases/business-and-consumer-surveys/methodology-business-and-consumer-surveys/national-questionnaires_en.

Pew Research Centre (2020), Methods. Accessed 1 July 2020 at https://www.pewresearch.org/methods/u-s-survey-research/questionnaire-design/.

Qualtrics (n.d.), Survey template. Accessed 9 September 2020 at https://www.qualtrics.com/marketplace/survey-template.

Reid, E. and Duffy, K. (2018), A netnographic sensibility: Developing the netnographic/social listening boundaries. *Journal of Marketing Management*, 34(3–4), 263–86.

Salmons, J. (2016). *Doing Qualitative Research Online*. Los Angeles, CA: Sage Publications.

Skålén, P., Aal, K.A. and Edvardsson, B. (2015), Cocreating the Arab spring: Understanding transformation of service systems in contention. *Journal of Service Research*, 18(3), 250–64.

Smith, A.E. and Martinez-Moyano, I.J. (2012), Techniques in teaching statistics: Linking research production and research use. *Journal of Public Affairs Education*, 18(1), 107–36.

Sowey, E.R. (1995), Teaching statistics: Making it memorable. *Journal of Statistics Education*, 3(2).

Sprout Social (n.d.), Social listening: Your launchpad to success on social media. Accessed 23 May 2020 at https://sproutsocial.com/social-listening/.

Sprout Social (n.d.), Social media monitoring vs. social media listening. Accessed 24 June 2020 at https://sproutsocial.com/insights/listening-vs-monitoring/.

Stern, B.L. and Tseng, L.P.D. (2002), Do academics and practitioners agree on what and how to teach the undergraduate marketing research course? *Journal of Marketing Education*, 24(3), 225–32.

Takahashi, S. (2008), *The Manga Guide to Statistics*. San Francisco, CA: No Starch Press.

The Economics Network (2020), Type of classroom experiments. Accessed 9 September 2020 at https://www.economicsnetwork.ac.uk/handbook/experiments/4.

Thyroff, A. (2019), Teaching qualitative marketing research: An experiential approach. *Marketing Education Review*, 29(1), 75–87.

Udall, A.M., de Groot, J.I., de Jong, S.B. and Shankar, A. (2020), How do I see myself? A systematic review of identities in pro-environmental behaviour research. *Journal of Consumer Behaviour*, 19(2), 108–141.

Vriens, M. and Vidden, C. (2019), The Linux Compete strategy: An analytics case study. *Applied Marketing Analytics*, 5(2), 129–36.

Vriens, M., Brokaw, S., Rademaker, D. and Verhulst, R. (2019), The marketing research curriculum: Closing the practitioner–academic gaps. *International Journal of Market Research*, 61(5), 492–501.

Wilk, V., Soutar, G.N. and Harrigan, P. (2019), Tackling social media data analysis: Comparing and contrasting QSR NVivo and Leximancer. *Qualitative Market Research*, 22(2), 94–113.

Wilson, H., Neeley, C. and Niedzwiecki, K. (2009), Content and method in the teaching of marketing research revisited. *Journal of Instructional Pedagogies*, 1.

Wilton, N. (2008). Business graduates and management jobs: An employability match made in heaven? *Journal of Education and Work*, 21(2), 143–58.

10. Teaching social marketing

Ariadne Beatrice Kapetanaki and Fiona Spotswood

1. ABOUT SOCIAL MARKETING

Social marketing is part of the recent political history and future of behaviour change and large-scale, publicly funded social marketing interventions have become household names (e.g. Change4Life, Truth, This Girl Can). Although some studies have found that social marketing is not always a constant in taught marketing programmes (Wellman, 2017), we argue that social marketing is a vital element of any well-rounded marketing programme (Kelly, 2009, 2013). Box 10.1 shows why marketing and policy-oriented programmes, such as sustainability and public health, should include social marketing in their curriculum.

> ### BOX 10.1 REASONS TO INCLUDE SOCIAL MARKETING IN MARKETING AND POLICY-ORIENTED PROGRAMMES
>
> 1. Younger generations are more engaged with environmental and public health issues as well as ethical business practices (Hancock, 2017). Therefore, the appearance of social marketing in the curriculum can appeal to potential students.
> 2. Teaching social marketing will encourage students to enhance their critical skills and develop a more responsible mentality towards business. Students can be critically engaged with marketing concepts and practices through the introduction of marketing in the context of wider societal, ethical, environmental and political issues which are often not so prominent in the marketing curriculum (Catterall et al., 2002; Heath et al., 2019).
> 3. Upon graduation, many marketing students will be asked to apply their marketing knowledge within a healthcare, charity, social enterprise[1] or public sector context and these are the places where social marketing

knowledge, understanding and application is vital. These sectors have seen a considerable growth, with about 30 per cent of UK workers in 2017 employed in public administration, education and health, the highest percentage across all sectors (Office for National Statistics, 2019). Social enterprises contribute £60 billion each year to the UK economy and are being recognised as the future of business (Kay, 2018). In the US, one out of every ten people works for a non-governmental organization (NGO), there are more than 600 000 NGOs in Australia and more than 129 000 public-benefit foundations in Europe, while if NGOs were a country, they would have the fifth largest economy in the world (Nonprofit Action, 2015). Given these statistics, it is vital to equip our students with the skills required to enable them to find work in these areas.

4. Students with a range of non-marketing backgrounds are likely to be asked to consider effective approaches to social and behaviour change programmes. These may include health-related disciplines such as health promotion and public health, subjects relating to sustainability and environmental studies, and medical students, nutritionists and dieticians. These students may draw on ideas from social marketing as principles in their academic studies and future careers and social marketing modules can be useful resources for programmes in many different faculties.

Social marketing:

> seeks to develop and integrate marketing concepts with other approaches to influence behaviours that benefit individuals and communities for the greater social good. Social marketing practice is guided by ethical principles. It seeks to integrate research, best practice, theory, audience and partnership insight, to inform the delivery of competition sensitive and segmented social change programmes that are effective, efficient, equitable and sustainable (iSMA, ESMA and AASM, 2013).

It sits at the intersection of marketing and policymaking and is known as an approach to behaviour change deployed by public and governmental bodies at various levels of governance across the world (e.g. United Nations, Avon and Somerset Fire and Rescue, Public Health England, New Zealand's Health Promotion Agency).

Social marketing is increasingly debated as one of the approaches to behaviour change which can help tackle 'wicked problems',[2] such as non-communicable diseases, but it also has a burgeoning membership interested in critical and macromarketing considerations in relation to the role of commercial marketing activities in creating and fuelling societal challenges

(Kemper and Ballantine, 2017). It has its own dedicated special interest group of the Chartered Institute of Marketing, a World Conference, and regional conferences in Europe, Australia, North and Latin America as well as numerous academic research groups including Social Marketing @ Griffith (Australia), the Social Marketing Group at the University of South Florida (US) and Stirling Institute for Social Marketing and Health (Scotland). The discipline contributes a recognised part of contemporary marketing theory and debate through contributions to top marketing academic journals (e.g. Andreasen, 2012; Dibb and Carrigan, 2013; Gordon et al., 2016).

Social marketing is often taught in relation to business, management, public health and sustainability programmes across a range of schools and faculties in Higher Education. It has been taught in universities for more than a decade either as a full course (for example, MA Health and Social Marketing in Middlesex University, UK; MSc Marketing [Social Marketing] in University of Brighton, UK and Master of Public Health concentrating on Social Marketing in University of South Florida, USA) or a module (for example, UG Strategic Social Marketing at the University of Sydney, Australia; UG Introduction to Social Marketing in University of Kent, UK and UG Social Marketing at the Victoria University of Wellington, New Zealand). In a number of other cases, social marketing is included as part of a module, for example at the University of Bristol's 'Contemporary Issues in Marketing' PGT unit on the MSc Marketing and within 'Sustainability and Social Impact in Marketing' on the same programme. With university schools increasingly aligning their research and teaching with global challenges (Charlton, 2020; Global University Network for Innovation, 2017), social marketing will remain a staple as part of taught marketing programmes at undergraduate and postgraduate level.

This chapter seeks to introduce some of the key issues to include and explore in social marketing teaching at undergraduate and postgraduate level, drawing on the authors' experiences of teaching social marketing at BSc, MSc and CPD levels, to marketing and non-marketing audiences, and in grappling with tensions in exploring crux ideas alongside innovations in theory and practice.

2. FRAMING SOCIAL MARKETING IN THE BEHAVIOUR CHANGE MARKETPLACE

The uniqueness of social marketing is that it incorporates traditional marketing theories and tools along with a vast range of social, behavioural and political sciences concepts to help mobilise society and solve complex societal problems that have a behavioural component. It is increasingly recognised that the complexity of behaviours relating to ill-health or environmental damage demands interdisciplinarity (Science and Technology Select Committee,

2011). Before moving on to discuss key components of social marketing teaching, it is important to frame social marketing in relation to contemporary debate. Indeed, in more detailed social marketing courses, this framing is an important starting point for teaching.

First, it is useful to explore how social marketing is 'misunderstood' (Eagle et al., 2013; Shaw et al., 2014). In the face of this confusion there is a considerable amount of academic column inches dedicated to exploring what social marketing is not (Smith, 2010), and to competing with more politically popular approaches (French, 2011). Indeed, social marketing is considered as needing better marketing in the 'social change marketplace' (Andreasen, 2002). Confusion about social marketing stems from sounding similar to 'social media' or 'social media marketing', and due to uncertainty over its difference to health communication, social advertising and health education. Social advertising and social media marketing can be used as tools and tactics of social marketing interventions. In terms of communications and advertising for the purposes of social change, the difference is that social marketing goes beyond just informing people or changing their attitudes and beliefs, to influence and change behaviours. In order to achieve this, it often takes more than the use of communication tools, such as advertising and social media. Moreover, Griffiths et al. (2009) argue that health promotion and social marketing are separate but complementary disciplines and it would be wrong to focus on delineating them, but it would be preferable to explore ways that their ideas can be integrated to promote health and wellbeing. In this context, public health students will benefit from learning about both health promotion and social marketing as the combination of the two can equip them with the necessary tools to succeed in the workplace and bring about effective social and behavioural change. These longstanding confusions help frame the starting point for many social marketing courses, which start by scoping out the definition of social marketing and encouraging students to engage with early seminal texts to understand their core routes and purpose (e.g. Wiebe, 1951; Kotler and Zaltman, 1971). These will be discussed in section 3.1.

Secondly, it is important to sketch out the political context of social marketing. Social marketers cannot claim dominance in the behaviour change marketplace, and indeed have lost some political favour in the most recent decade (Shaw et al., 2014). Any approach to behaviour change adopted by governments is inevitably philosophically, ontologically, ethically and politically charged. Weighing up and comparing approaches and their theoretical underpinnings can be insightful to students interested in political ideology. For example, after the 2010 general election, the new UK administration led by David Cameron supported the establishment of the 'Behavioural Insight Team', or what became known as the 'nudge unit', which focuses on approaches to behaviour change underpinned by behavioural economics (Thaler and Sunstein, 2009).

Although 'nudge' has remained popular among governments worldwide (Benartzi et al., 2017; Dibb and Carrigan, 2013), there has been considerable and wide-reaching critique about its poor real world efficacy, lack of power in tackling intractable problems, and its alignment with neoliberal governance (Editorial, 2020; NSMC, 2016; Spotswood, 2017; Spotswood et al., 2017). When teaching social marketing it is important to explore the ideas within the 'nudge' thesis, for example through the MINDSPACE (Dolan et al., 2010) and EAST policy tools (Behavioural Insights Team, 2018). This is useful to open discussion about the way social marketing has long deployed ideas that can be found in 'nudge' in the course of delivering behaviour change programmes but also how, in effective social marketing programmes, these are found in combination with other approaches (Lefebvre, 2011). So, ideally, social marketing is not aligned to any one intervention approach, but draws on an intervention mix, and always with a deep understanding of the citizen at the centre of strategy and tactics (NSMC, 2016). Indeed, it is social marketing's interdisciplinarity that is part of its core strength (Dibb and Carrigan, 2013) and interdisciplinarity is needed to achieve effective behaviour change in the face of complex societal problems (Benartzi et al., 2017; Science and Technology Select Committee, 2011; Ulasevich, 2015).

3.   WHAT TO TEACH

Social marketing can be taught as the focus of a whole module or part of a module. The following areas can be covered in more or less depth depending on the time devoted to teach social marketing. When social marketing is just part of a module there are two options. The first option is when the tutor spends one or two weeks introducing the main principles of social marketing. For example, social marketing can be part of a principles of marketing module or contemporary marketing issues. The second option is when the tutor devotes a substantial amount of the module teaching about social marketing principles and tools along with another relevant topic which can be, for example, ethics, sustainability or non-profit marketing.

The 'Sustainability and Social Impact in Marketing' unit at the University of Bristol (developed and directed by one of the authors) is a good example. The range of topics explored in the module include sustainability marketing, macro marketing and social marketing, and they are brought together to consider the global challenges of climate change and sustainable systems of production and consumption. In this case the assessment is focused on social marketing, but the students are invited to draw on ideas from across the theoretical and substantive areas of the module. The assessment is to design (part of) a social marketing plan focused on a sustainability problem.

We suggest that the following learning outcomes are part of every social marketing module with further outcomes to be added by the tutors based on the focus of the class, general curriculum needs, interactions with other modules of the curriculum and students' level.

1.   Understand the definition and scope of social marketing.
2.   Understand the contexts where social marketing is applied.
3.   Recognise what makes a social marketing programme effective.
4.   Critically understand the challenges of using marketing for behaviour and social change.

Regardless of the teaching mode, teaching social marketing should incorporate the following four essential areas: the history and definition of social marketing; social marketing paradigms; social marketing planning and practice; and the benchmark criteria. The latter section is really an umbrella for the main thrust of social marketing teaching topics, including core principles of citizen-centredness, theoretical underpinnings and intervention approaches. We believe that these are the basics that every social marketing student should learn and understand to ensure that they are academically and practically equipped to debate and apply social marketing principles.

3.1   Establishing the Basics: Definition and Domain

It is important to introduce students to the way the social marketing concept has evolved since its conception. This can include a timeline from Wiebe's (1951) article, which posed the question 'Why can't you sell Brotherhood like you sell soap?' that meant to change the way marketing was conceptualised and used, to twenty-first-century social marketing and the evolution of social marketing definition from Kotler and Zaltman (1971), who first coined the term 'social marketing', to the integrated social marketing definition of three social marketing associations[3] (iSMA et al., 2013).

To avoid definitions of fields and concepts feeling dry, a useful discussion can focus on identifying the evolving concepts that are reflected in the evolution of the social marketing definition. Changes include moving from seeking to shape 'social ideas' (Kotler and Roberto, 1989; Kotler and Zaltman, 1971) to always including behavioural goals (Gordon et al., 2016), to the inclusion of 'voluntary behaviour' (Andreasen, 1994) and the specification that benefit should be for individuals and society (Albrecht, 1997; Hastings, 2007). Consistent throughout all the key definitions since 1971 has been an emphasis on the use of marketing techniques, although that has been expanded to emphasise the integration of 'marketing and other' approaches. The most recent definition specifically mentions ethical principles and equity. Some other useful exercises that might be deployed to encourage students to think about the broad concept and contribution of social marketing are included in Box 10.2.

BOX 10.2 EXERCISES TO THINKING THROUGH THE CONCEPT OF SOCIAL MARKETING

a. Framing Social Marketing through the Nuffield Council on Bioethics Intervention Ladder

Having explored the concept of 'intervention', ask students to consider how marketing might contribute to interventions at different levels of the bioethics ladder (Nuffield Council on Bioethics, 2007, pp. 41–2). Consider where social marketing would NOT contribute. Compare social marketing with other approaches in the ladder.

b. Framing Social Marketing through Comparison

Using a comparison approach, students in groups can be asked to list the differences between social and commercial marketing, based on prior reading. There are examples of this exercise in French and Gordon (2019). Examples of differences are that social marketing 'sells' desired behaviour whereas commercial marketing sells goods and services; or that social marketing seeks societal gain whereas commercial marketing seeks financial gain. All these comparisons form fruitful opportunities for debate and discussion, such as about brands with social 'purpose' or the ethics of corporate social responsibility.

c. Framing Social Marketing through Debate

For students with experience of marketing or studying marketing, a discussion about the 'role of marketing in change behaviour' can be a useful way of introducing students to the ideas at the heart of social marketing. Students can be asked to prepare a position statement and to think through specific questions such as 'why do governments not regulate every problematic behaviour?' and 'why might social marketing be seen as appealing/unwelcome?' Students might engage in debate about the possible benefits of using social marketing to generate behaviour change, taking the position of different stakeholders, such as 'Health Minister', 'fast food industry' or 'low-wage parent'.

d. Framing Social Marketing through What it is Not

It can be useful to dispel misunderstandings early on about what social marketing is 'not', such as:

- It is not just advertising, although advertising can be a useful communications component but in social marketing it is likely to be included as one of many components in the marketing mix.
- It is not just SOS marketing (sending out something). Designing, printing and 'sending out' leaflets in a way that is not strategically linked with a project's targeted goals is unlikely to form part of a social marketing programme.
- It is not education. Education informs as an end goal whereas social marketing influences awareness, knowledge, attitudes, behaviours, practices and structures. The end goal is what people do.
- It is not social media, although social media is likely to be part of an overall social marketing intervention mix.

Having introduced the basic premise and core definitions of social marketing, students can be introduced to the idea of social marketing as a strategic approach to social change (French and Gordon, 2019) that includes downstream, midstream (Luca et al., 2016; Wood, 2016a) and upstream (Gordon, 2013) approaches. The 'streams' approach is a common teaching point in public health and there are numerous clips on YouTube explaining and illustrating the concept, which can be useful. Students should be able to differentiate between these definitions and understand how different approaches to social marketing can be used and are necessary to achieve sustainable societal shift (French and Gordon, 2019). To facilitate this, examples can be used such as the US truth campaign (https://www.thetruth.com/take-action), which very well reflects a strategic social marketing approach. A good exercise is to ask students to spend time on the Truth website and identify components from each of the three 'streams'.

3.2   Social Marketing Paradigms

Students who have understood the basic premise of marketing for social good can be introduced to the scholarly field of social marketing as a way of introducing some interesting tensions, developments and innovations in the field. Gordon and Gurrieri (2014) explain the three social marketing paradigms as 'traditionalist', 'social ecologist' and 'critical' and these are summarised in Table 10.1.

Gordon and Gurrieri (2014) argue that the traditionalist school dominates, matching rather than questioning the marketing messages and social issues that it is often designed to counter. They point particularly to the downstream focus, which has been critiqued as loading responsibility onto individuals and overstating their capacity to achieve behaviour change in the context of socio-material conditions, leading to health inequity in some cases (Langford and Panter-Brick, 2013). To some degree, scholars working in the social-ecological and critical paradigms may overlap, but it is useful to separate these in order to emphasise the innovation and evolution occurring in social marketing as a field of scholarship as well as practice.

Table 10.1   The three social marketing paradigms

Traditionalist social marketing	
'This narrow interpretation may have influenced misinterpretations of social marketing as communication or product-focused' (Gordon and Gurrieri, 2014, p. 262).	• Dominated by downstream, individual and voluntary behavioural change with little focus on structural conditions; • Adherence to traditional marketing frameworks e.g. 4Ps; • Little criticality; • More practitioner focused.
Social ecological social marketing	
This 'argues for a broader and deeper focus for social marketing beyond individuals to consider the wider environment, policy, structural conditions and social norms that influence social outcomes' (Gordon and Gurrieri, 2014, p. 263).	• Focus is beyond targeting citizens; • Focus can include policy and regulation; • Social marketing will include upstream, midstream and downstream intervention components.
Critical social marketing	
This 'espouses critical research on the impact of commercial marketing, and … critical debate and reflexivity in the field' (Gordon and Gurrieri, 2014, p. 263).	• The broadest conceptualisation of social marketing; • Critical reflection drawing on multiple theoretical bases, beyond traditional psychological routes; • Engaging with literature including studies of feminism, power, political economy, equality, social forces and governance; • Questions and critiques ethical, social and moral forces of social marketing.

Source: Adapted from Gordon and Gurrieri (2014).

3.3   Ethics

Ethics is an important feature of any social marketing course and closely relates to some of the work that falls within the 'critical social marketing' paradigm, although it has been an important part of social marketing from its earliest days (Andreasen, 2001). Students should understand that social marketing practice must be informed by 'ethical considerations including acceptability, transparency and the balancing of potential benefits and costs associated with programme interventions' (French and Gordon, 2019, p. 36).

There are a number of key subjects from which ethical debate will emerge. For example, social marketers often have to design programmes for vulnerable or high-risk groups and so questions of power must be considered. Furthermore, segmentation brings with it a range of ethical dilemmas; for example, how can a social marketer choose the 'low hanging fruit' to achieve the project's behavioural goals, but know they cannot move the hardest-to-reach groups with the most need of behavioural change. Another area for debate is whether social marketing should include the use of non-voluntary forms of behaviour change (Spotswood et al., 2012), while another is the ethical dilemma that comes from the end of projects which reach the limits of their funding. Community engagement projects have been criticised for being left 'in the lurch' when social marketing budgets run dry. Moreover, partnerships with and funding from corporations may be 'competitors' of the desirable behaviour (Bhattacharya and Elsbach, 2002; Hastings and Angus, 2011). In addition, unintended consequences of behaviour change (Eagle et al., 2015) have created ethical debates in social marketing. Finally, there is the powerful example of 'fear' in social marketing (Hastings, 2007; Kennedy and Santos, 2019) that warrant discussion.

The need for social marketing to comply with ethical standards is undeniable, and practitioners must at the very least demonstrate strong compliance with the research code of conduct (Market Research Society, 2019). In this context, a social marketing ethics report was prepared for the National Social Marketing Centre (Eagle, 2009). Carter et al. (2017) explain that no consensus code of ethical conduct exists for social marketing, but they draw on items from several papers in the history of social marketing thought – including Laczniak et al. (1979) and Truss and White (2010) – to create a series of questions that should underpin social marketing ethical consideration. Thus, where modules allow time, students can be introduced to key debates and theories from the history of debate and scholarship exploring ethical issues in social marketing.

The discussion around social marketing ethics will give students the chance to see social marketing through a critical lens. In addition to lively debate and discussion, students enjoy engaging in an activity where they are asked to consider ethical considerations stemming from social marketing activities and from commercial marketing activities (see Box 10.3).

BOX 10.3   ETHICS IN SOCIAL MARKETING

Students could be asked to decide and explore the ethical considerations in each of the following cases:

- Covert observational research with children into what influences their sweet (candy) eating to inform a social marketing programme.
- Coca Cola sponsoring healthy teeth brushing campaigns or sports events.
- Community consultation about a stop smoking intervention that involves talking to an existing community activism group.
- Pop-up ads showing mortality rates from smoking on a teen video game.
- A campaign targeting parents telling them to keep their children's weight within a certain range or they will be at risk of a range of health problems.
- Tracking the phones of teenagers to send targeted messages to warn them about unsafe sex when they go to night clubs, bars and pubs.
- Rewarding children for suggesting to their friends that they sign up to a doll manufacturer's website.
- A social marketing campaign offering free limousine rides to men who drink too much and would otherwise drink-drive.

3.4 Benchmark Criteria

The thrust of social marketing teaching will inevitably revolve around the benchmark criteria. These criteria emerged from debates around what social marketing is not (e.g. social advertising) and what its added value is. The criteria to benchmark social marketing were introduced by Andreasen (2002) to elaborate social marketing principles and to support social marketing practitioners in the design and implementation of social marketing initiatives. The original six criteria were enriched to include two more and the new eight benchmark criteria are now used to illustrate what makes an effective social marketing programme (NSMC, 2014). Tutors can develop their teaching around these criteria as it is described in the following sections.

3.4.1 Consumer insight and citizen-centredness

The importance of making informed decisions that are based on research must be highlighted to students of all backgrounds. Marketing students should already have developed the mindset of consumer-centric initiatives and value co-creation (Domegan et al., 2013; Grönroos, 2011) as these are fundamental marketing principles and so they are expected to appreciate the importance of research to understand their target audience. However, students from a health sciences background may have a more 'one-fits-all' approach which is common in public health and health promotion interventions (Horton, 2018; Poland et al., 1999) and so understanding the importance of research-informed programmes is essential. A fundamental principle of social marketing is that an understanding of the everyday lives of the target audiences is at the heart of every decision made. This requires rigorous consumer research and the development of insights from those research findings that can be fed into the development of social marketing interventions.

Social marketers employ qualitative, quantitative and mixed methods depending on the project objectives and so these options must be introduced to the students along with their relevance to the problem and the stages of the programme planning process. For example, formative research at the early stages of the planning process often employs qualitative approaches to get insights into the target audiences while during monitoring and evaluation experiments, surveys and control trials can be adopted to present quantifiable results. It is important to highlight that reliance on just a few methods may lead to narrow understanding of the problem and inadequate monitoring of the programme. Budget constraints are one important reason behind this practice; however, when budget allows, multiple methods are recommended to maximise the effectiveness of social marketing programmes (Carins et al., 2016).

Kubacki and Rundle-Thiele's (2016) book includes chapters that focus on a range of methods for formative social marketing research. Chapters 11, 12 and 13 of French and Gordon's (2019) book provide a detailed exploration of the various research perspectives, from qualitative to quantitative, that can be used to understand the target audience and inform and monitor social marketing interventions.

In order to create citizen-centred social marketing, a 'situation analysis' is also required to understand what factors of the macro and micro environment surrounding the individual can facilitate or hinder the adoption of the desirable behaviour, and to understand what assets are available to help create social change. A holistic understanding of the individual (internal factors) and the environment (external factors) can lead to the development of a SWOT analysis that can drive social marketers' decisions, partnerships, strategy and approach. Despite the fact that students of a marketing, management or business background will be familiar with the concepts of situation and SWOT analysis, it is important to highlight how these can be applied in a social marketing context by providing relevant examples. Most textbooks (e.g. Eagle et al., 2013; Hastings and Domegan, 2013; Lee and Kotler, 2019) include examples of how to conduct a situation analysis and these can be used in class.

BOX 10.4 IDENTIFYING CITIZEN-CENTRED INSIGHTS

A useful way of encouraging students to think about 'citizen centredness' and the importance of situation analysis is to provide small case studies for them to consider and discuss. This activity overlaps with the next benchmark criteria (representing the interconnection between all the elements of social marketing). It involves providing a summary of research findings from a scoping report including situation analysis and asset mapping. The students are required to identify insights that are critical in forming the basis of a social marketing project, identify possible partnerships and begin to identify a social marketing plan. An example might be 'teenage pregnancies', with a report highlighting social deprivation and poor educational outcomes for young women in areas of the UK. The students are asked to use principles of citizen centredness to understand the 'problem' of teenage pregnancy and work towards thinking about social marketing solutions. This is a useful exercise to ensure students are using the scoping research summary rather than their own cultural assumptions to consider the problem. For example, were the pregnancies accidental or planned? What agencies and people are already working with and trusted by the target audience? What are the related behaviours and contexts which frame the young women's health harming behaviours? These insights will be important for framing what social marketing actions are then suggested.

3.4.2   Behaviour and behavioural goals

Students must be able to identify what is the desirable behaviour and set SMART behavioural objectives which will later on be used to monitor and evaluate the social marketing initiative. It is often challenging to decide what the aim of a social marketing intervention will be and to identify the behavioural focus (Eagle et al., 2013). Students can be given examples of multifaceted social problems (e.g. high obesity rates, teenage pregnancy and environmental conservation) and asked to come up with alternative behavioural goals that a social marketing programme could adopt.

As an activity, students can be presented with a short case study that could be an extract or summary from preliminary research, and asked to identify behavioural goals and associated SMART objectives. There are a number of excellent resources that tutors can draw on to create and present case study material, which we present in section 4.3.

3.4.3   Theory

A crucial social marketing benchmark criterion is the use of theory to inform social marketing interventions. A key point for students is that theory is a useful way of helping social marketers understand where people 'are' in relation to a desirable behaviour, what influences them towards or away from this behaviour and how they can be moved closer to the desirable behaviour. It helps frame our understanding of 'competition' (see section 3.4.4) and the techniques that are likely to work as well as the theoretical assumptions that underpin the use of different approaches. We consider this a 'crux' criterion because it underpins the conceptualisation of the insights on which social marketing is based. It also triggers ethical and critical reflection about the role of intervention, and the responsibility and capacity of social marketers to act in society's best interests. It is worth scheduling a larger amount of time for this section.

The concept of theory-informed programmes must be clarified to the students by showing examples of how theoretical frameworks have been used effectively to support the development of social marketing programmes. Discussion can be teased out as to precisely *how* theories have been used to inform the programmes, for example to guide the insights underpinning the development of the intervention mix, to guide understanding about how the behaviour change might happen, or to guide the focus of evaluation. To gain a sound understanding of theory in social marketing, students must be exposed to the main theories used in social marketing as well as to the critiques towards certain theoretical approaches. Truong (2014) lists the main theories used in social marketing between 1998 and 2012 as:

- Social cognitive theory;
- Theory of reasoned action/planned behaviour;
- Health belief model;
- Stages of change model/transtheoretical model;
- Social/behavioural – ecological model;
- Diffusion of innovation.

This list is likely to have changed somewhat in the past decade, but a leaning towards social psychology remains.

BOX 10.5 USEFUL RESOURCES TO UNDERSTAND THEORY IN SOCIAL MARKETING

A good resource explaining the theoretical pillars of 'behaviour change' is Chatterton's (2011) report that lays out the differences between individually oriented theory (economic, educational and psychological theories) and socially oriented theories (theories of practice and distributed agency). He explains the different theories very clearly using 'energy use' as the context and makes the important point that 'in reality, energy use is simply what it is, and these are just different ways of looking at it that focus on different aspects of behaviour' (p. 7). Another good resource is Lefebvre's (2013) Chapter 3, which provides a very good reading for students to understand the need for using theory to inform social marketing initiatives and a detailed discussion around various theoretical models.

Social ecological models (McLeroy et al., 1988) are an important theoretical approach with which students of social marketing should be acquainted. Amidst the programme of rapid theoretical advancement that is seeing social marketing respond to calls to move beyond the limits of individualistic thinking (Dibb and Carrigan, 2013; Rundle-Thiele et al., 2019), social marketing has adopted social-ecological thinking to both understand influences on behaviour and to frame intervention planning (Hennink-Kaminski et al., 2018; Kapetanaki et al., 2014; Lindridge et al., 2013; Wood, 2016b). A social-ecological lens is commonplace in health promotion (Adamowitsch et al., 2017) and takes a 'wider and deeper' view that acknowledges the influential role of community groups, organisations, family and friends in behaviour and behaviour change and highlights the societal and cultural contexts of health and government decision making into which social marketing programmes fit (Brennan et al., 2016; Russell-Bennett et al., 2013). Other theoretical frameworks that have been considered and used by social marketers include the relationship marketing thinking (Marques and Domegan, 2011), systems thinking (Domegan et al., 2016), social movements (Daellenbach and Parkinson, 2017) and social practice theories (Hargreaves, 2011; Kapetanaki et al., 2019; Spotswood et al., 2017).

Exposing the students to all these different disciplines, theories and concepts can lead to thought provoking discussions and better design and application of social marketing interventions in the future. A common critique of the use of theory in social marketing is the tendency for programmes and published studies to over-rely (Truong, 2014) on social psychological foundations such as the Theory of Planned Behaviour (Ajzen, 1991) to explain and eventually influence behaviours around multifaceted health and social issues such as healthy eating and physical activity. The critique (e.g. Spotswood et al., 2017) questions the capacity for linear, individualist theory to account for the entangled nature of society in which socio-material structures, temporalities, spatial and technological as well as political forces shape everyday patterns of often unreflexive action (Maller, 2015). Another critique focuses on the use of commercial marketing models (Eagle et al., 2013; Peattie and Peattie, 2003) that cannot account for the complexity of shifting cultural conventions towards problematic behaviours. Furthermore, developments in health promotion that heavily lean towards embracing complexity and whole systems thinking in intervention conceptualisation and design have been found to be hard to implement in practice (Keshavarz et al., 2010; Moore and Evans, 2017). Social practice theory has been critiqued as difficult to implement in practice and ontologically problematic as a basis for intervention (Sahakian and Wilhite, 2014).

An activity to familiarise students with the use of different theories is to divide the class into groups with each group assigned a different theoretical perspective (e.g. Theory of Planned Behaviour, Socio-Ecological model, Social Practice Theory or the Transtheoretical Model). Given the same scenario students can be asked to apply their assigned theory and then present their findings in class, followed by a discussion on the differences found based on the theoretical approach that they adopted.

3.4.4   Exchange and competition

Inherently entangled with previous criteria are those of exchange (Bagozzi, 1975) and competition. Based on rigorous, theoretically informed insights that put understandings of citizens' lives at the heart of all strategy, social marketing will always seek to understand what might be offered and packaged for the target audience in exchange for the desired behaviour. For example, teenagers might be more receptive to offers relating to avoiding social ostracisation in exchange for quitting smoking, whereas pregnant women might be more open to a health-related offer. Decisions about an appropriate exchange offer will depend on the outcomes of formative research. Students should acknowledge the challenges and complexities of the exchange process in social marketing. For a more practical understanding, students could be introduced to the four types of exchange; Hug (incentives-based approaches), Nudge (choice architecture approaches), Shove (restriction-base approaches) and Smack (ban-based approaches) (French, 2011). They must also discuss value creation and co-creation in social marketing (Desai, 2009; Gordon et al., 2013), which emphasises that those targeted by the social marketing programme are not passive consumers involved in a monetary exchange, rather they are actively involved with the design and implementation of the social marketing offer (Hastings, 2003). For a more detailed discussion and critique of the use of exchange in social marketing, tutors and students can consider the articles by Duane et al. (2016) and Wood (2008).

Understandings of exchange and offers of 'value' to the target audience must be formulated within an understanding of the target audience's context, specifically the competition they are facing in shifting their behaviour. In other words, social marketers must make their offer appealing by considering the benefits as well as the costs of adopting the desirable behaviour. These can include a combination of tangible and intangible benefits and costs. Lynes et al. (2014) offer a useful study that develops the idea of costs and benefits further in the context of a sustainability-focused social marketing programme. What makes a social marketer's job more difficult is that often the desirable behaviour has long-term benefits (e.g. reduce the chance of lung cancer) and short-term costs (e.g. reduced pleasure or increased stress levels from smoking cessation). This combination of short-term versus long-term costs and benefits between the desirable behaviour and its competitors can be highlighted with several examples such as smoking cessation, healthy eating, safe sex and binge drinking. In the contexts in which social marketers work, the competition for the adoption of the desired behaviour can be complicated, ingrained and culturally embedded. The various levels and types of competition must be clarified along with the fact that different competitors may emerge at the adoption or the maintenance level of the desired behaviour (Schuster, 2015). For a more detailed analysis of the different types and levels of competition in social marketing, tutors and students can refer to Noble and Basil's (2011) chapter.

An indicative activity for the students at this point can be to ask them to identify the competition of healthy eating, drawing from their own experiences and discussions with their peers. The context could be specified. For example, students can be asked to think about healthy eating within their university. What are the different types and levels of competitors and what can the exchange be to adopt healthy eating habits? Kapetanaki at al.'s (2014) paper can provide examples of competition and exchange in this specific context for the students to consider.

3.4.5 Segmentation and targeting

The remaining criteria move into the managerial realm of social marketing, but remain crucial underpinnings of the approach. They draw particularly strongly on commercial marketing techniques and theory. The concepts of segmentation and targeting are vital to ensure that the social marketing offer is appropriate for the target population, and various, tailored offers should be used to target different segments.

Since social marketing focuses on changing behaviours, it is important to understand what the influences of the behaviour are and so segment the target population based on these understandings. This often leads to social marketing segmentation using cultural values to identify population segments (Raval and Subramanian, 2004). Other methods used in social marketing include: attitudes towards specific behaviours; actual behavioural activity; psychographic characteristics such as lifestyle and family life cycle; stage of the decision process; benefits sought from behaviour and psychological characteristics such as motives, beliefs and perceptions. A useful activity is for students to apply different segmentation methods (geodemographic, behavioural, psychographic) to tackle certain social problems and identify those hard-to-reach, unresponsive groups.

3.4.6   Intervention mix

One of the marketing tools adopted from commercial marketing by Kotler and Zaltman (1971) to design and implement a social marketing intervention is the marketing mix or the 4Ps. Students must be presented with the original 4Ps (product, price, place, promotion) and how these can be adapted to fit behaviour change purposes (Hastings, 2007) and also the ideas for replacing the 4Ps with new vocabulary that better fits social marketing purposes. According to Peattie and Peattie (2003), social propositions (instead of products), costs of involvement (instead of price), accessibility (instead of place) and social communication (instead of promotion) would better reflect the needs of social marketing interventions. The effectiveness of the marketing mix lies in its simplicity and in stressing that social marketing is not only about promotion (social advertising) but it is also about the other three elements which are often ignored. For a detailed analysis of the 4Ps along with specific examples and ethical implications, Lee and Kotler's (2019) book dedicates five chapters on these elements. Moreover, a systematic review (Luca and Suggs, 2010) of social marketing mix strategies provides examples that can be used in class.

The 4Ps model has some established shortcomings because of its narrowness. It does not integrate the abundance of tools available to social marketers to influence behavioural and social change. The marketing mix might seem relevant when a product is involved; however, often social marketing interventions are more complex and require a variety of approaches targeting various groups and levels from downstream to upstream. It is also recognised that one-level interventions are less effective than multi-level interventions and this is also something that the marketing mix fails to address. Furthermore, the internal orientation of the marketing mix which is controlled by the 'producer' of the social marketing offer ignores the importance of relationship thinking and value co-creation which are fundamental principles of effective social marketing interventions when it comes to addressing complicated behaviours.

To overcome these issues, scholars have designed other models that better capture the tools available to social marketers as part of an intervention mix. For example, the COM-SM links behavioural analysis with social marketing solutions and it is based on the capability opportunity motivation framework (Tapp and Spotswood, 2013). Another model is the deCIDES intervention mix which adopts a more strategic approach than the marketing mix framework and identifies five domains for influencing behaviour and refers to five basic public sector tools that can be used to deliver social marketing programmes (French et al., 2010). A third model is the retooled social marketing mix

(Gordon, 2012), which is influenced by the relational thinking paradigm. This model recognises the circumstances in which social marketing operates; the organisation and competition which also includes the role of stakeholders; the cost of performing or not certain behaviours; the consumer centredness; the process of designing and implementing the social marketing programme; and finally, the channels/strategies that can be utilised. The fourth alternative is a more holistic intervention mix model that French and Gordon (2019) introduce to reflect all the approaches available at various levels and from various disciplines. This model shows the sheer wealth and variety of options available to social marketers.

A case study activity is ideal for teasing out the potential intervention approaches that social marketers might take. Students can be asked to work in groups and assigned the same case study asking each group to use a different model (4Ps, COM-SM, deCIDES, social marketing mix, French and Gordon's intervention mix) to design their intervention plan. These can then be presented in class and opened up to discussion about the advantages and challenges of using each one of these intervention frameworks. Alternatively, the tutor can assign different case studies to different groups and ask the students to design interventions based on the same framework across the groups followed up by a discussion on how this framework was adopted to apply to different contexts.

3.4.7 Monitoring and evaluation

We discussed earlier (section 3.4.1) that students should understand the importance of research and the various research approaches that can be adopted at the different stages of the social marketing planning process. For example, formative research often employs qualitative approaches to get insight into the target audiences, while monitoring and final evaluation can be quantitative so that the initiative's efficacy can be measured. Social marketers have a toolbox of different types of research that they can use to monitor (process evaluation) and evaluate (summative evaluation) social marketing interventions to ensure that they are well designed and effective in meeting the agreed project objectives (Eagle et al., 2013). For an evaluation process to be effective, there must be constant communication and jointly set evaluation plans between those responsible for the planning, implementation and evaluation of the social marketing programme. It is important to highlight that evaluation should not be a one-off activity (Lefebvre, 2013) but that it should be integral to a learning organisation. Rather, effective social marketing programmes must be designed with clear objectives that underpin predetermined evaluation plans.

The theoretical perspectives used to inform the social marketing programme will influence social marketing evaluation. For example, Hargreaves (2011) shows what happens when practice theory is used to design, monitor and evaluate a workplace intervention. The evaluation process followed in this case was different from the ones used when more mainstream theories of behaviour change (see section 3.4.3) are adopted. Moreover, evaluations can be politically driven because government agencies' and funding bodies' political perspectives inform the way 'social good' is perceived and consequently how funding is prioritised and how initiatives are evaluated. Funders often set their own evaluation standards and processes, which in turn influence what will get done and how the programme will be managed.

Students should be introduced to the need to go beyond just outcome evaluation towards a dynamic and reflexive process evaluation approach where reflexivity helps to assess 'how' change is occurring or why change is not happening. This reflexive evaluation process also considers 'who-to-engage with, what-to-work-on together and how-change happens on small and large scales' (McHugh and Domegan, 2017, p. 137). Evaluation planning is also vital when there are multiple partners involved to ensure a smooth collaboration and long-term relationships among them. The more complicated the programme, the more complicated the evaluation to answer the various research objectives.

A good example of a multifaceted programme is the UK national social marketing programme Change4Life (https://www.nhs.uk/change4life/about -change4life). Students can see how different aspects of the programme have been evaluated through different methods including in-store observations, store mapping and qualitative interviews for the Change4Life Convenience Store Programme (Adams et al., 2012); cluster-randomised trial to evaluate the mass media campaign (Croker et al., 2012) and a quasi-experimental evaluation for the 'Change4Life Smart Swaps' campaign (Wrieden and Levy, 2016). Overall evaluation of the Change4Life programme can be found in the National Social Marketing Centre website (https://www.thensmc.com/resources/showcase/ change4life). Moreover, Basil's (2019) chapter on research and evaluation in social marketing provides guidance along with examples about monitoring and evaluation at various stages of the social marketing process. Fynn et al. (2020) have done a scoping review of 71 physical activity and dietary change programmes' evaluation frameworks, which led to a typology based on the programme type, evaluation objective and framework's format.

A case study activity will be ideal to help students practise their knowledge about monitoring and evaluation. Students can be given a case study and asked to map the project objectives with monitoring and evaluation actions. It may be a good alternative or additional activity to ask students to work on the case study they have used for the intervention mix (section 3.4.6). In this case they can be asked to link objectives with the interventions they had identified and with evaluation approaches.

4.   HOW TO TEACH

In terms of social marketing module delivery, it has been found that lecture-seminar and guest speakers are commonly used (Kelly, 2009, 2013). Alternatively, tutors can consider building the module around a live project and bring into class a real social marketing problem. The advantages of this approach are that students get to interact with social marketing practitioners and along with their academic understanding, which develops during lectures, they develop practical skills and they are exposed to real life challenges during the seminars and as part of their assessment. However, there are trade-offs in terms of the time available for grappling with crux ideas such as theory, which is particularly important when students are entirely new to marketing. To overcome this challenge, students with no prior marketing understanding should be introduced more slowly to theoretical bases of marketing and then proceed to the details about social marketing, including cases. This again may lead to a trade-off between the basic marketing concepts and the more advanced theoretical and philosophical aspects of social marketing.

Finally, it is worth emphasising the difference in pedagogical approaches between teaching social marketing to a higher education audience in comparison to a practitioner audience. Practitioner audiences may be engaging with social marketing techniques, theory and approaches in order to enhance existing skills and knowledge about behaviour change, public health, health promotion and so on. There are some trusted 'training' centres in social marketing available in the UK and globally, including the National Social Marketing Centre (https://www.thensmc.com/service/training-and-mentoring -services). These courses are shorter and have a heavy focus on understanding core principles and tools for effective practice. For example, the total process planning model (Eagle et al., 2013, pp. 44–6) would be a feature of such training, whereas in academic social marketing teaching the focus is more on debate, theoretical underpinnings, political context and published evidence. Nonetheless, the social marketing planning process, or the STELa alternative (French, 2017, p. 35), will support students in higher education to understand the practicalities of developing a social marketing programme and can provide a useful structure to support with their assessment if this includes a social marketing plan.

4.1   Textbooks and Reading

Using one core textbook is helpful because it provides structure for both tutors and students and there are many textbooks about social marketing to choose from. Most social marketing textbooks cover the areas we presented above in more or less depth and breadth along with useful case studies that can be used as activities during the seminars or as examples during the lectures. However, it may be useful to direct students to chapters in different books that focus on certain areas in more depth. In addition to this, and to enhance the critical discussion, students should be directed towards academic articles. Depending on the students' level they can be asked to read at least one article relevant to each of the areas that we covered earlier in this chapter. Our reference list is a good start to identify relevant academic papers and textbooks and section 3 shows how these are linked to the various social marketing areas.

4.2   Tutorials/Seminars

Seminars (or tutorials) are an excellent way to support students with the practical side of their learning and to apply their social marketing knowledge. If tutors decide to work with case studies it may be useful to introduce workshops that last between 90 to 120 minutes instead of hourly seminars. In case this is not possible and only one hour is available, then a case study can be used to cover more than one unit (e.g. intervention mix and evaluation or citizen insight, competition and exchange). For the seminars, tutors can also consult our suggestions for activities and find examples through this chapter's reference list.

4.3   Case Studies

Case studies can form a useful way of encouraging critical and reflexive thinking about social marketing approaches. There are many available case studies about the application of social marketing to a range of problems in both developed and developing countries. Many social marketing case studies focus on health-related issues including disease control and prevention, substance abuse and alcohol consumption. However, there are case studies on other areas, such as climate change and conservation (Veríssimo, 2019), financial crises (Duffy et al., 2017), border protection (Sherring, 2019) and human trafficking (Badejo et al., 2019).

Social marketing tutors may try to adopt examples and case studies about various types of behaviours and from different countries to support their teaching sessions so that students are exposed to different contexts and challenges. It will also be useful to use case studies that present both successful and unsuccessful social marketing interventions so that students understand what went wrong and how this could have been done in a more effective way. Tutors can find case studies and examples in social marketing textbooks, through the two dedicated social marketing journals: *Social Marketing Quarterly* and *Journal of Social Marketing*, as well as through the National Social Marketing

Centre (https://www.thensmc.com/resources/showcase/browse) and the Community-based Social Marketing (https://www.cbsm.com/) websites.

4.4 Assessment

There is much evidence that students are more engaged and perform better when there is a clear link between the learning outcomes, the way they are being taught and the assessment methods (Rust et al., 2005). For this reason, it is important that each one of the areas covered during the lectures are then discussed using case studies and examples during seminars. Consequently the assessment should be either case study based (in the case of an exam) or the development of a social marketing plan (in the case of an assignment) for a particular case (note that the main areas that we have highlighted above as essential to be taught are the blueprint for the development of an effective social marketing plan). Postgraduate students should be expected to expand on their critical analysis by discussing ethical, practical and methodological issues in more depth than undergraduate students. Presentations and written plans can be considered based on the number of students and the assessments at a curriculum level to ensure that students are exposed to different types of assessments across their studies.

Kelly's (2013) investigation showed that the most common assignment for social marketing modules is the development of a comprehensive social marketing plan with extra focus on certain aspects based on the school orientation, for example communication departments focus more on the promotion element while public health schools focus on the problem and audience identification.

Another important consideration for the tutor is whether the assignment is individual or group work. We argue that the development of a social marketing plan may be better done through group work to resemble real-life conditions. Group work has been found to enhance students' interpersonal skills that are very important in the workplace (Bobbitt et al., 2000). However, often students prefer individual assessments as they do not have to rely on the performance of their group members. Other types of assessments can be done individually and a mixture of individual and group work will both enhance students' skills development and increase satisfaction from their studies.

This constructivist[4] approach to teaching and learning incorporates the use of case studies and supports active learning (Lilly and Stanley, 2016). Students can apply their understanding and what they have learned during lectures to real-life case studies during seminars and as part of their assessment. The effectiveness of experiential activities that promote active learning has been demonstrated by many scholars who have linked it with higher levels of inter-personal, employability and reflective practice skills development; learning to learn from experience, which can be a useful lifelong skill; and enhanced learning experience that facilitates students' learning and helps some students attain knowledge. This active learning approach has also been recommended for social marketing teaching (McKay-Nesbitt et al., 2012).

In sustainability studies, Remington-Doucette et al. (2013) recommend the use of real-world problems that students are expected to solve. Thomas and Day (2014) argue that students should develop certain capabilities that are important for the workplace and this can be done through the incorporation of a critical, systemic, holistic and interdisciplinary thinking, a big-picture perspective and involvement in action. To do so, they highlight the importance of the involvement of practitioners in curriculum design and teaching delivery. This approach will help students understand the complexities of 'solving' wicked behavioural and social issues. Therefore, we argue that guest lectures should be an integral part of social marketing modules. A step further is to develop an authentic assessment (Fook and Sidhu, 2010; Gulikers et al., 2004) by working with behaviour change practitioners to introduce a real-life problem to students as part of their assessment. Tutors can collaborate with local charities, public sector and other organisations that work around behaviour and social change and engage with them to develop an assessment for their students. If this approach is adopted, group work is probably inevitable (Bobbitt et al., 2000). This problem-based learning approach can lead to a unique learning experience and it has been linked to community-based learning, which is a pedagogical approach that provides learning opportunities for tutors, students and organisations participating in real-life projects. Community involvement in social marketing teaching has also been found to be an effective way for students to learn and apply their knowledge in a more engaged way (Bardus et al., 2019). For those interested in adopting a problem-based approach, the book by Walker et al. (2015) is an excellent source.

CONCLUSION

This chapter focused on three areas: what social marketing is and why it is important to be part of the curriculum; what elements to include in a social marketing module; and what is a good pedagogical way to teach social marketing. The reference list provides a plethora of sources that social marketing tutors can use to design their lectures, seminars and workshops, as well as to share with their students as part of their core reading (textbooks) and as additional reading sources to deepen their understanding and critical analysis of certain topics. This chapter is designed in such a way to support the tutor by providing an outline of what and how to teach social marketing so that the students become familiar with the core principles, emerging paradigms, debates and critiques. Depending on students' level of studies and familiarity with marketing concepts, tutors can spend more time on different areas and adjust their examples and activities to fit their audience. To support this flexibility, we provided indicative activities as well as references to additional sources that tutors can use to guide their search for teaching material. We appreciate that everyone's teaching style is different so our aim was not to prescribe, but to create a set of resources for thinking and planning social marketing teaching.

Social marketing is a dynamic field that attracts a variety of professionals from academia, public health, non-governmental organisation and government, and it is applied in various contexts to improve individual and societal wellbeing. For this reason, it is a relevant curriculum element for various schools and departments. Those who are responsible for designing programme curricula in HE should consider what social marketing can add to their students' skillset and this chapter provides a lot of evidence to help towards this direction.

Given the challenges our societies face, from pandemics, climate change, migration and hunger to substance abuse, obesity, domestic violence and anti-vaccination movements, HE has a duty in shaping responsible future leaders, employers, employees and citizens. Social marketing is an important approach to enable social change and social good and so it should not be neglected within the HE curriculum.

NOTES

1. Social enterprises are 'not-for-profit private organizations providing goods or services directly related to their explicit aim to benefit the community' (EMES definition as cited by Defourny and Nyssens, 2008, p. 204).
2. According to Gordon et al. (2016, p. 1059), wicked problems 'have multiple and interlocking causes and are continually changing over time – usually for the worse. Typically, these problems have been long-standing and are seemingly intractable, as multiple efforts to address them over the years have shown few signs of encouragement ... wicked problems are socially complex and have at their root a need for people to change behaviours in order to improve the social good and promote well-being.'
3. Social marketing associations include the international Social Marketing Association (iSMA), European Social Marketing Association (ESMA), Australian Association of Social Marketing (AASM), Social Marketing Association of North America (SMANA), Latin American Social Marketing Association (LAMSO), Pacific Northwest Social Marketing Association (PNSMA) and Africa Social Marketing Association (ASMA).
4. 'Constructivist learning involves delivering education so that a high component of sensory input is involved; learners become very involved through interactive behaviors that enable them to "construct" their understanding of why different solutions work, or fail to work' (Lilly and Stanley, 2016, p. 50).

REFERENCES

Adamowitsch, M., Gugglberger, L. and Dür, W. (2017). Implementation practices in school health promotion: Findings from an Austrian multiple-case study. *Health Promotion International*, *32*(2), 218–30.

Adams, J., Halligan, J., Watson, D.B., Ryan, V., Penn, L., Adamson, A.J. and White, M. (2012). The Change4Life convenience store programme to increase retail access to fresh fruit and vegetables: A mixed methods process evaluation. *PLOS ONE*, *7*(6).

Ajzen, I. (1991). The theory of planned behavior. *Organizational Behavior and Human Decision Processes*, *50*(2), 179–211.

Albrecht, T.L. (1997). Defining social marketing: 25 years later. *Social Marketing Quarterly*, *3*(3–4), 21–3.

Andreasen, A.R. (1994). Social marketing: Its definition and domain. *Journal of Public Policy & Marketing*, *13*(1), 108–114.

Andreasen, A.R. (2001). *Ethics in Social Marketing.* Washington, DC: Georgetown University Press.

Andreasen, A.R. (2002). Marketing social marketing in the social change marketplace. *Journal of Public Policy & Marketing*, *21*(1), 3–13.

Andreasen, A.R. (2012). Rethinking the relationship between social/nonprofit marketing and commercial marketing. *Journal of Public Policy & Marketing*, *31*(1), 36–41.

Badejo, F.A., Rundle-Thiele, S. and Kubacki, K. (2019). Taking a wider view: A formative multi-stream social marketing approach to understanding human trafficking as a social issue in Nigeria. *Journal of Social Marketing*, *9*(4), 467–84.

Bagozzi, R.P. (1975). Social exchange in marketing. *Journal of the Academy of Marketing Science*, *3*(3–4), 314–27.

Bardus, M., Domegan, C.T., Suggs, L.S. and Mikkelsen, B.E. (2019). Engaging students and communities through service learning and community–academia partnerships: Lessons from social marketing education. In M.M. Pinheiro, A. Estima and S. Marques (eds), *Evaluating the Gaps and Intersections Between Marketing Education and the Marketing Profession* (pp. 84–116). Hershey, PA: IGI Global.

Basil, M.D. (2019). Research and evaluation in social marketing. In D.Z. Basil, G. Diaz-Meneses and M.D. Basil (eds), *Social Marketing in Action: Cases from Around the World* (pp. 45–57). Cham: Springer International Publishing.

Behavioural Insights Team (2018). EAST (Easy Attractive Social Timely). Accessed at https://www.behaviouralinsights.co.uk/wp-content/uploads/2015/07/BIT -Publication-EAST_FA_WEB.pdf.

Benartzi, S., Beshears, J., Milkman, K.L., Sunstein, C.R., Thaler, R.H., Shankar, M., Tucker-Ray, W. et al. (2017). Should governments invest more in nudging? *Psychological Science*, *28*(8), 1041–1055.

Bhattacharya, C.B. and Elsbach, K.D. (2002). Us versus them: The roles of organizational identification and disidentification in social marketing initiatives. *Journal of Public Policy & Marketing*, *21*(1), 26–36.

Bobbitt, L.M., Inks, S.A., Kemp, K.J. and Mayo, D.T. (2000). Integrating marketing courses to enhance team-based experiential learning. *Journal of Marketing Education*, *22*(1), 15–24.

Brennan, L., Previte, J. and Fry, M.-L. (2016). Social marketing's consumer myopia. *Journal of Social Marketing*, *6*(3), 219–39.

Carins, J.E., Rundle-Thiele, S.R. and Fidock, J.J. (2016). Seeing through a Glass Onion: Broadening and deepening formative research in social marketing through a mixed methods approach. *Journal of Marketing Management, 32*(11–12), 1083–1102.

Carter, S.M., Mayes, C., Eagle, L. and Dahl, S. (2017). A code of ethics for social marketing? Bridging procedural ethics and ethics-in-practice. *Journal of Nonprofit & Public Sector Marketing, 29*(1), 20–38.

Catterall, M., Maclaran, P. and Stevens, L. (2002). Critical reflection in the marketing curriculum. *Journal of Marketing Education, 24*(3), 184–92.

Charlton, M. (2020). Universities will be essential to meeting the SDGs in 10 years. *Times Higher Education,* 1 February.

Chatterton, T. (2011). An introduction to thinking about 'energy behaviour': A multi-model approach. London: Department of Energy and Climate Change. Available at: https://uwe-repository.worktribe.com/output/957138/an-introduction -to-thinking-about-energy-behaviour-a-multi-model-approach.

Croker, H., Lucas, R. and Wardle, J. (2012). Cluster-randomised trial to evaluate the 'Change for Life' mass media/social marketing campaign in the UK. *BMC Public Health, 12*(1), 404.

Daellenbach, K. and Parkinson, J. (2017). A useful shift in our perspective: Integrating social movement framing into social marketing. *Journal of Social Marketing, 7*(2), 188–204.

Defourny, J. and Nyssens, M. (2008). Social enterprise in Europe: Recent trends and developments. *Social Enterprise Journal, 4*(3), 202–228.

Desai, D. (2009). Role of relationship management and value co-creation in social marketing. *Social Marketing Quarterly, 15*(4), 112–25.

Dibb, S. and Carrigan, M. (2013). Social marketing transformed: Kotler, Polonsky and Hastings reflect on social marketing in a period of social change. *European Journal of Marketing, 47*(9), 1376–98.

Dolan, P., Hallsworth, M., Halpern, D., King, D. and Vlaev, I. (2010). MINDSPACE: Influencing behaviour through public policy. Institute for Government. Accessed at: https://www.instituteforgovernment.org.uk/sites/default/files/publications/ MINDSPACE-Practical-guide-final-Web_1.pdf.

Domegan, C., Collins, K., Stead, M., McHugh, P. and Hughes, T. (2013). Value co-creation in social marketing: Functional or fanciful? *Journal of Social Marketing, 3*(3), 239–56.

Domegan, C., McHugh, P., Devaney, M., Duane, S., Hogan, M., Broome, B.J., Layton, R.A. et al. (2016). Systems-thinking social marketing: Conceptual extensions and empirical investigations. *Journal of Marketing Management, 32*(11–12), 1123–44.

Duane, S., Domegan, C., McHugh, P. and Devaney, M. (2016). From restricted to complex exchange and beyond: Social marketing's change agenda. *Journal of Marketing Management, 32*(9–10), 856–76.

Duffy, S.M., Northey, G. and van Esch, P. (2017). Iceland: How social mechanisms drove the financial collapse and why it's a wicked problem. *Journal of Social Marketing, 7*(3), 330–46.

Eagle, L. (2009). Social marketing ethics: Report prepared for the National Social Marketing Centre. Technical Report. Accessed at https://uwe-repository.worktribe .com/output/1002174.

Eagle, L., Dahl, S., Carter, S.M. and Low, D. (2015). Social marketing ethical dilemmas: Pursuing practical solutions for pressing problems. Paper presented at the World Social Marketing Conference.

Eagle, L., Dahl, S., Hill, S., Bird, S., Spotswood, F. and Tapp, A. (2013). *Social Marketing*. Harlow: Pearson Education.

Editorial (2020). Nudges that don't nudge. *Nature Human Behaviour*, *4*(2), 121–21.

European Centre for Disease Prevention Control (2014). *Social Marketing Guide for Public Health Managers and Practitioners*. Stockholm: ECDC.

Fook, C.Y. and Sidhu, G.K. (2010). Authentic assessment and pedagogical strategies in higher education. *Journal of Social Sciences*, *6*(2), 153–61.

French, J. (2011). Why nudging is not enough. *Journal of Social Marketing*, *1*(2), 154–62.

French, J. (2017). Social marketing planning. In J. French (ed.), *Social Marketing and Public Health: Theory and Practice* (2nd edn, pp. 27–46). Oxford: Oxford University Press.

French, J. and Gordon, R. (2019). *Strategic Social Marketing: For Behaviour and Social Change*. London: SAGE Publications.

French, J., Blair-Stevens, C., McVey, D. and Merritt, R. (2010). *Social Marketing and Public Health: Theory and Practice*. Oxford: Oxford University Press.

Fynn, J.F., Hardeman, W., Milton, K. and Jones, A.P. (2020). A scoping review of evaluation frameworks and their applicability to real-world physical activity and dietary change programme evaluation. *BMC Public Health*, *20*(1), 1000.

Global University Network for Innovation (2017). *Higher Education in the World 6. Towards a Socially Responsible University: Balancing the Global with the Local*. Accessed at http://www.guninetwork.org/files/download_full_report.pdf.

Gordon, R. (2012). Re-thinking and re-tooling the social marketing mix. *Australasian Marketing Journal*, *20*(2), 122–6.

Gordon, R. (2013). Unlocking the potential of upstream social marketing. *European Journal of Marketing*, *47*(9), 1525–47

Gordon, R. and Gurrieri, L. (2014). Towards a reflexive turn: Social marketing assemblages. *Journal of Social Marketing*, *4*(3), 261–78.

Gordon, R., Domegan, C., Collins, K., Stead, M., McHugh, P. and Hughes, T. (2013). Value co-creation in social marketing: Functional or fanciful? *Journal of Social Marketing*, *3*(3), 239–56.

Gordon, R., Russell-Bennett, R. and Lefebvre, R.C. (2016). Social marketing: The state of play and brokering the way forward. *Journal of Marketing Management*, *32*(11–12), 1059–1082.

Griffiths, J., Blair-Stevens, C. and Parish, R. (2009). The integration of health promotion and social marketing. *Perspectives in Public Health*, *129*(6), 268–71.

Grönroos, C. (2011). Value co-creation in service logic: A critical analysis. *Marketing Theory*, *11*(3), 279–301.

Gulikers, J.T., Bastiaens, T.J. and Kirschner, P.A. (2004). A five-dimensional framework for authentic assessment. *Educational Technology Research and Development*, *52*(3), 67.

Hamer, L.O. (2000). The additive effects of semistructured classroom activities on student learning: An application of classroom-based experiential learning techniques. *Journal of Marketing Education*, *22*(1), 25–34.

Hancock, A. (2017). Younger consumers drive shift to ethical products. *Financial Times*, 23 December.

Hargreaves, T. (2011). Practice-ing behaviour change: Applying social practice theory to pro-environmental behaviour change. *Journal of Consumer Culture*, *11*(1), 79–99.

Hastings, G. (2003). Relational paradigms in social marketing. *Journal of Macromarketing*, *23*(1), 6–15.

Hastings, G. (2007). *Social Marketing: Why Should the Devil have all the Best Tunes?* Oxford: Elsevier.

Hastings, G. and Angus, K. (2011). When is social marketing not social marketing? *Journal of Social Marketing*, *1*(1), 45–53.

Hastings, G. and Domegan, C. (2013). *Social Marketing: From Tunes to Symphonies.* Abingdon: Routledge.

Heath, T., O'Malley, L. and Tynan, C. (2019). Imagining a different voice: A critical and caring approach to management education. *Management Learning*, *50*(4), 427–48.

Hennink-Kaminski, H., Ihekweazu, C., Vaughn, A.E. and Ward, D.S. (2018). Using formative research to develop the healthy me, healthy we campaign: Partnering childcare and home to promote healthy eating and physical activity behaviors in preschool children. *Social Marketing Quarterly*, *24*(3), 194–215.

Horton, R. (2018). Offline: In defence of precision public health. *The Lancet*, *392*(10157), 1504.

iSMA, ESMA and AASM (2013). Consensus Definition of Social Marketing. Accessed at https://www.i-socialmarketing.org/index.php?option=com_content&view=article &id=84:social-marketing-definition&catid=28:front-page.

Kapetanaki, A.B., Brennan, D.R. and Caraher, M. (2014). Social marketing and healthy eating: Findings from young people in Greece. *International Review on Public and Nonprofit Marketing*, *11*(2), 161–80.

Kapetanaki, A.B., Halliday, S.V., Wills, W. and Dickinson, A. (2019). Reducing food insecurity and vulnerability for older people. Paper presented at the 6th World Social Marketing Conference, Edinburgh, UK.

Kay, L. (2018). Social enterprises 'contribute £60bn to the economy each year'. *ThirdSector*. Accessed at https://www.thirdsector.co.uk/social-enterprises-contribute -60bn-economy-year/social-enterprise/article/1493336.

Kelly, K.J. (2009). Social marketing education: The beat goes on. *Social Marketing Quarterly*, *15*(3), 129–41.

Kelly, K.J. (2013). Academic course offerings in social marketing: The beat continues. *Social Marketing Quarterly*, *19*(4), 290–95.

Kemper, J.A. and Ballantine, P.W. (2017). Socio-technical transitions and institutional change: Addressing obesity through macro-social marketing. *Journal of Macromarketing*, *37*(4), 381–92.

Kennedy, A.-M. and Santos, N. (2019). Social fairness and social marketing: An integrative justice approach to creating an ethical framework for social marketers. *Journal of Social Marketing*, *9*(4), 522–39.

Keshavarz, N., Nutbeam, D., Rowling, L. and Khavarpour, F. (2010). Schools as social complex adaptive systems: A new way to understand the challenges of introducing the health promoting schools concept. *Social Science & Medicine*, *70*(10), 1467–74.

Kotler, P. and Roberto, E.L. (1989). *Social Marketing: Strategies for Changing Public Behavior.* New York: The Free Press.

Kotler, P. and Zaltman, G. (1971). Social marketing: An approach to planned social change. *Journal of Marketing*, *35*(3), 3–12.

Kubacki, K. and Rundle-Thiele, S. (2016). *Formative Research in Social Marketing: Innovative Methods to Gain Consumer Insights.* Singapore: Springer.

Laczniak, G.R., Lusch, R.F. and Murphy, P.E. (1979). Social marketing: Its ethical dimensions. *Journal of Marketing*, *43*(2), 29–36.

Langford, R. and Panter-Brick, C. (2013). A health equity critique of social marketing: Where interventions have impact but insufficient reach. *Social Science & Medicine*, *83*, 133–41.

Lee, N.R. and Kotler, P. (2019). *Social Marketing: Behavior Change for Social Good* (6th edn). Thousand Oaks, CA: SAGE Publications.

Lefebvre, R.C. (2011). An integrative model for social marketing. *Journal of Social Marketing*, *1*, 54–72.

Lefebvre, R.C. (2013). *Social Marketing and Social Change: Strategies and Tools for Improving Health, Well-being, and the Environment*. San Francisco, CA: John Wiley & Sons.

Lilly, B. and Stanley, S.M. (2016). Leveraging partnerships with local companies as a method of teaching sales: A Constructivist Approach. *Journal for Advancement of Marketing Education*, *24*, 49–56.

Lindridge, A., MacAskill, S., Gnich, W., Eadie, D. and Holme, I. (2013). Applying an ecological model to social marketing communications. *European Journal of Marketing*, *47*(9), 1399–420.

Luca, N.R. and Suggs, L.S. (2010). Strategies for the social marketing mix: A systematic review. *Social Marketing Quarterly*, *16*(4), 122–49.

Luca, N.R., Hibbert, S. and McDonald, R. (2016). Midstream value creation in social marketing. *Journal of Marketing Management*, *32*(11–12), 1145–73.

Lynes, J., Whitney, S. and Murray, D. (2014). Developing benchmark criteria for assessing community-based social marketing programs: A look into Jack Johnson's. *Journal of Social Marketing*, *4*(2), 111–32.

Mainemelis, C., Boyatzis, R.E. and Kolb, D.A. (2002). Learning styles and adaptive flexibility: Testing experiential learning theory. *Management Learning*, *33*(1), 5–33.

Maller, C.J. (2015). Understanding health through social practices: Performance and materiality in everyday life. *Sociology of Health & Illness*, *37*(1), 52–66.

Market Research Society (2019). Code of Conduct. Accessed at https://www.mrs.org .uk/pdf/MRS-Code-of-Conduct-2019.pdf.

Marques, S. and Domegan, C. (2011). Relationship marketing and social marketing. In G. Hastings, K. Angus and C. Bryant (eds), *The Sage Handbook of Social Marketing* (pp. 44–60). London: Sage.

McHugh, P. and Domegan, C. (2017). Evaluate development! Develop evaluation! Answering the call for a reflexive turn in social marketing. *Journal of Social Marketing*, *7*(2), 135–55.

McKay-Nesbitt, J., DeMoranville, C.W. and McNally, D. (2012). A strategy for advancing social marketing: Social marketing projects in introductory marketing courses. *Journal of Social Marketing*, *2*(1), 52–69.

McLeroy, K.R., Bibeau, D., Steckler, A. and Glanz, K. (1988). An ecological perspective on health promotion programs. *Health Education Quarterly*, *15*(4), 351–77.

Moon, J.A. (2004). *A Handbook of Reflective and Experiential Learning: Theory and Practice*. Psychology Press.

Moore, G.F. and Evans, R.E. (2017). What theory, for whom and in which context? Reflections on the application of theory in the development and evaluation of complex population health interventions. *SSM – Population Health*, *3*, 132–5.

Noble, G. and Basil, D.Z. (2011). Competition and positioning. In G. Hastings, K. Angus and C.A. Bryant (eds), *The Sage Handbook of Social Marketing* (pp. 136–51). London: Sage Publications.

Nonprofit Action (2015). Facts and stats about NGOs worldwide. Accessed at http:// nonprofitaction.org/2015/09/facts-and-stats-about-ngos-worldwide/.

NSMC (2014). Social marketing benchmark criteria. Accessed at https://www.thensmc .com/resource/social-marketing-benchmark-criteria.

NSMC (2016). Social marketing and behavioural economics. Accessed at https://www .thensmc.com/content/social-marketing-and-behavioural-economics.

Nuffield Council on Bioethics (2007). Public health: ethical issues. Accessed at https:// www.nuffieldbioethics.org/publications/public-health/guide-to-the-report/policy -process-and-practice.

Office for National Statistics (2019). Employment by sector. Accessed at https:// www.ethnicity-facts-figures.service.gov.uk/work-pay-and-benefits/employment/ employment-by-sector/latest.

Peattie, S. and Peattie, K. (2003). Ready to fly solo? Reducing social marketing's dependence on commercial marketing theory. *Marketing Theory*, *3*(3), 365–85.

Poland, B.D., Green, L.W. and Rootman, I. (1999). *Settings for Health Promotion: Linking Theory and Practice.* Thousand Oaks, CA: Sage Publications.

Raval, D. and Subramanian, B. (2004). Cultural values driven segmentation in social marketing. *Journal of Nonprofit & Public Sector Marketing*, *12*(2), 73–85.

Remington-Doucette, S.M., Connell, K.Y.H., Armstrong, C.M. and Musgrove, S.L. (2013). Assessing sustainability education in a transdisciplinary undergraduate course focused on real-world problem solving. *International Journal of Sustainability in Higher Education*, *14*(4), 404–433.

Rundle-Thiele, S., David, P., Willmott, T., Pang, B., Eagle, L. and Hay, R. (2019). Social marketing theory development goals: An agenda to drive change. *Journal of Marketing Management 35*(1–2), 160–81.

Russell-Bennett, R., Wood, M. and Previte, J. (2013). Fresh ideas: Services thinking for social marketing. *Journal of Social Marketing*, *3*(3), 223–8.

Rust, C., O'Donovan, B. and Price, M. (2005). A social constructivist assessment process model: How the research literature shows us this could be best practice. *Assessment & Evaluation in Higher Education*, *30*(3), 231–40.

Sahakian, M. and Wilhite, H. (2014). Making practice theory practicable: Towards more sustainable forms of consumption. *Journal of Consumer Culture*, *14*(1), 25–44.

Schuster, L. (2015). Competition and its influence on consumer decision making in social marketing. *Journal of Marketing Management*, *31*(11–12), 1333–52.

Science and Technology Select Committee (2011). *Behaviour Change.* London: House of Lords. Accessed at https://publications.parliament.uk/pa/ld201012/ldselect/ ldsctech/179/179.pdf.

Shaw, G., Barr, S., and Wooler, J. (2014). The application of social marketing to tourism. In S. McCabe (ed.), *The Routledge Handbook of Tourism Marketing* (pp. 76–87). Abingdon: Routledge.

Sherring, P. (2019). Declare or dispose: Protecting New Zealand's border with behaviour change. *Journal of Social Marketing*, *10*(1), 85–104.

Slater, M.D., Kelly, K.J. and Thackeray, R. (2006). Segmentation on a shoestring: Health audience segmentation in limited-budget and local social marketing interventions. *Health Promotion Practice*, *7*(2), 170–73.

Smith, B. (2010). Behavioral economics and social marketing: New allies in the war on absent behavior. *Social Marketing Quarterly*, *16*(2), 137–41.

Spotswood, F. (2017). Beyond behaviour change. *Social Business*, *7*(3–4).

Spotswood, F., Chatterton, T., Morey, Y. and Spear, S. (2017). Practice-theoretical possibilities for social marketing: Two fields learning from each other. *Journal of Social Marketing*, *7*(2), 156–71.

Spotswood, F., French, J., Tapp, A. and Stead, M. (2012). Some reasonable but uncomfortable questions about social marketing. *Journal of Social Marketing*, 2(3), 163–75.

Tapp, A. and Spotswood, F. (2013). From the 4Ps to COM-SM: Reconfiguring the social marketing mix. *Journal of Social Marketing*, 3(3), 206–222.

Thaler, R.H. and Sunstein, C.R. (2009). *Nudge: Improving Decisions About Health, Wealth, and Happiness.* London: Penguin.

Thomas, I. and Day, T. (2014). Sustainability capabilities, graduate capabilities, and Australian universities. *International Journal of Sustainability in Higher Education*, 15(2), 208–227.

Truong, V.D. (2014). Social marketing: A systematic review of research 1998–2012. *Social Marketing Quarterly*, 20(1), 15–34.

Truss, A. and White, P. (2010). Ethical issues in social marketing. In J. French, C. Blair-Stevens, D. McVey and R. Merritt (eds), *Social Marketing and Public Health: Theory and Practice* (pp. 139–49). Oxford: Oxford University Press.

Ulasevich, A. (2015). Behavioral economics and social marketing: Toward integrated approaches to behavior change. In W.D. Evans (ed.), *Social Marketing: Global Perspectives, Strategies and Effects on Consumer Behavior.* New York: Nova Science Publishers.

Veríssimo, D. (2019). The past, present, and future of using social marketing to conserve biodiversity. *Social Marketing Quarterly*, 25(1), 3–8.

Walker, A.E., Leary, H., Hmelo-Silver, C.E. and Ertmer, P.A. (2015). *Essential Readings in Problem-based Learning.* West Lafayette, IN: Purdue University Press.

Wellman, N. (2017). Are marketing degrees fit for purpose? Thesis. Cardiff Metropolitan University.

Wiebe, G.D. (1951). Merchandising commodities and citizenship on television. *Public Opinion Quarterly*, 15(4), 679–91.

Wood, M. (2008). Applying commercial marketing theory to social marketing: A tale of 4Ps (and a B). *Social Marketing Quarterly*, 14(1), 76–85.

Wood, M. (2016a). Midstream social marketing and the co-creation of public services. *Journal of Social Marketing*, 6(3), 277–93.

Wood, M. (2016b). Social marketing for social change. *Social Marketing Quarterly*, 22(2), 107–118.

Wrieden, W.L. and Levy, L.B. (2016). 'Change4Life Smart Swaps': Quasi-experimental evaluation of a natural experiment. *Public Health Nutrition*, 19(13), 2388–92.

11. Teaching international marketing

Jonathan Wilson

INTRODUCTION

As a discipline, international marketing covers everything from cultural issues to market entry strategies. In terms of research into international marketing, some areas are more popular with scholars than others. For example, Malhotra et al. (2013) analyzed the 29 years of research published in *International Marketing Review* since its inception. The authors found that articles often focus on export and global marketing. These continue to be popular areas of research and form an essential part of the international marketing curriculum.

Although certain areas of international marketing may not have changed in the last 40 years, globalization, the rise of brands from the BRIC (Brazil, Russia, India and China) economies, together with advances in technology, have dramatically changed the discipline both inside and outside of the classroom. Leading global brands, such as IBM and Google, are now witnessing their dominance being challenged by a plethora of technology brands, especially from China. For example, in the Brand Z Top 100 Global brands for 2018, 14 Chinese brands appear in the Top 100 ranking compared to just one (China Mobile) in 2006 (Brand Z, 2018). As a result, brands such as telecommunications giants Huawei Technologies and Lenovo are fast becoming household names outside of their home market.

My personal experience of working in marketing and doing research on Chinese brands has shaped my own pedagogical approach. The approach forms the basis of this chapter. Specifically, my argument is that international marketing education must reflect the changing nature of the international marketing landscape. First, this means taking a non-Western-centric approach. Second, as educators, our role is to prepare students for a career in international marketing beyond the classroom. The increased emphasis on employability requires now, more than ever, students learning skills that match the real-world tasks of professionals.

Approaches are needed that introduce students to the types of problems they would be likely to encounter if working in international marketing – for this reason, my contention in this chapter is that our central approach to international marketing education should be to engage in authentic learning pedagogy. In essence, authenticity is all about resembling students' (future) professional practice (Gulikers et al., 2004). By introducing students to real-world international marketing problems during their course, we are preparing them for a role in marketing practice.

Authentic learning and assessment includes activities that reflect real-world experiences. In terms of assessing students' learning, we need to move away from traditional assessment such as essays and closed book exams to more authentic assessment tasks (Sambell et al., 2019). For example, rather than setting students a closed book exam on an international marketing case study, students actually undertake a project on the case. Moreover, as educators we should be adopting an inclusive approach by recognizing student diversity and adapting how we deliver international marketing as a result. By way of an example, on my international marketing module, students have the option of choosing one of four brands to research. Each of these brands comes from a different country and sector. Typically, one from the UK, US, Europe and Asia. Why? Well, two reasons. First, choosing a mix of brands reflects the "international nature" of international marketing. Second, we have a large number of international students on the module. By giving students the choice from a selection of brands, there is a greater level of fairness in the assessment task. Having a diverse group of students also means in-class discussions benefit from a wide range of personal experiences and perspectives on local and global brands.

ORGANIZATION OF THE CHAPTER

This chapter is organized into three parts. First, I provide a short chronology on the history of international marketing, including how international marketing education has dramatically changed over the last several decades. Second, I will examine the nature of authentic learning pedagogy. My intention with this section is to provide a short introduction. The final part in this chapter presents a series of exercises you can use with your students to help them to develop their knowledge of international marketing. Each exercise is designed with an authentic learning experience in mind and covers a particular area of international marketing. Furthermore, consideration is given to students learning the "How" to be an international marketer, and not merely looking at "What" international marketing is all about. This is a central tenet of authentic learning so that students can become more comfortable with addressing the complexities of real-world problems (Lombardi, 2007).

A BRIEF HISTORY OF INTERNATIONAL MARKETING

This section presents a brief chronology of international marketing. The purpose is to examine how international marketing has dramatically changed since the latter half of the twentieth century. There are a number of approaches to periodization in marketing history; in this case, it is based on turning points in international marketing material (Hollander et al., 2005). My focus is on three distinct periods.

1960s–1970s

Before examining this period, it is important to briefly consider one of the fundamental questions in international marketing education, that is: how much emphasis should be placed on theory and practice when teaching international marketing? The history of marketing can be distinguished on the basis of marketing thought and marketing practice. Marketing thought examines how marketing has been taught and studied over time, while marketing practice focuses on the changing nature of the ways marketing has been practiced. In recent years, teaching international marketing practice has received greater consideration. This is largely due to the increased attention given to employ-ability in higher education and emphasis on transferable skills. Moreover, the inclusion of guest speakers as part of an international marketing class, in particular those who have worked abroad, means that students can hear about the first-hand experiences, stories and challenges associated with working in an international environment. It is important to note that marketing theory and marketing practice are not mutually exclusive, but teaching international marketing requires a set of practices grounded in theory. Hence, for this reason, this brief review of international marketing examines both aspects of marketing theory and practice.

International marketing practice pre-dates the biblical age, as witnessed by the development of trade routes linking Europe and Asia. Multinational organizations have been a force in global trade since the days of the East India Company (Bordo et al., 1999). In the early 1600s, this private English company had a monopoly on all trade between Britain and Asia, bringing Asian luxuries to Europe, such as spices, textiles and tea (Robins, 2012). Emphasis on trade is reflected in early international marketing work which was a practical extension of the international trade field (Omar, 2009). "An examination of some of the early work in marketing education reveals that the term 'commerce' was used to designate international marketing and to distinguish such international deal-ings between nations from domestic commerce, frequently labelled as trade." (Cunningham and Jones, 1997, p. 89).

In the 1960s, international marketing was not a key subject area for major business schools. By way of illustration, Meloan and Taylor (1968) found that only two out of 101 schools in their research offered international marketing as a major or an area of study at that time. It was not until the late 1950s and the early 1960s that scholars had started to recognize and study the differences between the domestic and international environment (Li and Cavusgil, 1995). In his article titled "Are domestic and international marketing dissimilar?", Bartels (1968) argues that by placing greater emphasis on the essential similarities at home and abroad, as opposed to differences, companies will have a better understanding of foreign marketing. In this sense, "foreign marketing" means the marketing to foreign nationals. He came to the conclusion that academic marketing should focus on environmental analysis both at home and abroad. Similarly, in relation to marketing practice, marketing managers should approach the international situation with expectation of both similarities and differences relative to domestic marketing. Bartels (1968) goes on to note the semantics in relation to the terms "comparative" and "international" as applied to marketing. International marketing has certainly developed a comparative approach over time. By examining differences and similarities across markets, firms are able to determine appropriate international marketing strategies.

In the late 1960s, Perlmutter (1969) examined the nature of a multinational firm by discussing the three types of headquarters orientation towards subsidiaries in an enterprise, namely: ethnocentrism (home country orientation); polycentrism (host country orientation); and geocentrism (a world orientation), otherwise known as the EPRG Model. The international orientation model was extended in 1973 with the introduction of "regiocentrism" (Wind et al., 1973). The authors explored the use of the EPRG framework as a guideline for planning and developing international marketing strategies, together with the conditions under which international marketers are likely to adopt these orientations and associated strategies. They concluded that the advantages and disadvantages of a particular orientation vary depending on a number of factors, including – a firm's financial situation, product line and size of potential overseas market. Certainly, at this time, many firms adopted the domestic market extension orientation, or ethnocentrism. However, as a firm evolves, it may also be guided towards another paradigm as its international marketing goes through different stages of development.

The 1970s brought increasing globalization in the international marketplace. More specifically, new economic relationships developed. In 1978, Deng Xiaoping announced China's new Open Door Policy, opening the country to foreign investment. America continued to dominate international marketing; evidence of this is that the country's 1970 exports were greater than the UK and Japan combined (Terpstra, 1987). The significance of standardization or adaptation of marketing strategies gained attention. For example, Sorenson and Wiechmann (1975) investigated the issue of marketing strategy standardization/adaptation in the consumer packaged goods industry. Interestingly, in many cases they found the multinational standardization of marketing activities, in spite of significant country-to-country differences in market and competitive conditions. This approach to marketing can have a detrimental effect on marketing success and suggests that some companies during this time were lacking in environmental awareness.

1980s–1990s

International marketing went through fundamental changes in the 1980s, such as the opening up of new markets in Eastern Europe and a move toward economic liberalization in the developing world (Aulakh and Kotabe, 1993). These changes were accelerated by the demise of the Soviet Union. Definitions of international marketing during this time tended to focus on the organizational level. For example, Fayerweather (1982) defined international marketing as a firm that has a permanent presence in two or more countries. Exporting remained the primary mode of international marketing. This was a time with increased focus on globalization and technology. In his 1983 seminal article "The globalization of markets", Levitt (1983, p. 102) commented that "two vectors shape the world – technology and globalization. The first helps determine human preferences; the second, economic realities." These two vectors are equally applicable today as they were in the early 1980s, arguably more so. Yip (1989) considered globalization from a strategic perspective by making a distinction between a multidomestic strategy and a global strategy. Features of the former include adopting a local marketing approach and products fully customized in each country. In contrast, features of global strategy comprise fully standardizing products and adopting a uniform marketing approach worldwide.

During the 1980s scholars carried out more empirical studies on environmental issues, in particular on culture. This included the impact of different cultures on international marketing decisions, the influence of culture on business negotiations and verbal and non-verbal communication of business executives (Li and Cavusgil, 1995). The period saw a growing interest in international marketing. This is evidenced by the launch of several journals in the late 1980s and early 1990s, including: *Journal of Global Marketing* (1987), *Journal of International Consumer Marketing* (1988), *Journal of Euromarketing* (1991) and *Journal of International Marketing* (1993). All are committed to advancing international marketing theory and practice (Javalgi et al., 1996). The 1980s also witnessed a decline in American dominance in international markets: "Looking at the micro side of international marketing in the mid-1980s, the most dramatic change is the prominent position of Japanese firms. Their tremendous growth has been largely at the expense of American firms who lost their previous dominance. European firms have also suffered from the Japanese success." (Terpstra, 1987, p. 51).

How international marketing education is delivered in the classroom received critical consideration. For example, Zimmer et al. (1996) examined marketing educators' approach to teaching international marketing as part of an introduction to marketing course. In their study based on a sample of 372 marketing educators from US institutions, they found that "instructors'" coverage of international topics lacked consistency and was infrequent. One-third of the instructors reported not including international marketing as a key theme in any particular week. Eleven percent of instructors did not devote any part of a week "exclusively" to covering the international component. Moreover, more than one in five instructors did not deliver a separate international marketing lecture, but instead relied on integrating international topics throughout the course. This study shows that marketers in this instance focused on "embedding" international marketing within an introductory marketing course, as opposed to teaching international marketing as a stand-alone module or course. Interestingly, this research shows that little attention was given towards the "international element" in marketing, even for a study conducted in the mid-1990s. However, it is essential to note that this is an American study. It is, therefore, not possible to generalize to other countries.

In research focusing specifically on the teaching of international marketing, Andrus et al. (1995) carried out an extensive survey of 144 academics who teach international marketing in the US and found that the majority of the faculty members were satisfied with the internationalization efforts of their departments. Moreover, "the cultural environment, competitive environment, and strategic planning were gauged to be the three most important topics" (Andrus et al., 1995, pp. 15–16). Although this study is encouraging from an international perspective, clearly, curricula need to change in line with a changing international environment. It is also worth noting that these findings are in contrast to earlier studies where international marketing mix elements were deemed to be the most popular topics (see McDaniel and Smith, 1987). Furthermore, there is often a close relationship in content and structure of most international business and international marketing courses.

By the late 1990s, a course in international marketing was typical at most accredited colleges and universities in the United States (Crittenden and Wilson, 2005). In their article titled "Undergraduate marketing education in the 21st century: views from three institutions", Smart et al. (1999) concluded that three underlying themes associated with marketing education are: the impact of technology; globalization; and changes in students' learning style. In the context of international marketing education, this can be viewed as immersing students in global learning communities, with a desire for a more participatory, experiential learning experience. More than twenty years later, these remain key themes associated with international marketing education.

Understanding a student's perspective on international marketing is important and can inform teaching and learning. In the late 1990s, Turley and Shannon (1999) analyzed undergraduate students' perceptions of international marketing as a career, together with their preparedness for working in international marketing. The findings indicated that students did not feel adequately prepared for careers in international marketing, only 2.9 percent of a US national sample of 832 marketing majors strongly agreed that their school had prepared them for a potential career in international marketing. These findings imply that students may not have the option or ability to travel abroad, or in short, do not have the opportunity to experience marketing in an international context. It is important to add that virtually all the empirical studies mentioned here are based on the USA. Studies in different cultural contexts may generate a different set of findings.

Post-2000

At the start of the twenty-first century China entered the World Trade Organization (WTO). The country's economic growth has been spectacular over the last two decades. In 2018 China experienced a sales volume of approximately 28 million vehicles, making it the largest automobile market in the world (Statista, 2018). Large domestic auto brands have also emerged – such as BYD and Geely. However, certainly in the automobile sector, these brands have largely failed to penetrate non-Chinese markets. This is not the case in all sectors, as evidenced by the success of Chinese tech brands such as Huawei Technologies and Tencent.

What is interesting about China's growing dominance across international markets is its approach to growth. Strategies typically involve mergers or more commonly acquisitions of leading Western companies. By way of illustration, the Chinese state-owned automobile giant Geely acquired the Swedish car brand Volvo in 2010. Furthermore, they also took over the British taxi maker – The London Electric Vehicle Company in 2013, meaning that the London black cab can now be found on the streets of China!

During this period, decentralization has allowed companies to make, sell and buy products and services throughout the world by being able to adapt to local and regional needs. In the early part of this century, it is clear that the emerging market economies of Russia and China present many new challenges for international marketing (Czinkota and Ronkainen, 2007). Dramatic changes in the political, economic, social and technological environments, such as Brexit, the COVID-19 pandemic and increasing online usage, create both threats and opportunities for international marketers. International marketing education needs to keep pace with these changes in order to prepare students for the real world. Unfortunately, the lack of applicability to real-world scenarios and problems faced by international marketers is not always addressed in text-books. By way of illustration, Vos (2013), when discussing the redesign of an MA International Marketing course, noted that in textbooks, "little attempt is made to show how political and economic issues can become deeply integrated with day-to-day operations of the business and why their evolution and change should be tracked, assessed, and managed along the way." (p. 99). Authentic learning pedagogy is one way in which international marketing educators can address the issues of real-world problems such as this. Just as marketing practitioners are constantly adapting their perspectives of marketing, so must educators continue to reshape what topics are important to teach in the class-room (Ferrell et al., 2015).

Examining international marketing education post-2000, there is no one universal definition of "international marketing". Ghauri and Cateora (2010) define it as "the performance of business activities that direct the flow of a company's goods and services to consumers or users in more than one nation for profit" (p. 7). In terms of the international marketing curricula, in 2005, Crittenden and Wilson (2005) conducted a review of teaching scholarship in international marketing and suggested three major curricula focuses: "content (knowledge) coverage, pedagogical approach, and learning outcomes. Traditionally, such shared information has been based on surveys of students, professors, and/or practitioners or the profiling of successful peda-gogical approaches" (Crittenden and Wilson, 2005, p. 85). The authors refer to "content knowledge" as primarily three perspectives: (1) the academic; (2) the student opinions; and (3) the practitioner perspective. Notably, this view goes beyond the academic and student relationship to consider the international practitioner, essential when focusing on authentic learning.

During this period, international marketing has been hugely influenced by major technological change. In the early part of this century Bell et al. (2001) discussed what they refer to as the "Internetalization" of international marketing education, arguing that "international marketing educators should seek to gain first mover advantage in the design and delivery of internetalized programs" (Bell et al., 2001, p. 79). Since the early part of the twenty-first century, technology has played a much greater role in the delivery of inter-national marketing education. This is certainly true at the time of writing, the COVID-19 pandemic having forced the pivot to online learning. The use of social media, video conferencing and game-based learning platforms such as Kahoot! can all help to enhance students' learning. By way of an example, Galan and Khodabandehloo (2016) implemented blogging within a LinkedIn study discussion group in an international marketing course. The authors found that engaging in this activity contributed to the students' acquisition of knowledge in international marketing, development of multicultural awareness, improvement of critical thinking, reasoning, analysis and interpretation. Students perceived blogging in LinkedIn as a more valuable activity when compared to traditional written assignments.

In recent years, there has been greater attention to corporate social responsibility, both from a consumer and organizational perspective. The delivery of international marketing education needs to recognize these changes. This point is echoed by Perera and Hewege (2016) who argue that:

> International marketing curricula mostly aim at developing marketing skills in designing, organizing and implementing marketing activities of business firms in a rapidly changing global environment. The recent developments in the global business environment pertinent to sustainability (e.g. carbon emission taxes on international business firms, eco-labelling) should be given a special attention in international marketing curricula. (p. 140).

In summary, this section has provided a brief chronology of international marketing. The key topics include globalization, the rise of Chinese brands, and new technologies. Once again, the vast majority of literature on international marketing is often viewed in the context of a Western-centric approach. Or more specifically, US-centric. Clearly, US hegemony is reflected in the development of the literature on the subject. However, in recent years, the rise of brands from BRIC economies is just one example why international marketing educators need to move away from Western-centrism.

A FOCUS ON AUTHENTIC LEARNING

In 2006, Kuster and Vila published an article comparing marketing education methods in Europe and North America. The authors found that the most commonly used teaching methods in both environments were: practical exercises, case studies and lectures. European marketing academics tended to favour practical exercises for their connection to the real world. In contrast, Americans focused more on technology-based alternatives, such as business games. However, although referring to the "real world", their article does not go beyond "teaching methods". Only a few studies have examined international marketing education in the context of authentic learning pedagogy.

The importance of real-world learning in relation to global geographical knowledge was argued by Hise et al. (1999). The authors conducted research into the geographical knowledge among US undergraduate international marketing students based on their ability to locate countries of the world. Surprisingly, students were only able to locate about one-sixth of the world's countries. Clearly, research in other countries, such as those in Europe, may well generate different results. However, these results are rather startling. Why? Well, if students are to work in international marketing they need to have geographical knowledge. This extends to knowledge about natural resources, climates and their implications for effective decision-making in international markets (Hise et al., 1999). Certainly, an authentic context should include scenarios that further a student's geographical knowledge, for example, analyzing cases across different international markets and not just those that are largely Western-centric.

The word "authenticity" is interpreted in a number of ways in current literature about learning and curriculum, although it can be viewed as giving student learning a similar emphasis to that of the "real-world" context and community of practice (Stein et al., 2004). Herrington et al. (2010, p. 18) argue that authentic learning consists of the following elements: authentic contexts; authentic tasks; expert performances; multiple roles and perspectives; collaborative construction; reflection; articulation; coaching and scaffolding; and authentic assessment. These nine elements that characterize authentic learning are summarized below.

- *Authentic context*: the curriculum should not be simplified and broken up into step-by-step processes, but should mirror real-world situations. An authentic context can lead to an intense feeling of engagement with the learning. Yet student engagement may also depend on the type of assessment. In their study into the use of authentic assessment among Masters students in Malaysia, Fook and Sidhu (2010) found that authentic assessment involving small group work resulted in approximately only 25 percent of students meeting with their lecturer to discuss their progress. The authors argue this is perhaps due to the nature of the assignment. However, there are other factors that impact student engagement, such as support and guidance from the educator.
- *Authentic task*: the task should be ill-defined, complex, comprehensive and completed over an extended period of time, mirroring activities that are relevant to the kinds of problems to which knowledge is applied in the real world.
- *Access to expert thinking and modeling of processes*: both students and lecturers can enhance learning for each other by sharing their different levels of expertise.
- *Provide multiple roles and perspectives*: students should be enabled to examine problems from more than one point of view to ensure expertise in areas.
- *Support collaborative construction of knowledge*: providing opportunities for students to work on a common task that is assessed collaboratively is important.

- *Promote reflection to enable abstractions to be formed*: it is essential to provide opportunities for students to reflect on their work. Reflecting on learning does not come naturally to students and they need instruction in how to do it well (Moon, 2004).
- *Promote articulation to enable tacit knowledge to be made explicit*: opportunities should be provided for students to speak and write about their growing understanding within communities of professional practice and in public forums.
- *Provide coaching and scaffolding by the teacher at critical times*: the idea is that rather than transmitting knowledge, the teacher's role is a supportive one, guiding and supporting students.
- *Provide for authentic assessment of learning within the tasks*: the assessed task is the polished product at the end of the learning period that has taken a significant period to produce and is integrated with the learning tasks (Herrington et al., 2010, p. 18).

Each of these elements of authentic learning can contribute to more engaged learning and promote higher-order thinking skills. For example, students working on an authentic task, such as carrying out international marketing research on behalf of a local business, are developing higher-order thinking skills such as decision-making, evaluating data and problem solving.

Does an authentic learning environment need to have all of the nine elements in order for it to be authentic? Herrington et al. (2010) argue that there is no such thing as a perfect task, in other words, one that matches exactly all of the elements of authentic learning. Thus, a better way to think about the elements is as a continuum. The authors propose an evaluation matrix where you can gauge the level of authenticity with each element (for more detail see Herrington et al., 2010).

Authentic learning can be viewed from the point of view of addressing real-world problems in the classroom. For example, Bozalek et al. (2013) noted that authentic learning has been suggested as a way to bring the necessary complexity into learning to deal with challenges in professional practice that students will encounter following graduation. In short, by students working on real-world international marketing scenarios and problems, they are preparing for a career in professional practice following their course. Creating this type of authentic learning environment has been shown to be of benefit to students (see Herrington and Oliver, 2000; Herrington and Herrington, 2007). The pedagogical and practical benefits are that students develop key transferable skills that prepare them for professional practice.

Although there is no one universal definition of authentic learning, Rule (2006) conducted a qualitative analysis of 45 articles on authentic learning and came to the conclusion that there are four themes supporting authentic learning. These are:

1.   The activity involves real-world problems that mimic the world of professionals in the discipline with presentation of findings to audiences beyond the classroom.
2.   Open-ended inquiry, thinking skills and metacognition are addressed.
3.   Students engage in discourse and social learning in a community of learners.
4.   Students are empowered through choice to direct their own learning in relevant project work (Rule, 2006, p. 2).

You will note that Herrington et al. (2010) and Rule (2006) focus on different elements and themes respectively. This illustrates the lack of consensus in the literature on what constitutes "authentic learning". Yet what they do have in common is a consensus that authentic learning is associated with students working on the type of real-world problems associated with professional practice.

In summary, this section gives a brief overview of authentic learning. The main focus here has been to discuss the nature of authentic learning rather than examine types of authentic assessment. The key benefit of authentic learning pedagogy over more traditional teaching methods is its emphasis on students developing higher-order thinking skills and knowledge critical for a career in international marketing. The final section in this chapter presents five international marketing exercises. Each exercise examines a different international marketing topic and briefly highlights an associated authentic learning element.

INTERNATIONAL MARKETING EXERCISES

The international marketing exercises presented here are designed to enhance students' knowledge of international marketing. The exercises have been purposely chosen as they address international marketing topics that students often find challenging. The nature of each topic is briefly explained at the start of every exercise together with the associated authentic learning element and how this benefits students' learning.

Exercise 1: Projective Techniques for International Brands

Introduction to the exercise
A fundamental aspect of international marketing, branding involves everything from deciding on the number of brands across markets, to whether to adopt

a global approach or to produce local, country-specific brands. The main focus of this exercise is on brand equity. Aaker (1991, p. 15) defined brand equity as "a set of brand assets and liabilities linked to a brand, its name and symbol that add to or subtract from the value provided by a product or service to a firm and/or to that firm's customers". Assets and liabilities are grouped on the basis of the following five dimensions: brand loyalty; brand awareness; perceived quality; brand associations; and other proprietary brand assets such as trademarks and patents.

The exercise provides students with an opportunity to learn about the significance of brand equity in an international context, and to reflect on their own views on brand equity using projective techniques. This type of qualitative research method is often used by marketers when aiming to understand participants' views that might be difficult to capture using more traditional data collection methods, such as an online survey or face-to-face interviews. In this sense, based on the nine elements of authentic learning (Herrington et al., 2010), it is primarily associated with "promote reflection". This is because the task requires students to articulate their beliefs on selected brands and provides collaborative groups to enable articulation of ideas and arguments. Moreover, it promotes higher-order thinking skills such as analyzing and evaluating brand equity of different brands.

This exercise works well with students at all levels, including undergraduate, postgraduate and practitioners. The session is best introduced following an introduction to the subject of brand equity. In order for this exercise to work, it is essential that students do not talk to each other. Explain that they should write no more than two or three words, and the first word(s) that comes to mind when they see the brand name.

What is interesting about using the projective technique of word association is that some students write down the literal meaning of the word. This may have little resemblance to the brand. For example, one year I had a student write the words "fruit" and "worm" as being associated with the global brand Apple!

Time
This is an exercise designed for inclusion within a seminar of 50 to 60 minutes. It typically takes students 30 to 35 minutes to work through the questions. This gives the instructor approximately 15 minutes to discuss the answers. This includes students sharing why they gave the answers they gave.

Learning objectives
- Identify how individuals perceive global brands (perceived quality).
- Assess the importance of brand associations (values and personality).

- Understand how factors such as culture and brand stereotyping impact views of brands.
- Reflect and discuss the impact of perceived country-of-origin effect (COO) of a product on brand attitude as proposed by Magnusson et al. (2011).

Resources/set-up

A4 handouts showing the brand names for students to complete (see Table 11.1). The words in brackets are the reasons students gave for choosing their selected animals.

Exercise instructions

The instructor gives each student a copy of the worksheet, then reads the following instructions:

> We are going to use the projective techniques of brand personification and word association to see how you view aspects of brand equity. In particular, brand awareness, perceived quality and brand associations. During this exercise, it is important that you follow instructions, and in particular do not discuss your answers until told to do so. Each of you should have a worksheet that consists of four columns. The first column is the number of the respective brand, the second column contains the brand name, column three includes the first of our projective techniques, "Brand personification", while the fourth column refers to the second projective technique, "Association Technique".
>
> 1. Without discussing with your neighbour, write down your views for each brand based on type of projective technique. If you do not know the brand, simply write "Don't know".
> 2. Discuss your answers with your neighbour. Do you share the same views? If not, why not?
> 3. Share your answers in groups of 4–5. Discuss your answers in your group. Do you share the same views? If not, why not?
> 4. Apply the following dimensions of brand equity (Aaker, 1991) to your favourite brand on the list: brand loyalty, brand awareness, perceived quality and brand associations.

Table 11.1   An example of a completed worksheet

No.	Brand name	What type of animal do you associate with this brand? (Brand personification)	What 1–2 words do you associate with this brand? (Association technique)
1	Apple	Lion (king, dominant)	Dominant, ubiquitous
2	Tesco	Ant (everywhere)	Leader, established
3	Uber	Fox (sly)	Innovative, negative
4	Rolex	Horse	Luxury, prestige
5	Samsung	Magpie	Follower
6	Burberry	Deer (tradition, English, classic)	Traditional, classic
7	Lego	Monkey (playful)	Play, nostalgic
8	Nike	Cheetah (pace, speed)	Sporty, celebrity

Discussion/debrief

After the exercise, ask students plenty of questions, in particular, how they approached the exercise. Other questions you can ask include:

- Are there any brands you are not familiar with?
- What influenced your word choice when writing about each brand?
- Are your answers largely positive, negative or neutral?
- How do your answers compare to your neighbour's?
- Why should international brands consider how their brand is perceived across cultures?
- How would you describe the brand equity of your favourite brand?
- Why might brands differ in perception due to stereotyping? Can you think of an example(s)?
- How might projective techniques be combined with other international marketing research methods?
- Why might brand perceptions change over time?
- Why might COO (Country-of-origin) effects impact perceived quality of the brand?

Key takeaways

To summarize, this exercise familiarizes students with brand equity and projective techniques used in international marketing.

- COO of brand and a person's nationality may influence their perception of the brand (brand stereotyping) and ethnocentrism.
- A global approach to branding gives a brand a uniform worldwide image and allows for cost savings.
- A strong overall brand equity is a positive for brands in international markets.

Teaching tips

This exercise looks at the topic of brand equity and works particularly well with a group of students from different cultural backgrounds. Moreover, it can provide particularly interesting data on how students perceive quality and brand associations, the results of which can be shared with all students via the course or module page.

Exercise 2: Baking the International Marketing Research Cake

Introduction to the exercise

This exercise focuses on international marketing research. Gathering, analyzing and interpreting data is a key part of developing succssful international marketing strategies. Although the methods associated with marketing research are largely the same for domestic and international marketing, the environments are very different. The complexities associated with the international marketing environment mean that marketers need to be able to conduct international marketing research.

The exercise offers students an opportunity to learn about the marketing research process in an international context, including: international marketing information needs; sources of marketing information; data collection methods; the international marketing research environment; ethical issues; the research process; and analysis of research findings. Through a group activity, students will use the metaphor of baking a cake to discuss and show the relationship between the different elements of the international marketing research process.

Based on Herrington et al.'s (2010) nine elements of authentic learning, this exercise is mainly associated with the element "provide coaching and scaffolding". The reason for this is that the exercise involves collaborative learning in groups, meaning more knowledgeable students can assist with scaffolding and coaching. In addition, the instructor is available to provide contextualized support.

Allocate students into groups of four or five and provide each group with a sheet of A1 paper and marker pens. Although this is very much a creative task, do give students guidance on how to complete the task by explaining the metaphor – that the cake is the outcome of the research, but do think about the "ingredients" that go into making "the cake". Avoid giving rigid constraints on the creative process.

In the past, I have found that students enjoy the creativity and group work that is inherent in this task. For example, they may illustrate each layer of the cake as a step in the research process. Others have illustrated a chef and a list of ingredients as the elements that go into making the cake. Overall, the exercise allows students to recall the key elements of international marketing research and later present their findings to the class. Do encourage other students to comment on each group's presentation. The debriefing session can focus on any elements in the process left out or not fully addressed.

This exercise works equally well by using self-selecting groups or putting students into groups. Be explicit in terms of the purpose of the exercise – pulling together what students have learned and to express this in a creative way. In addition, be clear on the time allocated to this task. You can certainly encourage students to produce a draft first, but make sure that they do not spend too long on this stage of the exercise, otherwise they will run out of time.

The exercise can be used for both undergraduate and postgraduate students. It works particularly well with students who are practitioners and/or studying largely on practice-based courses. This session is best delivered towards the end of a module as it is designed to "pull together" everything students have learned. Of course, there is no one 'right way' to illustrate the cake, but do look for creativity and the extent to which students are able to recognize the relationship between each stage in the research process. Figure 11.1 shows an example of a 'baking the international marketing research cake' illustration.

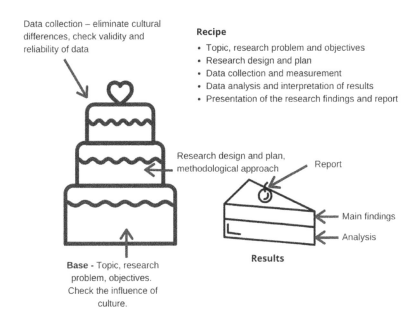

Figure 11.1   An example of a completed 'Baking the international marketing research cake'

Time

This is an exercise designed for a seminar of 50 to 60 minutes. Depending on the number of students, you can organize groups into four or five. Typically, allowing 25 to 30 minutes to work on producing their "cake" and 4 to 5 minutes for each presentation. Although not each member of the group is required to present, try to encourage each student to contribute to the task by directing questions to non-presenters.

Learning objectives

- Recognize the different steps in the international marketing research process.
- Understand the relationship between the elements associated with international marketing research.
- Learn about the considerations an international marketing researcher needs to take.

Resources/set-up

- A1 paper.
- Marker pens.
- A whiteboard and pen when debriefing.

Exercise instructions

The instructor gives each group a sheet of A1 paper and marker pens, then reads the following instructions:

> The purpose of this task is called "Baking the International Marketing Research Cake". Shortly, I want you to work in small groups to produce a cake to illustrate all of the elements associated with international marketing research. For example, this may include data collection methods, analytical techniques, ethical issues and cultural factors.
>
> Using the sheet of A1 paper and pens, in your groups, use the cake as a metaphor for conducting international marketing research. Think about what the layers of the cake may represent; what about the recipe and the ingredients? Do not simply list themes and/or keywords associated with international marketing research. In essence, I want to see how you "pull together" everything you have learned about international marketing research.
>
> For this exercise, I will give you 30 minutes to work on the task and 5 minutes for each group to present their cake. At the end of the session, if there are no objections, I will collect each group's work and post them to social media and the module/course page.

Discussion/debrief

Following each presentation, the instructor can ask the following questions:

- How did you approach the exercise? Did you produce a draft "cake" first?
- Are there any elements of the international marketing research process you are not familiar with?
- What influenced your allocation of words/themes to the cake metaphor?
- Is international marketing research a systematic process?
- Does all research start with a research problem?
- Why might the research objectives determine methodological approach?
- Why does an international marketing researcher need to take into account cultural differences?

Key takeaways

The key takeaways for this exercise can be summarized as follows:

- The research process when conducting international marketing research is not linear, it is in fact more of an iterative process.
- A framework for international marketing research includes the following environmental factors: marketing, government and legal, structural, socio-cultural, technological, economic and marketing.
- Cultural challenges in international marketing research include: hierarchy, time orientation, aesthetics and language.

Teaching tips

This exercise examines the topic of international marketing research. It is best to be absolutely clear when explaining what is meant by the metaphor "baking the international marketing research cake". Time allocation is also very important with this task. Although you can encourage questions from other students, try to allocate each group an equal amount of time to present their cake. Avoid using an exemplar from a previous year, as some students may use this as a guide for their own work. Remember that a key focus of this exercise is on creativity. Provide prompts and feedback during the task. One of the problems that can occur with this task is disagreement between group members. This is where the instructor can become a facilitator.

Finally, an alternative approach for this task is to give each group a scenario prior to baking their research cake. By way of an example: a Japanese manufacturer of electric powered scooters is considering entering the UK market. What research process might they go through when researching the UK market? Use the baking the international marketing research cake metaphor to illustrate your answer.

Exercise 3: International Advertising Reactions: Comparative Task (Real-time Reactions)

Introduction to the exercise

This exercise is about international advertising in the context of standardization compared to adaptation. It requires students to select two examples of international advertising. One of them adopts standardization, or in other words the same or similar advertising messages across countries. The second choice must refer to international advertising using adaptation, defined as using separate advertising messages in different markets.

Students are required to determine if their chosen advertising campaign adopts adaptation or standardization, the advertising message and effectiveness based on their attitudes towards the campaign. Sharing their real-time reactions helps students to share their views and creates transparency. To achieve this, you can set up a hashtag for students to live tweet their views. In relation to the nine elements of authentic learning, this exercise is based on "provide multiple roles and perspectives" (Herrington et al., 2010), as students are able to explore issues from different points of view. Moreover, they are able to use online learning resources for multiple purposes.

Time

The total time to complete the exercise and debrief is 50 minutes. Allocate 15 minutes for choosing videos via YouTube. The exercise works well by giving each pair a sector to search.

Learning objectives

- Evaluate the message in an international advertising campaign.
- Identify an advertising campaign that uses an adaptation approach.
- Learn the issues around standardization vs adaptation in international advertising.
- Identify an advertising campaign that uses a standardized approach.

Resources/set-up

- One laptop per group.
- Marker pens of different colours.
- Each group to have a laptop, iPad and access to the internet.

Exercise instructions
The instructor reads the following instructions:

> In pairs, conduct a search for two advertising campaigns for the same product or service on YouTube. One campaign must be a standardized campaign, while the other must be adaptation. In your pairs, discuss the following: why you believe each campaign adopts standardization or adaptation, the advertising message and your attitudes towards the campaign.

Discussion/debrief
After each group has chosen examples of their advertising campaigns, ask them to do a PowerPoint presentation showing the videos and their analysis. This task works best with small groups as it is difficult to do with large groups in 50 minutes.

Key takeaways
The key takeaways for this exercise are as follows:

• Students develop an understanding of how adaptation and standardization international marketing strategies are put into practice.
• The task illustrates the different factors that can be used to make a judgment on adaptation and standardization.
• Students are able to examine an advertising campaign critically and identify the intended message.

Teaching tips
One way to make this task interesting for students is to write well-known advertising campaigns on pieces of paper. Next, invite one student from each pair to collect a piece of paper – they must then watch, compare and analyze each advertising campaign based on the international marketing strategy and advertising message.

Exercise 4: Drawing your International Marketing Entry Strategy

Introduction to the exercise
The exercise looks at international market entry strategies. Why and how firms go abroad is the most important issue in international marketing (Ghauri and Cateora, 2010). This is an individual exercise that requires students to undertake three steps. First, to select a post-it note from the instructor. The post-it note features the name of a well-known brand. Second, to conduct a cursory search of the named brand to see which markets it has yet to enter and to undertake background reading. Third, to draw the following: brand, market entry strategy of their choosing, and finally, the developing world market. Drawing

these aspects of international marketing provides students with an opportunity to express their views visually. The purpose of the task is not to assess drawing skills! Based on Herrington et al.'s (2010) nine elements of authentic learning, this exercise is largely associated with "promote articulation" as the task requires students to discuss and articulate beliefs and understanding. In this case, this is their choice of market entry strategy and developing world market with their fellow students.

Time

The total time to complete the exercise and debrief is 50 minutes. The amount of time allocated to conducting research on the brand and drawing varies. For example, if students are likely to be familiar with a brand, then you may choose to reduce research time. However, as a guide, I suggest 15 minutes for research and 20 minutes for drawing. This allows time prior to the end of the session for some of the class to share their drawings.

Learning objectives

- Identify key sources of data on a chosen brand.
- Assess the different types of market entry strategies.
- Critique the implications of choosing a certain market entry strategy.

Resources/debrief

- White sheets of A2 paper, one sheet per student.
- Marker pens of different colours.
- Each student to have a laptop, iPad and access to the internet.

Exercise instructions

The instructor gives each student one sheet of A2 paper and marker pens, then reads the following instructions:

> The purpose of today's session is as follows. First, I am going to give each of you a post-it note with the name of a well-known brand written on it. Second, I want you to conduct some background research on the named brand using the university/ college digital library and web-based sources. Moreover, I want you to identify an international market your brand has yet to enter. You will spend approximately 15 minutes on this part of the task. Next, using the A2 paper and pens provided, I would like you to draw the following: the brand, your recommended market entry strategy, and finally, draw the developing country. By way of an example, let us say that you have been allocated the US automobile manufacturer Tesla. Based on your research, you discover that Tesla has yet to enter the Indian market. Further research produces a number of reasons supporting Tesla's entry to the Indian market via a strategic alliance. Therefore, you then decide that Tesla should enter the Indian market using

a strategic alliance as their chosen market entry strategy. Your drawing should illustrate these three choices – Tesla, India, Strategic alliance.

Once you have completed your drawing, share your illustration with your neighbour. Following this, a select number of students will be invited to share their work with the class. Prior to selecting your market entry strategy, consider the following two important points: first, think about why you have chosen your market. What might make this particular market attractive when compared to others? Second, try to justify why you have selected a particular market entry strategy. What are the advantages of your chosen method when compared to other options?

Discussion/debrief

At the conclusion of the research and drawing, the instructor asks students to share their drawing with their neighbour. In addition, following this, the instructor invites other students to ask questions.

Key takeaways

- When entering an international market it is important to consider the advantages and disadvantages of different international market entry strategies.
- There is no one "best" market entry strategy.
- Selecting a market entry strategy requires an understanding of the international marketing environment.
- Market entry strategies used by competitors can be used as a benchmark.
- Organizations need to consider a wide range of environmental factors before entering a market.

Teaching tips

Students are often concerned about their lack of drawing skills for this exercise. If this is the case, you might like to include your own example, perhaps using stick figures!

This task works equally well with small groups. Although, if using small groups, try to ensure that every group member is engaged with the task. This can be done by allocating roles to each student. For example, one student generates the ideas, while the other illustrates their ideas using the pen and paper.

The resources for this task may be adapted depending on the audience. For example, for MBA students and/or small groups, students may prefer to use technologies such as tablets to draw their marketing entry strategy.

Exercise 5: A Mind Map of International Marketing

Introduction to the exercise

In this final exercise, the emphasis is on students' ability to brainstorm the nature of international marketing and to show the association between sub-themes. Students generate ideas and structure them in a non-linear fashion around the central theme, international marketing, while the sub-themes are represented as branches. A mind map is a visual representation, in this case, of international marketing concepts. In short, the aim of mind maps is to find creative associations between ideas or themes. Thus, in this sense they can be primarily viewed as association maps (Davies, 2010).

The purpose of this exercise is to give students an opportunity to break down and structure international marketing in a visual form. It also allows them to show how different concepts in international marketing relate to each other. Brainstorming using mind maps is a useful way for an instructor to see how much students have remembered during their module/course. Furthermore, it can help to identify gaps in knowledge. Subsequently, any gaps found can be addressed in future sessions.

Students are likely to find mind mapping a helpful exercise when preparing for summative assessment, such as an end of module exam, as it promotes reflective thinking. The exercise also produces a permanent record (a mind map) that can be used as part of their revision process. Furthermore, in the context of the nine elements of authentic learning (Herrington et al., 2010), it primarily "supports the collaborative construction of knowledge" through group collaboration. Also, the incentive structure for whole group achievement is to produce a mind map that can be used as a helpful revision guide. Another core tenet of authentic learning is practice. This task gives students the opportunity to practice learning concepts or ideas more than once.

Time
This is an in-class group task that works best in an environment where students can work together in groups of four or five. Typically, allow groups 30 minutes to work on their mind maps and 20 to 25 minutes for presentations.

Learning objectives
- To create a mind map that represents your thinking about everything learned throughout the international marketing course/module.
- Analyze the relationship between the different central topic and sub-topics associated with international marketing.
- To produce a mind map that can be used as a useful revision guide when preparing for an international marketing exam.

Resources/set-up
- Show students an example of a mind map (ideally in a cognate subject).
- A1 paper.

- Marker pens.
- A whiteboard and pen when debriefing.

Exercise instructions

The instructor gives each group one sheet of A1 paper and marker pens, then reads the following instructions:

> For this session, I would like you to work in groups of four or five. The purpose of this group task is for you to create a mind map that represents your understanding of international marketing. On your desks, you will see an example of a mind map. Although the example is based on a different subject area, note how the map illustrates the central topic or theme and sub-themes. In short, it is a visual representation of a person's own thinking about the topic. In this task, I would like to see a similar outcome, although, clearly, your mind maps will be based on international marketing. Using your paper and marker pens, start to work on your mind maps. You can work on a draft first, but make sure to allow sufficient time to work on the final map. Remember that there is no definitive way of constructing a mind map. However, upon completion of the task, I will be looking for each group to deliver a short 5-minute presentation on their mind map. This will involve each group explaining how they approached the task, together with explaining the association between themes.

An example of how a mind map might look for international marketing is illustrated in Figure 11.2.

Discussion/debrief

After groups have produced their mind maps, ask each one to present in turn. The instructor asks questions about the mind map and invites questions from observing students. Questions may include:

1. How did you approach this task? Did each student take on a specific role?
2. Which international marketing theme/topic did you start illustrating first and why?
3. Were you able to fully recall the international marketing topics covered throughout the module/course?
4. How might you use your mind map for your revision? What have you learned from this exercise?

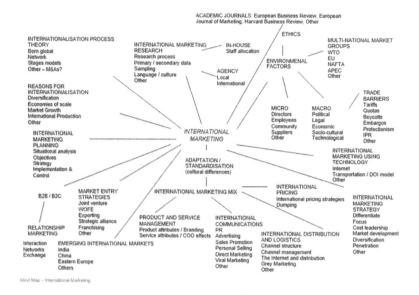

Figure 11.2   A mind map of international marketing

Key takeaways
The key takeaways for this exercise are as follows:

- Students develop an understanding of how themes covered within international marketing are connected.
- The finished product or mind map can be a useful point of reference for future exams or assignments.
- The task can help the instructor to identify any gaps in knowledge. If this is the case, these gaps can be revisited in later sessions.

Teaching tips
Students will find it helpful if you provide an example of a mind map. However, avoid providing an example based on marketing or international marketing. Take an active approach during the task by visiting each group to monitor progress. In some cases, students may need prompting to move from draft stage to final mind map. You can encourage students to ask questions by stipulating that each group must ask fellow groups a minimum of one question.

SUMMARY

The chapter has discussed a chronology of international marketing and highlighted the importance of concentrating on authentic learning pedagogy. This involves preparing students for the "real world" by focusing on activities and assessment that mimic international marketing practice.

The relevance of the review of the history of international marketing shows that as a subject, it was once very US-centric. However, there is an increasing focus on other countries and non-US brands, particularly those from the BRIC economies. This is in addition to a wider range of issues, such as the impact of technology, politics, economics and geography. Thus, educators need to take this into account when teaching.

I have argued that teaching international marketing should be viewed from the perspective of authenticity as opposed to more traditional methods. Furthermore, the old model of traditional assessment using closed book exams and essay writing is no longer suitable. As educators, we need both to focus on authentic learning pedagogy and to move away from a Western-centric approach to teaching and learning, thereby preparing our students for professional practice.

Finally, by participating in authentic learning experiences, students engage in higher-order thinking skills required in a real-world setting. In the words of John Keats: "Nothing ever becomes real 'til it is experienced".

REFERENCES

Aaker, D.A. 1991. *Managing Brand Equity*. New York, NY: The Free Press.

Andrus, D.M., Laughlin, J. and Norvell, W. 1995. Internationalizing the marketing curriculum: A profile of the international marketing course. *Marketing Education Review*, 5(2), 9–18.

Aulakh, P.S. and Kotabe, M. 1993. An assessment of theoretical and methodological development in international marketing: 1980–1990. *Journal of International Marketing*, 1(2), 5–28.

Bartels, R. 1968. Are domestic and international marketing dissimilar? *Journal of Marketing*, 32(July), 56–61.

Bell, J., Deans, K., Ibbotson, P. and Sinkovics, R. 2001. Towards the "Internetalization" of international marketing education. *Marketing Education Review*, 11(3), 69–79.

Bordo, M.D., Eichengreen, B., Irwin, D.A. 1999. Is globalization today really different than globalization a hundred years ago? Working paper, 7095, National Bureau of Economic Research.

Bozalek, V., Watters, K., Gachago, D., Alexander, L. Wood, D., Ivala, E. and Herrington, J. 2013. The use of emerging technologies for authentic learning: A South African study in higher education. *British Journal of Educational Technology*, 44(4), 629–38.

Brand Z. 2018. Brand Z Top 100 Most Valuable Global Brands. *WPP.com*. Accessed at https://www.wpp.com/news/2018/05/brandz-top-100-most-valuable-global-brands -2018.

Crittenden, V.L. and Wilson, E.J. 2005. Content, pedagogy, and learning outcomes in the international marketing course. *Journal of Teaching in International Business*, 17(1–2), 81–101.

Cunningham, P. and Jones, D.G.B. 1997. Early development of collegiate education in international marketing. *Journal of International Marketing*, 5(2), 87–102.

Czinkota, M.R. and Ronkainen, I.A. 2007. *International Marketing*, 8th edn. Mason, OH: Thomson South-Western.

Davies, M. 2010. Concept mapping, mind mapping and argument mapping: What are the differences and do they matter? *Higher Education*, 62, 279–301.

Fayerweather, J. 1982. *International Business Strategy and Administration*. Cambridge, MA: Ballinger.

Ferrell, O.C., Hair, J.F., Marshall, G.W. and Tamilia, R.D. 2015. Understanding the history of marketing education to improve classroom instruction. *Marketing Education Review*, 25(2), 159–75.

Fook, C.Y. and Sidhu, G.K. 2010. Authentic assessment and pedagogical strategies in higher education. *Journal of Social Sciences*, 6(2), 153–61.

Galan, N. and Khodabandehloo, A. 2016. Learning with LinkedIn: Students' perceptions of incorporating subject-related blogging in an international marketing course. *Interactive Technology and Smart Education*, 13(2), 166–83.

Ghauri, P.N. and Cateora, P. 2010. *International Marketing*, 3rd edn. Maidenhead: McGraw-Hill.

Gulikers, J.T.M., Bastiaens, T.J. and Kirschner, P.A. 2004. A five-dimensional framework for authentic assessment. *Educational Technology Research and Development*, 52(3), 67–86.

Herrington, A. and Herrington, J. 2007. What is an authentic learning environment? In L.A. Tomei (ed.), *Online and Distance Learning: Concepts, Methodologies, Tools, and Applications* (pp. 68–77). Hershey, PA: Information Science Reference.

Herrington, J. and Oliver, R. 2000. An instructional design framework for authentic learning environments. *Educational Technology Research and Development*, 48, 23–48.

Herrington, J., Reeves, T.C. and Oliver, R. 2010. *A Guide to Authentic E-learning*. London: Routledge.

Hise, R.T., Davidow, M., and Troy, L. 1999. Global geographical knowledge of business students: An update and recommendations for improvement. *Journal of Teaching in International Business*, 11(4), 1–22.

Hollander, S.C., Rassuli, K.M., Jones, D.G.B. and Dix, L.F. 2005. Periodization in marketing history. *Journal of Macromarketing*, 25(1), 32–41.

Javalgi, R.G., Cutler, B.D., Rao, S.R. and White, D.S. 1996. The international marketing literature: Topics, trends and contributors. *Journal of Teaching in International Business*, 8(3), 21–43.

Kuster, I. and Vila, N. 2006. A comparison of marketing teaching methods in North American and European universities. *Marketing Intelligence & Planning*, 24(4), 319–31.

Levitt, T. 1983. The globalization of markets. *Harvard Business Review*, 61(3), May–June, 92–102.

Li, T. and Cavusgil, S.T. 1995. A classification and assessment of research streams in international marketing. *International Business Review*, 4(3), 251–77.

Lombardi, M.M. 2007. Authentic learning for the 21st century: An overview (ELI Paper No. 1). Accessed at http://www.edna.edu.au/edna/referral/rss/http://www .educause.edu/ir/ library/pdf/ELI3009.pdf.

Magnusson, P., Westjohn, S.A. and Zdravkovic, S. 2011. What? I thought Samsung was Japanese: Accurate or not, perceived country of origin matters. *International Marketing Review*, 28(5), 454–72.

Malhotra, N.K., Wu, L. and Whitelock, J. 2013. An updated overview of research published in the International Marketing Review: 1983 to 2011. *International Marketing Review*, 30(1), 7–20.

McDaniel, S.W. and Smith, L.M. 1987. Industry views on content of the international marketing course. *Journal of Marketing Education*, 9(3), 9–14.

Meloan, T.W. and Taylor, D. 1968. Internationalizing the marketing curricula, in *Internationalizing the Business Curricula*, Bloomington, IN: Bureau of Business Research.

Moon, J.A. 2004. *A Handbook of Reflective and Experiential Learning: Theory and Practice*. Abingdon: Routledge Falmer.

Omar, O. 2009. *International Marketing*. Basingstoke: Palgrave Macmillan.

Perera, C.R. and Hewege, C.R. 2016. Integrating sustainability education into international marketing curricula. *International Journal of Sustainability in Higher Education*, 17(1), 123–48.

Perlmutter, H.V. 1969. The tortuous evolution of the multinational corporation. *Columbia Journal of World Business*, 4(1), 9–18.

Robins, N. 2012. The corporation that changed the world: How the East India Company shaped the modern multinational. *Asian Affairs*, 43(1), 12–26.

Rule, A.C. 2006. The components of authentic learning. *Journal of Authentic Learning*, 3(1), 1–10.

Sambell, K., Brown, S. and Race, P. 2019. Assessment to support student learning: Eight challenges for 21st century practice. *The All Ireland Journal of Teaching & Learning in Higher Education*, 11(2), 1–15.

Smart, D.T., Tomkovick, C., Jones, E. and Menon, A. 1999. Undergraduate marketing education in the 21st century: Views from three institutions. *Marketing Education Review*, 9(1), 1–9.

Sorenson, R.Z. and Wiechmann, U.E. 1975. How multinationals view marketing standardization. *Harvard Business Review*, 53(3), 38–167.

Statista 2018. Growth rate of vehicle sales in China from 2009 to 2019. Accessed at https://www.statista.com/statistics/281168/growth-rate-of-vehicle-sales-in-china/.

Stein, S.J., Isaacs, G. and Andrews, T. 2004. Incorporating authentic learning experiences within a university course. *Studies in Higher Education*, 29(2), 239–58.

Terpstra, V. 1987. The evolution of international marketing. *International Marketing Review*, 4(2), 47–59.

Turley, L.W. and Shannon, J.R. 1999. The international marketing curriculum: Views from students. *Journal of Marketing Education*, 21(3), 175–80.

Vos, L. 2013. Improving international marketing programs to reflect global complexity and risk: Curriculum drivers and constraints. *Journal of Teaching in International Business*, 24(2), 81–106.

Wind, Y., Douglas, S.P. and Perlmutter, H.V. 1973. Guidelines for developing international marketing strategies. *Journal of Marketing*, 37(2), 14–23.

Yip, G.S. 1989. Global strategy…in a world of nations. *MIT Sloan Management Review*, 31(1), 29–41.

Zimmer, R.J., Bruce, G. and Lange, I. 1996. An investigation of marketing educators'
    approach to teaching international marketing in the introductory marketing course.
    Journal of Teaching in International Business, 8(1), 1–24.

12. Teaching marketing science

Dag Bennett

INTRODUCTION

This chapter begins with a description of a simple exercise to generate data that can be manipulated with basic maths to create a body of evidence from which lessons can be drawn. The exercise is the first step in helping students on a journey not only to discover patterns of human behaviour, but also to develop an understanding of how to approach the study of marketing evidence. Along the way, the accumulation of knowledge leads to a deeper understanding of the implications of underlying behaviours to establish what marketing interventions can and cannot do. The data from the exercise are analysed in different ways as the chapter progresses, and key lessons are laid out step by step. This sequence of data, evidence, analysis, pattern and explanation is an inducto-deductive approach to helping students develop a marketing science mindset. It is designed so that they can begin to develop an understanding of how to go about solving marketing problems and come to reasonable, evidence-based strategies in response. Marketing science here is meant to be applied, not abstract, and to be useful for students in their business careers.

1.   START SIMPLE, USE YOUR OWN DATA: CHOOSING MARBLES PART 1

BOX 12.1 CHOOSING MARBLES PART 1

In a principles of marketing class, a bucket of marbles was passed round the room and students chose one, then put it back, and passed on to the next student, noting their selection of red, green, blue, etc. All choices made by the students were recorded in Excel.

The class was asked to describe the market for marbles based on the choice data. First, they listed the colours and added up the number of choices, which should have been 720 (120 students × 6 trips round the class), but turned out to be 664 – a discrepancy needing explanation. Eyeballing the data showed that some colours were chosen more often than others and also that no one chose only one colour. The main pattern was that most people chose three or four colours, including red and green.

Using Excel's counting functions, we worked out the following, as shown in Table 12.1:

- number of times each colour was chosen;
- the share of choices (100 × (choices of colour/total choices));
- penetration (total number who chose a colour at least once/ total number of choosers).
- Loyalty was measured in two ways:
  - repeat buying – % of choosers who choose the same colour again;
  - share of category requirements (SCR) – number of purchases of a colour/total purchases by people choosing the colour.
- Purchase frequency was calculated as the sum of choices/ penetration.

Table 12.1   *Choices of colour are determined by the popularity of the colour in the bucket*

Number of marbles	chosen	share %	Pen %	Repeat %	SCR %	Freq
35 Red	220	36	79	66	61	2.7
20 Green	127	19	6	55	55	2.0
15 Blue	88	13	55	51	39	1.6
10 Yellow	55	9	36	34	36	1.5
8 Silver	50	8	31	32	24	1.6
5 Clear	24	4	21	18	21	1.1
5 White	26	3	16	20	18	1.5
4 Turquoise	25	4	21	21	17	1.2
3 Cat-eye	27	4	22	22	16	1.2
Average	11	41	35	31	1.6	–

Arranging the results by share made it easy to see that the most-chosen colours were the ones with the most marbles in the bucket. Popularity or penetration was about availability. The most popular colours were also the ones chosen most frequently.

It was also clear that penetration varied much more, from 16 to 79 per cent, a factor of five, than did purchase frequency, which varied from 1.1 to 2.8, or a factor of just over two. Higher penetration also went with higher loyalty. This is double jeopardy (DJ) in action – big brands have many more customers, who are more loyal, while small brands are punished twice by having far fewer, less loyal customers who buy less often (see Ehrenberg, 1969).

The simple exercise above illustrates the importance of developing facility with numbers and basic maths, and presenting data for analysis and understanding. The data are used again to discuss the sharing of customers to demonstrate the Duplication of Purchase law (DoP). DJ and DoP are examples of empirical generalizations in marketing that are building blocks for strategy formulation and core elements of marketing knowledge that supports theory development.

2. TEACHING MARKETING SCIENCE

This chapter proceeds much like a taught course in marketing, but it starts not with theory or questions designed to stimulate discussion (those come later), but with a simple exercise in making choices. This is after all what consumers do all the time. These choices, the data, are the "what" that we have to work with in teaching marketing science. A set of observations can be used to describe an outcome or choice situation. Looking at the results, a bright spark might jump to an explanation or theory about why the data fell out the way they did. And the explanation might be right. But when the exercise has been done a few more times, perhaps with different classes, different colours of marbles, or perhaps stones or rubber balls and the results are consistent, then they begin to look like a general finding, or an empirical generalization (see section 6). From there a theory of explanation might be elaborated for "why" the finding occurs the way it does. In this way, students can gather, process, analyse and present their own data and findings in the context of previous work and in the process they can learn about marketing, and how marketing science works.

This process can be described as induction that proceeds from concrete information and experiences to abstract explanatory theory where conclusions are based on repetition. Topics are introduced by presenting specific observations, case studies or problems, and theories are taught by guiding students to discover them by establishing the need for an explanatory theory. Commonly used inductive teaching methods for marketing science include: inquiry learning, problem-based learning, project-based learning, case-based teaching, discovery learning, and just-in-time teaching. The inductive process is in contrast to, for example, traditional deductive instruction in engineering or the harder sciences that begins with theories and progresses to their application. While the strength of the evidence varies from one method to another, the reason for focusing on inductive methods in marketing science is that they are consistently found to be at least equal to, and in general more effective than, traditional deductive methods for achieving a broad range of learning outcomes (Prince and Felder, 2007). Once principles or theoretical explanations are established, then further studies can take a deductive approach to test the limits of theory.

The following sections lay out some of the key tools, skills and abilities that students need to build an understanding of marketing science and to put it into practice. We start in the next with numeracy, because not only are numbers the core language of business, but they are at the heart of scientific analysis. Being numerate also equips marketers with the language needed to talk to the people in accounts, finance, production, logistics, and so on.

We then use the marbles data in a more detailed exercise to introduce new concepts and set the stage for understanding empirical generalizations in marketing. This is followed by a set of rules for presenting data designed to make it clearer and more understandable.

3.   TEACHING AND LEARNING STEP BY STEP

Marketing science teaching can be enhanced through experiential learning, a technique where learning comes from direct, hands-on experience (Hagan, 2012; Kolb and Kolb, 2005; Lewis and Williams, 1994). This includes not only applied experience, but also observation, leading to the formation of abstract concepts and the opportunity to test hypotheses in new situations. Experiential learning is important because it provides educators with the opportunity to link core theory to situations replicating those that occur not just in the marketplace, but also in the workplace. Passive learning, on the other hand, falls short in developing the critical thinking and analytical skills necessary for modern marketing careers.

While marketing science can be taught at any stage in a degree programme, it can be most effectively taught at early stages because it helps students embed a critical mindset and develop skills with which to evaluate taught content and theory. Early-stage students engaged in experiential learning can take what they learn incrementally to build their knowledge. And because it comes from experience that tallies with the world as they know it, it makes sense to them both empirically and as an explanation for their own observations.

Late-stage students, on the other hand, may well feel that the scientific approach challenges accepted marketing theories. The evidence from marketing science is often at odds with common practice, the latest fads, textbooks and the business press, all of which make unsupported assertions such as: it costs over five times as much to get a new customer as to retain an old one (Jandaghi et al., 2011; Kuusik, 2007; Tu et al., 2011), brands must differentiate or die (Trout and Rivkin, 2010), marketing should be highly targeted (Kotler, 2012), and so on. With a scientific mindset, such assertions are open to question, or better yet, to examination – such questions make excellent subjects for dissertations. But for late-stage students who have been diligently imbibing such beliefs and learning the systems behind them, marketing science can be frustrating because it requires them to un-learn or discard unsupportable theories and ideas. Take the idea that brands can be built by attracting new customers via price-reducing promotions. While this seems sensible because everyone likes a bargain, when tested, however, price promotions tend not to gain new customers (Blattberg and Neslin, 1990; Bogomolova et al., 2017; Srinivasan et al., 2004, Tiltman, 2012). Instead, they reward existing customers with lower prices. This might be a good thing, but it comes at a high price, and it won't build the base and help the brand grow. So if growth in the customer base is the goal then other strategies or tactics will have to be found.

The same is true in teaching marketing science to company executives where fresh-out-of-university managers struggle to reconcile empirical results against what they have been taught. New marketers are often tasked with projects like reinvigorating a loyalty programme, driving up a Net Promotor Score, feeding the social media machine – all schemes that seem to hold great promise, but rarely deliver, much to the frustration of the eager young marketers. More experienced peers, on the other hand, eschew such unrewarding projects because they know better. On the plus side, learning about marketing science often helps them to find explanations for their accrued experience – they know what works and what doesn't, and marketing science can help them understand why.

4. NUMERACY AS A CORNERSTONE FOR SCIENCE

One way to understand numeracy is to think of it like mathematical literacy. Literacy is the ability to read and write and a bit more – the Latin root *litteratus* means learned. In the same way, numeracy can be functional – the ability to understand numbers and perform mathematical functions, or expressive – the ability to use numbers as a means of communication. For today's business students numeracy is essential. This is true even in marketing, to which some business students flee in the belief that it is much less dominated by numbers than, say, finance or accounting (Bhowmick et al., 2017). Even so, they are likely to be disabused of this notion in the workplace when confronted with marketplace data, spreadsheets, the need to make sales projections, and the myriad metrics generated by digital marketing and social media. Numeracy is therefore a key foundation for marketing science and for coping with the evolving nature of modern marketing practice.

Numeracy is also critical to the scientific method involving hypothesis testing, tests of significance, correlations, and so on. Fortunately, many programmes such as Excel make calculations of all sorts quite simple.

Unfortunately, that simplicity does not translate into knowledge or under-standing of either the calculations or the results, increasing the likelihood of imperfectly understanding them, especially for the maths refugees. For example, most people have an idea of what average or standard deviation mean, but when they come to work out their ideas in Excel, they will find four different definitions for each. This can be confusing, and potentially may lead to wrong results, and to results that are inexplicable to the person presenting them. Spreadsheet programmes are like pianos – they require time and practice to develop proficiency.

Playing with marbles can enhance numeracy and introduce core elements of marketing knowledge. By using simple tools, to create their own data, then manipulate that data with simple and hopefully familiar maths, learners begin to progress toward understanding more complicated concepts. Take market share, a term used by all marketing students, many of whom struggle to define it mathematically, or to calculate it from simple data. By laying out calculations as above, students rapidly begin to internalize the idea and will be able to repeat the exercise on other data. The marble exercise or other simple exercises give them a way to refresh and operationalize their understanding. From there, other terms such as share of category requirements (SCR) can be introduced. This is a small but important increment because SCR is one of the most common measures of loyalty used in consumer packaged goods (CPG) businesses and it links to other ideas like share of wallet, share of voice, and so on. And while SCR is a simple concept, it implicitly acknowledges that most customers are not 100 per cent loyal, and that leads into a second, more advanced set of calculations for duplication of purchase analysis along with profound managerial implications.

Numeracy for marketing can build from simple foundations, learning by doing, and using student-generated data. The marble exercise typically takes three sessions, after which more concepts can be added. For most students it is a lesson in applied maths, and also a refresher in the use of spreadsheets that enhances their technical capabilities.

Table 12.1 was meant to be accessible and easy to understand. This is hardly the case for most of the data that we generate or that are presented by research-ers. This is partly because numbers are a different sort of language, but it is mainly because numbers are often very poorly presented. For example, tables are often organized alphabetically, which is better than no ordering, but still presents big difficulties in identifying patterns or deriving meaning.

4.1   Presenting Numbers

Andrew Ehrenberg's seminal work in data reduction (Ehrenberg, 1975) led to his formulation of five simple rules for presenting data. These rules underpin the tables used in this chapter and are straightforward, but are not built into analytical or spreadsheet software, and so must be thoughtfully applied.

1. *Order the rows and/or columns by some measure of size*: Table 12.1 was organized by size or share – from 35 Red marbles down to 3 Cat-eyes. Market share was a derived measure of size based on the choices made by students. When organized by size, the underlying pattern of choices was immediately evident, including for measures of loyalty.
2. *Round to two effective digits*: The table used rounded numbers (percentages) which make them easy to comprehend and to remember. They are also easy to compare against each other. It would of course be more "accurate" to include some decimal points but this would in no way improve our reading or understanding.
3. *Calculate an average to give visual focus*: Row and/or column averages help to provide a visual/mental focus. In Table 12.1 we can easily compare two- and one-digit numbers with each other and compare them to the average, helping us know whether a number is big or small because we have something to compare it to.
4. *Use table elements to guide the user's eye*: Tables should be laid out so that it is easy to scan down the columns. This is because it is much easier to scan downward than across – simply put, bigger numbers look bigger because they are longer.
5. *Give a brief verbal summary*: The brief verbal summary is in the title of the table. It could also have a paragraph of explanation, so the reader understands the main point of the table and doesn't have to search for meaning or work it out for themselves. A title like "Student choices of marble colours" is technically accurate, but also rather meaningless – it is much more useful for titles to deliver meaning, as in, "Choices of colour are determined by the popularity of the colour in the bucket".

4.2 Deepening the Analysis

Table 12.2 is a typical switching table created using the rules for presenting data. The table is designed to give the reader an almost immediate understanding of how marble choices are spread across the colours.

WHAT WE CAN LEARN FROM HABITUAL BEHAVIOUR: CHOOSING MARBLES PART 2

BOX 12.2 CHOOSING MARBLES PART 2

Since people chose more than one colour of marble, was there any pattern to their choices? Since the number of each colour was important, the next step was to lay out a matrix, ordered by popularity as in Table 12.2, from top to bottom and from left to right. The choosers of any colour were tracked for their other colour choices and it became clear that choosers of any colour also chose more popular red and green at the left of the table than unpopular turquoise or cat-eye on the right.

Table 12.2   The choosers of all colours of marble also chose other more popular colours

Choosers of	% Who also chose								
	R	G	B	Y	S	C	W	T	C
Red	–	71	63	60	65	29	40	33	44
Green	66	–	59	60	50	44	45	32	38
Blue	70	67	–	55	55	44	41	31	31
Yellow	61	65	53	–	47	36	38	34	41
Silver	59	60	58	55	–	43	39	44	28
Clear	71	67	54	51	45	–	28	33	41
White	72	66	55	54	24	42	–	42	38
Turquoise	58	55	61	53	45	41	22	–	44
Cat-eye	75	57	56	54	43	20	30	52	–
Average	**68**	**63**	**57**	**55**	**47**	**37**	**35**	**36**	**36**

To describe the table, start with the obvious – the numbers in the rows decline from left to right. Of those who chose white for example, 72 per cent also chose red, 66 per cent green, and so on. The pattern is the same for all colours and, on average, red was about twice as likely to also be chosen as cat-eye. Describing this relationship can be reduced to saying that the choosers of all colours of marble also chose other colours in line with the popularity of the other colour.

Describing the pattern in the columns is simple because all the numbers in each column are about the same. Just over half of the choosers of all colours also chose yellow, whereas just under half also chose silver, and a third, cat-eye. The pattern is the same for each colour, and having chosen any colour to start, the likelihood of choosing another particular colour is about the same regardless of the colour chosen first – about two-thirds of all choosers also chose red, and about a third also chose cat-eye, and so on.

The exercise opens a discussion about loyalty and switching for any competitive category of goods. Rather than marbles, consider mobile phone services – when it is time to renew a contract many customers stay with Vodafone, the largest brand. If they switch though, will they choose O2 or T-Mobile next? Since O2 has about 20 per cent market share and T-Mobile about 6 per cent, a reasonable guess is that they would be more likely to choose O2. Another way to think about it is that mobile service providers share their customers unequally, in line with how big they are in the marketplace. Phone services vary more than marbles, but in real-life buying situations, the choice patterns are much the same, and are dominated by the size of the competing brands.

The exercise makes key points:

1. Marketplace data is imperfect (as seen here, with fewer choices than expected, a declining base, e.g. the bucket started with 105 marbles, but ended with 97) but even so can be organized and analysed to reveal patterns.
2. Such patterns include similarity of customers – most chose 3–4 colours. In contrast, no one was 100 per cent loyal and a few always chose different colours.
3. Doing simple calculations (counting, percentages, etc.) helps to embed marketplace metrics and their meanings.
4. Organizing market data by size helps make patterns apparent.
5. Spotting patterns between metrics establishes relationships between them.
6. Spotting exceptions in the data (e.g. turquoise and cat-eye had higher penetration than expected), leads to questions to be answered.
7. Finding explanations – what customers chose is clear, but not why – which might be answered by different research, e.g. asking the customers to explain their choices, perhaps using qualitative data to explore meanings that lie behind the patterns in quantitative data.
8. Routine or habitual choosing is seen to be almost thought-free, with clear implications for brand choice in other categories.
9. Tying the data and insights back to existing knowledge (the exercise is novel to the students, but the patterns, laws and implications are well established) reinforces patterns such as the dominance of size over other marketplace metrics.
10. Deriving managerial implications, e.g. strategies to increase size – number of marbles in the bucket – will drive up loyalty metrics through availability, etc.
11. Extrapolate to real-world markets – marbles are marbles, but are candy bars much the same? Or airlines? Or cars?

5.   PRACTICE WITH PURPOSE

Being able to manipulate simple numbers and present them to tell a story helps us understand the data, observe patterns and exceptions and then eventually recognize established empirical generalisations. The marbles exercise introduces double jeopardy and then duplication of purchase, two very well-established empirical generalizations that apply in competitive choice situations. And while these empirical generalizations (EGs) are somewhat counterintuitive, they form a solid foundation for developing marketing strategy and tactics.

Double jeopardy is why every manager wants their brand or company to be the biggest, though they may not say it that way. Being big, of course, brings bragging rights, but it also improves all the performance metrics. And since size matters so much, most marketing strategy is focused on getting bigger. Double Jeopardy says the way achieve growth is to get more customers – because there are always customers in the market who don't buy even the biggest brand (some people did not choose green or red marbles either). It is therefore possible to raise penetration (increase the size of the customer base) and grow. Trying to grow by getting existing customers to buy more is very difficult because the purchase rates vary very little across competitors (in theory, it does not have to be this way, but in practice it always is). DJ means that raising the purchase rate requires getting more customers, and not the other way round (Ehrenberg, 1988).

DJ (Ehrenberg, 1959) has been a prominent concept in marketing for over fifty years (Ehrenberg et al., 1990). Through hundreds of replication studies it has been identified across time, in different markets and market situations, different countries, industries and services (Sharp, 2010). It is the classic case of an empirical generalization that through a process of marketing science has come to be known as a law of marketing (Uncles, et al., 1995).

Empirical generalizations are discussed in the following section, followed by an unexpected real-world application in section 7.

6.   USEFUL KNOWLEDGE – EMPIRICAL GENERALIZATIONS

An empirical generalization (EG) is a *relationship* between two or more variables that has been observed across a range of conditions, such as water boils at 100°C, more or less. Because the relationship is observed repeatedly it is regarded as a pattern, regularity or sometimes as a law. By knowing that an observed relationship holds under a range of conditions (and that it does not hold under other conditions – water boils at less than 100°C at lower air pressure) it is possible to use knowledge of the relationship for practical purposes, such as making routine predictions and stating principles. It is also possible to start to theorize about why the relationship occurs, and why it holds under some conditions and not others, thereby moving from empirical description to theory-building (Barwise, 1995).

EGs can be viewed as core knowledge much like the laws of physics, without which engineers and architects could not build things that remain standing. Marketing has few laws, but it does have academics who take a scientific approach to research and the development of marketing theory. Such academics typically employ a "data first" rather than "theory/model first" approach to search for law-like patterns in many sets of data. In this approach, initial findings tend to be simple, but repeated testing and extension to new contexts then add depth and identify boundary conditions. This approach views science as a gradual process of knowledge accumulation and refinement, rather than as a quest for revolutionary new ideas and places great value on theories and knowledge that are useful. In the marketing literature, replication and the growth of empirical knowledge have been a constant theme in the work of Scott Armstrong, and periodically leading journals like *Marketing Science* call for more replication studies and publish special issues on empirical generalizations (1995), while the *Journal of Advertising Research* published two issues on the topic in 2009 and 2013.

Two famous advocates of the EG approach were Andrew Ehrenberg and Frank Bass (Bass, 1995), both of whom made huge contributions to establishing useful EGs. One reason they were influential is that they usually based their research on industry-sourced data and metrics and therefore produced results that became popular with the managers who use them. Another reason for their continued influence is that they both set out to produce reusable knowledge by design, applying a scientific approach to studying issues in marketing.

EGs are important to marketing for four main reasons:

1. First, *they are a basic form of marketing knowledge* (see Rossiter, 2002 on forms of marketing knowledge). EGs describe relationships that exist over a range of different contexts that have been studied systematically. DJ is an example that has been observed over fifty years in varied countries, industries and product categories.
2. Second, *EGs are fundamental building blocks for developing knowledge.* The NBD-Dirichlet model (Ehrenberg et al., 2004) shows how a model can be refined, elaborated and extended. The Generalised Bass model (GBM) in the diffusion literature is another example of how a model can be built up from partial models with new observations.
3. Third, *EGs are useful.* For instance, a manager who knows about DJ understands what to expect from sales-oriented interventions: growth is

more likely to come from adding more customers than from increasing the purchasing frequency of existing customers. The strategy of securing more purchases from existing customers could be attempted, perhaps with a loyalty programme, but DJ suggests that would be going against the grain and will not work.

4. Fourth, *EGs help protect against falsehoods and unsubstantiated claims to knowledge.* Falsehoods take many forms – in research, a falsehood may be a reliance on a dubious result, as from a single innovative, un-replicated study. For managers there is also the danger of believing the hype surrounding fads or blindly following the herd into TQM, 6 Sigma, Marketing funnels or any number of compellingly promoted ideas that sound good, but have little of substance behind them, and may also be difficult in application.

Science and understanding advance when systems are in place for building logically from a base of existing knowledge. New studies may then reconcile conflicting findings, identify boundary conditions, and consolidate understanding. Ongoing marketing science also reveals both important gaps and suggests promising new directions for research to follow. None of this happens by accident, however, and inefficiency emerges when studies are ad hoc, one-off treatments based on single sets of data that do not link systematically to the underlying body of knowledge. There is therefore a need to seek to build empirical generalizations, which has driven calls for papers from top journals soliciting systematic reviews and meta-analyses to consolidate existing EGs and generate new ones.

The next section is a surprising example of the same sort of data exercise that was performed on marbles, however here the subject is large commercial aircraft.

7.   SEEK AND DISCOVER

BOX 12.3 SEEK AND DISCOVER

There are records for every large commercial aircraft ever sold and these records can be treated in the same way as other choice data to determine whether aircraft and marbles have anything in common in terms of how they are chosen. They really shouldn't because planes are hugely expensive, involve capital allocations processes, all manner of experts from finance to logistics, along with sales and purchasing engineers, banks and regulatory authorities. Also, they have lead times of up to five years during which volcanoes can erupt or pandemics break out that cancel the reasons airlines have for buying the planes in the first place. What could marbles possibly have in common with jumbo jets?

To answer that question, data were gathered from the Federal Aviation Administration in the US, the European Aviation Safety Agency in Europe, and from plane-spotting organizations that are fanatical about planes and data. Applying the same metrics and rules as to the marbles data, organizing by size and so on, produced a table showing how airline manufacturers share their customers. There are both expected results – Airbus and Boeing are very big (much higher penetrations), and surprises – lots of customers buy both Airbus and Boeing. There is also a split between those who buy Boeing and Airbus, and those who buy from everyone else. The overall pattern is similar to that for marbles, but messier.

Big Questions
Why would any airline buy from both Boeing and Airbus? After all, each manufacturer and every model adds a huge increase in fleet management complexity and therefore cost. Why don't airlines drive down costs through rationalization, simplification and concentration? Why spread purchasing between the manufacturers in this way?

These questions and many others can link analysis of market structure to strategic and managerial implications. The questions come out of the data as reduced and manipulated so that the market's underlying competitive structure is exposed. Table 12.3 looks like the marbles table, but is much lumpier and irregular. The table has a familiar form, but the irregularities and deviations cry out for explanation. Why does the table look like this?

Exceptions and irregularities need explanations
It turns out the structure is based on size – Boeing and Airbus make big planes of 150 to 450 seats, while others sell smaller planes of 50 to 160 seats. There is therefore a functional basis for choosing between suppliers. Large aircraft are bought by airlines with intercontinental routes, smaller ones by airlines with shorter, regional routes. Of course, some airlines have both longer and shorter routes, and will therefore need both large and small planes. In addition, at every size and specification level, at least two or more manufacturers offer very similar planes, so customers are choosing between very competitive offerings. Planes are not exactly like marbles, but customers choose them almost as if they were.

So what? What should the competitors do, or do differently? Does knowing the structure of the market matter? Should manufacturers vary their strategies for different customers? Should customers play one rival against another? What should new entrants do, a Chinese manufacturer perhaps, keen to enter the market for commercial aircraft, should they make big planes or small? Who should they target?

Table 12.3   Duplication of purchase in the Aviation industry (2009 to 2019)

% Buyers of brand		Who also bought...						
	Pen (%)	Airbus	Boeing	ATR	Embraer	De Havilland Canada	Bombardier	All Other
Airbus	46	–	32	8	6	2	4	2
Boeing	39	37	–	7	9	3	4	2
ATR	18	20	15	–	7	11	4	0
Embraer	12	24	28	10	–	7	13	3
De Havilland Canada	6	14	19	3	14	–	11	0
Bombardier	6	34	25	13	6	13	–	3
All Other	4	16	20	0	8	0	4	–
Average	–	24	23	7	8	6	7	2
Theo. Dup.	–	25	22	10	7	4	3	2

Source: Bennett and Anesbury (2021, in review).

The competitive structure in the market does in fact suggest that new competitors should enter via the more competitive, smaller aircraft subsector, not just because development costs are lower, but because customers in that subsector are inclined to buy from more suppliers. This is exactly what Comac of China did in 2016 when they introduced a 160-seat aircraft. By 2017 they had 517 orders and began deliveries in 2019. In turn, existing suppliers could respond in many ways, but given the nature of the marketplace, they should seek to gain (and keep) as many customers as possible. This is despite the fact that many small customers make only occasional purchases, so this amounts to targeting the entire market, most of which are light buyers. This may seem paradoxical, but these smaller airlines buy nearly half of all aircraft.

The large commercial aircraft case above demonstrates what can be done with data to illuminate core concepts as a starting point for exploring, and doing, marketing science. As part of the student learning journey, a market or data set like the one used here could form the basis for a live case study to enable deeper exploration of the laws of marketing and also to establish more connections with actual marketing strategy and practice.

Real data are important, but as with marbles, do not have to be complex. Real data enable students to develop competences and skills to master the tasks they want to learn. As much as possible the aim should be to design activities and exercises that approximate what students will do when they are either conducting their own academic research or as part of their job.

8.   LIVE CASE STUDIES

Mixing real world elements into the curriculum entices students to think critically in new environments. Live case studies are one way to bring real companies with real business issues into the classroom. This is especially valuable to final year students to bring business frameworks to life, but also to place them in unpredictable and challenging situations that further their learning (Charlebois and Foti, 2017).

In a typical live case, leaders from a participating company visit the classroom and present a business problem or brief that they need to tackle. Students are then asked to develop solutions. They generally do this as a team that works during the semester and then presents solutions to the professor, classmates, and the company. When a company visits and lays out a specific problem, students are suddenly put inside the business. They have to develop solutions and strategies, think about the implications, and then apply real performance and sales numbers to see how their proposed solutions affect company performance. The real-world application helps them attain deeper, more meaningful understanding.

Students must also work out how to present, explain and justify their solution to a manager or company owner. This gives them a level of responsibility, ownership and involvement that can only come from real-world interaction. This in turn means that they put in a lot more effort because they are not just going for a mark, but they also put themselves up to scrutiny when they stand up in front of a company and make a proposal to it (Kolb, 1984).

8.1   Setting up Live Cases

Live cases generally fall within a class curriculum designed without knowing which company or problem will be studied. The company brief is critical and may require extensive discussion between the tutor and managers to lay out the problem to be solved, but also why the exercise is valuable to both company and students.

It is important to understand both the company's and students' boundaries. Live cases take a lot of time, effort, and involvement from all parties to be successful, and it is important to agree not just a process, but who does what and when. Live cases are valuable learning experiences because they not only help develop marketing science skills, but they also help nurture a scientific mindset for approaching marketing problems. The marketing science mindset will be explored further in section 9.

BOX 12.4 GALBUSERA (SEE WWW.GALBUSERA.IT)

At the beginning of 2020 Stefano Cutrona, Managing Director of Galbusera, presented a challenging brief to a marketing class at London South Bank University. Galbusera is a family company that has grown over the last 100 years into one of the most progressive and innovative bakery companies in Europe, becoming the leader in "healthy bakery" in Italy. In 2014 the company expanded into the "indulgent" segment by acquiring the Tre Marie brand, growing it to the second largest in the wafer segment in Italy. In both healthy and indulgent bakery, Galbusera brands stand out for high quality, innovative flavours, advanced technological solutions, and being able to command price premiums vs the competition.

Students were asked to define an effective go-to-market strategy for Galbusera brands in Europe. Using marketing databases to evaluate market potential and strategies for launch, they were asked by the company to tackle real-world problems, and with no teaching notes or pro formas, they had to come up with their own solutions. The company provided background and market research data and sample products.

Students soon discovered they knew little about the business of biscuits. So Galbusera provided detail about products, competitors, logistics and so on, and outlined their budgeting processes. By the end of the briefing, the students realized they needed to pull together what they had learned to develop proposals and make real decisions.

To begin, student teams organized available category data country by country, following the rules of data presentation. Since they had participated in the marble-choosing exercise, they knew about DJ and DoP, and in analysing the category data found that big brands had much higher penetration and slightly higher repeat rates and that people who bought crackers (savoury biscuits), or cookies (biscuits), or wafers, bought across the baked goods spectrum. In other words, the baked goods categories conformed to DJ and DoP expectations. This was important when they began to formulate market entry and market development strategies.

The next step was to research consumer attitudes to "healthier" and "indulgent" as applied to baked goods. They developed a questionnaire that was circulated online across Europe and each student gathered 20–40 responses which were pooled into a dataset of 1100 respondents with cross-tabulatable data on attitudes towards salt, fat, sugar and natural ingredients in baked goods and what would improve baked goods' healthiness.

The survey showed that many consumers don't see cookies as particularly healthy even though they are the most popular regular snack, while the most-healthy baked good, crispbread, was the least popular.

Table 12.4   Snacks

| | % Claimed regular snack | Perceived healthy minus not healthy | To improve healthiness | | | |
			Less sugar	Natural ingredients	Less fat	Less salt
Fruit/Veg	31	58				
Crisps	18	−54				
Cookies	18	−37	49	22	14	6
Crackers	15	15	15	22	16	23
Wafers	6	−50	45	26	19	5
Crispbread	1	32	12	28	11	14

The popularity of the snack did not seem to depend on whether it was seen as healthy – crisps and cookies were seen as unhealthy but were nonetheless very popular.

On the other hand, the perceptions of regular users were much less negative. This was important because it hinted that usage or trial might change marketplace perceptions, and also that users' views can be very different from those of non-users.

The market entry and development strategies proposed by the teams generally emphasized the importance of targeting bigger markets with established baked goods categories. The main goal on entry was to maximize trial and penetration through wide distribution and extensive marketing activity using traditional and digital media. Some teams emphasized health advantages, some indulgence, and some healthier indulgence, but most emphasized driving penetration up to capture repeat purchasing. This was a direct and focused application of what they had learned from studying empirical generalizations.

Table 12.5   *To improve healthiness*

| | Perceived healthy minus not healthy | To improve healthiness | | | |
		Less sugar	Natural ingredients	Less fat	Less salt
Cookies	−19	34	27	16	11
Crackers	37	9	32	21	23
Wafers	−26	39	9	22	2
Crispbread	69	7	33	6	11

After the project, the students did reflective assessments of their experience and talked about the skills and tools the case enhanced. Taken altogether the reflections had three main themes: the live case helped build confidence, it prepared students for their future by enhancing relevant skills, and it helped make their theoretical or "book" knowledge practical. Many saw the live case as a stepping-stone to professional life. They felt it had immediate benefits from learning by doing (Experiential learning). This included greater engagement and sense of ownership than they had experienced before. Some students added that it was hard, but that having done it, they felt prepared to take on other real problems beyond the safe university context, and ready to explore the wider world.

9.   THE MARKETING SCIENCE MINDSET

It is too much to ask that marketing students have great technical knowledge, but they do need to develop a mindset of learning, breaking down problems, and developing solutions. Live cases such as Galbusera showcase how non-technical people often struggle with problems, for example they can't find an example to match their issue, or they aren't able to break it down into workable pieces, so they feel overwhelmed. Problems are like puzzles, and while scientists may not know exactly how to solve them, they do understand how studying a problem through iterations and varied approaches can help them build sufficient understanding to achieve their goals. Developing a scientific mindset requires acknowledging lack of initial understanding and not knowing what to do, but also the need to be comfortable with the struggle to find a solution. Adopting this mindset is not easy, especially for numerically challenged, non-technical students, but practice and reinforcement help. The Galbusera teams traveled a challenging intellectual path, the same path as technical people who were also once novices struggling with the same problems.

The scientific mindset is an asset to students who increasingly see higher education as a total experience that encompasses lectures and tutorials, but only as small parts of their learning world. That world can include part-time jobs, side hustles, clubs, societies, extra-curricular travel, and online communities in huge and shifting variety. Students, or as some call them, education customers (George, 2007) are also increasingly diverse, and so delivery of education is becoming more personalized, reflecting different learner motives for study, different patterns of study from full to part-time, modularization, apprenticeships, on-demand remote-access – anytime, anywhere, and outcomes including traditional degrees, professional certifications and micro-credentialing of course components.

As the educational horizon shifts and atomizes, practical, job-ready skills are becoming increasingly important. Today's student CVs typically list levels of proficiency in widely used software and business tools. Among these are data handling skills including knowing what data to search for, and how to retrieve, select, analyse and present it. While a toolkit and skill base are important and also reflect students' orientations to problem solving, it is critical that these are applied within a framework of useful knowledge – the basic principles that govern the practice of marketing.

Marketing science requires scientific method (Houston and Hulland, 2021), which is an approach to answering a question. For example, what happens when a brand influencer is pictured on social media wearing a fur coat? The answer might be obvious because fur coats are loved by some and abhorred by others (a hypothesis), so the predictable answer is likely to be that some people will react negatively – which can be tested in a variety of ways. From there it is possible to make more refined hypotheses and predictions, and more importantly, to make managerial decisions about the influencer, influencers in general or even about fur coats.

Marketing science is not just about mathematics and statistics. Marketing happens in a business context with social and behavioural aspects and it requires knowledge or context to make sense. Moreover, it goes beyond statistics because data analysis can seldom be done well with automated software of the sort that most people don't understand. How does a marketer choose between JMP, KNIME, Orange, Python or R – all popular data analysis software packages? A reasonable person might fall back on IT professionals, statisticians or consultants, but this is really just kicking the can down the road because eventually they will have to try to understand what the experts say in order to make a business decision.

The meaning to decision makers is the important thing, and judgment and experience are essential to the scientist, or to a new marketer who has to justify a recommendation – usually on the basis of a quantified measure of something. An obvious exception to this rule is when all that is really wantes are predictions that are likely to come true, of the sort that experienced marketers can make, for example, if we have a two-for-one deal in June we're likely to triple our sales that month. This prediction is based not on understanding the underlying data or behavioural mechanisms or the "why" (though it might be) but is instead based on knowledge of the "what". Common sense and pricing theory say that two-for-one deals increase sales, while the tripling forecast comes from experience and judgment.

Being able to understand the qualitative aspects of quantitative research, therefore, is an aptitude that good marketing scientists must have. Good scientists are tenacious but, at the same time, creative problem-solvers who can feel what the data are saying. There are analogies with music – a technically gifted classical musician is unlikely to go very far without the ability to play with feeling.

Interpersonal and communication skills are important for many jobs, and marketing science is no exception. An analyst who is technically clever will be underutilized if he or she can't get along with people or communicate with them in language they can understand. A core task of the marketing scientist is therefore to translate and communicate data in the context of marketing knowledge so that it can be acted upon by decision makers.

10.   THE PROBLEMS OF KNOWLEDGE

The development of knowledge faces two big hurdles. First, any knowledge may be based on fallible observations (Hunt, 1990, 1991), and second, it is logically impossible to prove any statement to be universally true. This may sound a bit stark, but while empirical knowledge may be fallible and there is uncertainty in searching for it, it is still possible to obtain reasonably objective knowledge about the world through observation and experience.

Karl Popper (1935) dealt with the impossibility of conclusive proofs of universal statements or theories, saying that we should not try to prove theories to be true, but instead try to prove them to be false by subjecting them to stringent tests and comparing them to *competing theories* to determine which provides the best predictions with the least falsifying instances. Any theories or ideas that survive rigorous examination can then be accepted as "true". Modern marketing scholars (Armstrong et al., 2001) suggest that a practical way of ensuring that theories are strong is to test multiple competing hypotheses, and prefer the one that, over time, performs the best for given conditions.

In the real world theories are rarely tested per se because managers are not very concerned with making testable predictions (Hubbard and Armstrong, 1994). Instead, they examine data on consumer behaviour looking for insights that may improve their decision making. This is the approach of many marketing textbooks – that *understanding* leads to better decisions, for example managers who want to satisfy consumers need an in-depth understanding of those consumers in order to develop effective marketing strategies. This is why empirical generalizations matter so much – they provide benchmarks for expectations and guidelines to shape strategy. In the next sections we discuss where marketing science can play a role for managers.

10.1   In the Real World

Less than 1 per cent of businesses achieve long-term growth, according to a study of over 3900 brands in 58 consumer packaged goods categories in 21 countries (Kantar, 2019). This is despite nearly every marketing plan having growth as a goal. For most businesses, becoming a member of the "1 per cent club" is a wish, like a kid's dream of playing professional football. Marketers know growth is hard, but with experience they learn to write strategies with achievable KPIs like increasing penetration, engagement, the number of mentions on social media, or incremental sales growth, if not market share growth, when the economy is good.

But the 1 per cent dream can also be dangerous because it makes marketers believe the promises for growth made by wily management consultants, crafty advertising gurus and sophisticated data-wonks. Customer Relationship Management (CRM) is a case in point – in the name of improving customer service, CRM drove big far-reaching changes in staff training and investment in IT systems, some of which were useful, but also expensive. To be sellable, the high investment costs were set against other desires and so improved brand loyalty and lower customer defection were added, both of which promised astonishing gains in revenue and profit.

Understanding why CRM failed to deliver as promised requires clear-eyed examination and scientific evidence (see Reichheld et al., 2002). The bottom line is that the incremental returns from CRM didn't cover the costs of investment. Now consider the promises made for content marketing (where valuable content is shared). Or Artificial Intelligence (AI), where a trained computer thinks about data, or influencer marketing where media mavens move markets, or blockchain systems that are meant to randomize data and protect competitive intelligence. These and many more hot ideas are promoted as game-changers that just might take a business into the 1 per cent.

That's where marketing science comes in. By approaching marketing from a foundation of evidence it allows marketers to place the promises made for any form of marketing activity into the context of knowledge about that activity. For example, much is known about how advertising works – or what to expect from direct-response or brand-building campaigns, leading to calculations for advertising ROIs. It is also evident that price elasticity is generally about −2.0 (a 10 per cent change in price generates a 20 per cent change in

sales in consumer packaged goods), and that big brands have more loyal customers than small ones do. And while experienced managers know all this and
a great deal more, their knowledge is usually confined to a few companies, and
is not systematic or generalized across industries, which is where marketing
scientists come in.

10.2   Marketing Science or Science in Marketing?

In short, there is science in marketing – it even has some laws. Ries and Trout
(2017) claim that there are 22 immutable laws of marketing, which is probably
over-claiming, possibly in reaction to those who doubt the scientific status of
social sciences in general. This re-opens the old question of, "Is marketing
a science?" (Brown, 1948), which after seven decades still embroils scholars
(though probably not practitioners) in heated debate. Social sciences, such
as marketing, are seen as complex because they involve people. The point of
any field of scientific enquiry however, is the derivation of principles, or laws
which can serve as the basis of prediction, decision and action. Prediction of
anything is possible only when there is great uniformity in the phenomena
under study, as can be found in nature. And since the conditions and events in
nature are found to have high uniformity, predictions concerning them are seen
as reliable, and the methods by which such phenomena have been studied have
become the standard for scientific research.

The fundamental belief for marketing scientists is simply that the methods
of the physical sciences also apply in social science. The laws of buyer behaviour and the principles of discovering such regularities are the same as in other
science: collecting enough of the right kind of facts and studying them. And
because humans, despite all their complexities, exhibit a great deal of regular
behaviour, so studying their behaviour leads to the discovery of regularities.
Science can be simple. All one has to do is to pick regular things to study.

For students and marketers, the debate above is entirely academic. They are
not very bothered that much of what we know about science remains confused
and contentious. To them, it is more useful to know that implicit in observed
phenomena are many lawlike relations saying that if this occurs, so does that.
The systematic uncovering of such relationships and their subsequent applications to practical problems are how science and technology progress.

And marketers who take decisions based on knowledge can make better
decisions. M&M Mars for example has many leading businesses and takes
a scientific and systematic approach to marketing. To do this, Mars trains
its staff repeatedly in marketing science. As a result, most Mars marketing
interventions have a central goal of increasing penetration – the size of the
customer base. That singular goal, however, can be addressed with any number

of strategies, from repetitive brand-building advertising, to edgy and exciting influencer marketing.

Marketing science is an approach to marketing that uses scientific methods in the pursuit of "truths" in marketing. It is related to, but more general than marketing research, which is oriented towards a specific product, service or campaign.

11. CHALLENGES AND DEVELOPMENTS

As goes marketing, so goes marketing science. In the coming year, both will look very different. It might be that for marketing, COVID-19 is like the asteroid that killed off the dinosaurs. Or maybe not – many fundamental changes such as Big Data, the Internet of Things, User Generated Content (UGC), AI, and Data security were already afoot. They may just have just been accelerated by COVID.

The effects on marketing science are likely to be seen in an increasing requirement for high levels of technical sophistication (e.g., Bayesian statistics, programming languages) and advanced computer science skills. In some ways, marketing science has long been a sort of black-box advantage that sophisticated, well-resourced companies use to dominate their markets. Now anyone can draw on analytical tools that are deceptively accessible, but don't require any knowledge of research or statistics or scientific method. As a result, though people can now perform analytics and generate presentations that were unheard of a few years ago, the risk of shoddy analytics has also risen.

This is a problem with many marketing trends. Take the hype about Artificial Intelligence (AI) for marketing. A tremendous amount is written about AI but practising marketers read little of it because it is quite technical. Even so, they might want AI for what it is good for: performing very complex calculations, pattern recognition (with training), prediction, translation and collation of documents and languages, text mining. On the other hand, AI is not good at going beyond what has been programmed – it has no curiosity, can't make abstractions, read or feel emotions. AI is just one among many exciting developments that challenge marketers to keep up.

Teaching and learning marketing science and the associated quantitative skills is a priority area for companies, universities and governmental organizations. For example the ESRC has the Quantitative Methods Initiative or Q-Step in the UK (ESRC, 2009) to assist teachers to improve the research skills of undergraduates, and the Applied Quantitative Methods Network (AQMeN, 2017) for postgraduates.

In modern classrooms, students come from many academic and professional backgrounds, are enrolled in very different university degree programmes, and have highly varied knowledge and skills bases. Sheer diversity complicates the organization and structure of any course, but for marketing science it also requires teachers to make complex decisions about the purpose of the course and who it is aimed at. They will also need to determine what it will cover; the balance between theory and practice; the order in which ideas, concepts and skills will be introduced and built upon; how to engage students in the subject; and how to use data.

Attitudes towards scientific thinking are far from uniform – academics and those employed as marketing scientists care a lot about it, while managers tend to want reliable solutions they can apply with confidence. There is also an element of fear or apprehension when it comes to quants and statistics, not to mention programming and data analytics. In teaching marketing science this anxiety is more than just something to overcome because it affects confidence and ability to learn. Anxiety can result in a sort of mind-lock that precludes learning unless carefully unpicked and remedied with patience, practice and positive feedback.

11.1   Course Design

Structure and sequence are critical to designing any learning experience, and especially important when developing online learning. This chapter was built on the experience of teaching marketing courses, not all of which were Marketing Science courses. Whether entry level or final year, however, they followed a similar progression from small student-generated data sets (sometimes involving marbles), to analysis of business data sets (sometimes in live case studies), to formulation of marketing strategy.

Design of marketing science courses either in-class or online should follow well established guidelines. To begin, it is important that courses have a clearly explained structure that is easy to understand and navigate. This also applies to the user experience of the platform and course. Second, content and tasks should be structured so that students can progressively build competence. Content should be incremental so that it is easy for the learner to understand why it matters and what it is about. Complex tasks can be broken into a number of stages, with constructive feedback at each stage. As the learner progresses and builds competence the number of stages can be reduced. Considered structure and sequencing also allow students to move at their own pace, especially if they require re-learning of some concepts, or need to refresh their skills in maths and numeracy.

12.   FROM ART TO SCIENCE

Science, not art, drives marketing. Yet there is a certain artistry required to marketing as science. Inaccurate data, biased readings, poorly defined experiments and woolly hypotheses represent just some of the dangers of ill-applied marketing science.

Students of marketing who want to pursue marketing as a science as opposed to an art need to both understand marketing and have a decent set of skills in a data-related field such as statistics. Potential career candidates need to have a thorough understanding of marketing terms and techniques, data collection, and analysis.

Students in a marketing science course will learn about data techniques and how to analyse the gathered information. This is useful for a career in scientific marketing as it allows students to expand the tools needed for data handling and analysis. It is important to learn not only how this data is tracked and analysed, but how to use this data to create and implement powerful and effective marketing campaigns.

Marketing science as a discipline applies equally to different subjects within marketing. While the discussion in this chapter is mainly about purchasing or brand buying, a marketing science approach applies equally well to courses on advertising, social media marketing, marketing research, branding and so on, but with data and metrics appropriate to each. The marketing science mindset allows students, teachers and practitioners to look at any subject with the intent to develop reliable and useful understanding.

REFERENCES

AQMeN (2017) Applied Quantitative Methods Network, Training for business and industry. Accessed at http://www.aqmen.ac.uk/home.

Armstrong, J.S., Brodie, R.J. and Parsons, A.G. (2001) Hypotheses in marketing science: Literature review and publication audit. *Marketing Letters*, 12(2), 171–87.

Barwise, P. (1995) Good empirical generalizations. *Marketing Science*, 14(3), G29–34.

Bass, F.M. (1995) Empirical generalizations and marketing science: A personal view. *Marketing Science*, 14(3), Part 2 of 2: Special Issue on Empirical Generalizations in Marketing, G6–G19.

Bennett, D. and Anesbury, Z. (2021) How do airlines buy aircraft? An empirical study of industrial buying behaviour. *Marketing Letters*, in review.

Bhowmick, S., Young, J., Clark, P. and Bhowmick, N. (2017) Marketing students' mathematics performance: The mediating role of math anxiety on math self-concept and math self-efficacy. *Journal of Higher Education Theory and Practice*, 17(9).

Blattberg, R. and Neslin, S. (1990) *Sales Promotion: Concepts, Methods and Strategies.* Englewood Cliffs, NJ: Prentice-Hall.

Bogomolova, S., Szabo, M. and Kennedy, R. (2017) Retailers' and manufacturers' price-promotion decisions: Intuitive or evidence-based? *Journal of Business Research*, 76, 189–200.

Brown, L.O. (1948) Toward a profession of marketing. *Journal of Marketing*, 13(1), 27–33.

Charlebois, S. and Foti, L. (2017) Using a live case study and co-opetition to explore sustainability and ethics in a classroom: Exporting fresh water to China. *Global Business Review*, 18(6), 1400–411.

Ehrenberg, A.S.C. (1959) The pattern of consumer purchases. *Applied Statistics*, 8(1), 26–41.

Ehrenberg, A.S.C. (1969) Towards an integrated theory of consumer behaviour. *Journal of the Market Research Society*, 11(4), 305–37.

Ehrenberg, A.S.C. (1975) *Data Reduction*. London, UK and New York, NY, USA: John Wiley.

Ehrenberg, A.S.C. (1988) *Repeat-Buying: Facts, Theory and Applications*. Oxford: Oxford University Press.

Ehrenberg, A.S.C., Uncles, M. and Goodhardt, G. (2004) Understanding brand performance measures: Using Dirichlet benchmarks. *Journal of Business Research*, 57(12), 1307–325.

Ehrenberg, A.S.C., Goodhardt, G. and Barwise, P. (1990). Double jeopardy revisited. *Journal of Marketing*, 54(3), 82–91.

ESRC (2009) Economic and Social Research Council Q-step funding programme on Quantitative Methods training for UK social science undergraduates. Accessed at https://esrc.ukri.org/files/research/qmi/final-report-strategic-advisor -for-quantitative-methods-proposals-to-support-and-improve-the-teaching-of -quantitative-research-methods-at-undergraduate-level-in-the-uk/.

George, D. (2007) Market overreach: The student as customer. *Journal of Socioeconomics*, 36(6), 965–77.

Hagan, F. (2012) *Essentials of Research Methods for Criminal Justice*. Pearson.

Houston, M. and Hulland, J. (2021) Call for papers for a special issue and thought leaders' conference on generalizations in marketing: Systematic reviews and meta-analyses, *Journal of the Academy of Marketing Science*, forthcoming.

Hubbard, R. and Armstrong, J.S. (1994) Replications and extensions in marketing: Rarely published but quite contrary. *International Journal of Research in Marketing*, 11(3), 233–48.

Hunt, S. (1990) Truth in marketing theory and research. *Journal of Marketing*, 54(3), 1–15.

Hunt, S. (1991) Positivism and paradigm dominance in consumer research: Toward critical pluralism and rapprochement. *Journal of Consumer Research*, 18(1), 32–44.

Jandaghi, G., Alireza, A., Parvaneh, P., Zahra, A. and Hasan, K. (2011) Survey the role of brand in formation of customer loyalty in financial services marketing by the approach of small firms. *Far East Journal of Psychology and Business*, 3(3), 50–61.

Journal of Advertising Research (2009) What we know about advertising: Advertising Empirical Generalizations: Implications for Research and Action, June, 49(2).

Journal of Advertising Research (2013) What we know about advertising II: Research and Action, 53(2).

Kantar Worldpanel (2019) Kantar Inspiration report. Accessed at https://www.kantar .com/uki/inspiration/brands/mastering-momentum-fewer-than-one-percent-of -brands-master-growth-momentum.

Kolb, A.Y. and Kolb, D.A. (2005) Learning styles and learning spaces: Enhancing experiential learning in higher education. *Academy of Management Learning and Education*, 4(2), 193–212.

Kolb, D.A. (1984) *Experiential Learning*. Englewood Cliffs, NJ: Prentice-Hall.

Kotler, P. (2012) *Kotler on Marketing*. London: Simon & Schuster.

Kuusik, A. (2007) *Affecting Customer Loyalty: Do Different Factors Have Various Influences in Different Loyalty Levels?*, No. 366, Tartu: Tartu University Press.

Lewis, L.H. and Williams, C.J. (1994) Experiential learning: Past and present. *New Directions for Adult and Continuing Education*, 62, 5–16.

Marketing Science (1995) Special Issue on Empirical Generalizations in Marketing, 14(3), Part 2.

Popper, K. (1935) *Logik der Forschung*, trans. into English under the title *The Logic of Scientific Discovery* (1959), London: Routledge.

Prince, M. and Felder, R. (2007) The many faces of inductive teaching and learning. *Journal of College Science Teaching*, 36(5).

Reichheld, F.F., Schefter, F. and Rigby, D. (2002) Avoid the four perils of CRM. *Harvard Business Review*, 80(2), 108–109.

Ries, A. and Trout, J. (2017) The 22 immutable laws of marketing. Online. Accessed at: dln.jaipuria.ac.in.

Rossiter, J.R. (2002) The five forms of transmissible, usable marketing knowledge. *Marketing Theory*, 2(4), 369–80.

Rust, R. (2020) The future of marketing, *International Journal of Research in Marketing*, 37(1), 15–36.

Sharp, B. (2010) *How Brands Grow*, Oxford: Oxford University Press.

Srinivasan, S., Pauwels, K., Hanssens, D. and Dekimpe, M. (2004) Do promotions benefit manufacturers, retailers, or both? *Management Science*, 50(5), 617–29.

Tiltman, D. (2012) Trends report on shopper marketing. Online. WARC.

Trout, J. and Rivkin, S. (2010) *Differentiate or Die, Survival in Our Era of Killer Competition*, 2nd edn. Hoboken, NJ: John Wiley & Sons.

Tu, Y., Lin, S-Y. and Chang, Y-Yi (2011) Relationships among service quality, customer satisfaction and customer loyalty in chain restaurant. *Information Management and Business Review*, 3(5), 270–79.

Uncles, M., Ehrenberg, A.S.C. and Hammond, K. (1995) Patterns of buyer behavior: Regularities, models, and extensions. *Marketing Science*, 14(3), G71–G78.

Zaltman, G. (2000) Consumer researchers: Take a hike! *Journal of Consumer Research*, 26(4), 423–28.

Index

Printed and bound by CPI Group (UK) Ltd, Croydon, CR0 4YY

16/04/2025

14658491-0005